History and Legend

History and Legend

WRITING THE INTERNATIONAL BRIGADES

ROBERT STRADLING

UNIVERSITY OF WALES PRESS
CARDIFF
2003

© Robert Stradling, 2003

British Library Cataloguing-in-Publication Data.
A catalogue record for this book is available from the British Library.

ISBN 0–7083–1774–X

All rights reserved. No part of this book may be reproduced, stored in a retrieval system, or transmitted, in any form or by any means, electronic, mechanical, photocopying, recording or otherwise, without clearance from the University of Wales Press, 10 Columbus Walk, Brigantine Place, Cardiff CF10 4UP.
www.wales.ac.uk/press

The right of Robert Stradling to be identified as author of this work has been asserted by him in accordance with the Copyright, Designs and Patents Act 1988.

Typeset by Mark Heslington, Scarborough, North Yorkshire
Printed in Great Britain by Dinefwr Press, Llandybïe

Contents

List of Illustrations		vi
Preface and Acknowledgements		vii
List of Acronyms		xvi
Note to Text		xvi
1	Introduction: The Virtuous Republic versus the Philistines	1

Part I: Writers, Fighters and Bloody Scribblers

2	Comrade – Lover – Victim: Cornford, Spender and Friends	25
3	Battle on Monte Oscuro: The Surreal Landscape of Orwell's Spain	48
4	Ballad of Heroes: Britten, Auden and the British Battalion	74

Part II: Other Parts of the Field

5	Crusades in Conflict: Idealism, Perception, Motivation	99
6	Necessary Murders: The British Battalion at Brunete	123
7	Between the Bullet and the Sonnet: Poetry and Propaganda in the Trenches	145
8	Conclusion: Writers, Politics and the War for Art	169
9	Epilogue: The Real Fifth Column	188
Appendix: 'Necessary Murders' – The Texts		196
Notes		203
Bibliography		255
Index		274

List of Illustrations

Between pages 96 and 97

The body of Alfonso Ponce de Léon in a Madrid morgue

Salamanca's memorial to Unamuno

John Cornford in September 1936

Spender, Hyndman, Worsley and Helen Gibb, *c.* 1935

W. H. Auden and Benjamin Britten, early 1940s

Auden in Valencia, 1937

Different views on the International Brigades: wall graffiti in Albacete, 2001

Memorial stone to the Nationalist commander in Villanueva

Puyol's cartoon *El Rumor*

Graffiti tribute to Hernandez

Plaque to English International Brigade poets

Koltsov at the Anti-Fascist Writers' Congress

Preface and Acknowledgements

'You are History! You are Legend!' This was the rhetorical climax of a famous eulogy to the International Brigades delivered by the Spanish Communist leader, Dolores Ibárruri ('La Pasionaria') in October 1938. The phrases have resonated down the decades as an inspiring reminder of heroic and voluntary sacrifice in the cause of freedom. The words are inscribed, for example, on the National Memorial to the Welsh volunteers which stands in my native city of Cardiff.

Those who by being merged into them, become free of both History and Legend are truly, sempiternally and more than any imperial spouse, beyond reproach. This poses a problem for the critic – a category which I take to include historians. Of course, the most rewarding and exciting history has always been revisionist in inspiration; and a critical, even sceptical, approach to the secondary antecedents and primary sources of its subject is an ethical given for professionals. Moreover, the essential libertarian–poststructuralist query: 'who benefits from this argument/conclusion?' – still startling to some disciplines – has long been inherent in historical dialectics. But more than ever in the postmodern age, the historian cannot aspire to disentangle Legend from History. We no longer enjoy the luxury of procedures which presumptively decode time's complex text. In exchange for the loss of these privileges, modern theories of cultural criticism have given us a more democratic hermeneutics of history. Richly plural and wide-ranging, productive of more utilitarian understandings of past and present society, it also tends to a radical scepticism in its procedures, and reaches for conclusions which are candidly subjective and ephemeral. In a phrase, we are all culturalists now.

In few areas of historical enquiry does the cultural power of myth subsist with such elemental force as in the case of the Spanish Civil War. This book attempts an independent discussion of the processes which invested the 'History and Legend' of the International Brigades with such potent meaning. What happened in Spain in 1936–9 proved to be the twentieth century's most explosive catalyst of political tensions. It excited commitment across the whole westernized world, expressed, above all, through sympathy for, assistance to, or participation in the International Brigades. It produced a matrix for and a metanarrative about the 'besieged' Spanish Republic: the good old cause of 'Spain'. At the time, support for the Republic was often spontaneous as far as individuals and small groups were concerned. But neither the International Brigades as an institution, nor the creation and dissemination of 'Spain', were left to chance. On the contrary, both involved conscious and deliberate acts of policy. In societies which by the 1930s had achieved near-universal literacy, the main medium of politics was the written word. Accordingly, writing was the means by which 'Spain' entered the bloodstream of western culture. Within Spain itself internecine conflict produced the most urgently important literature since the seventeenth century. Amongst anglophone peoples, it stimulated, some scholars believe, more (at any rate, more influential) writing than either of the two world wars.

By the start of 1937, intellectuals could not avoid the insistent question 'Are you going to fight in Spain?' and its distressing supplementary 'If not, why not?' This book considers (mainly) English writing, and explores various cases of writers who were driven to seek some positive association with the International Brigades. In the context of 'Spain', an issue which was both dominant and urgent, it seeks to uncover the power struggles of its subcultural and micro-cultural ambiences – often 'marginal', but always intense, clashes of political principle, personal feelings, propaganda, gender, clique and class – in which dozens of writers, famous and forgotten, were caught up. It examines the relationship of these struggles to the more universal issues of freedom and tyranny which permeated propaganda and the press. The experience and influence of the volunteers in Spain are looked at from various perspectives established by the literary-romantic myth of the International Brigades. The Internationals have frequently been apostrophized as a regiment of writers in arms – a claim which, if subject to important misgivings, still seems broadly plausible. More importantly, the 'Volunteers for Liberty' were projected as men whose sufferings gave the cause a concrete reality of lived suffering and sympathy, existing above and beyond bookish representation and subjective weaknesses. For bourgeois intellectuals, martyrdom in the workers' cause was the ultimate proof of their identification with it. The killed and maimed, of whatever class, offered a blood sacrifice which hallowed the cause, thus constituting the central tragedy which is endlessly inscribed in its literature. It is not by happenstance that characters in many novels and screenplays set during the Spanish War – particularly those featuring heroes linked to the International Brigades, and beginning with notable contemporaries like Hemingway's Robert Jordan and Malraux's Manuel – are intellectuals, artists or (above all) writers.

The book's introduction explores the relationship between the Second Republic and the world of the creative intellect which was mobilized in its support during the Civil War. The consequent identification of the Republic with 'Culture' conferred a halo of humanist stature upon its cause. It acquired a reputation so powerful that, in the moral reckoning of later generations, it easily counterweighted the Republic's resort to the protection of Stalin's USSR, with its triple machinery of military hardware, political control and police terror. The hegemonic ethos of western societies in the middle decades of the last century was a liberal civilization which valued art, writing and the expressive intellect above all other human considerations. As part of this culture, almost as one of its constitutional enactments, the Spanish Republic became 'the last great cause'. The apparently 'natural' alliance of radical left politics with bourgeois 'Culture' (that is 'The Arts') during the age of the Popular Front (1934–48) succeeded not only in establishing an interpretative orthodoxy about the overthrow of freedom by Fascism, but also in setting the anti-Fascist agenda on a plane of spiritual absoluteness which almost precluded dispute amongst intellectuals. The International Brigades became a vast global network for the creation and mobilization of anti-Fascist commitment, based on an assumed monopoly of liberal-humanist ideals. To this day, their epic-heroic reputation has remained at the core of a profound cultural legacy, sedulously preserved by dedicated organizations with widespread support in the popular and academic media. In exposing the historical conditions of this construction, I argue that the relationship between the Republic and the intellectuals was more complex and more compromised than is widely believed.

> Nor ask what doubtful act allows
> Our freedom in this English house
> Our picnics in the sun.
>
> The conscious acceptance of guilt in the necessary murder.

'Doubtful Acts' and 'Necessary Murders'. Both main parts of the book are concerned with explaining the meanings of these acts of confession/contrition by W. H. Auden, as well as the relationship between them. The first part looks at the ethical, political and personal dilemmas involved in commitment to the Spanish Republic, through the experiences of English writers who were inspired by the International Brigades or (in Orwell's case) by their non-Stalinist equivalents. Many of the themes and arguments explored here developed out of my parochial interest in the Cardiff-born International Brigader, T. A. R. Hyndman. As a sixth-former, I was set to read examples of the lyric verse of Auden and Spender. I was deeply moved by their expressive formulations of love and empathy, and simultaneously embarrassed by my adolescent awareness of being moved. My embarrassment had nothing to do with the homosexual dimension of the poems, of which I was ignorant, and everything to do with my domestic class and religious contexts, which were rebarbatively suspicious (respectively) of poetry and love. At the time, Hyndman, subject of much of Spender's writing, and especially his poems of the Spanish War, was living only a short walk from my parental home. This fact – even had I known it – would then have held little or no significance for me. But the fortuitous discovery of this conjunction (or non-conjunction) more than thirty years later, just as I was incubating a research obsession with the Spanish Civil War, was the epiphany of this book. It helped produce its interplay of largely conventional historical discourse, to do with the universals of war, class and myth, with newer agencies which foreground the political dynamics of small groups, of desire, social charisma and gender.

The International Brigades were the forcing-house of politics and writing in the Spanish Civil War. As the priority context of personal commitment and sacrifice, their desperate struggles on distant battlefields epitomized the tragic grandeur of the war. The experience of the Brigades also defined standards of heroism (and its opposite) across class and culture divides. The core of the book's second part is an examination of the ways in which the image and history of the Brigades were constructed during the war itself. The treatment selects various propaganda presentations of the Republican war-effort and the role within it played by the Internationals. It juxtaposes familiar and elevating nostrums about the war's meaning with more sordid banalities concerning the volunteers' situation at the battle fronts as the 'shock troops' of the Republic. At several points the approved images of the Internationals and the Republican cause are compared with those elaborated on the Nationalist side, taking the argument into the parallel sphere of the 'propaganda war'. It ends with a direct critical investigation of the Republic's 'cultural mission' amongst men of the 'Popular Army', and the International Brigades' encouragement of working-class writing as a medium of political solidarity.

The book concludes by taking the argument into a different dimension. The Spanish Civil War, more than any other conflict in history, has always been understood as a defining ethical contest between truth and falsehood. In a sense I return to this conventional discourse, but by positing the war as representing the climax of a philosophical struggle, initiated by the Enlightenment, between the autonomy claims of mandarin 'culture' and 'art' (on the one hand) and the demands of socio-political commitment, deriving from humanist ideology and traditions of revolution (on the other). By the 1930s, what I have elsewhere called 'Artism' and its hieratic 'Artistocracy' nurtured an autochthonous agenda which was both elitist and totalitarian, many of its agents representing a constituency which sought to exploit the Republican cause for its own ends. The site of struggle of these competing moral imperatives was the history and legend of the International Brigades.

Just as its gestation has brought more unsatisfied curiosity than secure understanding, the book's completion has left me – at least in one sense – in the red. Like others in the field, I have constantly turned to Jim Carmody for help in answering nitty-gritty queries about the volunteers themselves. He is a veritable encyclopaedia about the personnel histories of the Brigaders. Though our common obsession in one sense makes us both eccentric, he is the utterly non-eccentric and much more amiable personification of a character in Robert Goddard's novel *Hand in Glove*, 'Sylvester Kilmainham', who pursues the impossible mission of a complete prosopography of the volunteers who went to Spain. Another fellow-sufferer from the obsession, Lala Isla, has provided much information, interest and encouragement. The same goes for Luna Luna, an assiduous tutor who introduced me to many of the Spanish writers of the Civil War, providing voluminous research materials and food for thought. Richard Baxell and Michael O'Shaughnessy were stimulating work-companions during a testing assignment in Moscow. Both will recall with grateful delight the assistance provided by our inimitable interpreter, Vladimir Koverznev. In connection with my Moscow research, I received willing help from Natalia Wase at the British Council's Moscow office, whilst the timely advice of Professor Bob Davies, doyen of Soviet studies, was of great importance. I am most grateful to Dr Tom Buchanan for his material help and expert guidance on various issues. My thanks also go to the Warden and Fellows of All Souls College, Oxford, Gill Bird, Benito Vázquez Iglesias, José Ramón Pelayo Loscertales, María Dolores Requena Manzano, Martin Blinkhorn, Terry Hawkes, Gustav Klaus, Dave Turner, Scott Newton, Meirion Hughes, Josie McLellan, Anna Hearder, Robin Briggs, Helen Stradling, Ed Stradling and Rob Stradling (jnr) for practical assistance and intellectual stimulation. At a late stage chapter 4 benefited considerably from the attention and advice of the distinguished Britten scholar Dr Donald Mitchell and Mr Tony Scotland of the Lennox Berkeley Estate. Amongst all these its benefactors are several who will not be happy with the entire contents of the book: I take spiritual comfort from the fact that knowing this did not deter their support and collaboration.

As always, archivists and librarians deserve acknowledgement and thanks. At the RGASPI Archive in Moscow, the director, Dr Kirill Anderson, Svetlana Rosenthal of the International Brigade Section, and many other staff, were always sympathetic and resourceful in finding ways to cope with sometimes difficult conditions. My Moscow agent, Liudmilla Selivanova, experienced and resourceful ex-archivist, also worked wonders. In addition to recording a formidable debt – contracted over a period to be counted in decades rather than years – to the staffs of the British Library, the Bodleian Library and Cardiff University Libraries, I offer particular thanks to: Terry Cooke (British Library), Tish Collins (Marx Memorial Library), Jenny Doctor (Britten–Pears Library), Victoria Ramos (PCE Archive, Madrid), Pilar Casado Liso (Ministry of Foreign Affairs Archive, Madrid); nearer home, to Dennis Pratt (librarian at HTV Wales Studios, Cardiff) and Peter Keelan (Salesbury librarian, Cardiff University).

Some documents cited here from sources in Moscow and Madrid have since appeared, in slightly differing versions, in R. Radosh et al., *Spain Betrayed: The Soviet Union in the Spanish Civil War* (New Haven, Yale University Press, 2001).

Finally, I am deeply obliged to the Society of Authors for a generous grant towards the costs of my researches in Russia and Spain.

The author and publisher gratefully acknowledge the permission granted by the following to reprint extracts from:

W. H. Auden, 'Night covers up the rigid land', from *The English Auden* first published by Faber & Faber Ltd, 1937
Copyright © 1936 by W. H. Auden
Reprinted by permission of Curtis Brown, Ltd

W. H. Auden, 'Spain, 1937', from *The English Auden*, first published by Faber & Faber Ltd, 1937
Copyright © 1937 by W. H. Auden
Reprinted by permission of Curtis Brown, Ltd

W. H. Auden and Louis MacNiece, *Letters from Iceland*, first published by Random House
Copyright © 1937 by W. H. Auden
Reprinted by permission of Curtis Brown, Ltd

W. H. Auden, 'Ode to the New Year'
Copyright © 1939 by W. H. Auden
Reprinted by permission of Curtis Brown, Ltd and Christ Church Library, Oxford

W. H. Auden, *Plays, 1928–1938, On the Frontier*, first published by Random House, 1939
Copyright © 1938 by W. H. Auden
Reprinted by permission of Curtis Brown, Ltd

W. H. Auden, letters to Benjamin Britten
Reprinted by permission of Curtis Brown, Ltd

W. H. Auden, 'Spain, 1937' and 'Night covers up the rigid land', from *The English Auden*
Reprinted by permission of Faber and Faber Ltd

W. H. Auden, 'A Summer Night', 'Danse Macabre' and 'In Memory of W. B. Yeats', from W. H. Auden, *Collected Poems*
Reprinted by permission of Faber and Faber Ltd

W. H. Auden, 'Pardon them their Mistakes', 'On the Frontier' from *The Ascent of F6 and On the Frontier*
Reprinted by permission of Faber and Faber Ltd

W. H. Auden, 'A Summer Night', 'In Memory of W. B. Yeats', copyright 1940 and renewed 1968 by W. H. Auden, from *W. H Auden: The Collected Poems* by W. H. Auden, copyright © 1976 by Edward Mendelson, William Meredith and Monroe K. Spears, Executors of the Estate of W. H. Auden. Used by permission of Random House, Inc.

Hugh MacDiarmid: 'An English War-Poet', in *Complete Poems*, reprinted by permission of Carcanet Press Limited

W. B. Yeats, 'Three Marching Songs' and 'Politics' reprinted with the permission of A. P. Watt Ltd on behalf of Michael B. Yeats, and Scribner, an imprint of Simon and Schuster Adult publishing group, from *The Collected Poems of W. B. Yeats, volume I: The Poems, Revised*, edited by Richard J. Finneran. Copyright © 1940 by Georgie Yeats; copyright renewed © 1968 by Georgie Yeats, Michael Butler Yeats and Anne Yeats

Roy Campbell, *The Flowering Rifle* (1938), reprinted with permission of Jonathan Ball Publishers (Pty) Ltd

Benjamin Britten, *Letters from a Life: Selected Letters and Diaries of Benjamin Britten*, edited by D. Mitchell and P. Reed, reprinted by permission of Faber and Faber and the University of California Press

Quotations from the letters and diaries of Benjamin Britten are © the Trustees of the Britten-Pears Foundation and may not further be reproduced without the written permission of the Trustees

Quotations from the letters of W. H. Auden and Lennox Berkeley to Benjamin Britten are reproduced courtesy of the Britten–Pears Library

Quotations from the letters of Lennox Berkeley are reproduced courtesy of Lady Berkeley and the Lennox Berkeley estate

Every effort has been made to trace the copyright holders of material reproduced in this volume. In the case of any query, please contact the publisher.

To
Tony Hyndman, writer
and
Lance Rogers, socialist

List of Acronyms

AIA	Artists' International Association
BUF	British Union of Fascists
CNT	Confederación Nacional de Trabajo
CPGB	Communist Party of Great Britain
CTV	Corpo Truppe Voluntarie (Italian Expeditionary Force)
FAI	Federación Anarquista Ibérica
IBA	International Brigade Association (GB)
ICF	Irish Christian Front
ILP	Independent Labour Party
PCE	Partido Comunista de España
POUM	Partido Obrero de Unificación Marxista
PSOE	Partido Socialista de Obreros Españoles
PSUC	Partido Socialista de Unificación Catalana
SIM	Servicio de Inteligencia Militar (Republican Security Police)

Note to Text

Please note that, from p. 130 onwards, an asterisk is used in the text to indicate those contemporary accounts from which longer, contextual extracts (with source references) are given in the Appendix (pp. 196–202).

~ 1 ~
Introduction: The Virtuous Republic versus the Philistines

Many have heard it on remote peninsulas,
Or sleepy plains, in the aberrant fisherman's islands
   Or the corrupt heart of the city,
Have heard and migrated like gulls or the seeds of a flower.

They clung like burrs to the long expresses that lurch
Through the unjust lands, through the night, through the alpine
                                                tunnel.
   They floated over the oceans;
They walked the passes. All presented their lives.[1]

More than sixty years after its military defeat, political overthrow and physical extinction, Spain's Second Republic remains the sacred cow of the western intellectual tradition. For many who have led their ethical lives within that tradition and take their most fundamental assumptions from it, the meaning of the Republic is evoked – in the appropriate context – by the single word, 'Spain', the title of Auden's magniloquent ode of 1937.[2] In so far as the broad humanitarian ideals of social freedom and progress, along with the spirit of sacrifice which must ultimately deliver them, now have an authentically global resonance, then the mythology of the Spanish Republic stands at their core. Few pause long to consider that the cause which this mythology serves embodies more than an abstract ethical construction; it also encapsulates a specific politico-ideological interest. And fewer still realize (or acknowledge) that the myth of 'Spain' by its very nature and function, excludes and suppresses half of Spain and half of the history of its Civil War.[3]

The myth is powerful enough to cross ideological frontiers, even where these still exist, as it were physically. Auden's poem SPAIN is (arguably above all) an encomium to those who 'presented their lives' for 'Spain' – that is, the International Brigades. It is not surprising that the USSR should have invoked the deathless reputation of the Brigades in its disputes with Communist China in the

1960s.[4] This was, after all, in line of descent from Stalin's claim to have created the army which – a part of the myth assures us – saved Madrid from Fascism in 1936. The Soviet Union's investment in 'Spain' was even at the time used to strengthen Stalin's regime in its own ideological internecine war against Communist dissidents. What is more remarkable, because so laden with irony, is that in 1989, the protesting Chinese students in Tiananmen Square should have reached for the rhetoric of the besieged Madrid of 1936. 'They Shall Not Pass', along with extended reference to the heroic myths of 'Spain', studded the text of their appeal for support to the outside world. Perhaps unknowingly, they even appropriated, for a future democratic China, Stalin's words about 'Spain' which summed up the sanction of the Popular Front: 'The struggle for democracy in China is the common cause of all progressive peoples in the world.'[5]

But the most seductive aspect of the mythology of the unlost Republic, an aspect which lends ineffable moral authority to its more strictly political heritage, is its identification with artistic aspiration. No political regime since Pericles' Athens has become more identified in the western mind with the arts in all their forms. In common perception it was, as a contemporary dubbed it, the 'Republic of Professors'.[6] Spain's first democracy was designed and (mostly) ruled by intellectuals, whose mission was to educate the people and to protect the profound artistic legacy of Spain, whilst simultaneously patronizing innovation and modernity, in a spirit of progress inspired by its commitment to freedom. During its struggle for survival against the violent challenge of the rebel generals, the Republic explicitly sought and duly received the world's accolade as being a civilization which lived and died for Art, and by that token worthy of all imitation and eternal honour.[7]

1 Cultures and Martyrs

The construction of 'Spain', by definition, consigns the Nationalist cause to the fate of being the perennial 'other', the anti-Spain existing in a darkness only made visible by the forces of light. The movement which was victorious in the military struggle, a wide coalition of principled forces opposed to the Republic, is ubiquitously presented as the ethical antipodes of its victim. In much of its treatment outside Spain, the Francoist regime is pictured as avowedly philistine, to the point of vandalism.[8]

It is true that the 'National-Catholic Spain' of the postwar years had limited time and resources to spare for the refinements of High Art, which in the course of the twentieth century came to be accepted as a required attribute for a 'civilized' nation-state. It sanctioned a neo-classical, weakly fascistized art, which privileged images of religion, patriotism and triumph. As it happens, the results resembled the official public art of Soviet Russia quite as much as that of Nazi Germany.[9] Within the Spartan Spain of the *postguerra*, José Antonio Primo de Rivera, founder of Spain's Fascist Party, was sacralized as *presente*. The supreme 'martyr' of national Spain, judicially murdered by the 'Reds' in 1936, he achieved immortality by decree. His remains were placed before the high altar at the core of the Nationalist sepulchre, the Valley of the Fallen. This vast sanctuary-ossuary, laid out on a windswept platform amongst mountain peaks to the north of Madrid, was constructed by the forced labour of Republican prisoners, to hundreds of whom this act of compulsory atonement brought early death as a blessed release. Here, in triumph and justification, were brought the bodies of their enemies, the Nationalist soldiers, from shallow graves on battlefields all over Spain, to form the storage silos of blood sacrifice, the primitive spiritual accumulation sustaining over forty years of dictatorship. In 1975, Franco himself was laid alongside José Antonio – like some Philip II, or as others less deferential remarked, some Pharaoh – with all the panoply of military Spain and the Catholic Church.[10] The image of a barbaric, grandiose, almost pre-literate civilization is often found in descriptions of this site; and seems borne out by the fact that its square kilometres of blank granite surfaces carry fewer than ten words which might offer some explanation of the Nationalist cause to the curious visitor.[11] Like the Arch of Victory, which Franco placed at the exact location where his armies had been stalled for most of the Civil War by Madrid's resistance, the Valley of the Fallen is steadily being overgrown with weeds.[12] In time, its massively self-reflective silence will be broken only by the occasional coachload of puzzled tourists from remote locations. It has now become a symbol, not of the triumph of God and Spain, but of the apparently logocentric vacuum at the core of Francoist politics.

For its first two decades, its victory being admittedly hard-won, and having very little else to celebrate, Franco's regime continued to proclaim victory, in a tedious, noisy and essentially introspective ritual of triumphalism. But all the time it was slowly becoming clearer, to all but the most dedicated cohabitants of the dictator's 'bunker', that in the most meaningful senses, it was the Republic which had triumphed. Almost everywhere outside Spain, even amongst the peoples of Franco's erstwhile allies, Germany and Italy, the posthumous influence of the Republic was celebrated whilst that of Nationalist Spain was null and void. This phenomenon had little to do with the activities of republican 'governments in exile' which stuttered on into the 1960s.[13] Rather, memory of the struggle, perennially renewed by the ongoing cultural programmes of exiled intellectuals and International Brigade veterans, created the mystical aura of 'Spain'. For a surprising range of otherwise differing political affiliations, the Republic became the florescent spiritual location of libertarian politics. In this populous community, having perhaps a majority of subscribers from the New World, the object of desire was the 'New World' which Buenaventura Durruti, killed defending Madrid in 1936, and his anarchist followers claimed to carry in their hearts.[14] But by far its most resonant symbol was another 'martyr'. In August 1936, Federico García Lorca was murdered by Fascist thugs in his home town of Granada. It was Lorca, not José Antonio, who was to be *presente* in the minds of academics, artists and intellectuals the world over, a hero to yet unborn generations, and thus an infinitely more potent icon than his Fascist acquaintance and admirer.[15] No single victim of the military rising and its ruthless campaigns of repression was to be more regretted by the directors of Francoist Spain. No personality better qualified than Federico to represent the Second Republic could have been constructed by some multidisciplined team of programmers working towards an ideal template. By its involvement in the death of this polymathic genius the Nationalist cause stood condemned 'before the bar of history' for all time.

In his lifetime, Lorca achieved fame on both sides of the Atlantic, New York as well as Madrid, Buenos Aires as well as Barcelona. He was poet, painter, dramatist, musician, actor, director, teacher. Art itself, it seemed, had been murdered with him – buried anonymously, at night, and so obscurely that its bones were never to be found. There was an added factor, emerging years later, but which reinforced the cult of the dead poet by reason of its affinity with the political causes of the second half of the century. Lorca was a target of the Fascists because he was gay. This made a big impact on the young of the 1970s. The Vietnam War generated an atmosphere of popular radicalism, within which the mythology of 'Spain' experienced a revival, proving superbly adaptable to the shift in cultural perspectives.[16] Lorca became the archetype of the modern transgressive writer, destroyed partly because he questioned the cultural and racial shibboleths of Spanish identity, partly because he gave voice to the miseries of oppressed Andalusia (the landless *braceros* and the women of the *pueblos*), but mostly because his sexual orientation was an intolerable affront to the tenderest sensitivities of his classically 'macho' society.[17]

But as it happens, young, glamorous, radical artists were not a reserved species of the Republican side in the Civil War. On the night of 20 September 1936, Alfonso Ponce de León was arrested after strolling with his wife in Madrid's Paseo de la Castellana, taken away, tortured in order to extract information about suspicious associates, and finally shot. His body was found in a gutter of an outlying suburb the next day. This fate was the fate of thousands of so-called 'Fascist fifth-columnists'. Ponce de León was a painter whose career had just begun to blossom when the war broke out. Coming, as did his friend, Lorca, from a privileged background, he too came to empathize profoundly with the poor and oppressed. For a time, indeed, he worked with Lorca as a scene painter and occasional actor in the famous theatre company, La Barraca, which toured the most deprived regions of Castile. This experience radicalized his ideas still further, and in search of an effective, revolutionary solution to Spain's socio-economic crisis, he joined the Falange. In January 1935, he held his first individual exhibition in Madrid. In the year leading up to July 1936, Alfonso worked on important commissions, and contributed some mordantly anti-capitalist cartoons to the Falangist magazine, *Arriba*. He became associated with a group of Fascist intellectuals (including the young poet, Dionisio Ridruejo) who used to meet regularly in a Madrid café.

On 20 July, Ponce de León's elder brother was among the rebel officers of the Montaña Barracks, and was killed after the besieging mob had broken into the building. His father and another brother were arrested and murdered at around the same time as Alfonso; his mother killed herself after spending a year trying in vain to find out what had happened to her loved ones. The Ponce de León family were relatively wealthy, Catholic members of the conservative right. Doubtless, it was known that Alfonso was a Falangist and brother to a proven traitor. If not already an active member of the Fifth Column, he was reckoned a likely recruit to its ranks. His murderers were members of the Checa (irregular security militia) of Madrid's Barrio Fomento; in effect, like the killers of Lorca, 'uncontrollables' for whose actions the official authorities took no responsibility. Quite unlike the case of Lorca, however, Ponce de León and his work were forgotten for nearly half a century. 'It is curious', remarked Ridruejo (perhaps disingenuously) forty years later, 'that such an interesting painter should have disappeared, as it were from the map.'[18]

A few weeks after the massacre of the Ponce de León family, as Franco's armies approached the banks of the Manzanares, García Lorca's arrangements of Andalusian folk songs were pressed into service as hymns of resistance. Provided with topical texts offering defiance to the rebel generals, they were played and sung in public meetings, in the trenches and at the barricades.[19] The significance of these songs was grasped by the political commissariat of the International Brigades. One of these was Gustavo Durán, a communist musician-turned-soldier, on the staff of the XI Brigade. Durán too was an associate and friend of Lorca, who was admired by André Malraux. In exile after the war, he was to make his own arrangements of Federico's folk songs.[20] Such men – many themselves writers – took Lorca into their kitbags, and thence back to Paris, Moscow, London, Boston, Havana; and after 1945, to East Berlin and to Rome.[21]

2 University Politics: (1) Contest of Faculties

The International Brigade received its baptism of fire in Madrid's University City in November 1936. This site had been allocated as the new campus of the Universidad Complutense in the 1920s. Building began during the relatively benign military dictatorship of José Antonio's father, Miguel Primo de Rivera. Under the Republic, construction went on apace, its prevailing architecture being state-of-the-art varieties of Bauhaus. It was to be a showpiece of Republican virtue, an expensive testament to its constitutional commitment to enlightenment and progress. But in November 1936, when the University City was selected by General Varela as the target zone for the 'final' assault of the Nationalist Army of Africa upon Madrid, several important buildings were still incomplete. The Republican government, along with its senior bureaucrats and most of the diplomatic corps, abandoned the capital. With the world looking on and expecting a rapid Franco victory, only the soldiers – and, of course, the people – were left to offer the sacrifice and face the suffering.[22]

At the critical point of military outcome, on the cusp of two competing ideas of 'civilization', the front line was drawn between the faculty buildings of Law and Philosophy. In an epic Contest of Faculties, as if obeying the decree of some potent, presiding metanarrative, the 'Fascists' occupied Law, whilst Philosophy was defended by a force of Communists. The former included the lamentably untutored Moroccans, led by Spanish officers. The latter were newly formed battalions of foreign volunteers, the International Brigade, representing the workers and intellectuals of the world. On the one side (that is) the ignorant drones and mindless slave-drivers of colonialism; on the other, the most politically conscious military units in world history. Bullets and insults were exchanged over makeshift barricades of books. For thirty months, the complete works of Cervantes and Schopenhauer on one side, and the *New Collection of All the Laws of the Kingdom of Castile* on the other, were peppered into dust. The University City, object of incessant bombardment, was reduced to rubble. Its destruction seemed to offer symbolic proof of the nihilism at the core of international Fascism.

Sparkling with the literary stars of a dozen nations, the XI and XII International Brigades included Ludwig Renn and Gustav Regler (German), Jeff Last (Dutch) and Maté Zalka (Hungarian) as commanders and commissars. The Republic usually balked at publicizing the presence of Internationals at the front; but there were times when the propaganda value of artistic reputations outweighed any negative impact that knowledge of a foreign military contribution might have on the Non-Intervention Committee. A prominent frontline newspaper, *La Voz del Combatiente*, refrained from mention of the International Brigades even during the crisis of Madrid. But during the battle of Jarama, one report enthused that 'whilst we're talking of culture, there seems no alternative but to boast about the magnificent fact that the Dutch poet and writer Jeff Last is a lieutenant in the 37th Brigade. What a lesson and an example for those who think that writers are good for little more than singing to the moon.'[23]

John Cornford (British) was a political commissar in the XI Brigade. The image of the twenty–year-old poet, rifle in hand, bloodied bandage around his head, could have been in the mind of Malcolm Muggeridge, already the cynical scourge of the British left, when he wrote of the 1930s 'fashion for the soldier-poet, agonised at having to shed blood, listening to birds singing when the guns paused, with his Keats or Shakespeare sonnets in the pocket of his tunic; yet not less courageous and effective for that; if anything, more'.[24] In the bigger picture, too, Muggeridge seems to have been reading accounts of the University City's resistance, perhaps that of the Communist writer John Sommerfield, Cornford's comrade-in-arms, when he noted of this generation:

> Barricades of knowledge were erected, piled ever higher; Maginot Line, impregnable let us hope, composed of small and large masterpieces, pocket, crown octavo, and other editions, lucid accounts of this and that, surveys historical, sociological, psychological, calculated to increase understanding. Ye are instructed, they are ignorant; the pen is mightier than the sword, and to demonstrate its might, must be active. When Dr Negrin, Spanish Prime Minister, visited France, it was counted to him for virtue that he found time to visit the bookstalls by the Seine. Would Goering have so employed his time?[25]

One of Negrín's predecessors as prime minister was Manuel Azaña, intellectual and writer, acknowledged leader of the reforming administrations of 1931–3. He supervised an ambitious programme of secular education, aimed at fashioning a new spiritual culture for a nation which (he felt) had ceased to be Catholic in anything but the ritual and individual sense. Azaña himself was not wholly unaware that he stepped on the primary fault-line which might sunder Spain. But it was through a series of mistakes and misunderstandings, by way of acts of commission and ommission, in which many supporters of the Republic were complicit, that this 'civilizing mission' turned out to be the primary issue which divided the nation against itself. The demands of education and bourgeois culture came to be seen by many Catholics as part and parcel of a conspiracy to secularize Spain by destroying its traditional religion.

In principle, Church reform was intended to be limited to those social and educational influences seen as inimical to a progressive twentieth-century democracy. In practice, however, reform was soon construed as (and, in detail, often degenerated into) persecution of Catholic institutions and observance. Of course, the final breakdown of 1936 evolved through a complex mess of converging issues and events, often unconnected with religion. But without the *basso ostinato* of ideological suspicion, without the conflict over the Church, which inevitably involved all Spaniards, the relapse into violent polarization and civil war is inconceivable.[26]

All the same, the Republic's claim to stand for freedom of intellectual inquiry was based on real concern and solid achievement. As one Spanish expert admits, from a basically Francoist perspective, even during the Civil War, 'the Republican left's obsession with culture was not simply a matter of propaganda.'[27] It must be remembered that many a political crisis before 1936 was accompanied by swingeing measures against the press, from censorship to jail sentences. The hyperbole of wartime propaganda thereafter was often specious, the more so as these freedoms became compromised by the exigencies of war. Nevertheless, there was at first a purer reality. The 'Reforming Republic' (1931–3) opened thousands of new schools, modernized the curriculum, and increased teachers' salaries.[28] Influenced by Manuel Cossío, art historian and radical educationalist, the minister for Public Instruction, ex-schoolteacher Marcelino Domingo, instituted travelling libraries which criss-crossed Spain, visiting the remotest *pueblos*. Lorca's La Barraca was only the best-known of several state-sponsored caravans of performing artists who were hired to amaze and delight the rural masses. In the university of Lorca's Granada, as also in Madrid, institutes for the study of Spain's Arabic heritage were opened. A disciple of Cossío was promised the headship of a new Institute of Education, whilst the Humanities Faculty of Madrid's Universidad Complutense was granted unprecedented freedom of curricular innovation.[29]

Even when the rate of improvement slowed down under the centre-right Madrid administrations of 1933–6, reform continued apace in Catalonia, which under its autonomy statute had charge of its own education policy. Once the left regained control of central government following the 'Popular Front' election of February 1936, the national programme went ahead with renewed zeal. This certainly made the desired impact in the localities: during the Civil War, local councils pressurized both government and sub-governmental authorities for help in creating lecture halls and libraries. Statistical evidence of the spread of enlightenment impressed observers like José Castillejo Duarte. A distinguished educationalist, exiled in Britain during the Civil War, Castillejo was only half-convinced by the Republic's general project, but accepted that its work in this dimension had been of tremendous value. In his view, creating this popular infrastructure was to fashion 'the essential instrument for the selective functioning of a true democracy' – a policy all the more impressive for avoiding a slavish imitation of foreign examples.[30] Recognition of such achievement by experts like Castillejo, Alberto Jiménez and Lorenzo Luzuriaga – and of E. Allison Peers, a British Hispanist who fully shared their views – was more impressive for being, in part, a grudging one. The Spaniards were in Britain as voluntary exiles from the Republican zone, Castillejo having narrowly escaped with his life after being held by a Checa in Madrid.[31] For such men, most of whom had served it in some capacity, the stumbling block to support of the Republic remained its religious policy. They feared the Republic was creating a new culture, not for its own sake, but for the purpose of engineering a laicist civilization in which the Church could have no meaningful role. A political animal did not have to be a fanatical (or even a practising) Catholic in order to nurse such reservations. Not surprisingly, the revolutionary events of 1936 itself, with their apparent attempt once and for all to have done with the Church – to cauterize it both from the present and from the past – intensified these anxieties.[32]

None of this mattered in the judgement of the Italian academic Aldo Garosci. For Garosci, writing in the late 1950s, the difference of 1936–9 was simply between those who embraced the Goddess of Reason, and those who rejected her. The former, by definition, included the intellectuals. Garosci, himself a veteran of the International Brigades, suggested that the exodus of writers from the defeated Republic held greater significance for twentieth-century thinking than that from post-1933 Germany; indeed, it was the modern equivalent of the diaspora of scholarship from Constantinople in 1453, alleged genesis of the European Renaissance. The literature produced by the anti-Franco exiles was of 'unique spiritual significance' because it crucially advanced our

The Virtuous Republic versus the Philistines

understanding of basic issues of freedom, tolerance and sacrifice.[33] Garosci's book was a contribution to the polemic of political struggle. But just as by no means all teachers and academics (or, for that matter, creative artists) had espoused 'Spain', similar divisions existed among a related group with much more general influence, the intellectuals. Here I make the distinction which existed in certain European countries until relatively recently, referring to freelance *savants* whose relationship with the formal academic world was loose (and frequently disdainful). Often men of private means, their opinions on politics and society were regularly solicited by magazines and newspapers. Some enjoyed an aphoristic influence which reached well beyond the common rooms of the Complutense or the Ateneo. The pro-Republican interest had no hegemony in this area. In the aftermath of the military rebellion of 1936, most of Spain's great thinkers attempted (at least at first) to hold themselves 'above the quarrel'.[34]

Prominent among them was José Ortega y Gasset, world-renowned philosopher and social scientist. Ortega had been an active supporter of the Republic in its early days, organizing the 'Agrupación al servicio de la República, in effect an Intellectuals' Party, which won several seats in the Constituent Cortes.[35] But his positive feelings about the new dispensation were in essence produced by his negative reaction to the old, the dictatorship of General Primo de Rivera, which had imposed a wayward censorship and an equally random proscription of ideas. Earlier still, Ortega's essay, *The Rebellion of the Masses*, expressed his deep apprehensions about the nature of democracy. Whilst always standing in a liberal-humanist window of ethical perception, his dialectic was profoundly linked to art-centred preconceptions of 'civilization'.[36]

In the 1920s Ortega concluded that Fascism was in essence a reflection of the weaknesses of any system within which it flourished; and that it flourished commensurately with the seriousness of that malaise. It followed that any democratic regime which was overthrown by Fascism suffered a fate which was both deserved and inevitable.[37] This odd variant of Social Darwinism enjoined that Fascism represented a truth which could not be resisted – exactly the reverse of Marxian–Hegelian prescriptions of history. Thus (Ortega might argue) once Franco had conquered more than half of Spain, which arguably came about with the fall of the Basque Country in June, 1937, the logic of the 'II Año de la

Victoria', proclaimed in the documentation of the Franco regime, neither could nor should be further resisted.

In the mid-1930s, alienated by the attitudes of the Azañista radicals, and fearful of the side-effects of radical democratization, Ortega distanced himself from the Republic. At the war's outbreak, he went to Paris, and at first refrained from endorsing either side. Several disciples (such as Francisco Pérez de Ayala) followed his example. However, as the violent social revolution in Spain unfolded, Ortega found it increasingly difficult to remain silent. In 1937 he publicly rebuked Albert Einstein for intervening in a dispute which he knew little or nothing about. Ortega tartly enquired what right Einstein possessed, as a foreigner with no Spanish connections, to use his fame to influence world opinion over the fate of the Spanish people.[38] Few were surprised when during the second year of the war, Ortega began to put out feelers in the direction of the Burgos regime.[39]

The political *cursus honorum* of Gregorio de Marañón was not dissimilar. One of an increasing fellowship of Spanish scientists who gained fame in the non-Hispanic world during the first quarter of the century, Marañón was a pathologist who (in the 1920s) resigned his Madrid chair and renounced research medicine in favour of his hobby, history. He produced biographical studies of the autocratic rulers of Golden-Age Spain (King Philip II, the Count-Duke of Olivares) in which he combined his diagnostic insights, and a linked interest in psychology, with *sub-rosa* criticism of the ruling dictator, Primo de Rivera.[40] Under the Republic, Marañón was associated with Ortega's group, and was content to be used as a flagship intellectual for democratic Spain. With the military uprising, however, he sought exile in France. Unlike Ortega's, his decision to accommodate with Burgos was not derived from an intellectual position previously elaborated. Marañón's motivation was more mundane. He could see clearly enough that Franco was no improvement on Primo, leave alone the Republic. But his two sons had both enlisted in the Nationalist armies. In gratitude for his support, Franco was later to name a square in Madrid's main thoroughfare, the Paseo de la Castellana, in Dr Marañón's honour.[41]

3 University Politics: (2) Death to the Intelligentsia

As the above examples illustrate, to seek exile from the Republic did not necessarily indicate that the subject was a Franco supporter. On the contrary, many were repelled by his regime and never offered it sustenance, public or otherwise. Of course, in practical terms it was less difficult for intellectuals who had fled the Republican zone, and never endorsed its cause, to make their peace with the victors after 1939, and (as in many cases) to return to Spain. But accommodation with the new regime did not always represent comfort. In the Nationalist zone itself these dilemmas were even sharper. Here, intellectuals and academics were given little opportunity to leave the country. Those who escaped the process of 'purification' and kept both their lives and livelihoods had no alternative to support for Francoism. It is commonly believed that the case of Don Miguel de Unamuno typifies how the truly great thinker could never tolerate such shabby conformism. In fact, although the tragedy of Don Miguel sensationally dramatized the relevant issues, his story has a more ambiguous ambience.

In terms of prestige, Unamuno had no equal in the Spain of his day. Pre-eminent as philosopher and literary critic, renowned for his imaginative fiction, he was the supreme interpreter of Spain's cultural traditions (in the widest sense of the term). Like all the elite 'intellectuals' defined and commented on above, he supported the early Republic, which had rescued him from the self-imposed exile of the Primo years. In 1936, it was therefore a matter of some satisfaction to the Nationalist junta when their actions met with his approbation. Moreover, this endorsement was not the result of some geographical accident, of the fact that Salamanca University, Spain's oldest and most prestigious seat of learning, where Don Miguel was vice-chancellor, happened to be located at the heart of a solidly conservative region which had opted for the Nationalists in the first days of the war. Unamuno's support for the Nationalists was no opportunism. Like Ortega, he was convinced that the democratic experiment had failed, at least for the time being. After the Popular Front elections, he felt that Spain had collapsed into a tide of anarchy which threatened to engulf all its institutions and inundate its traditions. Only swift and authoritative action could remedy the situation.[42]

The fact that Unamuno was a Basque offered a bonus for

Franco's publicity men. The great Spaniard hailed from Bilbao, a city which in October 1936 became the capital of an autonomous Basque Republic, following a statute rushed through the Madrid Cortes in recognition of Basque support. Bilbao was the epicentre of resistance to Franco in northern Spain. But this did not please Unamuno. Throughout his career Don Miguel, in exemplary fashion, had placed love of his region (*patria chica*) firmly below the duty of loyalty to historic Spain, a people united in one nation which nurtured plural identities.[43] But his moral dilemmas were soon to force themselves upon his consciousness – and in a manner which could have provided the setting for one of his own novellas. Unamuno was the representative figure of the so-called 'Generation of 1898', Spain's original group of radical, proto-modernist intellectuals. For this reason, the traditional institution with which he was least comfortable was the military – as his reaction to Primo's dictatorship had demonstrated. In the summer of 1936, he nevertheless collaborated with the military junta which had installed itself in Burgos. He made personal donations of money to its war effort, and went so far as to carry out a purge of pro-Republican professors on his staff.[44]

In late September, however, Franco was chosen as *generalísimo* by his peers, and appointed himself head of state into the bargain. The provisional Junta was dissolved, the apparatus of autocratic government was set up in Burgos, and Salamanca became the base for Franco's military direction of the war. Soon afterwards the *Día de la Raza* (12 October, the national holiday commemorating Columbus' sighting of the New World) was celebrated by a ceremony in the ancient womb of the university, a medieval lecture hall called the Paraninfo.[45] Franco himself was absent at the front, dealing with a series of Republican counter-attacks launched as his forces closed on Madrid. Alongside Don Miguel and a bevy of other academic dignitaries were Doña Carmen, Franco's wife, and General Millán Astray, his military mentor and close friend. Unamuno was, evidently, content to grace this strongly profiled Nationalist ritual with his presence, so that his subsequent behaviour seems to have been genuinely spontaneous. Millán's characteristically robust speech, which infringed academic protocol by making contemptuous reference to the 'anti-Spain' of the Republic, was volubly encouraged from the floor. There were shouts of '¡Viva la Muerte!' – the slogan of the elite shock-troop regiment called 'El Tercio', which Millán and Franco had founded – and some supporters jumped to their feet to give the Fascist salute.

As the meeting proceeded, Unamuno was observed to be frantically scribbling notes. He was expected to deliver a routine speech in praise of the eternal greatness of the Spanish spirit as enshrined in the 'Discoveries' and the 'Golden Age' of the sixteenth century. But when he finally spoke it was with barely controlled anger. Millán and his noisy clique had traduced everything he held dear. Basques and Catalans were condemned as traitors, intellectuals vilified as peddlers of anarchy, the sanctuary of Spanish learning defiled. Unamuno felt himself personally insulted. Don Miguel's righteous indignation knew no bounds, and though this gave an added eloquence and resonance to his words, it also clouded his judgement. He proclaimed in unforgettable phrases the centrality of education and the cultivation of elite intelligence to any civilized community. He insisted that by no means all Basques or Catalans were fighting on the side of the Red Republic. He struck out at the military ethic, which, if left to its own devices would turn the national cause into a mindless and brutal juggernaut. Stung further by shouts of '¡Muere la Inteligencia!' from equally angry opponents, he referred to himself as 'the high priest of intelligence', and even took personal revenge on Millán Astray, using the general's physical condition as the most famously wounded soldier in Spain – to his admirers, evidence of patriotic self-sacrifice – as a metaphor instead for the spiritually crippled Spain which, in Don Miguel's opinion, Millán proposed to establish.

Unamuno's speech was a prophecy, but also in many ways it became a self-fulfilling prophecy. His most telling remark, all the more effective for its poetic encapsulation, was saved until last, and was to resonate for generations around the groves of academe: 'Venceréis, pero no convenceréis'.[46] Yet at the moment of its utterance, this announcement seemed to be at variance with the facts. After all, the speaker himself (that is the 'high priest of intelligence') had been, until that very moment, more or less convinced of the superior case of the Nationalists. The *escándalo* at Salamanca was censored in the Nationalist media, and only random whispers about the circumstances of Unamuno's disgrace and death reached Republican ears. It was only much later that the event entered mainstream mythology as the definitive rejection of Francoism by the world of the intelligence. But once that construction was in place, the confrontation of 'Long Live Death' and 'Death to the Intelligentsia' with 'You will conquer, but never convince' provided fecund evidence on which to indict Franco-Fascism on the charge of philistine nihilism. Like Lorca, and equally inadvertently, Unamuno had helped to deny the Nationalist cause any representation before the bar of history.[47]

We may move forward a few years, and shift the scene from the Paraninfo of Salamanca to the equally sacred space of the Sheldonian Theatre, Oxford. In 1946, the Francoist government neatly reciprocated the British Council's ambiguous 'gift' of English books to Spanish universities by sending a consignment of Spanish books to their British equivalents. As A. J. P. Taylor later recalled, 'At Oxford the University Council put down a routine decree in Congregation expressing gratitude. Memories of the Civil War were revived. Some Oxford people did not want to express gratitude to the Spanish Fascists for books or anything else.' The indignant young historian organized resistance which had echoes of '¡No pasarán!', and 'Venceréis pero no convenceréis', and was able to produce a majority in the Sheldonian meeting for a motion rejecting the decree of thanks. 'The affair became quite a diplomatic incident', Taylor continued in self-congratulatory mode, 'telegrams flowing in from the British Embassy in Madrid, the Foreign Office trying to dictate a renewal of the decree and many hard words exchanged in Oxford.' No matter. The conscience of English scholarship was not to be compromised by even the most formal connivance with Franco-Fascism's pretence to civilization.[48]

4 The Disasters of War

During the Spanish 'war of independence' against the Napoleonic occupation, Francisco Goya produced his celebrated series of sketches with the above title. Of shocking documentary realism, they were the most harrowing images of war made since the work of Jacques Callot in the seventeenth century. It might be argued that, with their adumbration of post-Freudian surrealism, their grisly emphasis on the consequences of political breakdown, civilian suffering and local reprisals, Goya's pictures served as perfectly for 1936 as for 1812. But by the mid-twentieth century, radiotelegraphy and newsprint could not be denied. Spain was putting on, in the consciously sardonic words of a young Catalan bureaucrat, 'the most photogenic war'.[49] Spain, the 'Tragic Spain' of so many headlines and captions, moved to the forefront of world attention, becoming the first war to be recorded on cine film and covered comprehensively by the newspaper industry. In the aftermath of Franco's failure to take Madrid, which (of course) was also the Republic's triumph in resisting him, there was an almost audible hiatus. Both sides suddenly became conscious of the need to respond to the world's attention, and especially concerned at the consequences, in terms of external sympathy, of the previous five months of vicious battle and fanatical terror. Many aspects of the orgy of bloodletting which had taken place behind the lines had been widely reported and (within the limits of prevailing taste) pictured. For Valencia as for Burgos, the immediate imperative of propaganda was to make it clear that their cause stood for 'civilization', and that of their enemies for 'barbarism'.

Though the pause in the military struggle for the land was only momentary, the Republic never again lost sight of the almost equally important task of recapturing the ground of representation. As, on one level, the atavistic genie of the revolutionary masses was gradually squeezed back into its bottle, on another a new image of the Republic, more reassuring to the outside world, was carefully prepared. Both the rhetoric and the practice of revolution were actively discouraged by the Soviet Union, which in September had committed itself to rescuing 'la niña bonita' from the Fascist dragon. The staff of the Soviet embassy which then arrived mostly comprised military, intelligence and propaganda experts.[50] In the last-named team were Mikhail Koltsov and Ilya Ehrenburg, who from their own experience in moulding the external image of the USSR, were already familiar with the problems in focus. They quickly took charge of censorship and propaganda in Madrid.[51] On the Spanish Front, what better antidote to the poison broadcast by the world communications media than to demonstrate that the typical loyalist in arms was not a criminal priest-killer, but an intellectual dedicated to the spread of literacy, or an ordinary soldier hunched in the trench over the holograph of his first poem?[52]

The embattled Republic thus promoted education, art and culture to the forefront of its propaganda. One means to this was the mass production of pamphlets and posters, which richly repaid the effort involved, successfully bequeathing an impression to the world which has never been effaced. Many of its posters, in particular, were subsequently seen as works of art in themselves, indeed as virtually creating a new genre of representation.[53] They pictured a people aspiring towards the basic human dignity of education, with no greater (even no other) aspiration than that of enlightenment, yet in constant danger of being crushed back into the slime by the Fascist jackboot.

> *El mayor enemigo es el analfabetismo*
>
> *La ignorancia es arma del fascismo*
>
> *El analfabetismo ciega el espíritu*
> *¡Soldado instruyente!*[54]

One of the most intensively exploited themes was the Republic's guardianship of Spain's 'artistic heritage', apparently under direct attack by the enemy. The growing corps of foreign pressmen (and presswomen) in Madrid was constantly directed to scenes in which paintings were saved from the vandal Junkers overhead, and carefully stored in underground shelters; where the minor religious artworks of the convents were reverentially protected; where even the sixteenth-century palace of the Duke of Alba, Franco's emissary to London, was saved from a fire started by a Nationalist air-raid.[55] (This was the Palacio de Liria, which had in fact been taken over as a barracks of the PCE militia.)[56] The Republic put considerable energy into convincing the world that the destruction of Spain's artistic heritage was a specific – indeed a priority – war aim of the Nationalists. These campaigns were subtly extended via thematic interplay. For example, Madrid's Prado Museum, site of Spain's world-famous collection of paintings, was frequently alleged to be under deliberate attack from the air.[57] During one raid in November 1936, Junker pilots seemed to single out Goya for special attention, three incendiary devices falling on or close to the gallery dedicated to his work.[58] Amidst considerable publicity the priceless masterpieces were moved from Madrid to a secret destination in order to secure them from Fascist barbarism.[59] The evil alliance of Franco with Hitler was summed up in the notion that the Condor Legion selected libraries and art galleries on the one hand, and women and children on the other, as its two preferred targets. Louis Delaprée, a French reporter in Madrid, encapsulated this trope carefully, noting that 'all the precious books of the National

Library . . . went out this morning with a children's convoy. On a lorry two little lads of seven sat on a case.'[60] In this way the basic human values of civil society were linked to the alleged centrality of their expression in art, a link which would be recognized as valid and crucial by educated people everywhere.[61]

This campaign was stimulated by the attention paid by the world press to the systematic incineration of churches and their artistic contents, embarrassingly unwelcome publicity which, to begin with, handed the palm of 'defenders of culture' to their enemies. Throughout the summer of 1936, newspapers and newsreels played up the apparently wholesale artistic iconoclasm carried out by 'uncontrollable' anarchist gangs.[62] During this period, the expatriate English novelist, Ralph Bates, soon to be a commissar in the XV International Brigade, encountered a CNT militia column in a Catalan village. Bates was conscious that art-loving people outside Spain would find it hard to understand the vandalism of the masses, and needed deflecting from the suspicion that such behaviour hardly suggested a civilizing mission on the part of the Republic. He sent an article to *Left Review*, 'wishing only to explain the feelings of the Spanish workers', relating how he had personally advised, using only his own aesthetic judgement, on which images from a local church should be burned. 'You have to get right into the imagination of Spain to feel it the way I do, or a Spaniard does . . . It is the legendary heroic quality of this struggle that I am trying to make clear, not its violence.'[63]

In January 1937, the bulletin of the Artists' International Association announced that 'Franco is destroying Spain's art from the air', whilst the British Hispanist J. B. Trend called for protests against the burning of Lorca's books ('a new *auto-da-fe*') by the Nationalists.[64] Later that year, Nancy Cunard and John Banting visited the Prado Museum. 'In the basements', Banting recalled, 'experts had partly restored El Grecos taken from attics and churches . . . The work was going on steadily with semi-famine, bombardment and icy weather outside.'[65] When the delegates of the Anti-Fascist Writers' Congress arrived in Madrid in July 1937, they were addressed by Gustavo Durán on the work of the Junta Delegada del Tesoro Artístico, which (it was claimed) had saved 10,000 great paintings, 100,000 other artworks and 400,000 important books.[66] By 1938, even Hollywood had got the message, the feature film *Blockade*, set in wartime Spain, including a scene in which art treasures are protected by loyalist militiamen.[67] But this was not enough to allow pause. With Catalonia about to fall, the Ministry of State again urged all agencies abroad to alert the press to the measures being taken to safeguard Spain's artistic heritage.[68] Nancy Cunard was on hand to embroider the sacred fabric of myth for readers of the *Manchester Guardian*.

> One of the last official documents to bear the signature of Señor del Vayo in the old Castle of Figueras was that accepting that the Spanish paintings and works of art be taken to Geneva for safe keeping . . . At the moment of signing a violent bombing of Figueras took place, the electric current was cut off and the signatures had to be apposed by the light of matches. The report that some of the lorries transporting works of art were attacked by planes is confirmed in the local press here today.[69]

Despite Franco's efforts, Goya and his distinguished colleagues did not became another disaster of war, and the canvases survived the journey. In Geneva a few months later, like many other artistic exiles 'sheltering from the Spanish Civil War', mute but voluble witnesses to 'Spain', they were duly inspected and approved by A. J. P. Taylor and his wife during a touring holiday.[70]

Elsewhere, too, even after the death of the Republic, in places which existed as far removed from Swiss art galleries or Oxford common rooms as could be imagined, the candles of enlightenment continued to splutter. The phenomenon was witnessed by a Belgian monarchist, Charles d'Ydewalle, who in 1943 was arrested in Barcelona on suspicion of espionage, and interned in the POW camp at Miranda del Ebro, where many ex-International Brigaders were also held. In this punitive environment he rubbed shoulders with men of many nationalities. Though by no means either politically or personally sympathetic to most, he identified with them in one crucial respect:

> All these men, coming from such diverse conditions and environments, recognized each other by their choice of literature. What a medley of books I came across in that camp – detective stories, novels by Claude Ferrere, pious books, obscene books, revolutionary manuals redolent of dynamite, the stories of Alphonse Daudet, and treatises on political economy. Yellowed they were, and torn and dirty, dog-eared and broken-backed from much use, passed a hundred times from hand to hand, but in all of them the mind found refuge from the ever-present menace of boredom.

D'Ydewalle noted with surprise that much of the literature thus consumed was prohibited in the world outside the barbed wire. He was puzzled at the atmosphere of apparent toleration by the authorities. One may infer from his treatment that they simply did not realize the importance of literature to resistance, and thus were ignorant of the effects which d'Ydewalle (himself, it almost goes without saying, a writer) was keen to apprehend:

> The International Brigade had their own library in their hut. So had the Poles in No. 17. The Belgians had another, in No. 26, and the British in No. 18. All this literary give and take must have produced some odd results, scarcely analysable at the moment, but such as will certainly leave their mark on history.[71]

This mark had already been bid for in more ambitious and less ambiguous terms by Ralph Bates, who, it would seem, aspired to succeed Unamuno as the Republic's 'high priest of the intelligentsia'. In 1939, writing for an American middle-class audience, Bates apostrophized the death of the Spanish Republic as an apocalyptic event tantamount to the extinction of art and culture themselves. He told of 'the men of the Fifth Regiment [who] saved the books from the Faculty of Philosophy' in the University City. As Hemingway's fictional hero, Robert Jordan – professor of Spanish turned-guerrilla fighter – might have done, Bates recruited the great names of Spanish literature into his elegy. But recruitment did not stop there; for even the Godhead was conscripted for the cause. A talk on art and culture which he gave to the American volunteers of the Lincoln Battalion at the front, 'was [Bates recalled] like a High Mass of the Holy Ghost'.[72]

I

Writers, Fighters and Bloody Scribblers

~ 2 ~

Comrade – Lover – Victim: Cornford, Spender and Friends

1 Hyperion and the Satyr

In the early days of 1937, a young Communist made a pilgrimage to Cambridge. Michael Straight was an American, and heir to a substantial fortune. He was going back to the university where he had graduated the previous summer, but not in order to attend a gaudy reunion of contemporaries or to respond to a don's invitation to spend social time at his old college. His errand was to inform Cambridge parents of their son's death in action in Spain. The son was John Cornford. The parents were Francis, Fellow of Trinity College, and Frances, familiar as a poet in certain circles. The messenger, who probably acted on the orders of the Communist Party, was one of the dead man's closest friends. Having discharged his sad duty, Straight went to report to the leader of the Cambridge cell, Anthony Blunt. Just as he had admired Cornford and other Communist contemporaries – only just the right side of idolatry – Straight also had great respect for Blunt. Despite this, he was taken aback when Blunt informed him that he was expected to undertake a long-term espionage mission in the United States on behalf of the Soviet Union. Straight (as his name eloquently attests) was not homosexual, and his purely ideological commitment was limited. He expressed reluctance to accept the Party's commission, but Blunt insisted on obedience. Straight was eventually driven to ask for what reason he might be expected to betray his country. The reply was quick and decisive: 'For the same reason that John went to Spain.'[1]

In the heritage of my generation – I was a student in the 1960s – John Cornford was the supreme exemplar of the International Brigader, an epitome of 'Spain'. From every angle demanded by constructors of iconic representation, he was the perfect subject: possessor at once of the hot bloom of youth and the cool temper of maturity, Byronic poet and lover of women, promising historian, leader and teacher, fearless warrior on the battlefields of Spain, selfless martyr for the people's cause. Indeed, no political movement of modern times has been vouchsafed such an invulnerable advocate. But above all came the one thing that Cornford himself placed above all. High over all other qualities fluttered like a banner atop a fortress the hero's most stainless feature: he was an intense and dedicated Communist. On the night before battle in the hills of Aragon he wrote to his girlfriend, 'I shall fight like a Communist if not like a soldier' and enclosed a new poem:

> Our fight's not won till the workers of all the world
> Stand by our guard on Huesca's plain,
> Swear that our dead fought not in vain,
> Raise the red flag triumphantly
> For Communism and for liberty.[2]

Cornford's death on (or about) his twenty-first birthday was, therefore, the model sacrifice of the model victim. The latent power this event generated and bequeathed to his spiritual heirs, the Communist Party, for them to use *in aeternum* for political advantage, was tremendous. It seems analogous to the investment of vast capital finance in a Swiss bank. Appropriately, the offspring of New York millionaires was to be its first target, victim of a moral blackmail to which, in various ways, thousands of other men in Europe and the United States were later subjected. As implied above, this power was not just an epiphenomenal influence associated with contemporary responses to the Spanish Civil War. Rather, it radiated down the generations, with little diminution in its seductive appeal. Even in the 1960s, age of the 'Ché' poster, the well-known image of the 1930s poet, with his Romany good looks, wry smile and cigarette, was never effaced.[3] The portrait dates from September 1936, when Cornford was on leave, charged with the recruitment of fresh heroes to accompany him on his return to Spain. Michael Straight, who took the photograph in the grounds of Dartington Hall, his Devon home, had made large donations to Communist Party coffers from his own allowance whilst a student. He wrote to his mother,

> I'd lived in fear that I'd become incapable of loving. Now I've learned that I'm able to love the Communist students even if I don't love communism itself ... I'm filled with a violent, uncontrollable love for them; and extraordinary sense of comradeship. It's unreasonable and inexplicable. It burns within me and I can't express it.[4]

During his interview with Blunt, Straight was therefore in a heightened state of emotional receptivity. His sense of guilt over not going to Spain was intensified to remorse by Cornford's death. Nonetheless he resisted the Party's orders. During the Second World War he dedicated a book 'For John Cornford and all the young men who have given and will give the last full measure of their devotion in the struggle for the liberation of all mankind'. Cornford was perceived, not only as martyr of 'Spain', but also as prototype hero of what later became known as 'premature anti-Fascism', and of the 'People's War' against the Axis powers.[5]

It was not the heir to a fortune, but rather the down-and-out, who replaced the hero. On (or about) the day that Cornford was killed in the first action of the British Battalion, another young man enlisted in its ranks. Tony Hyndman hailed from a working-class background in south Wales. He had joined the CPGB whilst working in the office of the literary-political magazine *Left Review*. Getting involved in 'Aid for Spain' work, Hyndman was befriended by Giles Romilly, a nephew of Winston Churchill. Romilly was not just another public schoolboy: he and his younger brother, Esmond, were the most celebrated public schoolboys in England. In 1934–5, the teenagers embarrassed their family, irritated their elders and entranced thousands of their class contemporaries by 'deserting' from Wellington and producing a mimeographed magazine, *Out of Bounds*, which attacked the authoritarian culture of the public schools in irresistible style.[6] In October 1936, Esmond became one of the first recruits to leave for Spain under CPGB auspices. Like Cornford, he took part in the defence of Madrid in November, and later escaped from the battlefield of Boadilla, where most of the rest of the British contingent of the XII Brigade were killed.[7] Again like Cornford, though (since not a Party member) with less missionary zeal, Esmond Romilly did some recruiting after his return. His example fired his more studious brother with enthusiasm. Before the end of his first term, Giles abandoned Oxford. He and Hyndman visited the latter's friend Christopher Isherwood in Brussels for a last fling before the trials of war.[8] As this suggests, the two men had become lovers as well as comrades.

They arrived in Spain late in 1936, joining the British Battalion which had been established some weeks earlier as part of the new XV Brigade. Hyndman had been brought up in Cardiff's docklands, and later spent three years in the Coldstream Guards. The company he now entered provided a shocking reintroduction to these hard worlds. He was appalled at the drunken loutishness of a group from Glasgow's gangland, whose attentions were aroused by the relationship between Tony and the obviously upper-class Giles. At any rate, Hyndman found himself in jail, ostensibly for indiscipline, more likely for his own protection, whilst Giles, whose VIP identity had been discovered, was assigned to a non-combatant unit. Even before the battalion moved to the front, Hyndman's morale was undermined. The experience of the first day at Jarama (12 February 1937) was shattering. Many of the 580-strong 16th Battalion broke and fled before the terrifying onslaught of the Moroccan fighters. Hyndman was among those whose nerves melted in the horrific heat of battle.[9]

After three ferocious days, a lull settled on the Jarama battlefield. Along with others rounded up from various places of refuge, Hyndman was forced back into the line, and set to the urgent work of entrenchment. One night, Cuthbert Worsley, Hyndman's friend and Romilly's ex-teacher, made a foray from Madrid to seek them out. Hyndman was evidently a nervous wreck.[10] Not long after Worsley's visit, counter-attacks were ordered on enemy strongpoints. The newly arrived American battalion was thrown into the fray and badly mauled. On 27 February, a last attempt was made to capture the dominating position, a ridge of the Sierra de Pingarrón. This time Hyndman refused outright to join an action which, as it turned out, was tantamount to suicidal and incurred huge casualties. He was placed under arrest, and taken to Albacete to face the commissars' judgement.[11]

The subsequent ruling was merciful. Though disappointed at the extent of their misplaced confidence in an ex-guardsman, the leadership decided to make use of Hyndman's other qualifications, an ability to type and general office experience. He agreed to remain enlisted on the understanding that under no circumstances would he be sent back up the line. However, on 8 March, Franco's Italian allies began a further offensive to the north-east of Madrid. It seemed that the city would be cut off. The authorities at Albacete were ordered to send every fit man to help to stem the advance of the Fascist army.[12] In company with an office colleague, John Lepper, Hyndman abandoned the base and made his way to Valencia. They were refused shelter in the British consulate, and soon picked up by police. Hyndman was, in effect, a triple deserter, and there was talk of making a radical example of him.[13] In jail awaiting his fate, he composed a poem about his trauma at the Jarama:

> ... he was dying
> And the blanket sagged.
> 'God bless you, comrades,
> He will thank you.'
> That was all.
> No slogan,
> No clenched fist
> Except in pain.[14]

2 Tiger Bay to Big Spender

Among the books which appeared in Spain to mark the fiftieth anniversary of the Civil War (1986) was a bilingual anthology of poetry originally written in English. Its editors acknowledged the fact that the war had involved two sides, yet the poets they selected were overwhelmingly of the pro-Republican persuasion, the most numerous category being members or literary camp-followers of the International Brigades. Moreover, it was asserted that poems written by direct participants in the conflict were, quite simply, better. They smelled of the sweaty fear of battle; they reflected an authentic empathy with suffering and sacrifice. In contrast, the stuff produced by observers – from 'tourist' visitors to the Madrid front, who fired a ritual shot at the 'Fascists' across no-man's-land, to those who never went to Spain at all, only contributing in the line of poetic propaganda – tended to be more empty and less convincing.[15]

The construction of 'A Poet's War' is one which historians, despite their cultural presuppositions, have frequently found bothersome. Their reasons are mixed up with the complex of left-liberal myths about the Spanish War. It is a discourse which foregrounds the artistic/elitist aspects of the struggle, whilst functionally marginalizing the demotic feelings of ordinary soldiers. It presents a Romantic, imagined war of epic novels and university seminars, tending to diminish the significance of the blood and guts of butchered workers on the battlefields. It privileges Art above Memory, 'Literature' above mere 'Record'. The 'Poet's War' tag confirms and conforms to a disturbing teleology, asserting the values of a hieratic elite which alone can endow the struggle with 'spiritual' meaning, providing the transmutation – better, the transubstantiation – of experience into art. Suffering, inspired by commitment, became converted into artistic monuments of eternal value, testaments of 'humanity' whose meaning and influence float free of history, party and even (in the end) ideology.

Many who fought for 'Spain' and who had no connections to the world of letters have also objected to the dominion of High Culture within its historiography. For them, it seems crucial that attention should not be deflected from the working-class – and thus, by definition, non-literary – element among the 'volunteers for liberty'.[16] The authentic understanding of proletarian destiny possessed by the latter, along with their direct, unflinching faith in the cause of democracy, underwrote the value of a cause which exists independently of the consolations and contradictions of philosophy. This is the pure, unmediated vein of memory which forms an honoured ritual of post-war political commitment, and is still the sacred stuff of meetings and marches, activities seen by the left as contributing to the 'continuing struggle against Fascism and imperialism'.

The coiner of the resonant phrase 'A Poet's War' was a significant British writer of the last century, Sir Stephen Spender.[17] The editors of the *Antología Bilingüe*, in the mistaken belief that Spender actually fought in the British Battalion, gave his contributions pride of place. Spender's Spanish War lyrics were (of course) already widely known in anglophone circles, with a canonic status in modern 'Eng. Lit.' studies. But few realize that these poems were largely inspired by the experiences of his homosexual lover, Tony Hyndman (1911–82). As we have seen, the latter – unlike his mentor – *did* volunteer for the International Brigades. Moreover, Hyndman himself was among the less-known writers to whom the *Antología* drew special attention. As a result, his poem 'Jarama Front' (quoted from above) made an impact in Spain, and has since been reprinted several times.[18] Spender's patronage meant that the piece originally appeared in what is arguably the twentieth century's most celebrated anthology of English poetry, *Poems for Spain*, published shortly after the end of the Spanish war.[19] This striking accomplishment encouraged the author of 'Jarama Front' in his aspirations to become a successful writer. Hyndman, who enjoyed many connections among the committed gliterati, could (it seemed) look forward to future achievements, perhaps even a career, in the world of 'literature'.

As in numberless other cases, such a career failed to materialize. Instead, Hyndman had to wait for nearly forty years before seeing another word of his own in print.[20] In all this time, his failure to become a writer never ceased to be a source of mental distress and emotional bitterness. Towards the end of Hyndman's life, a friend of the present writer occupied a room in the same Cardiff house. One day Hyndman knocked on his door to borrow something and found him reading a book by Spender. 'Did you know *I'm* in that book?' Hyndman asked excitedly. In 1975, he wrote an essay on his Spanish experiences for a volume edited by Philip Toynbee.[21] He told a reporter that 'people who knew me [in London] won't have to ask what happened to Hyndman any more. They'll read the book, oh, they'll all read the book and they'll know I'm still around.' In his autobiography Spender described life with Hyndman as 'being with someone whose life was empty', adding revealingly: 'the uncreativeness of Jimmy's life often left me with a feeling that my own work was a kind of disloyalty to him, the exercise of an unfair advantage.' The Cardiff local-interest story played up a feeling of vindication, even revenge. 'Satisfaction. At last. And dignity. Now Tom Hyndman can sit in his room and say the hell with the world'; ending with the assertion that things were OK for Hyndman now, after all his troubles: 'He's in hard covers. And no-one can say he's "uncreative".'[22]

The inner frustration which haunted much of Hyndman's life was brought about by an accidental and an accident. The accidental was his working-class origin. Born the son of a publican, he was the eldest of seven children – significantly enough, all his siblings being female. His father's passion was boxing, and the developing signs of his only son's lack of drive towards the normal sexual and sporting pursuits of his class did not conduce to a good relationship. Tony 'ran away' to the army on losing his first job in a solicitor's office. After being discharged from the Coldstream Guards in 1933, he drifted to London. Loitering with intent in (or near) the underground toilet of Piccadilly Circus, the original 'cottage', he met the slightly older Spender, who was engaged in a complementary exercise. At this point, the latter's first book of poetry was in the press. Shortly afterwards it was published, bringing wide acclaim, literary prizes and writing commissions. In a decade when the prestige of 'being a writer' was at its zenith,

Spender became instantly famous; and, if not rich, then at least a person of independent means.[23]

As this glamorous scenario assembled, Spender and Hyndman became partners. They lived together, on the whole monogamously, for three years. So far as we can judge from Spender's writings, they were romantically in love with each other. Almost immediately, Spender began to write poetry inspired by his 'significant other' (several examples being added to the second edition of his inaugural collection);[24] and within a year had dedicated to him a book of short stories in which he appears in various guises as the catalyst of sexual and psychological crisis.[25] Further to Tony's fame and excitement, the joint recipient of this dedication was W. H. Auden, acknowledged leader and aesthetic nucleus of a coterie of young writers who were the cynosures of Oxbridge, Bloomsbury and Fitzrovia. To it, in addition to Spender, belonged Christopher Isherwood, Louis MacNeice, Cecil Day Lewis, John Lehmann, and others now of fainter canonical stamp. All of these men were Communists or fellow-travellers of the 'people's front' persuasion.[26]

Hyndman became part of this milieu – if only as a sort of mascot. Aesthetically and ideologically, it was the most energetic force for change in British intellectual life between the wars. In the left-liberal academic culture which has prevailed amongst us hegemonically since the 1960s, its concerns have been seen as almost more meaningful than any contingent speculations or debates going on in the spheres of scholarship or politics *per se*.[27] The agonized Marxiose-Freudian dialectics in which the Auden circle was engaged, along with the essential dynamic of their social lives, were intensified by the ubiquitous rise of Fascism. In 1933, with Hitler jumping about in the Reichstag, Mussolini thumping his chest and Mosley stumping Britain's cities, it was easy to identify the beasts slouching towards Bethlehem. In no other decade have the truths of history, philosophy and art seemed to meld so indistinguishably with the concrete realities of everyday life, ineffably guiding right understanding of the past, unerringly pointing the true path into the future. Thus Marxist scripture and the Party priesthood were apprehended as arbitrating the whole range of personal choices: the psychological subject; ethical beliefs and social values; political allegiance; the forms, content and aims of writing; questions of familial, social and sexual relationships; places of residence and material lifestyle.[28]

For Hyndman, being caught up in this community was like landing on a different planet, a place as dangerous as it was seductive. Born with alien lungs, he desperately needed to learn how to breathe its perfumed atmosphere. Though often included in the socio-intellectual space around Spender, Hyndman found it a constant challenge.[29] He made the fair copies of Spender's writings, a role culminating in 1936, when he prepared the typescript of a major commission from the Left Book Club, the political treatise *Forward from Liberalism* (*FFL*).[30] He relished all this, along with Spender's speaking engagements at places where the *jeunesse dorée* were brilliantly assembled. But there was another side to things. Despite its exotic and emotional aspects, the relationship had originated in a business deal, and ultimately could not escape the undertones of master and servant – the surnames of the contracting parties being evocative in this context as well as in the sexual one. Hyndman kept Spender's flat tidy, cooked the meals, and – when others called round – did the requisite making and waiting. Inevitably, and however inadvertently, he was sometimes reminded of the fact that, as far as most visitors were concerned, he was merely a privileged menial in the presence of greatness. His condition was one of constant (if relative) degradation; yet one which, rather than crushing his spirit, on the contrary stimulated its desire to compete on their terms.

Word soon got around literary London about Spender's 'bit of rough'.[31] Virginia Woolf told her nephew, Julian Bell, that Spender 'is married to a sergeant in the Guards. They have set up a new quarter in Maida Vale: I propose to call them the Lilies of the Valley.'[32] Hyndman accompanied Spender on extended holidays to obscure Mediterranean destinations. Spender wrote, Hyndman shopped and cooked, they sunbathed. Hyndman became the subject of Spender's writings, portrayed as obsessively as a painter might treat an adored model. At the same time he provided a useful audience for the ideas on political economy which were developed in *Forward from Liberalism*.[33] In spring 1936 the couple made their usual trip, via a visit to Isherwood in Portugal, and thence passing through Madrid and Barcelona. By the time they returned home with the completed text of *FFL* the Civil War was under way and 'Spain' had come to dominate the world of literary London. The Spender–Hyndman relationship had weathered the summer badly. In September, they parted for the first time. Tony took 'a small flat' with financial help from Spender and their mutual friend, Worsley.[34] For his part, Spender was sucked into the 'Aid Spain' movement, and within a few months had met and married an Oxford research student working on Spanish literature.

His publisher's advance and assurance of future royalties encouraged Spender to embrace 'conventional' married life. But there was a deeper reason for his attempts to acculturate himself to the heterosexual sphere. Like all gay writers of this epoch, Spender lived in dread at the prospect of exposure, and the sordid cycle of blackmail, arrest, court proceedings, newspaper stories, fines and jail which had become an occasional purgation ritual of 'society' since the Wilde case. It was this besetting fear which, even as late as the 1950s, obliged homosexual authors (and not only the members of what Cyril Connolly called 'the Homintern') to adapt their public writings in order not to provide criminal testimony against themselves.[35] Another reason for long foreign jaunts was that they offered the security of exile. This was a logic that Auden, Isherwood and others were later to take to its obvious conclusion. An alternative refuge from the opportunist police informer or ruthless literary enemy was marriage. But what represented an escape hatch for Spender was a trapdoor to perdition for Hyndman. Their domestic partnership now definitively ended, and Tony (metaphorically, at least) was back on the streets.[36]

3 The Narrative of Quest

Hyndman soon found a new lover in Giles Romilly, and a new protector in the Communist Party. He joined the CPGB soon after his initial break with Spender, in October 1936. The step was consequent upon his immediate problem, but also derived from his intellectual experience of the Spender circle; and above all, the arguments elaborated in *FFL*. For his part, Spender assumed that Hyndman had joined the International Brigade as an uncomplicated act of emotional pique, much as he had joined the British army on the run from his father.[37] All the same, when Hyndman's sister wrote to accuse him of responsibility, his feelings poured out:

> Once, about a month ago [he told Isherwood] when I did think he was going [to Spain] on account of our marriage, I dissuaded him. But this time I didn't try to do so because I felt, as he does, that he was

particularly well qualified to go . . . All I know is that I love him & that whenever he comes back I shall be extremely happy and that I wish he were now here, and that I miss him very much.[38]

Around this time, Spender was contacted by Harry Pollitt, secretary-general of the CPGB. Pollitt had seen a review of *FFL* in the *Daily Worker*, and was attracted by the prospect of recruiting another Cornford to the cause of 'Spain'. As it happened, Spender's reputation as writer and artist was far higher than Cornford's.[39] Moreover, he had published an influential piece of pro-Communist dialectic in the inspiring livery of the Left Book Club. Pollitt sought to exploit the logical conclusions of *FFL*, conclusions which Hyndman had already acted upon. He asked Spender to join both the Party and the International Brigade. The latter offer was firmly rejected, but the former met with a less discouraging response, since Spender was looking for a pretext to visit Spain in search of Tony. Shortly after meeting Pollitt, Spender and his friend Cuthbert Worsley were commissioned by the *Daily Worker* to fly to Spain in order to investigate and report on the disappearance of a Soviet aid-ship.[40]

Spender was now in flight from his troubles in much the same way as Hyndman. The mission to Spain, accompanied by a casual male lover, was a comic-opera adventure more absurd than anything recounted by Orwell about the lighter moments of the war in Aragon.[41] They were denied entry to the Nationalist zone and returned home after various fruitless peregrinations and a stopover in Barcelona. Though no lead was forthcoming on Hyndman, the trip convinced both Spender and Worsley that they wanted to be part of 'Spain'. Not long after getting back to London, Spender was offered a job in the English broadcasting section of the Republican Ministry of State in Valencia. His conversion to Communism was now formally announced in the *Daily Worker*, with a feature article over the poet's signature and accompanied by a portrait photo.[42] The night before publication, Spender joined a very different kind of party, dinner at the home of Leonard and Virginia Woolf. The sensitive hands which earlier that day had been placed in fealty between the rough mits of the chief tribune of the people now clasped the cut glass of Bloomsbury. Spender's hostess noted that he was 'somewhat metalled because, having married, his friend, the male, joined the F[oreign] Legion, [and] is fighting in

Spain ... [Spender] said that the CP, which he had that day joined, wanted him to be killed in order that there may be another Byron.'[43]

Indeed, at first Pollitt must have congratulated himself on a minor propaganda coup. But things started to go badly awry. In Barcelona, Spender met Worsley: 'Tony [has] appealed to me through Cuthbert to get him away from the Brigade at all costs.'[44] Reaching Valencia, he learned of Hyndman's desertion at Jarama. Spender became convinced that Tony was in danger of execution. Overcome by remorse, he decided to intervene. Government sources of advice and help were closed to him. The previous autumn, an article of his (in the *News Chronicle*) had denounced consular officials and businessmen living in Barcelona for their alleged anti-Republican bias. The Foreign Office considered taking action against the newspaper for 'wantonly endangering the lives and interests of British subjects', and Spender became *persona non grata*.[45] Harry Pollitt, in contrast, provided a sympathetic hearing. Hyndman was only one among a group of recalcitrant deserters who refused to face the enemy again after the horror of Jarama. The CPGB leadership was involved in an internal debate over how to treat them; within the Spanish team, voices were (indeed) heard in favour of execution. As it happened Pollitt, personally on the moderate side of the debate, was also in Spain at this point, helping to deal with this crisis.[46] Spender's notion was to get Hyndman transferred to work as his secretary in Valencia.[47] Reaching Albacete, he gained access to representatives of the Brigade Judicial Commissions, and was allowed to meet the subject of his quest.[48]

The battle of Jarama inspired dozens of applications for repatriation from fearful and disillusioned volunteers. But the military efficacy and moral integrity of the British Battalion were threatened by an indiscriminate fallout of resentful men. Discharge was granted only to cases where compelling arguments existed: a disabling wound; personal grounds combined with a good combat record; or an impeccable Party attitude in men who were reckoned to be more useful at home. Hyndman boasted none of these qualifications.[49] When Spender was reunited with his protégé at Albacete he persuaded him to stay and behave, like a trustee awaiting a meeting of the parole board. Spender then travelled to the British positions on the Jarama, where he carried out observations for his contracted propaganda work. He found the whole experience depressing and embarrassing; the latter, in particular, when asked awkward questions by men in the dugouts about his friendship with Tony Hyndman.[50]

No sooner had Spender fired his regulation shot at the enemy lines, and left the scene en route to Madrid, than the normally quiescent Jarama front suddenly burst into action. This was not an enemy reaction to Spender's challenge: Nationalist forces were accustomed to being fired on, literally as well as metaphorically, by famous foreign writers. The attacks were diversions, intended to dissuade the Republic from sending reinforcements to the real point of crisis, east of Madrid, where Mussolini's expeditionary force had launched a major offensive. The crisis of Guadalajara, described briefly above, ensued. Having deserted again, Hyndman and Lepper were apprehended in Valencia, and sent back to Albacete under guard.[51] Spender was now deeply fearful for Hyndman's life. Back in Valencia, he somehow gained the help of the British consulate, and with this and other assistance obtained an audience with the head of the War Commissariat, Julio Alvarez del Vayo. Though insisting on the primacy of discipline and morale, the minister agreed that so long as he first served an exemplary sentence short of the capital one, Hyndman should be allowed to leave Spain.[52]

When Spender took this news to Albacete, a deputation of British commissars (Kerrigan, Springhall and Tapsell) subjected him to a distinctly unpleasant interview. His Party credentials were now shot to bits: not only had he enlisted the help of the British government, but also had gone to the Republican government over the heads of both CPGB and Comintern.[53] Returning to London, Spender persuaded Kingsley Martin, editor of the *New Statesman*, to intercede with Pollitt. At this juncture, Pollitt was faced with growing disquiet among Party and quasi-Party intellectuals, sparked by the renewed wave of purges in Moscow, and intensified by rumours about firing squads and punishment camps in Spain. In great bad humour he replied to Martin that

> civil war is civil war – and Tony Hyndman went out with full knowledge of the consequences likely. He was working at the base and deserted from the base. He was not in the firing line when this took place and was subsequently arrested and is now in a labour camp ... When I see Spender I will have many interesting things to discuss – as well as the question of Tony Hyndman. If all the boys took the attitude of Hyndman, Madrid might well have been captured.[54]

Spender was called for a grilling at the Communist Party's office in King Street and seems to have suffered the full force of Pollitt's temper. In exchange for the general secretary's promise to investigate the Hyndman case, Spender was compelled to abase himself:

> Thank you for the consideration with which you spoke to me yesterday ... I shall tell Kingsley Martin myself tomorrow that I am quite satisfied ... Of course I guarantee absolutely that when Hyndman returns he will say nothing against the Brigade. I only mention this because at Albacete the Commissars seemed to think it was possible. Since you were angry at the whole situation towards the end of our interview, I do not know whether you will be pleased at my thanking you, but nevertheless I do thank you for what I understand to be a very generous decision.[55]

Pollitt was no longer comfortable in being embraced fraternally by Comrade Spender. Leaving aside the considerations dealt with below, he had every reason to feel misled and even betrayed.[56] Yet the interests of the Party, especially as regards the image of the Brigades on the home front, remained paramount. If possible, Hyndman had to be spared the worst punishment.

Hyndman had been sentenced to two months 'dans la compagnie de travail et de rééducation'.[57] Work detachments were often assigned to dangerous places, sometimes even producing circumstances in which 'undesirables' were unfortunately killed by enemy bombardment. But around this time a settlement was opened at Mahora, the so-called 'Camp Lucas', to which Hyndman was now consigned. He later claimed that his resentment of the Communist jailers led to suspicions of Trotskyist or other anti-Party sympathies.[58] The regime at Camp Lucas was certainly hard, but there is no evidence of torture or of excessive physical punishment having been dispensed there. Hyndman spent two months in the 're-education centre' and was then sent back to Albacete.

4 Gender War in Spain

Responding to Pollitt's enquiries about Hyndman in May 1937, Wally Tapsell wrote: 'this chap will be freed in a few days. They want to send him to work on a farm, but in view of your letter I am recommending – public disgrace, dismissal with ignominy for cowardice and desertion ... [He] is an arrant coward.'[59] The commissars had now learned the unpalatable truth about Spender's solicitude for the Party.[60] The issue of repatriation came up at the CPGB's central executive committee. Will Paynter, battalion commissar and senior British Communist at Albacete, had sent proposals to ameliorate the crisis. He added that 'Hyndman is with us again. I am opposed to his coming [home] to you [which] will not help us much.'[61] Hyndman's evidently figured among the most problematic cases. During discussion one member scribbled a note for Pollitt: 'I consider Paynter's proposal to return all men over 40, particularly those who have been wounded, should be agreed to. I also think that Hyndman (if this is Spender's Hyndman) should be left there.' He did not add 'to rot', but the mute feeling is almost palpable.[62]

Meanwhile, Spender published a *New Statesman* article in which he criticized Communist handling of the Brigades, particularly their propaganda exploitation.[63] Reaction within the Party leadership was strong, but they hesitated to expel him from their ranks, fearful of the negative publicity it would attract so soon after his fanfared induction. A barbed exchange of letters took place between Spender and Pollitt. The former, demanding Hyndman's immediate return from Spain, concluded with a barely veiled threat to make a further public stand against the Party:

> The whole question has become ... one of life and death. In these circumstances you can see that I am bound to take every possible means to get him home, regardless of the consequences to myself. I only hope that you will not force me into a position of opposition to you on a question which is not one of principle but of the future and perhaps the life of an individual.[64]

Pollitt replied that he had made strong recommendations, during a recent Spanish visit, that Hyndman 'should be sent back immediately', but added ominously: 'I can only express my continued surprise that you can write your letters in such a tone.'[65]

Though CPGB patronage was over, Spender had other cards to play. In Valencia he had impressed PCE leaders in the fields of both literature and politics. Constanza de la Mora, head of the Press Bureau, and her husband, air force chief Hidalgo de Cisneros, introduced him to the prominent Communist poet Manuel Altolaguirre, as well as smoothing his path to Alvarez del Vayo. Through these contacts he was invited to represent Britain at the

International Anti-Fascist Writers' Congress, organized in July 1937. During the Madrid sessions of the congress, Spender was taken to task by Claud Cockburn over his *New Statesman* article; then Ralph Bates, cultural commissar of the XV Brigade, and leader of the British delegation, took him aside to relate an apparently gratuitous story.

> He told me that, in his role as political commissar, he had been asked to decide the fortunes of a member of the Brigade who was a coward. He had had a long talk with the young man and persuaded him that he should go back to the fighting. Secretly he had arranged that he should be sent to a place where he was certain to be killed. 'I have just had a message to say that he is dead,' he said rather pompously. 'Of course I am a little upset, but the matter does not weigh on my conscience. For I know that I did right'. There was a pause. Then, looking at me, he added: 'I am telling you this because there is a moral for you in the story'.[66]

Through allegorical story – of which he was a minor master – Bates was warning Spender that Hyndman's well-being depended on his maintaining a loyal public demeanour as regards the Party. A recognizable version of this incident figures in David Leavitt's novel *While England Sleeps*, based on the Spender–Hyndman affair. In Leavitt's adaptation, the commander of the British Battalion threatens the Spender character ('Botsford') with exposure of his homosexual activities to the police in retaliation for any attempt to publicize the case of Hyndman ('Phelan') at home.[67] Claud Cockburn was later to express in print the hostility and contempt he felt for Spender over the Hyndman case.

> The intellectual homosexual of those days was really like an early nineteenth-century romantic – however political he might think himself, everything had to give place to his amour; for some reason this was considered respectable when it was a boy although it would have been laughable had it been a girl. Just as one thought he was going to sit down and write an article for a magazine, or go to Spain, it turned out he was getting his boyfriend out of the hands of the police. This was a number one priority. Homosexuality had a sort of prestige value that took precedence over politics, the end of the world and everything else.[68]

But Spender was now able to talk to more powerful people than Cockburn, Bates or even Pollitt. The Writers' Congress was a hugely important propaganda event: it was addressed by prime minister Juan Negrín, and its sessions were attended by other influential politicians.[69] Later that month, Pollitt interviewed Hyndman in Albacete. 'What with your family and friends [he told him] you have been more trouble to me than the whole British Battalion put together.'[70] According to Hyndman, Pollitt promised liberty would not be long delayed. But when (on 1 August) he was finally released, he owed his freedom more to Alvarez del Vayo than to Pollitt – if, of course, to Spender more than either. It was noted against his name: 'Recalled for political reasons. Undesirable.'[71]

Undesirable in the view of the Comintern, Tony Hyndman remained highly desirable to Spender, and to others of the Auden circle, for some years to come.[72] As one comrade later told him, 'In Harry Pollitt's opinion . . . I was an ordinary, decent, working class chap who had got into the hands of the sort of intellectuals the party could well do without.'[73] This remark reflects a feeling shared by most of Pollitt's leadership colleagues, especially those who, like him, belonged to its 'proletarian' element. Almost nothing was understood about the nature of homosexuality, which was something they found exceptionally difficult to manage. Partly out of sheer embarrassment, partly because no discourse existed to mediate it, at the official level, nothing was ever written down. Social background was significant: middle-class comrades, particularly those from public schools, were more likely to appreciate the ramifications of the issue, in both personal and intellectual terms, and were thus less vulnerable to homophobia.[74] For the proletarian, the categorization tended to be biblical, for the elite, classical. Confronted with sodomy, the former thought of the twin cities of the plain, the latter of Socrates and *Seven Against Thebes*. In any case, the subject brought into focus by the Hyndman–Spender affair was bound to exacerbate tensions within the British Battalion, both over its toleration of the 'sort of intellectuals' characterized by Pollitt, and as regards the presence of homosexuality in the trenches.

In some units, like the mainly German XII Brigade, led by ex-Weimar politicians, female brothels were set up during militarily inactive periods. These were consciously intended to have a prophylactic effect, reducing the impulse for casual homosexual acts.[75] The commander of the Thaelmann Battalion, the writer Ludwig Renn, who made his literary name in Weimar Germany, was known to utilize the special services of his messenger boys (*enlaces*).⁷⁶ Among the British, homosexuality came to be seen as both a disciplinary and moral offence. In the same volume which carried Hyndman's memoir, John Jump, also a British Battalion veteran, touched on the dread subject. An acquaintance in Albacete unaccountably went missing. 'It was difficult to obtain any information, but finally I was told that he had been sent to prison for homosexual activities.' The text continues directly with the remark that 'there were occasionally more serious crimes . . .'!⁷⁷ Nonetheless, this particular crime came to stand alongside – even becoming confused with – others, like desertion or Trotskyism, which carried implications of betrayal.⁷⁸ During the Teruel campaign, two Britons were tried for desertion. One was executed by a firing squad drawn from Battalion members; the other, placed in a punishment platoon, was soon killed. One comrade later hinted that the former had a sexual hold over the latter: 'he was, you know, not really the kind of type that we would want out there in any case.'⁷⁹ It was assumed that 'decent' working-class comrades, whose commitment to revolutionary progress did not conflict with – rather, confirmed – a yearning for social respectability, had an 'elemental' hatred of sodomy. Thus the feelings of the 'better elements' were engaged on the side of loyalty and discipline.⁸⁰

When visiting the Jarama trenches, Spender had been shown around by Captain George Nathan, who was accompanied by a young aide, a public schoolboy. Spender later recalled that Nathan, 'an elegant, cane-swaggering, likeable type of adventurous Jew . . . asked me to stay on for three or four days – perhaps a week'.⁸¹ Nathan had other, more relevant, qualities. He had commanded the first British company to go into action, at the battle in which Cornford was killed. Most accounts agree that he was the most gifted and courageous British military leader in Spain, and his popularity with the rank and file was widely acknowledged. The fact that he was also homosexual does not seem to have worried many of the latter unduly.⁸² On the contrary, since the Battalion's earliest days, Nathan had been the popular choice as its commander. As Brigade liaison officer, the same hospitality he offered to Spender had been extended to various volunteers who served as drivers and motorcycle riders.⁸³ However, his fall from grace was (on the surface, at least) not due to his sexual behaviour, but because it emerged that he had belonged to a British Army hit squad in Ireland during the War of Independence in the early 1920s. Irish comrades demanded an inquiry, and Nathan, his application to join the party rejected, was seconded to the XIV Brigade. When he left, he took Giles Romilly with him. Within a few weeks, however, he was accused by a senior officer of persistent drunkenness and anti-Party statements, and sent back to the British in disgrace. During the battle of Brunete, he was killed in somewhat dubious circumstances. Nathan's troubles, and perhaps his death, had a deeper cause than is recorded in the documents.[84]

Ostensibly, at least, Spender was not aware of Nathan's sexuality or his connection with Giles Romilly.[85] In his novel *While England Sleeps*, David Leavitt endowed the Battalion commander with the accentuated homophobia of the closet homosexual, an attribution that may be regarded as a political platitude amongst gay writers.[86] The Hyndman–Spender relationship was also studied by their friend Worsley, in a novel he worked on for some thirty years.[87] Though the finished product is, if only for reasons of its period, less homocentric than Leavitt's, it too interprets events in terms of sexual politics. Both books situate the political, personal and literary tensions of the 1930s, which, like static in thunderclouds stalked the intellectual climate and social atmosphere, in the context of the Spanish Civil War, the catalyst which released the storm. From these perspectives, Hyndman can be seen as a desirable entity, over whom predator-claimants with variously economic, political and sexual motives fought for possession. In the relevant discourses, whether homo- or heterotextuality, the victim loses his own identity, becoming in turn Tony (instead of his baptismal Thomas), Till, Jimmy, Harry, Edward, and so on.[88] When Tom Hyndman exclaimed '*I'm* in that book', he was intuiting a kind of transmigration of souls. By all the criteria to which experience had conditioned him, his real life was a shell, his subjectivity a vacuum. He was and is only in books; an orphan of the storm; a victim, who died on the day that he met Stephen Spender, the man who saved him from death.[89]

5 Hyperion in the Valleys

In 1933, John Cornford, direct descendant of Charles Darwin, became a convinced Marxist. For a time, he even gave up poetry in favour of politics.⁹⁰ In his first year as a history undergraduate at Cambridge, he published a critical essay, welcoming the 'revolutionary fermentation in the work of the younger poets – W. H. Auden, Charles Madge, Stephen Spender, C. Day Lewis . . .', but objecting to the philosophical stance taken by Spender in a controversy with Madge. With Spender, he asserted, 'the world of the artist is considered as a metaphysical abstraction unrelated to the world in which he lives, which produced him and his art.' For Cornford, on the contrary, the writer 'must actively participate in the revolutionary struggles of society'.⁹¹ He must work and write with the workers, using their speech and speaking their thoughts. Spender was unmoved. Later that year, approached by the magazine *New Verse* for comment on this issue, he refused to reply.⁹² In 1938, Cornford's poem 'As Our Might Lessens' was published posthumously. Its violently sexual metaphors pictured the Nazis as masochistic sodomisers of boys:

> . . . those whose tortured, torturing flesh
> Stirred at the body under the lash,
> The painted boy in the praetorian's bed . . .

and Communism as the fulfilling, honest enjoyment of girls:

> Where the nightmare faces grinned
> We, or our sons, shall wake to find
> A naked girl, the future, at our side.⁹³

There is no reason to doubt Cornford's physical courage. The man who spoke admiringly of 'necessary murders' carried out in aid of the revolution, was the same man who carried a wounded German comrade (whom he had recruited to the Brigade) for over a mile to safety at Boadilla.⁹⁴ Yet meeting Cornford's mother some time later, Spender told her that John had been completely disillusioned when he returned to England from the Aragon front, but was forced to go back to Spain by Harry Pollitt.⁹⁵ Meanwhile, in the summer of 1937, following Cornford's death, and fresh from the Congress of Anti-Fascist Writers, he collaborated wholeheartedly with Nancy Cunard on the production of the celebrated propaganda exercise *Authors Take Sides in the Spanish Civil War*.⁹⁶

In (or about) the same week of 1933 in which the original Spender–Hyndman encounter took place, Cornford also met a 'significant other' in London. He had qualified for Cambridge some eighteen months early, and his wealthy, liberal parents rewarded him with what would today be called 'a year out'. He devoted himself to political work and independent study at the LSE, organizing anti-Mosley demos and occasionally 'drinking with the peasants'.[97] Cornford was introduced to Ray Peters, a working-class comrade a few years older than himself, from the south Wales valleys. Hyndman has (more than once) been romantically misrepresented as a miner's son, but Peters really was the daughter of a Rhondda coal miner. Like Hyndman she had apparently run away from home for reasons not unconnected with sexual orientation.[98] John and Ray became lovers immediately, and later lived together in Cambridge whilst Cornford read for his degree and organized the student Communist group. This act of daring scandalized the community and caused intense embarrassment to his parents.

In the course of 1935, Peters gave birth to a son, James. By this time, Cornford had met a woman of his own class and intellectual interests, Margot Heinemann, a student of English. They excitedly welcomed the workers to Cambridge when a Hunger March passed through. In an earlier exchange with his mother, Cornford argued that the participants in such marches really were hungry: 'I don't know how much a baby costs to feed – certainly it is more than the 1 s[hilling] it's allowed under the present Means Test.'[99] Shortly after James's arrival, Cornford abandoned both mother and baby. Heinemann, like Hyndman, achieved fulfilment in becoming the great love and helpmeet of a significant writer. Cornford and Heinemann were absolute soulmates. He told her that 'revolutionaries should cut their connections with their bourgeois intellectual family and look and behave as much like a worker as possible'.[100] After meeting Ray, Cornford had been tempted back to poetry, and contributed to *The Listener* using the nom de plume of 'Dai Barton'. Not content with this quasi-felonious personation, he organized vacation trips from Cambridge to the Rhondda Valleys, where students lived in miners' cottages and studied the ways of the workers as if researching an essay or preparing a play. For Heinemann, this experience 'made me a Communist for life'.[101]

Cornford, like Orwell, was on his way from Wigan Pier to the sierras of Aragon. The love poetry written to Heinemann from Spain is as well known as that written by Spender to Hyndman, and both are meaningless without the fertilizing context of the Spanish Civil War.[102] After Cornford's death, Heinemann was left pregnant, but contented with her fate, and financially secure. In contrast, Ray Peters and James were homeless and penniless. Cornford's parents, poet and Plato scholar, who were barely able to accept Ray as a guest in their liberal home, rejected appeals to help, and even refused to acknowledge their grandchild.[103] Only the intervention of Michael Straight retrieved the situation. He took Ray home to Dartington Hall, where his parents ran a left-wing summer school, and found her a place amongst the domestic staff. History is silent about her subsequent existence.[104]

The cohabitation between the left intellectuals and the workers, in the south Wales valleys, in the struggle against Mosleyites, above all in Spain, can be seen as a vampirean transfusion of energy from a vital to a dying culture. Once drained, the donor body was cast aside. In the wake of the last miners' strike of 1984–5, another Ray, another Marxist critic, another Cambridge professor – above all, another Welsh person – Raymond Williams, wrote a novel in which Cornford's life is fictionally reprocessed against the backdrop of the Spanish War and the involvement of south Wales with the International Brigades. In *Loyalties*, evocatively titled (and partly confessional), Williams develops the hypothesis that the Communist elite of the 1930s colonized the workers on behalf of Stalin, hijacked their collective willpower, impregnated them with an alien culture, and finally abandoned them as helpless hybrids to the fate that free-market global capitalism had in store.[105] The 'Cornford' character is Norman Boase, who as a Cambridge maths student in the 1930s seduces a Welsh miner's daughter, abandoning her and their baby son, Gwyn. He becomes part of the Stalinist intelligence network in Spain, leading the investigation and repression of working-class British Brigaders suspected of 'Trotskyism'. In later life – now 'Sir Norman' – Boase transmogrifies into an 'Anthony Blunt' character, a revered establishment figure who reveals secrets about strategic computer science to the Soviets. During the miners' strike of 1984, Gwyn at last begins to grasp the political significance of his tormented, hybrid existence. He is nothing other than a failed experiment in genetic-social-political engineering, a James Cornford out of Lysenko out of Darwin. He confronts his natural father:

> You have been a class of betrayers ... You have always fought your internal battles by recruiting and using genuinely popular interests or by

lining up with some alien power. Or, as in your case, both. And then all that is new is that you damaged something authentic, something that had grown under the weight of you and in your own soil. You betrayed your own countrymen, but always and everywhere your class has been doing that, to serve its own interests. Your special betrayal was that you involved and damaged the only substance, the only hope of our people. You involved and damaged socialism: our own kind of hope but converted by people like you to a distant and arbitrary and alien power . . . A whole people is carrying the cost . . . It can never be forgiven. It will never be forgiven.[106]

As witnesses to this bitter indictment we may call onstage, for the last time, the tragical-historical *dramatis personae*. Stephen Spender and John Cornford on the one hand, Tony Hyndman and Ray Peters on the other, were antithetical examples of sacrificial victims in the Spanish Civil War. Spender enjoyed huge literary fame, and later accepted a knighthood, but knew and suffered the cost of both. Cornford, poet-hero, noble, beautiful and pure, became the immortal apotheosis of the drama of 'Spain'. Hyndman and Peters, in essence servile, common, and confused, melted back into the chorus from which chance had plucked them.

~ 3 ~
Battle on Monte Oscuro: The Surreal Landscape of Orwell's Spain

1 Reputation

In their own propaganda, the International Brigades were 'the most literate army in history'. The profile given to writers created the impression that Communist solidarity, battlefield courage and literary sensibility were components of the same package of collective heroism.[1] It is curious, therefore, that the writer who achieved universal fame as a socialist warrior fighting Fascism in Spain never joined the Brigades. Instead (one might almost say 'on the contrary') he became the literary partisan of a Marxist but anti-Stalinist revolutionary group; his writings about Spain proved inimical to the mainstream Communism established in the Brigades; and in the long run, his influence was more deleterious to the image of the 'Virtuous Republic' than those of any advocate of its Nationalist enemies.

George Orwell is perceived today as the brightest star in a galaxy of foreign writers who participated in the Spanish Civil War. He seems to shed the clearest light on issues which are notoriously resistant to 'reading'; issues which are as rebarbative as the Aragonese landscape itself, where he fought, on a hill called Monte Oscuro, in 1937. As subject of study, the war constitutes a perennially misty zone, haunted by danger, deception and double-dealing. More than sixty years later, interpretation must be attempted in a surreal landscape where nothing is what it seems at first- and often at third-hand. Since his premature death in 1950, Orwell's *Homage to Catalonia* (hereafter, *Homage*) has become the best-known contemporary commentary. For many, his limpid prose provides a safe guide through what Raymond Williams called 'the minefield' of this densely political war.[2] Orwell has played a pre-eminent role in forming subsequent opinion on its most controversial problems. But does he deserve his reputation as an accurate observer whose analysis is purged of prejudice and propaganda, a necessary (and for some, sufficient) model of Olympian detachment?

Homage was written during the second half of 1937, and in every sense it stands close to its subject, perhaps too close. In contrast to its later record, at first the book made no impact. Appearing in the unregarded livery of a new publisher, it was swamped by a tide of competitors. By the time Orwell died, the print-run (of 1,500) had sold little more than half. The first American edition did not appear until 1952, during the Korean War and McCarthyite crisis, as transatlantic pundits spotted the potential of its author as a Cold Warrior of the pen.[3] A French version came out in 1956. Three years later, when the Italian critic and ex-International Brigader Aldo Garosci placed *Homage* in a class of its own, hailing its author as a uniquely truthful 'artist of the moral life', no edition had been published in Italian.[4] In 1970, five years before Franco's death, the first Spanish translation became available.[5]

In the 1950s, the endorsement of Orwell's anti-Sovietism by ex-Communist Spanish War writers like Stephen Spender, Arthur Koestler and Louis Fischer had signalled a notable backsliding amongst the western intelligentsia.[6] The American liberal critic Lionel Trilling characterized Orwell as the virgin soldier of the Spanish Republic, preserved from the pervasive corruption of Auden's 'low, dishonest decade' by the honesty of his untutored intellect. One of the leading radical gurus of the 1960s, Noam Chomsky, likewise lent *Homage* his sanction. In the 1970s, essays by two eminent British Marxists, Raymond Williams and Edward Thompson, added to Orwell's laurels.[7] The first scholarly biography appeared in 1980.[8] By then, Orwell's opinions on the major socio-political issues of his time had reached a status almost beyond the realm of impeachment. From the headquarters of the military-industrial complex to the seminar rooms of the London School of Economics, his word was tantamount to holy writ.

In post-Franco Spain the trend was reinforced. The first censor-free compendium of criticism on civil war 'literature' gave Orwell a prominent place.[9] By 1984, most of his major writings had appeared in Castilian translation and even the minor essays excited attention.[10] In that year, to celebrate the first Catalan version of *Homage*, Barcelona's two universities combined with the regional government to stage an Orwell festival which included performance of a rock-opera based on *Animal Farm*. Meanwhile, Orwell's account of the war was given the imprimatur of various Catalan experts.[11] The glow of enthusiasm hardly dimmed with the 1990s. In 1994, a popular Spanish study of Civil War writers praised *Homage* above all for the unmediated essence of truth which, 'by one of those miracles of literature', established perfect empathy between writer and reader.[12] In 1997, another respected scholar found *Homage* to be 'perhaps the best report on the Spanish Civil War written by any eyewitness' – that is, including those by Spaniards!'[13] In France, where British intellectuals rarely grab headlines, Orwell's account has recently been acknowledged in the review pages of *Le Monde* as one of two 'principaux représentants des lettres anglaises' who 'a inspiré au cours du temps un indiscutable respect'.[14]

2 Polemic

When the 'Orwell Year' of 1984 arrived, the *ci-devant* Eric Blair had become a laureate of world literature, his works a staple of the academic syllabus in anglophone countries.[15] There were many *pièces d'occasion*. I contributed an essay on Orwell's Spanish writings to a collection of critical studies.[16] Unlike others, this was not a celebration of Orwell's greatness, but rather sought to 'demythologize' a writer who had been 'kidnapped by the forces of reaction'.[17] However, my pretentiously titled 'historical critique' discomfited the publishers, the official British Communist Party house of Lawrence & Wishart, for it seemed too often to resonate in sympathy with its subject. Unwilling to attempt overt censorship, but feeling the need for some 'corrective', the editorial staff instead inserted alongside the commissioned essay another on the same subject.

The author selected for this purpose was Bill Alexander, one-time commander of the British Battalion of the International Brigade, later prominent in the CPGB leadership. Alexander was a man of deep political convictions, who was badly wounded fighting for the Republican cause on the Aragon front. As it happens, he shared these character-shaping experiences with both Orwell and Garosci. Unlike the latter, however, Alexander's essay showed little spirit of communion with a man who might be validly regarded as his comrade, or at least as his comrade-in-arms. On the contrary, he attacked Orwell's account of the Spanish War in general, and his attitude to the USSR's role in particular, as the muddled speculations of a political innocent, at best a meddling dilettante, at worst an agent of Franco-Fascism.[18]

All this represented a mere skirmish in the war of words over Orwell which had been a major Communist Party propaganda concern ever since Victor Gollancz committed the tactical error of accepting *The Road to Wigan Pier* for the Left Book Club in late 1936. Far from subsiding after 1945, or following Orwell's death, the quarrel stretched into the Cold War era, fuelled by the anti-Soviet implications of *Animal Farm* and *Nineteen Eighty-Four;* and into the 1990s, when the feature film *Land and Freedom,* loosely derived from *Homage,* sparked off rowdy exchanges between competing leftist groups, to the bemusement of audiences arriving at cinemas to enjoy what was (after all) a rattling good movie. In the interim, the Orwell debate qualified as the most obsessive dispute over a home-brewed writer which has ever divided the British left.

In 1984 I blithely assumed that examining Orwell's credentials and the empirical substance of his relevant writings would reveal with statistical exactitude the extent of his reliability on such burning issues as the moral integrity of the Republic, the role of the Communist Party and the significance of atrocity and propaganda. I assessed the texts as if they were a cross between the files of a Treasury accountant and the draft dissertation of a promising postgraduate. Over the years several scholars challenged my interpretation.[19] This tendency culminated in 1999, when one referred to it as 'a quite disgraceful exercise'.[20] Such objections, added to the discomfiture of being chaperoned by Bill Alexander, gave me pause. Had I been too hard on Orwell? Teaching an undergraduate option on 1930s Spain involved frequent discussion of *Homage* with students. As a subject for seminars and essays, its political analysis and documentary status invariably inspired debate. Occasionally, an able student of left inclinations, usually 'mature' and of a militant tendency, disputed my conclusions. Meanwhile, I was increasingly attracted to the Spanish War as a research topic. Orwell influenced me in general, and in some particular ethical convictions, but above all in the sheer dogged courage which led him to tell a formidable ideological interest, and a whole culture, what they did not want to hear. I decided that when opportunity offered, Orwell should be allowed (as it were) a resit. Indeed I was confident that this time he would pass with flying colours.

3 War and Politics

For many, Eric Blair was a dedicated soldier of the Republic, who came within a millimetre of making the ultimate sacrifice for its cause. Furthermore, as the writer 'George Orwell', he was a powerful advocate of 'democratic socialism', enemy of privilege, warrior for social justice and economic equality. In contrast, to spokespersons of mainstream Communism he was a traitor, a heretic, a lackey of capitalism. For Bill Alexander, as for many comrades who, amongst the stormy waters of politics and history, remained anchored to a positive perception of the Soviet Union's mission to humanity, Orwell's original sin was that he fought not for the International Brigades, but for the 'Trotskyist' POUM militia.

In fact, Orwell's failure to enlist with the International Brigades was nothing more than a caprice of historical contingency. His interview with Harry Pollitt was a disaster: they clearly irritated each other, Pollitt perhaps too brusque in interrogation, Orwell refusing – by way of reaction – to drop his aitches.[21] Going to Barcelona (as it were) on the rebound, under the auspices of its British affiliate, the ILP, Orwell duly joined the POUM militia. Despite a general satisfaction with the 29th ('Lenin') Division, where military equality and revolutionary discipline impressed him, Orwell yearned to 'get on with the war'. There was impatience at being stuck in what Cornford had already discovered to be 'a quiet sector of a quiet front'.[22] Such feelings were aggravated by news of the Guadalajara battle (8–21 March 1937) when the International Brigades were prominent in routing the Italian Fascist Army (CTV), especially since this victory occurred in a zone relatively close to Orwell's trenches at Huesca. But even before Guadalajara raised the Internationals' profile, Orwell was arguing in favour of the main Communist policies: that the war took temporal priority over – even if its purpose was to enable – the revolution; and that final victory could only be gained with a united army, organized on conventional military lines, in which party militias were obediently subsumed. So persuasive was he during debates in the dugouts that no fewer than eight out of thirty-five English-speaking comrades agreed to join him in applying for transfer to the International Brigades when the company took leave in Barcelona on 26 April.[23]

If this furlough had been scheduled a week earlier, Orwell and his comrades would have become members of the British Battalion. The authorities in Albacete were worried at declines in recruitment. Yet in the wake of Guadalajara, with the successful training of a new Popular Army, the Republic was preparing an offensive. In addition, André Marty, the Brigades' political leader, was keen to reduce the POUM militia – regarded as little better than a wing of the Fascist Fifth Column – by any means.[24] A British commissar, Wally Tapsell, was sent to Barcelona to make contact with Orwell's group. Through his wife Eileen (a secretary at the POUM headquarters), Orwell had already agreed the transfer with Hugh O'Donnell, Comintern agent and British representative with the Catalan Communist Party (PSUC). Arriving in Barcelona, Orwell spoke to O'Donnell, and consulted another 'Communist friend attached to Spanish Medical Aid':[25]

> The leading personality and most respected man in the contingent at present is Eric Blair. This man is a Novelist who has written some books on proletarian life in England. He has little political understanding and says 'He is not interested in party politics, and came to Spain as an Anti-Fascist to fight Fascism'. As a result of his experiences on the front, however, he has grown to dislike the POUM and is now awaiting his discharge from the POUM militia. In a conversation with the writer on 30th [April] Blair enquired whether his association with the POUM would be likely to prejudice his chances of enlisting with the International Brigade. He wishes to fight on the Madrid front.[26]

Orwell later speculated on what might have happened had the transfer gone ahead. 'Quite possibly I should have been sent to Albacete before the Barcelona fighting started. In which case, not having seen the fighting at close quarters, I might have accepted the official [Communist] version of it.' In any other case, as a Brigader 'my position would have been impossible.'[27] We may add that the ex-POUM group would have been in the line at Brunete, a battle in which the British Battalion suffered seventy-nine dead, with 201 wounded and desertions, out of a total of some 320 effectives.[28]

But the plan was thwarted by the 'May Events' – four days of fighting in Barcelona between Communist-backed (Catalan) government forces and the CNT–POUM alliance. The former claimed to have forestalled a planned uprising against the Republic, into which the recalcitrant revolutionaries of the POUM – acting on the instigation of the 'Fascist' enemy – had seduced their majority anarchist soulmates. The latter argued that the fighting was provoked by a PSUC conspiracy, aimed at settling once and for all with those elements of the Popular Front which Stalin found unacceptable. The 'uprising' was the most important event of intra-Republican politics during the war, and dramatically altered its character. It remains an open wound in the side of 'Spain', which historical research has never been able to bind.[29]

Orwell's involvement in this affair forms the crux of his book, and provides the gravamen of his charges against the Republic. He argued that the democratic nature of the Popular Front had been subverted by Stalin, whose agents dictated its policy agenda, manipulating its propaganda and dominating its security apparatus, to the extent that it represented a totalitarian system no less oppressive than Fascism. But it was not the 'May Events' themselves which moved Orwell, but rather their consequences that produced his conclusions about the Republic's moral degeneration. For weeks following the Barcelona events he was isolated from regular news. Returning to the Aragon front on 4 May, he received a life-threatening wound about two weeks later. A month later still, following intensive treatment and extensive convalescence, he turned up at Eileen's Barcelona hotel, to learn – apparently to his astonishment – that a purge of POUM personnel was in full swing, and their lives were in danger. Although after the Barcelona fighting he had resolved not to join the International Brigade, this was mostly because of his sense of 'decency'. In this crisis, he drew back from abandoning his comrades and compromising loyalty to his commanders, Kopp and Levinski. It is notable that even by 20 June, when he rejoined Eileen, Orwell had refrained from joining the POUM. Yet during the following sixty hours – his last two days in Spain – he formed the whole dialectical basis of his Spanish War writings (and much else besides).[30]

During this terrifying episode, Orwell could have been captured, tortured, even murdered, by faceless thugs in some local hell-hole. Though in the event he and Eileen escaped the clutches of the intelligence services, several members of their circle suffered during the Republic's ruthless pursuit of the 'objectively Fascist' POUM. Some years later, Orwell read Arthur Koestler's *Dialogue with Death* and probably discussed with its author both the subjective implications of this experience and its wider context in terms of the Stalinist Terror.[31] In the meantime, it was understandable that Orwell should have reacted with a visceral fury to the persecution of friends and associates by Stalin-inspired agents, operating with (at least) the complaisance of the Republican government for which he had shed his own blood.

Orwell later commented apropos *Homage*, that it was 'a frankly political book, but in the main it is written with a certain detachment . . . I did try very hard in it to tell the whole truth.' Sincere as these claims were, and despite the surface coolness of his style, Orwell did not write with detachment (in the circumstances, a superhuman virtue). Of course, he could not know the 'whole truth', but this did not preclude a keenness – as with any political writer – to tell the reader what to think. Indeed, it was about the time of *Homage*'s publication in 1938 that he at last joined the ILP and began contributing to its proselytizing activities.[32]

This is what the ILP wanted from the start. The much-debated issue of whether Orwell went to Spain to fight or to write is otiose: one was meaningless without the other. Just as Pollitt was anxious to recruit intellectuals for the British Battalion – though in this case (in contrast to that of Spender) he evidently 'read' Orwell's political character – so equally were Brockway, McNair and other ILP leaders. No sooner had Orwell reached Monte Oscuro than the POUM's weekly magazine shone the spotlight of publicity on his trench. Under the heading 'British Author with the Militia', it described him as 'a well-known British author whose work is much appreciated in all English-speaking left circles of thought'.[33] This copy was by the American revolutionary, Charles Orr, ex-activist in the Socialist Party of America. Orwell had not yet entered any 'left circles of thought', and this was probably the first time that any American had heard of him. Furthermore, if Pollitt had reason to suspect Orwell's motives, the same was true of the ILP leadership. The controversial second part of *Wigan Pier* had been even less deferential to the ILP than to the CPGB, showing an attitude which (even allowing for rhetorics of style) could easily be construed as contempt.[34]

Bob Edwards, leader of the official contingent of ILP volunteers, was certainly wary of Orwell.[35] A model soldier but a political embarrassment, he seemed more trouble than he was worth. One of Edwards's tasks (similar to that of a commissar in the International Brigades) was to counter negative political influence. No one suspected Orwell of being a Stalinist agent provocateur – after all, he was merely enjoying one of the freedoms of their supposed utopia – but, inevitably, tensions were exacerbated by personal rivalry. At one point Edwards accused Orwell to his face of being a 'bloody scribbler' who was mainly out to enhance his career profile.[36] The phrase could be an ironic epitaph for all British writers in Spain, and especially those for whom 'bloody' is endowed with a double significance.

4 Propaganda

For all this, over the years Orwell has given the ILP a better return on their investment than (say) Spender, Auden, Koestler, Regler et al. gave the Communist Party. Despite the many condemnations of propaganda in his writings, Orwell was himself a willing propagandist. Though he had more awareness than other writers of the cultural context of his work, he was no more capable of escaping its moral implications. Certainly, he shared with Koestler the prophetic vision of 'History ending in 1936' – meaning that the propaganda writings of the Spanish War erected an impenetrable screen against future perception of 'the event itself'.[37] But both these writers were about to be sucked into the BBC's wartime propaganda machine, in the service of which Orwell even allowed moralistic reminders about 'Spain' to be censored out of his broadcasts.[38] His morning job for some years as a mild pre echo of Winston Smith may have led him to preach the salutary sermon of *Nineteen Eighty-Four*, but it does not change the fact of his own compromise with propaganda, just as he compromised with imperialist war, patriotism, and other 'bourgeois' cultural values.[39]

Reaching home in July 1937, Orwell immediately drafted a series of dramatic reports exposing the truth behind the mask of Republican propaganda. The Republic was indicted as a puppet regime of Stalin, guilty of waging a campaign of terror against its own citizens. He compared this action to similar policies in Germany and Italy, concluding that there was little to choose between them. Indeed he completed his ethical volte-face by stating unequivocally that 'the present [Republican] Government has more points of resemblance to Fascism than points of difference'.[40] But by the time Orwell settled down to compose (and revise) *Homage*, though the iron had entered his soul, the fire of its forging had apparently suffocated in his belly. Thus, despite the sustained attack upon the Comintern and all its works, Orwell went relatively easy on the Republic as such.[41] His feelings were confused, his opinions constantly shifting; things were by no means as clear and fixed to him as the text of *Homage* suggests. Each discrete piece of writing is (more or less) consistent within itself on the crux issues, and expressed in prose of compelling dynamism and dialetical clarity. However, viewed in chronological order they reveal that he failed to make up his mind for long whether or not the Democratic Republic was 'objectively Communist', whether or not (therefore) it was deserving of the support of decent men, or even of a (by now chimerical) victory over Fascism. In *Homage* itself Orwell was guilty of putting strong arguments across to readers whilst keeping his own fingers crossed behind his back.[42] True, he attempted to cover himself by constantly admitting his human fallibility; but surely he realized that the effect of these disclaimers was likely to be the exact reverse of that ostensibly intended – to augment rather than diminish the trust of the average reader?

In several cases of doubt over Orwell's probity that I signalled in 1984, he knew what 'the facts' were. Others he did not know, and subsequent research has supplied them. An instance of the latter is the state of the revolution in Barcelona at the time of Orwell's first visit, in the week which straddled 1936 and 1937. His description has become the outstandingly familiar piece of reportage from the Spanish Civil War, a stock-in-trade of history textbooks and literary compendia. These pages are a paean of praise to social revolution, apostrophized as beautiful and true, despite the ugliness of its violence and chaos. Not only are they 'white propaganda' for the 'revolution' – with a perennially persuasive effect on students – but they are also 'black propaganda' against Communism (and, in the second degree, Fascism) which are inimical to it.[43]

Yet the splendid shire horse which Orwell saw in the Ramblas with 'the working class in the saddle' was really more like a wooden pony, rocking asleep in the reins of counter-revolution. Since the heady days of summer 1936, the Catalan government (Generalitat) had gradually reasserted its power. Only two months after the popular insurrection, Franz Borkenau passed through Barcelona, noting that 'the town is quiet and empty, the revolutionary fever is withering away'.[44] In November, an American fellow-traveller lamented that 'since we first came here [in August] this town has become extremely bourgeois. All these women roaming the streets in their fur coats and men in their big expensive overcoats and shoes. Where, oh where, are the overalls of yesterday?'[45] Luis del Romero, based with an artillery regiment in the city, summed up this feeling: 'in rearguard Barcelona, everybody tried not to notice the war. Apart from the occasional air raid, things carried on much as normal. People displayed a total indifference to events.'[46] In spring 1937, the token POUM minister was removed from the Generalitat. Not long afterwards, the Committee of Anti-Fascist Militias, made up from the syndicalist parties (including the PSUC), and which had been accepted by the Generalitat as its enabling executive, dissolved itself, despite the protests of the POUM leadership. Meanwhile, in Moscow, *Pravda* announced that 'so far as Catalonia is concerned, the cleaning-up of Trotszkyist and Anarcho-Syndicalist elements there has already begun, and it will be carried out there with the same energy as in the USSR'.[47]

Only days after Orwell had left for the front, Borkenau again arrived in the city. To the Austrian observer, the defeat of the revolution was now palpable:

> [In August] it had overwhelmed me by the suddenness with which it revealed the real character of a workers' dictatorship. This time it struck the observer by the clean sweep of all signs of this same dictatorship. No more barricades in the streets, no more cars covered with revolutionary initials . . . no more workers in civilian clothes, but rifles on their shoulders; as a matter of fact very few armed men at all, and those mostly *asaltos* and *guardias* in brilliant uniforms; no more seething life around the party centres . . . and the red banners and inscriptions, so shining in August, had faded.[48]

Much of this stands in contradistinction, if not in actual contradiction, to Orwell's picture of a revolutionary utopia. Beneath the surface, things were even worse than Borkenau and Romero feared. By this time, as Michael Seidman has shown, the collective reforms of the anarcho-syndicalists had already failed. The war industries of Barcelona encountered difficulties with obtaining raw materials and foreign currency. The Republican government (based in Valencia) had reasons for treating Catalonia with suspicion, and the PCE/PSUC was determined to show its power by restricting Soviet supplies of food and arms to anarchist power centres. But the semi-paralysis of collectivized industry in Barcelona was compounded by widespread absenteeism and malingering amongst the workforce, which had little to do with with external pressures and everything to do with individual opportunism. Individual disputes with the new employers (that is the trade unions themselves) over pay, work conditions and political privileges were endemic, a problem with which the CNT found – for ideological and historical reasons – virtually impossible to cope. Seidman comments:

> Orwell ignored non-political factors which hindered revolutionary construction. Indeed, his analysis might actually invert the process. The popularity of 'working class control' and its 'egalitarian spirit' may have declined not so much because of the Soviet Union or the Communist Party, but rather because of worker apathy.[49]

In a striking remark about the 1930s, Orwell later asserted that awful events took place even though establishment worthies (like Lord Halifax) and rightist newspapers (like the *Daily Telegraph*) said they took place – in other words, that something can be true even though it is also propaganda. He did not always show a self-reflexive awareness of this principle. In the article 'Spilling the Spanish beans' he argues that the purpose of the Republic's formation of a new army (Ejército Popular) in 1936–7 was not to win the war, but to suppress revolution. The Communists, to the fore in its organization and command, were agents of capitalist reaction, enemies of the workers, and *ergo* (though Orwell stops just short of this conclusion) 'Fascists'. These charges were little less absurd than many forwarded by Cominternists against the POUM; making them in print meant that Orwell was behaving not very differently from 'Frank Pitcairn' (that is, Claud Cockburn), the *Daily Worker* correspondent whom he excoriated in *Homage*.[50]

Orwell always stoutly defended POUM comportment during the Barcelona events. A standing charge against the revolutionary parties was that they hoarded weapons which should have been sent to the front. This was used to justify the suppression of the POUM on the grounds that they were preparing a coup and thus – by logical extension – were effectively Fascists. In *Homage*, whilst (for some reason) finding himself able to admit this charge as regards the CNT, Orwell denies it on behalf of the POUM, on the basis of his own observations within the Hotel Falcón (their HQ). But the POUM, like all the other parties (including the PSUC itself) did retain quantities of arms against a day of internecine reckoning.

The need to defend sectarian interests in Barcelona was, indeed, a major reason for weapon starvation at the front, and the failure of Republican operations in Aragon. Morreres also confirms the allegation – made by the Communists, and denied by the POUM – that during the May Events units of the Lenin Division abandoned the line, intending (abortively) to march to the relief of their Barcelona comrades.[51] Orwell is unusually emphatic in denying this incident, a denial he verified by inquiry when he returned to his unit after the Barcelona interlude.[52] Presumably, even his English comrades were prepared to deceive him on this point, which encourages the suspicion that 'political solidarity' was becoming a greater priority for the POUM in the wake of the Barcelona events.[53]

Perhaps in some of the pro-Communist accounts – those books of 'shocking dullness and badness' which he reviewed in 1937–8 – Orwell found enough to persuade him that he had been misled on these or some other points. At any rate, he began to match his spilling of Spanish beans by letting Catalan cats out of bags. An essay on the POUM militia tended to confirm Communist criticisms of militia discipline and military effectiveness. Though similar points are made in *Homage*, in the book they are placed in a humorous context, or diluted with more positive observations. He now admitted that bitterly internecine suspicions existed between the POUM and CNT militias, to the extent that on one occasion many POUMistas (including Orwell) volunteered for a task force intended to prevent by force a rumoured CNT detection from the line. He also revealed that the political atmosphere inside the POUM division was not quite as distinct from that obtaining in the International Brigades as *Homage* would have us believe. Orwell himself had not (it seems) objected to the shooting of POWs of officer rank as a matter of routine. Like the Internationals, most POUM men agreed with their political leadership that desertion should be punished by death. Indeed, Orwell was forced to the conclusion – like any International Brigade commissar – that it was 'good party men' who made the best soldiers.[54]

Perhaps the supreme irony of these observations – which, in the context of the normative Orwellian moral code, amount to trenchant criticism of the POUM militia – is that Orwell never directly criticized the International Brigades. Rather, references to them are mostly fraternal. He recognized 'that the International Brigade is in some sense fighting for all of us – a thin line of suffering and often ill-armed human beings standing between barbarism and at least comparative decency'.[55] Another disconcerting Orwellian equivocation is the confession, amounting almost to a retraction, made in a letter to *Manchester Guardian* correspondent Frank Jellinek that

> Actually [in *Homage*] I've given a more sympathetic account of the POUM 'line' than I actually felt, because I always told them they were wrong and refused to join the party. But I had to put it as sympathetically as possible, because it has had no hearing in the capitalist press and nothing but libels in the left-wing press.[56]

It is difficult to reconcile this with the claim made in 1946 that 'I did try very hard [in *Homage*] to tell the whole truth'.[57] In sum, Orwell was actually serving 'the higher truth' – or, as he was later to put it, 'learning to love Big Brother'.

Even more unpalatable is that Orwell was prepared to betray not only the POUM, but the whole principle of the Spanish Revolution, and to write exactly like a *News Chronicle* correspondent. Early in 1939 he wrote an essay on Spain for the Workers' Educational Association magazine, *The Highway*. It appeared in a special issue designed (in its editor's words), 'to reveal the vitality and the potentialities of democracy, to hearten the timid and confound the Fifth Column'. At this time, as his other writings illustrate, Orwell could hardly find adjectives strong enough to convey his suspicion of democracy in general and his disgust over the Spanish example in particular. Here, however, he submitted a piece of official Labourist optimism. The essay praises the Spanish Republic's preservation of 'both the forms and the spirit of democracy', passing lightly over its 'internal power struggles'. It asserts, quite contrary to *Homage*, that 'any government which triumphs over Franco will be of liberal tendency', and elsewhere spiritlessly retails the Popular Front–liberal line. The Spanish War, claims Orwell,

> was acting as an educational force. If men were suffering, they were also learning. Scores of thousands of ordinary people had been forced into positions of responsibility which a few months earlier they would never have dreamed of. Hundreds of thousands of people found themselves thinking with an intensity which would hardly have been possible in normal times, about economic theories and political principles. Words like fascism, communism, democracy, socialism, Trotskyism, anarchism, which for the mass of human beings are nothing but words, were being eagerly discussed and thought out by men who only yesterday had been

illiterate peasants. There was a huge intellectual ferment, a sudden expansion of consciousness. It must be set down to the credit side of the war.[58]

As Lenin once said, 'If you are not prepared to adapt yourself, if you are not inclined to crawl on your belly in the mud, you are not a revolutionary but a windbag.' He was speaking of the infamous surrender of Brest-Litovsk.[59]

5 Art and History

In 1946, Orwell enunciated 'four great motives for writing'. We may assume that the order in which they appear represents the writer's order of importance. (Moreover, the words devoted to the first two outnumber those of the last two by a factor of five.) The first two are 'Sheer egoism' and 'Aesthetic enthusiasm'. Modern critics would see these two motives as powerfully complementary, indeed as overlapping. The last two are 'Historical impulse' and 'Political purpose'. These, contrariwise, modern opinion would view as mutually exclusive. Art inevitably embraces (without implying as necessary) a relationship with truth which is less than straightforward. I refer to so-called 'artistic licence'.[60]

Orwell's approach to ethics was that of a late nineteenth-century liberal dilettante; derived essentially from nostrums about art and history – if you like, 'writing' and 'real life'. 'Above the level of a railway guide', he noted, 'no book is quite free from aesthetic considerations.' Despite its embarrassing class overtones, Orwell considered himself an artist. He later stated that 'what I have most wanted to do throughout the past ten years is to make political writing into an art' (adding the typical disclaimer that 'when I sit down to write a book, I do not say to myself "I am going to produce a work of art"'). The first fruit of this mission was *Wigan Pier*, where his critique of British socialism was basically an aesthetic one, almost that of an art critic reviewing a new exhibition. In a deeply revealing sentence he described socialism in England as a 'frightful debauchery of taste'![61] Elsewhere, a similar vocabulary is used to draw the attention of the policy-forming elite of the left parties to the fact that their cosmetic image left much to be desired. He, Orwell, could prescribe remedies in order to stimulate the mass recruitment needed to engender revolutionary social change. In other words, a media message that could be canvassed successfully in the leafy suburbs of Sussex rather than the sordid lanes of Wigan.[62]

Orwell read other contemporary accounts of the Spanish War, if only in order to fulfil review commissions. His judgement on them as a genre was distinctly unfavourable: 'The immediately striking thing about the Spanish War books, at any rate those written in English, is their shocking dullness and badness. But what is more significant is that almost all of them . . . are written from a political angle, by cocksure partisans telling you what to think.'[63] This blanket dismissal was unjustified. Books by International Brigaders provide several contrary examples. Though John Sommerfield's *Volunteer in Spain* is a partisan work, it is also highly readable and strikingly original in structure, whilst Esmond Romilly's *Boadilla*, hardly less entertaining than *Homage*, is barely written from a political angle at all. The same is broadly true of the memoirs of Tom Wintringham, a founder-member of the CPGB who commanded the British Battalion during its first collective action at Jarama (February 1937). Orwell read these accounts, in addition to the works of academic Hispanist E. Allison Peers, produced from a solidly researched background, which fail to meet any of his criteria of condemnation.[64] Indeed, this is a typically pugilistic instance of the intolerance which marked all his writings of the late 1930s.

Moreover, these deep-set prejudices were not forced to the surface by his experience of Communist persecution. *Wigan Pier* immediately preceded *Homage*: he finished the manuscript only days before leaving for Spain, the book being published whilst he was on the Aragon front. It reveals a seething mass of grievances, precipitated by the plight of the British working class, but already latent in his intellectual make-up. There are many formal correspondences between *Wigan Pier* and *Homage*. More important, the two books are spiritually contiguous. In the closing pages of the former, Orwell dwells on the possibility of working-class resistance to oppression (a leitmotiv of his later writings) and cites the war in Spain as an opportunity to test this to the utmost.[65] Indeed, 'Spain' was the logical outcome of a search for effective action enunciated in the final pages of *Wigan Pier*. The concerns of the two books merge, the particular British crisis becomes universal in 'Spain'. In both parts of *Wigan Pier*, Orwell takes out a vicarious resentment on the leisured classes, whose luxuries were subsidized by proletarian suffering. The most frequent target, sometimes gratuitously dragged into the arena of shame and penance, was the hypocritical left-intellectual establishment, and above all its spoiled darlings the 'Nancy Poets'.[66] Mine-owners, civil servants, government ministers, tribunes of the trades unions: all these remained anonymous in their corporate guilt. But by the 'Nancy Poets' Orwell can only have meant three or four known individuals, specifically the 'Auden Group'.[67] In fact, these writers were deeply affected by the emotions of both class war and Spanish War, in a relationship marked – as was Orwell's own – by intense feelings of guilt. As it happened, Auden had already expressed his consciousness of the substance of Orwell's indictment, in some lines – written in 1934, thus before *Wigan Pier* – which contain a profoundly Orwellian sentiment.

> And, gentle, do not care to know
> Where Poland draws her Eastern bow,
> What violence is done;
> Nor ask what doubtful act allows
> Our freedom in this English house
> Our picnics in the sun.[68]

In his essay 'Inside the Whale' (1940) Orwell continued his vilification of Auden with an attack on his poem SPAIN. In effect, he accused the poet of espousing, in the phrase 'the necessary murder', the maxim of 'the end justifies the means'; making him guilty by association with Stalinist thugs who caused the death of his young friend Bob Smillie. Auden, already softened up pyschologically by his own experiences in Spain, was cowed into disavowing his poem.[69] But the construction that Orwell placed upon it was crudely literalist. Furthermore, he increased the force of his attack by the claim: 'it so happens that I have seen the bodies of numbers of murdered men – I don't mean killed in battle, I mean murdered. Therefore I have some conception of what murder means.'[70] In the circumstances, it seems necessary to enquire when and where Orwell had this experience. Readers are evidently intended to assume that the incident took place in Spain: but no such event is recorded in Orwell's writings, nor are his biographers forthcoming on the point.[71] The alternative explanation, that he invented the story to gain a moral advantage over Auden, though even more damaging to his reputation, seems nevertheless the more likely.

Furthermore, his whole comportment was dubious in that Orwell – unlike Auden – had actually espoused the principle that 'the end justifies the means' over Spain. As we have seen, even if he did not witness, he evidently accepted the need for the execution of deserters and the murder of prisoners. Moreover, in *Homage* and elsewhere, he stated unequivocally that he wished to see Franco defeated 'by any means whatever', a sentiment which may be held to cancel out all his moral dicta about the ethical dimension of the Spanish War.

Orwell carried his persecution of the Auden group from *Wigan Pier* over into *Homage*, where his anger, this time at the betrayal of the revolution and all that the death of Smillie epitomized, inspired venomous references to 'Nancy Poets' who supported the Comintern. In August 1937, in response to Nancy Cunard's invitation to contribute to *Authors Take Sides*, he told her roundly to

> stop sending me this bloody rubbish . . . I am not one of your fashionable pansies like Auden and Spender . . . By the way, tell your pansy friend Spender that I am preserving specimens of his war-heroics and when the time comes when he squirms for shame at having written it . . . I shall rub it in good and hard.[72]

Thereafter, Orwell shewed remorse, canvassing Cyril Connolly to arrange a meeting with Spender. During a hospital convalescence in 1938, he furthered this *rapprochement*, apologizing to the poet if any of his writings had been the occasion of hurt. When Spender replied that he had not noticed any slight, Orwell resorted to a wormwood vagueness in shuffling off the substantive nature of his slanders.[73] After the latter's death, Spender (who largely concurred with the conclusions of *Homage*) was to be a leading supporter of his reputation. It would be an exaggeration to say that they had become friends. Given Orwell's remark, 'you can have an affection for a murderer or a sodomite, but you cannot have an affection for a man whose breath stinks', their relationship might be better described as a sort of Nancy-Anti-Soviet Pact.[74]

In passing, we may note that Orwell had other categories of hate-object. Journalists emerge from *Homage* with even less credit than Nancy Poets (or Comintern agents). Orwell's contempt for reporters seems boundless – odd when we consider his original intention of 'writing some newpaper articles' about Spain.[75] There is more to this than the disillusionment of the Spanish war: intermixed, we may detect trace elements of the toxic feelings often present in writers with eternal longings in them but who need the income that only reporterage and other hack work can provide. It is the elite assumption (analysed and interpreted elsewhere in this book) that since art is truth, journalists necessarily stand in either a parasitical or a treacherous relationship to it, a relationship even more subordinate in terms of caste than that obtaining with politics.[76] Throughout his career, Orwell resorted to journalism to supplement an income which (he claimed in 1936) was no bigger than that of a coalface miner.[77] Of course, he may have regarded the articles he wrote for small literary-political magazines as having a higher aesthetic status than deadline-oriented hit-and-miss reporter work.

However sheepish one part of his personality felt about the flaw in the other, he could not escape the imperative urge of his generation to be an artist and a genius. However, it seems that (perhaps misled by his experience of Eton) Orwell assumed that his despised 'Nancy Poets', who fell unambiguously into the category of 'artists', were sons of gentlefolk. In fact none of the Auden group enjoyed financial independence; like Orwell himself, each cobbled together an income from casual commissions and/or editorial work. His rabid attacks on them were the spiteful results of prejudice, not so much unfortunate as outrageous, even allowing for adjustments of cultural-moral paradigms between our age and his. Orwell's non-fiction is punctuated by pharisaical outbursts against social types and institutions, often so strongly expressed as to constitute a kind of verbal violence: 'intellectual brutality' he called it.[78] This makes for lively reading, and is consistent with Orwell's *persona* as a writer who relished a good scrap. Whether or not he sought some kind of Olympian detachment from the ideological *mêlée* of the 1930s, he was in practice not only implicated in the street fighting of the sects, but also involved in the backbiting of the hacks.

This brew may be distilled further. In many studies of 1930s 'literature', the writings of Franco supporters such as Wyndham Lewis and Roy Campbell, who engaged in vitriolic onslaughts against the 'fashionable left intellectuals', are on the end of sharp criticism from the latter's academic descendants. In particular, their homophobic instincts – which, in Campbell, are given exuberantly adolescent expression – are the occasion of frequent disgust. If Orwell's divagations on this subject were to be placed alongside

Campbell's in a context of authorial anonymity, those of Orwell might be found less colourful, but never less objectionable by modern standards of political morality. It seems they are exempted from censure by virtue of their author's Brahmin status as a genius who was on the politically correct side in Spain.

Though his knowledge of political theory may have been stronger than is sometimes supposed, Orwell was not an academic writer. This may be attractive to academics, but does not invalidate their task of exploring the taxonomic locations of *Homage*: herein, after all, lies one key to the plurality of textual meaning. 'Spain' gave Orwell an intense awareness of the necessity of history, seen as inseparable from artistic freedom. By 1938, indeed, he was inclined to give artistic freedom a priority identical with that accorded it, for example, by Spender in *Forward from Liberalism*.[79] In his wartime articles, above all in 'Looking back on the Spanish War', he constantly restated a belief in the hermeneutic role of historical perspective and the pristine inviolability of the recorded past. One of the most chilling of *Nineteen Eighty-Four*'s horrors is the professional delight taken by the slave-journalist Winston Smith in his rape of something which his other self knows to be the most precious of humanity's resources – the 'historical truth'.

But perhaps the historian should resist being seduced by Orwell's respect for the subject. In 'Inside the Whale' he transposed Ranke's famous principle of historical writing ('wie es eigentlich gewesen') from the past to the present tense. His concept of history was the dim sense of the 'historian of the future' to whom the articulate layman sometimes gives rhetorical voice. In an early critical appraisal of Orwell, Tom Hopkinson pointed out that 'he was without any historical perspective. He saw the world of his day with peculiar intensity because he saw very little of its past.'[80] Orwell also imagined seminal 'facts' of history – atomic and indivisible except with nuclear consequences – which in the right conditions inevitably yield a harvest of literal and universal truth. Thus the historian may note the relevant problematic for the method used in *Homage*. As we have seen, Orwell here felt free to interfere with the chronology and detail of his Spanish experiences in the interests of aesthetic criteria. It follows that by Orwell's own standards 'art' is not in harmony with 'history' but, on the contrary, in conflict with it.

In any case, Orwell's distaste for the literature produced by

'Spain' was not simply an aesthetic judgement. He was filled with foreboding at the promiscuous distortion, manipulation, suppression, and invention of reality; lies, disseminated by established power-systems in the interests of oppression. The course of the war and of the revolution, and the aspirations and lives of Spaniards – perhaps as a prelude to those of all humanity – were being literally dictated by the written and broadcast word. As an inhabitant of the 1930s, Orwell's reaction was to be morally horror-stricken, in contrast with our present, relativist 'detachment'. He reached maturity in the first age of mass communication and mass reception, the first generation of near-universal literacy in Great Britain. By the mid-1930s most families had access to radio and cinema, the preconditions for an era of ubiquitous propaganda.[81] The dramatically altered context of global politics, and the significant struggles of the second half of the twentieth century which it produced, could only breathe in such an atmosphere. Nowadays these solids have (to paraphrase Marx) melted into air, and only the atmosphere remains, the global media phase of capitalism. Thus it stands to his credit that Orwell so famously deplored the use of history as a tool of power, and that we find this salutary message inscribed in all his Spanish writings.

6 Cause

Eric Blair the warrior was careless enough to let himself get fixed in the sights of an enemy sniper. The writer Orwell is more difficult to pin down. During the ten years which witnessed both the Spanish War and the Second World War (1936–45) Orwell's views on fundamental issues of political economy underwent mercurial changes from one piece of writing to the next.

What, then, *was* his cause? There is no reason to doubt his claims (a) that he had been anxious about the rise of International Fascism for some time before he went to Spain, and (b) that he had been at odds with the Communist Party for much the same time. A notable difference between Orwell's political writing and that of his contemporaries is his abstinence from sustained polemic. It is probably a matter of style rather than feeling, but we rarely find him ranting against Fascism or Fascists. Raymond Williams described Orwell as 'a natural Popular Front man'; and although he excoriated aspects of the 'People's Front' policy, especially the cynical Soviet tactics behind its propagation, I tend to agree with this assessment.[82] When considering the motives of International Brigaders, the conclusion is unavoidable that for the great majority, the political affiliation entered on their identity cards as *antifascista* was the only accurate description of their individual – and thus their common – cause. For all that he ultimately refused to fight with 'a Communist-controlled unit', Orwell was a partisan of this cause.[83] In 1938, around the time he joined the ILP, Orwell also agreed to join the committee of Solidaridad Internacional Antifascista, an organization in aid of 'Spain', mainly inspired by the American anarchist movement.[84] From the time of writing *Homage* until the outbreak of war with Germany two years later, Orwell's sympathies were basically pro-anarchist. This meant that he approved and sought to bring about violent social revolution, thus physically to destroy all elements of conventional social control – empire, state, Church, property, army and police. In this context, the fall of the government of Largo Caballero, which occurred in the wake of the May Events, marked the parting of the ways between Orwell and the Republican cause. After that it became increasingly clear to him that whichever side won the war made no difference to the fate of the Spanish Revolution.

In 'explaining' his decision to join the ILP he stated that 'if Fascism triumphs I am finished as a writer'; but he failed to cite reasons, other than the complementary assertion that 'the only regime which, in the long run, will dare to permit freedom of speech is a socialist regime'.[85] Yet Orwell did not reach the conclusion that Fascism and art were incompatible. In this, he really did stand apart. That Fascism and philistinism were synonymous was an article of faith to other left writers of his era, and thereafter became a structural presupposition of western intellectual life. But in *Wigan Pier* Orwell expressed the fear that if socialism did not get its act together, artists might eventually opt for the Fascist alternative. This was more than just another swipe at the capricious nature of the politics of effete, left intellectuals. In 1938, he told his friend Jack Common: 'I think it's really time someone began looking into Fascism seriously. There must be more to it than one would gather from the left press.'[86] Indeed: for Orwell's Spanish writings are limited by his exiguous treatment of the Nationalist side. If he did not consider the enemy as bestial, it was only because he did not consider them at all. There is much point in E. P. Thompson's marvellously Orwellian simile of Orwell's version of the 1930s; 'Like an endless football game in which one side (Fascism, Reaction) is invisible, while the other side (Anti-Fascism, Communism, Progress) spend their whole time fouling each other or driving the ball into their own goal.'[87]

Every reader remembers Orwell's picture of the Fascist in the opposite trenches trying to scuttle away from the target area holding up his trousers.[88] Here, he seems to express feelings for the enemy's humanity. Yet little more than a page of *Homage* (with a couple more in 'Looking Back') are expended on the Francoist movement. Where not dismissive, Orwell's comments are pure speculation, since he knew nothing about the enemy. He had no inkling of what inspired so many Spaniards to fight against the Republic, beyond what he uncritically accepted from the left-wing sources that he distrusted on every other matter. As the reviewer of *Homage* in the Catholic magazine, the *Tablet*, pointed out, 'it is curious that a man who tells us that for a year or two past the international prestige of fascism had been haunting him like a nightmare, should not display more intellectual curiosity.'[89] For Orwell, the question of any altruism or idealism on the other side simply did not arise. The enemy was actuated purely by vested interest, and regimented by power. To Orwell, the Nationalist *movimiento* was simply a horde of drones and coolies driven on to destroy the workers by the bosses – whether capitalist, landowner, army officer or priest made no difference – supplied and paid for by international Fascism.[90]

Throughout his 'Spanish' texts (though without notable rancour) Orwell invariably refers to the enemy as 'Fascist' yet makes no mention of José Antonio and the Falange, nor indeed of any other figure or party amongst the rebels apart from Franco – interesting tributes both to the *Caudillo*'s cult of personality and his programme of unification. In spite of using this conventional discourse strategy, Orwell perceived that Francoism was a phenomenon of the nineteenth century, not of the twentieth. Equally acute was his prophecy that, whichever side won the war, the ensuing regime 'would have to be a dictatorship of some kind of fascism', but that, Spain being Spain, this 'fascism' would be considerably less totalitarian, and more humanely inefficient, than the Italian, German or Soviet models.[91] However, these insights are wholly a product of his school training in the 'Black Legend' of Spanish history.[92] From the same subliminal font derives his ignorance of Spain's religious character. Indeed 'ignorance' is inadequate in describing his attitude to an issue which was one of the two most important long-term causes of the Spanish Civil War. He unquestioningly accepted that the destruction of churches was proof of a popular and universal distaste for Catholicism. In Barcelona 'almost every church had been gutted and its images burnt. Churches here and there were being systematically demolished by gangs of workmen.' 'In six months in Spain I saw only two undamaged churches.' Some had been converted into army stores or billets, or – as at Alcubierre – into a latrine. The disgusting condition to which some stately homes had been reduced by revolution even gave Orwell 'a sneaking sympathy with the Fascist ex-owners' – but he did not extend this sympathy to the Church.[93]

At Monflorite (near Huesca) Orwell visited a cemetery and, seeing very few religious symbols, concluded that the locals were indifferent to religion. 'No reverence for the dead here . . . It struck me that the people in this part of Spain must be genuinely without religious feeling.'[94] Almost certainly, he had happened upon a graveyard which had been secularized in accordance with the terms of the anti-clerical Republican constitution. In fact, the region where Orwell was based was a typical, strongly religious, agrarian community of northern Spain.[95] Village churches all around had been destroyed the previous summer, not by local parishioners, but by anarchist militias, usually gangs organized for the purpose in Catalan towns like Gerona or Lérida. At the time, and for months after his return, Orwell had no idea of the nature and extent of the revolutionary terror – attested to even by John Cornford, who at the time was serving with the POUM militia – which had swept through Aragon, and had been used deliberately to underpin the imposition of the rural collectives.[96] He later came to appreciate why pro-Franco writers were upset about the massacre of clergy. Whilst still insisting on 'the apparent absence of any religious feeling whatever among the mass of the people', he acknowledged that its being 'dangerous to admit openly to religious belief' in the Republican zone may have helped him form this impression.[97]

Around this time, at Wallington, the Blairs were visited by the vicar, and the Spanish War was discussed: 'of course we had to own up that it was true about the burning of the churches, but he cheered up a lot on hearing that they were only Roman Catholic churches.'[98] This anecdote is voluble testimony to the cultural suspicion of papism which lay at the heart of the Protestant-liberal English (and patriotic) tradition to which Orwell belonged.

7 Consensus

Perhaps the best summation of Orwell was that made by Juan Negrín. As executive head of the Spanish Republic in 1937–9, Negrín had presided over the policies which Orwell catalogued and condemned. He was the living symbol of the surrender of the cause to Stalin, and all that this entailed, from the suffocation of revolution to the death of Bob Smillie. Meeting in 1940, they enjoyed a pleasantly civilized little chat. Orwell seemed to the Spaniard 'decent and righteous, biased by a too rigid puritanical frame, gifted with a candour bordering on naivety, highly critical but blindly credulous, morbidly individualistic, and so supremely honest and self-denying that he would not hesitate to change his mind once he perceived himself to be wrong.'[99]

My re-examination of Orwell's writings on 'Spain' did not, after all, result in the resolution of previous doubts and reservations. In 1984, I asked readers to consider that Orwell may be wrong even where he says he may be wrong – a version of his own remark about Lord Halifax's confirmation of 'Fascist outrages' in Europe.[100] To this I would now add: *Orwell may be wrong even where the Soviet interest claims he is wrong.* Yet Orwell's equivocations, though vitiating the quasi-scriptural view of his works espoused by Trilling et al. on the one hand, do not compromise him in the fatal degree laid down by the Alexander camp on the other. Taken as a whole œuvre, Orwell's 'Spanish' texts betray their author's shift from an anti-democratic and revolutionary position to a democratic-socialist one. This represents an authentic political metamorphosis: after all, the unexampled force of experience in 1936–45 brought about a similar change of perspective in millions of others, Fascists as well as Communists, working-class as well as bourgeois. Thus these writings demonstrate the residual hegemony of nineteenth-century liberal humanism, despite (or perhaps because of) the threat to it of the politics of revolutionary catastrophism. It suggests that this ideology had become cultural in the

West, thereby escaping from the epiphenomenal status of being an ideological construction at all.

In this, Orwell's 'Spain' is effectively identical to the 'Spain' of another Englishman who wrote influentially about the Spanish War in these years, Gerald Brenan. Brenan was similar to Orwell in terms of social background and attitudes. He too started from (and returned to) the position of an English patriotic liberal – what might be called, in Thomas Mann's formulation, 'an unpolitical man'. He was moved by a sense of decency and fair play, and never joined a political party, even after the Spanish Revolution (which he witnessed at close quarters) sparked a rebellion against his own background. Like Orwell, he quickly decided to write a book about Spain, and began work after returning to Britain in late 1936. His empathy with the Republic was balanced by pragmatism and common sense. After his celebrated study *The Spanish Labyrinth* was published in 1943, he confessed to a friend: 'I saw what I had written was really an indictment of the follies and illusions of the left, with whose general aims I sympathised.'[101]

Even before his death, Orwell was converging with public opinion rather than leading it. Thereafter 'Orwell' became a prophet of the increasingly consensual, anti-totalitarian dispensation of the post-war world. A writer who stands for all that is 'decent' in political commitment may not be a comfortable companion for a critical reader, but is rather more so than one who espouses bloody revolution. For me, the problem remains that, rather because of than despite their determined onslaught upon the Communists, Orwell's writings on 'Spain' now constitute a classic contribution to the vaguely 'liberal' myth of the Spanish War; a myth so hegemonic that remorse over Franco's victory is part of the guilt-complex of the western intellectual, a stock-in-trade of a whole ethical culture. This time round, instead of bemoaning the end of history, Orwell has become one of those responsible for it.

~ 4 ~
Ballad of Heroes: Britten, Auden and the British Battalion

1

After failure in the battle of the Ebro, the cause of the Republic was doomed. The campaign which started so resonantly in July 1938, punching a great hole in Francoist lines and stimulating a wave of euphoria, ended, as had all its predecessors since Brunete, in defeat and retreat. True, each sierra, even each particular peak, which the Popular Army had captured in the first week of the offensive was turned into a fortress: many were defended to the death in near-impossible conditions as enemy counter-offensives developed inexorably and unremittingly. The battle front seared eastwards across the rugged terrain of north-eastern Aragon throughout August and September. It took Franco the best part of three months to re-establish the lines held at the outset of the campaign. But in the process the Republican Army of the East was reduced to a shambles, and in particular the International Brigades, its spearhead of attack and spinal column of its defence, were shattered. In late September, after many rumours of relief had raised and dashed the hopes of its zombie-like survivors, they were pulled out of the line for the last time. In accordance with an agreement brokered by Britain and France, all foreign units were to be repatriated from Spain. By the end of the year, most members of the British Battalion had reached home. Behind them, the inevitable offensive against Catalonia began. Francoist forces crossed the Ebro with scant resistance, and the ensuing campaign was little more than a procession. Early in the New Year (1939) the government abandoned Barcelona, which fell to the Nationalists on 29 January.[1]

During this grim struggle for survival, when the ubiquitous imperatives of *¡No Pasarán!* and *¡Resistir es Vencer!* were more desperately relevant than ever before, the 'Aid Spain' movement in Britain reached a peak of activity. Accomplished orators among the returned Brigade veterans (usually Communist Party members) were deployed to venues all over the country, where they displayed their wounds, eulogized their martyred dead and waxed elegiac about suffering 'Spain'. Fund- and consciousness-raising campaigns became more intense than ever. Assistance offered and provided to the Republic (short of primary military materials) became ever more comprehensive and widespread. New committees and branch organizations proliferated. Relief ships bound for Barcelona or Valencia sailed from British ports on an almost daily basis. All this reflected a level of humane commitment which by now had spread well beyond the social classes and interest groups represented in Popular Front politics. Indeed, it might be argued that – ironically at the last gasp – the Comintern had achieved its objective of creating a 'Home Front Abroad' for the Spanish Republican cause.[2]

As part of this phenomenon, the Workers' Music Association took the lead in organizing a series of London concerts, announced as a 'Festival of Music for the People'. The plan was to mount three spring evenings of music at the Queen's Hall with all proceeds to 'Spain', and ending up with one concert specifically dedicated to the memory of the British dead.[3] Edward Clark, fellow-traveller and moving spirit of the whole enterprise, was inspired to devise a programme which was well ahead of its time in almost every significant respect. Clark's vast experience and European-wide contacts enabled him to mobilize dozens of organizations in the performance of works by composers as diverse (indeed, divergent) as Vaughan Williams and Schoenberg. The final event was a choral-orchestral extravaganza with vocal soloists, various London choirs and the London Symphony Orchestra under the direction of composer-conductor Constant Lambert. The premiere of a new work, the only one of the festival, was announced, to be contributed by Lambert's younger contemporary, Benjamin Britten.[4]

The 25-year-old prodigy worked feverishly at his commission in the early months of 1939. This was the time when Catalonia was in its death-throes and the tide of refugees swept over and around the Pyrenees into France. Press and newsreels recorded the exodus of half a million men, women and children, whose miserable plight was eloquent evidence of their belief that defeat meant proscription and possible execution. The composer was deeply moved by these circumstances, producing a work of striking originality and power which, mindful of his commission, he entitled *Ballad of Heroes*. In search of appropriate texts with which to apostrophize the martyrs of the British Battalion, Britten turned naturally to the work of W. H. Auden, whose epic poem SPAIN of two years earlier had equally, in all but name, been dedicated to the International Brigades.[5]

2

Ballad of Heroes was by no means Britten's first collaboration with Auden, nor the first fruit of his dedication to the cause of the Internationals and 'Spain'. Auden and Britten met as a result of Edward Clark's initiative in putting Britten in touch with the GPO Film Unit, where Auden already worked. The unit was looking for a composer who could produce settings of Auden's verse, working under the same kind of pressure in which the texts themselves had been written.[6] This was mid-1935; and the two artists were soon involved in joint ventures. Their close friendship and artistic association was from the start hugely fortified by politics and later cemented by the crisis of Spain. Auden's impact on a young man who still looked and felt like an adolescent was deeply unsettling. Britten, though astonishingly gifted, and already immensely knowing within his vocation, was relatively untutored in nearly everything else which mattered in the 1930s, above all in literature and politics.[7] Perhaps more important, he was emotionally immature and confused. On both levels, Auden dazzled and captivated him.

Six years Britten's senior, Auden was not only recognized leader of 'the new poetry', but also a conversational virtuoso with the range of a polymath and the cogent insights of a philosopher.[8] In the winter of 1935–6, as they worked together on various projects Britten began to read widely. He found the subject areas difficult, even recondite, and Auden's company daunting: but increasing admiration for his mentor's mind and personality drove him on. For his part too, Auden was highly impressed by his new friend: Britten's coruscating array of musical talents combined with winsome good looks were enough to excite a comprehensive enthusiasm. Surely, Auden, of all people, had some inkling of the double-entendre implicit in the title of their celebrated film about the railway postal service from London to Scotland – *Night Mail*. Be that as it may, Auden was, and on the instant, a potential suitor.

They went to concerts together, and Britten was initiated into Auden's 'gang', a process which included at least one working session at Stephen Spender's flat (where he is likely to have met Tony Hyndman).[9] During the first half of 1936, as well as composing prolifically, Britten knuckled down to reading radical political literature, together with a selection of poetry, both recommended by Auden – and just as Hyndman had done under Spender's supervision. At the same time, all these areas were combined in Britten's first major concert commission. *Our Hunting Fathers*, an excoriating satire on the orthodox evils of the ruling class – oppression, violence, and a tendency to Fascism – set a sequence of allegorical verses by Auden. It was finished on 23 July 1936.

Three days earlier, Britten's diary noted the outbreak of a 'Spanish revolution – those bloody fascists trying to get back into power'.[10] This was the very day that the military uprising was challenged and bloodily overcome, mainly by the organized working class, in both Madrid and Barcelona. As recently as April, Britten had spent a week in the latter city, where a work of his was performed as part of the International Society of Contemporary Music Festival. He was enchanted by Barcelona and its popular music-making, noting down some tunes of the Catalan *Sardana* folkdance for future use.[11] Now suddenly a much less peaceful popular event in Barcelona's streets erupted into the world's media. On 22 July Britten scribbled down his feelings: 'News makes me sick from Spain. The rebel Fascists seem to be doing better . . . practically all N. Spain . . . is in their hands – including Barcelona . . . After dinner read a lot more Marx. Hard going, though edifying.'[12] He was especially moved by the fate of teenage boys allegedly lined up and shot by 'the Fascists'. He wrote to his mother – who, it seems, had dissented from his view of what was happening in Spain: 'But what about the fascists lining up all the little Popular Front boys against a wall & putting the machine guns on them? Imagine English boys of 14 even knowing what Popular Front means – much less dying for it.'[13] Already, on the day following completion of *Our Hunting Fathers*, he had drafted 'a funeral march to those youthful Spanish martyrs'. Written within days of the original military rising in Morocco, this was, perhaps, the earliest artwork dedicated by a major international figure to the victims of the Spanish Civil War.[14]

Once his commission was in the can, Britten called on an old schoolfriend, and found himself arguing about the Spanish situation over the dinner table with the father of the family, a 'true blue' and an admiral. Soon his pre-Auden friends began to complain that 'Ben can't talk about anything but the Spanish War'.[15] Thus began the 'naughty' phase, a quinquennium of delayed maturation (1936–40) in the life of Lord Britten of Aldeburgh, 'the best brought-up little boy you can imagine' as described by Rita Thomson, who nursed him in his final illness.[16] That summer of 1936, the mentor of misrule, Auden himself, was away on an extended trip to Iceland. Britten, renting a cottage in Cornwall, grew closer to an older composer, Lennox Berkeley, whom he had first met in Barcelona. Berkeley visited his young friend: 'we agree on most points & it is nice to discuss things we don't agree on.' One of the former was the moribund state of English music: one of the latter may have been aspects of the war in Spain, but another was certainly Britten's sexuality. He was aware of Berkeley's 'sexual weakness for young men of my age and form [but] he is considerate & open & we have come to an agreement on that subject.'[17] Whatever the precise meaning of the latter encryption, Berkeley was attracted to Britten, and in order to anchor their relationship he broached the subject of collaboration on a work to celebrate their common love of Catalonia.

3

Meanwhile, Auden, in the wilds of Iceland, was anxious to be brought up to date on Spain. 'Write and tell me if you know anything authentic', he asked Erika Mann, his wife of convenience, after an encounter with 'a selfish little English gentleman . . . who said, apropos of Spain, "Why can't these foreigners behave themselves. It's sickening. You can't travel anywhere nowadays. . ."'.[18] During the long bright nights of the Icelandic summer, Auden was stuck with the heterosexual writer, Louis MacNeice, as companion. To ward off boredom and frustration the two men compiled a spoof 'Last Will and Testament'. Auden tucked in a couplet which voiced a concern as besetting as that for Spain.

> For my friend, Benjamin Britten, composer, I beg
> That fortune send him soon a passionate affair.[19]

These lines referred back to sentiments expressed in a poem that Auden had dedicated to Britten in March, 1936. Little doubt can subsist today that this typically complex lyric represents a declaration of sexual love for its dedicatee.

> Night covers up the rigid land
>   And Ocean's quaking moor
> And shadows with a tolerant hand
>   The ugly and the poor.
>
> The wounded pride for which I weep
>   You cannot staunch, nor I
> Control the moments of your sleep
>   Nor hear the name you cry,
>
> Whose life is lucky in your eyes,
>   And precious is the bed
> As to his utter fancy lies
>   The dark caressive head.
>
> For each love to its aim is true,
>   And all kinds seek their own;
> You love your life and I love you,
>   So I must lie alone.
>
> O hurry to the fated spot
>   Of your deliberate fall;
> For now my dream of you cannot
>   Refer to you at all.[20]

In describing Lennox Berkeley's proclivities, Britten was well aware that he himself had a 'sexual weakness for young men'. In these years, he became infatuated with a series of male adolescent acquaintances, with an age discrepancy equivalent to that which divided him and Auden – or even him and Berkeley, who was ten years his senior. Indeed, his diary records feelings about several of these boys expressed in terms which might be described as avuncular or even as *in loco parentis*. One of the more spontaneous and troublesome of these encounters was with a Basque refugee, one of the 'orphans of the war' in Spain identified by sympathetic Britons with the victims of Nazi bombers at Guernica, and to whom he gave shelter in his Suffolk home for several months in 1937–8.[20] Yet underneath it all, Britten could not escape from the sanctions of his middle-class upbringing. Partly owing to his family history, he craved social respectability and financial security. Even in these rebellious years he was haunted by sexual taboos which inhibited him, not only from welcoming Auden's advances, but also (perhaps) from explicitly physical relationships with teenage protégés. On the other hand, 'Night covers up' and the Iceland couplet, in the context of Auden's very particular beliefs about love, lead me to conclude that during 1936, at least, the poet had not yet resigned himself to being one of 'the ugly and the poor' (that is, a victim of unrequited love); that he looked on Britten as a candidate for the ideal-unique romantic attachment he craved; and that he hoped that once his love had lost his inhibitions (that is, his virginity) the status quo would be changed utterly.[21]

Despite Britten's many diary entries describing his emotional feelings and even (up to a point) his sexual encounters, it remains impossible to be sure that the epiphanal event desired by Auden took place before Britten and Peter Pears became lovers, probably in 1939. In the intervening period, he often stayed at the homes of a wide circle of friends, including Christopher Isherwood and Lennox Berkeley, as well as Auden himself. It is true, too, that his diary is notably more reticent about Auden (in the present intimate context) than about several others. Nevertheless, once Auden was back from Iceland, their professional and personal relationship once again dominated Britten's agenda. *Our Hunting Fathers* was premiered in September and almost immediately thereafter the composer received the text of the second Auden–Isherwood play, *The Ascent of F6*, for which he was to provide the music.[22] At the same time the two men were collaborating on another documentary, this time for director Paul Rotha of Strand Films. Rotha commented later on how the Spanish Civil War became an obsession with those involved in the arts, an inescapable topic of conversation and concern. What had up till then been known as the 'International Column' was now developing into the International Brigades, whose recruitment and dispatch was being organized clandestinely by the CPGB. A thousand sources of personal and group emotion – love, fear, jealousy, empathy, aspiration, compassion, opportunism; all the drives which a cultural theorist might arrange under the category of 'desire' – poured into this turbulent watershed. 'The Spanish Civil War dominated so much of our lives [recalled Rotha]; should we give up our careers and go to Spain?'[23]

The successful defence of Madrid against Franco's army in November 1936 gave an enormous boost to the image of the International Brigades. Comintern–Republican propaganda picturing the victory as being won against overwhelming odds was all the more effective because of widespread predictions in the pro-Nationalist and neutral press that Franco's offensive would prove a walkover. Relief in leftist circles was almost palpable. Britten noted 'Thank God there is no more 1936 to be gone thro'. Of all the frightful years. Tragedy after tragedy . . . with only the miraculous Madrid stand, & at home FB's recovery to brighten it.'[24] The Internationals became the object of widespread admiration, reaching in many towards hero-worship. In December, two of the most plausible and attractive heroes, Esmond Romilly and John Cornford, arrived home on leave, partly in order to act as recruiting-sergeants for the new British Battalion being set up in Albacete.[25]

Auden was acquainted with the Romilly brothers, whose iconoclastic magazine *Out of Bounds* had expressed many of his own feelings about the public schools; and he had corresponded with Cornford about the latter's early attempts at verse.[26] In what was already coming to be seen as a 'generation' of writer-rebels, Auden was something more than *primus inter pares*. Indeed, as early as 1933, he was addressed by Cecil Day Lewis as a heroic warrior set to lead Britain's intellectuals in battle against the bourgeois philistines.[27] If Day Lewis's metaphors bordered on the infantile, on a more cliquish level, as their leader, Auden was obliged to follow acolytes like Cornford and Romilly with a certain degree of resolution if he was to retain his status as 'Uncle Wiz'. But linked to the negative motive of peer pressure was a more positive, if not exactly glorious one: the wish to impress the main object of his emotions, Benjamin Britten. In early December, Auden wrote to an academic friend, Professor E. R. Dodds, with the news that 'I have decided to go out in the new year, as soon as the book [about Iceland] is finished, to join the International Brigade.'[28]

4

Relationships of sexual desire are inescapably involved with power, the power that pleasure, satisfaction, control, self-esteem and manipulation of social networks all convey to the partners (if usually not in equal measure). In Isherwood's memoir of this period (written in the third person), Auden's closest friend and confidant attempted uncomfortably to disguise the jealousy which welled within him when the poet declared his intention to leave for Spain.

> The British press had turned Wystan into big news . . .] To thousands of young people he was now a hero – a Byron or at least a Rupert Brooke going forth to war . . . [But] Wystan's dedication to his chosen cause was certainly as sincere as theirs had been . . . Christopher could never have done alone what Wystan was doing . . . [But] he didn't feel guilty about this, only regretful for what he was missing.[29]

Quite obviously, Christopher *did* feel guilty, a reaction common to so many others who failed the acid test of commitment (not just 'Communist' writers – as even Isherwood felt himself to be); many being unable to shuffle off residual shame until their dying day. He confided to his mother that he hoped to join Auden in Spain.[30] In fact, Isherwood later had a chance to redeem himself in part, when he and Auden accepted an invitation to join

> a delegation which was to visit Spain and declare the solidarity of left-wing artists and intellectuals with the Spanish government . . . the lady organizer was a forceful character. She was rumoured to have sent white feathers to several young men who had failed to volunteer for the International Brigade . . . [Christopher] began to assume the air of a soldier on the eve of departure to the front. This was mainly to impress his young men . . . They were duly impressed.[31]

In his letter to Dodds, Auden made no mention of Byron or Brooke, but – in a revealing expression – claimed to have been 'seduced' by the precedent set by Wilfred Owen, the outstanding (homosexual) poet and hero of the Great War. Owen's influence was profound in the 1930s, as it was in the 1960s when Britten, also 'seduced', set his poetry in the immensely successful *War Requiem*. Explaining his motives to Dodds, Auden added that he did not

> believe that poetry need or even should be directly political, but in a critical period such as ours, I do believe that the poet must have direct knowledge of the major political events . . . I shall probably be a bloody bad soldier but how can I speak to/for them without becoming one?[32]

But even before writing to Dodds (on 1 December) Auden had revealed his intentions to Britten – who seems to have been the first to know about them, at least amongst the inner circle of Auden adherents. Here, too, the plan of action was 'to go to Spain after Xmas & fight'. Britten was duly impressed. He tried 'to dissuade him, because what the Spanish Gov. might gain by his joining [the Internationals] is nothing compared with the world's gain by his continuing to write'.[33] Whether on this occasion (the *mise en scène* was a flat which Britten shared with his sister in Finchley Road) seduction – meant literally this time – was added to the unction of feudal flattery, we shall never know. At any rate, Britten made no objection to Auden's volunteering on grounds of political principle, whether pacifist or otherwise. A few days later he noted: '[Wystan] is the most charming, most vital, genuine & important person I know & if the Spanish Rebels kill him it will be a bloody atrocity.'[34] It is possible to venture a little further. Britten's official memorialist – the only scholar to have noticed it to date – attaches no significance to the fact that exactly a year later, the composer himself was (in his own word) 'toying' with the idea of going to Spain.[35] On the face of things this seems a surprising development, however ephemeral and infantile the emotion concerned, in view of Auden's experiences in Spain – which had been unpleasant to an extent little short of trauma. In fact, Auden told no one (not even Isherwood) of what happened to him in Spain; but Britten surely had many opportunites to hear the grim realities from other informed sources.

The two men seem not to have seen each other again until 8 January 1937, when at Auden's instigation they met in London – an encounter which has passed into legend. Auden had now completed his preparations for Spain: he and Britten spent best part of a morning over coffee in a Lyons Corner House. There were some long pauses in the conversation, since in the endpapers of published scores which Britten happened to be carrying, Auden laboriously copied out two recent and thus unpublished poems, one of which ('Danse Macabre') occupied no fewer than fifteen quatrains.[36] The other is now among the best-known love lyrics of the twentieth century: 'Lay your sleeping head, my love'. 'I've Lots to do with them', enthused Britten to his diary, adding that he felt Auden was 'phenomenally brave'.[37]

It is possible that poet had composer in mind on two levels of collaboration when writing this verse. The whole encounter of

8 January betrays a carefully planned seduction scene, which was scripted to end with the two men booking a hotel room in Charing Cross; a version of the cathartic, ritual bedding performed by couples since time immoral on the eve of wartime separation. Perhaps Auden even suggested that Britten should go with him to Spain. In any case, they were very quickly in touch again (perhaps by telephone) since on 10 January, the composer noted 'Wystan hasn't gone yet – expects to go tomorrow – because the Medical Unit he was going with has been stopped by the government.'[38] Two days later, Auden finally left for Spain via Paris. On the same day, Britten also left Victoria Station on what was apparently a 'spur-of the-moment' trip to the French capital, accompanied by two friends, a musician and a writer. They were appalled by Josephine Baker banana dancing at Le Hot Club, but failed to locate Oscar Wilde decomposing in Père Lachaise.[39]

Notwithstanding these speculations, and the person-specific references in his new poems, it seems unlikely that Auden had Britten uniquely in mind. With notable exceptions (Dante and Beatrice, Shakespeare and his 'onlie begetter') poets tend to produce promiscuously rather than monogamously, and aim to influence (and thus exert power) over all and sundry; though it is true that sexual objectives are, more often than not, ontologically prioritized. 'Lay your sleeping head' is a poem of candid disorder and disloyalty in respect of any individual, privileging only the ideal of beauty. 'Danse macabre' bids farewell to all Auden's dears, not just Britten – despite the fact that the latter used as a child to think of himself as the one and only 'Dear'.[40] When Auden arrived at the Gare du Nord on 12 January, he was met by Isherwood, and they went straight to a hotel.[41] All this did not exactly represent what was known in those days as 'Gay Paree'.

Auden's 'Danse macabre' reflects not simply a facetious attitude to soldiering, such as that evinced in his letter to Dodds, but a forthrightly cynical one. Explanation of this change of heart lies in the shadowy interval of some five weeks between the two meetings with Britten discussed above. None of his biographers casts any light on the exact manner in which Auden pursued his intention to get to Spain. In order to join the British Battalion, Auden would have needed to obtain clearance from the CPGB. This normally entailed a potential volunteer turning up for interview at their Soho recruiting office and convincing the staff of his physical and political aptitude. Auden's acquaintances, Giles Romilly and Tony Hyndman, who along with several hundred others enrolled and left for Spain during these weeks, were either already members of the Party or felt it wise to join before going.[42] Admittedly, Auden was not a normal case and would probably have been felt to merit special treatment. His unique literary standing would surely have placed him in a different category even to the party's own intellectual luminaries like Christopher Caudwell and Ralph Fox. Be that as it may, no trace of Auden has yet been found in any Comintern or CPGB records.[43] Moreover, for whatever reason, at some point along the line, Auden surrendered the idea of fighting. Instead he opted for the less glorious role of driving an ambulance, an odd reversion to his work for the revolution a decade earlier, during the General Strike. This meant applying to the Spanish Medical Aid Committee in London, which organized the British Medical Unit. The unit itself was then in process of being incorporated into the International Brigades, the formation of which it had antedated by several months. But likewise, no evidence of Auden has so far been traced anywhere in the records of Medical Aid.[44]

He seems, therefore, to have reached the French border with Republican Spain – 'On the Frontier' with a vengeance – lacking accreditation from any of the relevant Spanish or British authorities. He needed to persuade guards and officials of his probity and the seriousness of his mission. Though lacking Spanish or Catalan, he somehow negotiated this obstacle. There can hardly be more eloquent testimony to the poet's charisma. But the underlying reason for his success was that his examiners were members of the CNT, the anarchist syndicate, whose militia units controlled Catalan border posts. As such, they were highly suspicious of incoming Communists, including any who may have wished to join the International Brigade. At any rate, Auden arrived in Valencia, then the capital of Republican Spain, on or about 15 January.

What is known about his subsequent activities can be pieced together and/or deduced from a patchwork of sources. These comprise a brief account by Cyril Connolly of two separate meetings;[45] Arthur Koestler's recollection of a drunken encounter in a hotel bar;[46] a reminiscence by Claud Cockburn who – evidently not to his relish – was appointed Auden's 'minder';[47] and a few feet of British newsreel film which accidentally captured him attending a bullfight – giving the Popular Front salute, and apparently in the company of a group of young men.[48] About ten days after his arrival, Auden wrote a brief magazine article about his 'Impressions of Valencia'.[49] On the same day or the next (c.25 January) he met a group of Comintern agents in a hotel bar – probably by appointment – the occasion briefly described by Koestler. As well as those Koestler recalled, at least two others seem to have been present: Cockburn, *Daily Worker* correspondent, and a fellow-travelling journalist, Philip Jordan. The last of these described

> The vultures in the Hotel Victoria ... from every place you could think of, spies, harlots, more spies, jobhunters, propaganda men, sap-headed intellectuals who had never been properly appreciated in their own countries, drunken aviators ... all riff-raff on the make ... All the fine people I knew were sorry to be there and were hating it.[50]

Auden potentially qualifies under several of these heads. A drunken aviator figures prominently in Koestler's story. Both Koestler and Cockburn were Comintern agents who specialized in propaganda. They were among dozens such who were present in Spain, often (*pace* Jordan) under cover of press passes obtained from sympathetic editors in various countries. Some, like Koestler, were effectively spies or informers. (Whether they acted against the real enemy or oft-imagined internal enemies makes little difference here.) But Koestler's anecdote also reveals that among the company on the night of 25 January was none other than Mikhail Koltsov. Stalin sent Koltsov, editor of *Pravda*, to Spain a few weeks after the war began.[51] Though his headline task was to supervise matters of publicity and propaganda, he was also charged with major political responsibilities, above all that of reporting directly to Stalin. These reports probably form the basis of the extensive 'insider' account of the first year of the war later published as Koltsov's 'Diary'.[52] His personal access to Stalin gave Koltsov the power of life and death, at least over other Soviet personnel in Spain. In *For Whom the Bell Tolls*, Hemingway pictured him as the mercurial and deadly 'Karkov', 'one of the three most important men' in Republican Spain.[53] Furthermore, in the estimation of Ian Gibson, Koltsov was the leading Soviet official involved in the plan to transport over 2,000 political prisoners from Madrid to Valencia in early November, 1936, as Franco's army arrived at the gates of the capital. This operation ended in the deaths of over 1,500 'Fascist' detainees in killing grounds to the east of Madrid.[54] Koltsov's diary, though exceptionally detailed for this period, is silent on the fate of the prisoners; moreover, for the week of 21–8 January 1937, entries are missing altogether.[55] Though it is unlikely that he travelled to Valencia merely to meet W. H. Auden, it is nonetheless reasonable to suppose that their encounter constituted an informal interview of some kind. Koltsov was an intellectual of tremendous vitality and certainly Auden's equal in charisma, or (if you like) garrulousness. Auden would have been liberally treated to the Russian's views on the war, and lectured to on the main planks of the Republic's propaganda platform. In the charged and alcoholic atmosphere which developed that night, he may even have been entertained by some salutary anecdotes concerning 'necessary murder'.

The rest is quieter, but not quite silence. Auden must have been aware of the dreadful casualties suffered by the British and American Battalions at the Jarama battle during February, when the hospitals of the Republic's Mediterranean cities filled up with wounded and their bars and doss-houses with deserters. He left Valencia in the last week of February, shortly before Stephen Spender arrived there in his quest for Tony Hyndman.[56] Auden left a note, poste restante, informing Spender that he was leaving for the Aragon front at Sariñena. This was a long and arduous journey, leading north of Zaragoza into the Pyrenean foothills, in the province whose capital was the town of Huesca, then under siege from Republican forces including the POUM division in which George Orwell was serving.[57] Sariñena itself, however, was a CNT/FAI bastion, serving as supply and rest centre for front-line anarchist units. Not surprisingly, when Auden turned up a week or so later at the PSUC offices in Barcelona, looking for a safe-conduct pass out of Spain, he was greeted with considerable reserve. O'Donnell, effectively the CPGB representative, refused to help him on the grounds that he had been consorting with anarchists on the Aragon front.[58] The circumstances of Auden's exit from Spain thus remain as obscure as those of his original entry. He reached London on 4 or 5 March; physically, at least, none the worse for wear.[59]

5

Because of, rather than despite its obscurities, this period of barely more than six weeks represents the most critical and formative in

Auden's life. One of the few revelations he later made about it was that the sight of burnt-out churches and stories of religious persecution stimulated a subconscious counter-revolution, of which the first evidence, a few years later, was a return to religion – eventually to Catholicism, if only of the Anglo variety. If his offhand reference to the now-celebrated poster ('If You Tolerate This. . .') is anything to go by, he seems to have had more instinctive sympathy for the priestly victims of the revolution than he could summon up for the children slaughtered by Nazi bombers.[60] His psyche, of course, reacted more honestly to direct evidence than to the synthetic prompting of propaganda. Nonetheless, Auden produced a propaganda poem, an epic, apostrophic ode to the Republican cause which has been acclaimed, justly in my view, as one of the two greatest artistic products of the Spanish Civil War (the other being Picasso's painting *Guernica*).[61] More importantly, SPAIN constitutes an immortal elegy to the International Brigades, whose fateful commitment, epitomized for Auden as much by the hapless Tony Hyndman as by the heroic-poetic dead like Cornford and Caudwell, evidently moved him to the marrow.

The experience of 'Spain', impels Auden, as it did Orwell, to allocate a supreme role in human affairs to the nature and function of 'History'. 'History' is presented as God the Father, at once author and judge of moral decisions, yet who – faced with the fact that the once-defeated Lucifer has 'dynamited his way out of prison' – has cynically abandoned Everyman to his free will.[62] In the very centre of the ode, immediately preceding the stanzas which so evocatively describe the response of the volunteers, Auden places the crucial quatrain. 'History the operator' speaks directly to its human petitioners:

> 'What's your proposal? To build the just city? I will.
> I agree. Or is it the suicide pact, the romantic
>   Death? Very well, I accept, for
> I am your choice, your decision. Yes, I am Spain.'

To a professional, reading the text as (say) a postgraduate essay, some of Auden's history (as opposed to his 'History') might seem a bit awry. For example, the notion that:

> The trial of heretics among the columns of stone;
> . . . the theological feuds in the taverns
> . . . the Sabbath of witches

were horrors that happened 'yesterday' is myopic and misjudged. Surely Auden, in the Spanish taverns, at some point witnessed 'theological feuds' amongst Republican partisans? Though he produced his poem in the days before the May Events in Barcelona, whilst he was in Spain the miserable defendants of the second episode of the Moscow show trials were being dragged from the NKVD torture dungeons in the Lubyanka prison to face their baying prosecutors amidst the stone columns of the House of the Unions, across the square and facing the Kremlin. This drama was played out according to a different kind of text, prescribed by Stalin the Operator.[63] A Spanish production was not long delayed. The witch-hunt of heretics began in Madrid and Barcelona just as sales of the original flysheet of SPAIN began in London and Paris. Within a few months, hundreds of rank-and-file POUMistas, and dozens of their (real or imagined) foreign supporters, were dead or in torture chambers, whilst their leaders awaited in dungeons a show trial among columns of stone.[64]

Yet SPAIN is remarkably solid with 'Spain'; that is to say, with the cause of the Soviet-backed Popular Front. This is true not only in the Marxian orthodoxy of its philosophical opening section, in which 'all the past' is presented (if with some individual touches) as a working-out of dialectical materialism, but in the immediate sense in which later stanzas reflect specific endorsement of the Republican government's propaganda, via the consequences of a 'decision' for 'Spain':

> For the fears which made us respond
> To the medicine ad. and the brochure of winter cruises
>   Have become invading battalions;
> And our faces, the institute-face, the chain-store, the ruin
>
> Are projecting their greed as the firing squad and the bomb.
> Madrid is the heart. Our moments of tenderness blossom
>   As the ambulance and the sandbag.
> Our hours of friendship into a people's army.

In prosaic translation, SPAIN means that the abstract fear of Fascism shared by Auden, Britten and their circle, haunting them with frequent sickness and constant dread, has now become a concrete, representational invasion of their lives by Fascism in alliance with international capital. The invaders proceed in their cruel and cowardly ways of war – firing squad and bomb – but the loyalty, tenderness and comradely resolution of the left offer the means of resistance and final victory. Whilst the votive volunteers at the front eke out

> ... their makeshift consolations: the shared cigarette,
> The cards in the candlelit barn, and the scraping concert,
> The masculine jokes ...

it is up to Everyman to support the cause of 'Spain' behind the lines. Thus will be advanced the artistic utopia of the poem's penultimate section. Victory must be now or never. Defeat would mean not the end of history (as for Orwell and Koestler) but the end of hope.

> We are left alone with our day, and time is short, and
> History to the defeated
> May say Alas but cannot help nor pardon.

Auden's address is couched, therefore, in terms which precisely convey the propaganda constructs of the Republic. In Althusserian terms it 'interpellates' the reader – hailing or calling the subject – who is thereby identified, in every sense, with 'Spain' – to its aid. 'Spain' represents an ideological Eden, invaded by the evil other (= international Fascism). In return for the support of the civilized world, 'Spain' – and only 'Spain' – offered it freedom.[65] These conceits were to be found everywhere and in every medium of government propaganda, managed as much of it was by Soviet experts like Koltsov and Ilya Ehrenburg. Indeed, it seems to me that Auden's presentation of them is as orthodox as (if considerably less cliché-ridden than) that of their official bard, Rafael Alberti.

But what did Auden mean by the somewhat equivocal promise of 'all the fun under/Liberty's masterful shadow'? Here he surely projected a vision of the people's inheritance of great urban squares and aristocratic gardens, moving within the ambient protection of gigantic statues of Marx, Lenin and Stalin; in short, what his disciple – and Communist Party activist – Day Lewis symbolically desired in the revolution, the exact fulfilment of the fears which haunted Ortega y Gasset in *La Rebelión de las Masas*.[66] Furthermore, the discursive calendar of Auden's utopia has more than a sniff of the Soviet and the Five Year Plan:

> Tomorrow . . . the research on fatigue
>   And the movements of packers . . .
> Tomorrow the hour of the pageant-master and the musician
> The beautiful roar of the chorus under the dome . . .
>   The eager election of chairmen
> By the sudden forest of hands . . .

'Tomorrow for the young' was a kind of salvation through the martyrdom of a people, but at the same time it was predicated precisely upon victory for the Virtuous Republic of Artistic Attainment.

Alongside his work on this poem, Auden was reading (for review) Christopher Caudwell's last volume of criticism, *Illusion and Reality*.[67] The book was published posthumously in March 1937, its author having been killed during the British Battalion's engagement at Jarama less than a month earlier. Caudwell was Auden's exact contemporary, as well as Britain's earliest Marxist literary critic. These facts seem to have moved Auden guiltily to adjust his programme of tomorrow nearer than he otherwise might have to that set out in Caudwell's chapter on Poetry. Here, Auden, Day Lewis and Spender are exhorted to make their work an intelligible expression of uncomplicated love for the people and unconditional solidarity with the Soviet Union – in essence, to abandon bourgeois notions of artistic freedom and join the Party.[68] Caudwell, poet, soldier of the British Battalion, martyr, from his shallow grave helped to mould Auden's elegy for the International Brigaders. What had moulded Caudwell's address to poetry were the words of Karl Radek, Stalin's adviser on intellectual matters, whose keynote speech at the 1934 Soviet Artists' Congress decreed that all left literature should express love for the proletariat. As Caudwell was offering up his life on Suicide Hill, Radek, found guilty of plotting against the people, whose forest of hands demanded that 'the Trotskyite-Zinovievite band of murderers be wiped off the face of the earth', was spared his life by Stalin. Instead, he was sent to a labour camp in the Arctic, where (in 1939) he was obscurely murdered by one of the people.[69]

6

Auden's successive shifts and compromises, chronicled above, were marked by the difference between his first declaration of going out to fight and his premature return to London in a state of (apparently) self-imposed and total silence, a condition surely alarming to his friends, if only by its dramatic contrast to the norm. But none of this seems to have altered Britten's regard for his mentor. In the months after Auden's return, Britten set several of his shorter lyrics to music, not only in his 'serious' compositional style, but also (and consciously 'apart') in a blues style approximating to popular taste.[70] The latter numbers formed the basis of a 'cabaret' which Auden and Britten put on later that year in the Seymour Hall with proceeds to Spanish Aid.[71]

During the whole of Auden's absence in Spain, Lennox Berkeley was living in Paris. However, he and Britten kept in touch, and their relationship continued to develop, to the point that in 1937 they decided to buy a house together. This was the Old Mill at Snape, not finally occupied until April 1938. Britten's biographer, Humphrey Carpenter, is persuaded ('convinced' would be too strong) that shortly thereafter the relationship passed through a sexual phase. At any rate, Berkeley fell in love with Britten, and over the next two years addressed to the younger man a series of passionate and adulatory letters, written in spite of the fact that 'I really ought to know better at my age'.[72] He could not conceal his jealous awareness of his rivals in the field, who by now included Peter Pears. Around this time he set two Auden poems to music and dedicated them to Britten; his choices – 'Night covers up' (addressed to Britten by the poet) and 'Lay your sleeping head' – are eloquent testimony to his intense and fearful feelings. He may (or may not) have derived reassurance from Britten's dedication to him of the work which gave its composer more trouble than any other in these years, the Piano Concerto premiered in August 1938. Meanwhile, Auden and Isherwood, after returning from a journalistic trip to the Sino-Japanese war, spent that summer in Brussels, attempting to recapture their halcyon days in Berlin. Auden wrote to Britten:

> If you are taking a holiday in Sept why not come here for a few days. I've got something waiting here for you that will make you crazy. 16, tries to pick up a living by singing in the street . . . Mother dead. Father drinks. Shall I get a photo? Such eyes, O la la love Wystan.[73]

Britten decided to fall in with this proposal, but Berkeley was horrified.

> Is Peter going with you? I think you must try and behave nicely there, in spite of being in possession of mysterious addresses. I hate to think of you doing . . . I mean – oh damn, well you know what I mean.[74]

Whether or not to please Berkeley, Britten eventually decided against joining the Brussels junket. Evidently miffed, Auden sent him a sarcastic and patronising letter on the techniques of seduction, apparently referring to one of the composer's teenage friends.[75] In the end, of course, Berkeley was pushed out of the magic circle not by Auden but by Pears. But if not the cause, Berkeley's political unreliability was certainly a symptom of Britten's loss of interest. The composer remained active in the field of 'Spain', and determined in his faith.[76] It is doubtful that (at this stage) he was able to read the signs of Auden's gradual retreat from commitment and from politics as a whole.[77] Berkeley, however, had never been a true ideological soulmate. In October 1936, when Britten's outrage over 'Fascist' atrocities was reaching a peak, he wrote:

> I haven't done anything more to the Spanish Tunes . . . you hardly have the heart. – only today I was reading of the trial and shooting of prisoners under the 'Tribunal Popular' on board the Uruguay in the harbour of Barcelona just under Montjuich . . . I know it's going on on both sides (this example is not meant in any tendentious spirit – only because it happened in Barcelona which we both know) . . . I am quite willing to believe that the Church is very much to blame. Anyhow it is no concern of ours . . .[78]

Berkeley was evidently nervous about the fate of his opinions, and thus of his suitorship, when exposed to the ardour of Britten's support for the Republican cause. His apprehension was fully justified. A few days after Britten and Pears left for America in 1939 a letter of his followed them: 'as you see I haven't committed suicide so far . . . I love you far too much.'[79] On the day that Britain declared war on Germany, he could not resist giving Britten his forthrightly patriotic views on Mr Harry Pollitt's reaction, but once again resistance collapsed into 'since I knew you, I've honestly felt that I understood and sympathised with the left point of view; but since the Russian-German pact . . .'[80] This ended his credibility and

Britten now expressed contempt for Berkeley's opinions to other friends.[81]

7

Following the fall of Catalonia, the Spanish Tragedy entered its last act. Loyalist territory was reduced to a slowly shrinking bubble (some 30 per cent of Spain) stretched between Madrid and Valencia. The civilian population had no morale left and merely prayed for the end. Only Communists and others who had everything to lose by defeat actively continued the struggle. In March 1939, non-Communist elements of the political and military establishment launched a coup in Madrid. After suppressing Communist opposition in the streets, they tried to negotiate with the enemy. Whilst the Negrín government finally abandoned Spain, Franco never deviated from his demand for unconditional surrender. On 30 March his forces entered Madrid without resistance, and on 1 April Franco announced that the war was over.[82] The atmosphere at the final concert of London's 'Festival of Music for the People', given on 5 April, must have been grim, so many people on stage, backstage and out front were plunged into a mood much worse than mourning. It was not, in fact, the end of 'Spain', though its supporters naturally thought so at the time: indeed, this concert was arguably the inaugural event of its metamorphological survival. In that sense, at least, we may audibly imagine 'the beautiful roar of the chorus under the dome'.

With Auden now too distant for consultation, Britten exercised political as well as artistic licence in adapting his lines from 'Danse Macabre' and *On the Frontier* (the third and last Auden–Isherwood play) to refer specifically to the fallen volunteers of the British Battalion. *Ballad of Heroes* opens with a funeral march: is this movement a revival and/or revision of the 'funeral march for those youthful Spanish martyrs' he had sketched and apparently abandoned in the first week of the war?[83] It closes with Auden's elegy to the dead of the war between Ostnia and Westland, here metamorphosed into the martyred International Brigaders:

> Pardon them their mistakes,
> The impatient and wavering will.

> They suffer for our sakes,
> Honour, honour them all.
> Dry their imperfect dust,
> The wind blows it back and forth,
> They die to make man just
> And worthy of the earth.[84]

But 'the people', whose festival this ostensibly was – according to one music critic – 'showed their lack of enthusiasm in this strange combination of music and political propaganda by leaving a large number of seats unoccupied'.[85] In 1942, however, when alliance with the USSR in a renewed – and this time government-sponsored – Popular Front meant that the International Brigaders were transformed from potentially dangerous red guerrillas into 'premature anti-Fascists', the BBC broadcast *Ballad of Heroes* as suitably anti-Fascist propaganda. Recently returned from America to do his patriotic penance, Britten nominated the Spanish Civil War along with the Second World War as 'world tragedies' which had deeply affected his work.[86]

Sixty years later, the guardians of Britten's memory remain reticent about the dramatic, contemporary issues of politics, desire and power which his association with Auden so strikingly reflect. In a recent Channel 4 documentary which charted the relationship between Britten and Pears, the composer's psychology was explained by repeated reference to an amazingly insightful and prophetic letter of Auden's, written when the couple decided to return to Britain from the USA in 1942. The letter marked, in more ways than one, the parting of the ways for composer and poet after seven years of fruitful collaboration, the products of which – as Donald Mitchell has rightly insisted – were as complex and meaningful as those of any artistic partnership in history.[87] Yet the programme gave no hint that the relationship between the two men was anything more than aesthetic-platonic; one contributor stoutly denied that Lord Britten had ever been interested in politics. For just one moment the ranks broke apart to reveal the agape. Britten's nurse, Rita Thomson, speaking about his last days, recalled attempting to reassure him when he asked what death would be like. '"Never mind," I told him, "old Wystan will be up there waiting for you." And he just laughed.'[88]

Corpus Delicti: the body of Alfonso Ponce de Léon in a Madrid morgue. From R. Inglada (ed.), *Alfonso Ponce de Léon* (Madrid: Museo Centro de Arte Reina Sofia, 2001)

'High Priest of the Intellect' – Salamanca's memorial to Unamuno. Photograph by the author

W. H. Auden and Benjamin Britten in New York, early 1940s. Courtesy of the Britten-Pears Library, Aldeburgh

(Top left) John Cornford snapped by Michael Straight in Dartington, September 1936. From P. Sloan (ed.), *John Cornford: A Memorial Volume* (London: Cape, 1938)

(Below left) All in the same boat – Spender, Hyndman, Worsley, plus chaperone (Helen Gibb), c. 1935. Photograph by Humphrey Spender; reproduced by permission of Humphrey Spender.

Auden – the moment of truth, Valencia, 1937

Different views on the International Brigades expressed in their old HQ – Albacete, 2001. Photograph by the author

Memorial stone to the Nationalist commander in Villanueva.
Photograph by the author

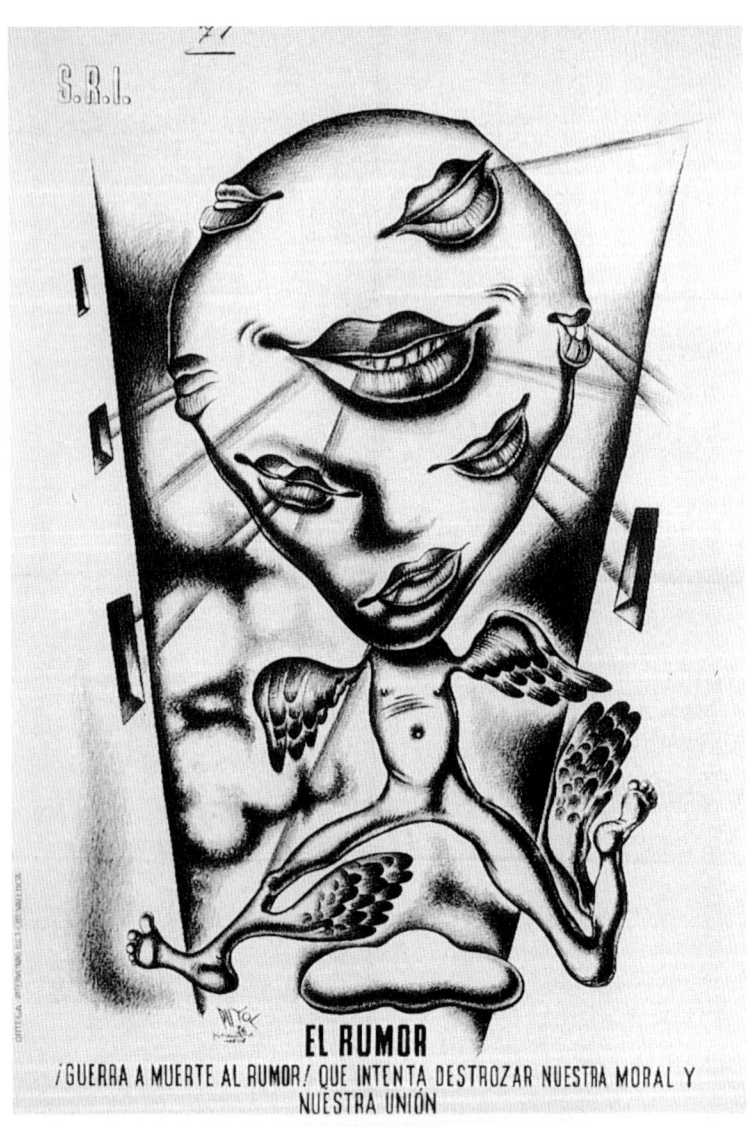

Ramón Puyol's cartoon *El Rumor*, painted full of tongues

Hernandez, people's poet – graffiti tribute spotted in modern Salamanca. Photograph taken by the author

English International Brigade poets – plaque in Madrid's *Residencia de Estudiantes*. Photograph taken by the author

Koltsov speaks at the Anti-Fascist Writers' Congress.
From J. L. Alcofar Nassaes, *Los Asesores Sovieticos en la Guerra Civil Espanola* (Barcelona: Editorial Dopesa, 1971)

II

Other Parts of the Field

~ 5 ~
Crusades in Conflict: Idealism, Perception, Motivation

> But the members of the International Brigade
> Were made of a different stuff,
> And will never fall back into the ranks.
> And the war in Spain – and everywhere else –
> Will never end till they win it,
> Since they fight for Spain and not
>   Just for castles in Spain.[1]

1 Sites of Struggle

In an event, Britten's 'miraculous Madrid stand', taking place in mid-November 1936, Madrid was saved from capture by what was widely heralded as the 'final assault' of Franco's army. Such was the expectation of the city's fall that one British newsreel company featured an item titled 'Insurgents Enter Madrid', showing Generals Franco and Mola entering a government building and Moroccans marching through the streets.[2] That the result of the confrontation turned out differently was (at least in part) owing to the intervention of the first International Brigade (that is the XI), which had been dispatched prematurely to Madrid after its hurried formation in Albacete. A few weeks later, having enjoyed a slightly more leisurely period of induction, the second Brigade (numbered XII) followed in the footsteps of the first. The soldiers, mainly from central European countries, de-trained at a village lying in the city's south-eastern environs. Whilst waiting for transport lorries to arrive, Alexei Eisner, an exiled Polish Communist, wandered into the parish church. The revulsion felt at the disgusting shambles he found inside the building was still strong when he compiled his memoirs some thirty years later. 'They had turned the church into a pigsty', he recalled. Eisner, a cradle Catholic, realized at the time that this was the work of anarchist 'uncontrollables', and not his own comrades. Eisner's response contrasts with the otherwise similar case of W. H. Auden. The experience did not affect the former's long-term ideological solidarity, which drew on profound historical and theoretical sources of European socialism, with a carapace of resistance made tougher by vicious persecution in his own country. His main problem with the desecration of the church was a pragmatic rather than a religious one: such barbarism represented a mad weakness which was likely to cause untold damage to the cause of 'Spain'. In this precise connection, he recalled that 'from Catholic Ireland a regiment of volunteers came to help General Franco, and to defend their Holy Church. These men were authentic volunteers, undoubtedly; and they did not delay too long before blooding their crusading swords.'[3]

One of Eisner's comrades in the XII Brigade was Bill Scott, the first volunteer from Ireland to fight in Spain, and a convinced Communist. The former was en route to his baptism of fire, but Scott was already a veteran, having joined a militia *centuria* in Barcelona in August 1936, later fighting alongside Esmond Romilly in Madrid. He wrote home to reassure a friend, who was evidently worried about hostile reactions amongst pious Dubliners: 'You needn't mind who knows I am in Spain, for it's the most sacred cause in history to defend freedom.'[4] Scott was a patriotic Irish Republican, who eventually left Spain and the cause rather than serve in the British Battalion. At the same time, he was also a militant anti-Fascist of the type who had struggled in the mean streets and sordid tenements of Dublin against oppressive forces which he believed were greater even than British imperialism in reach and significance. Yet to characterize the campaign being fought by the International Brigades as a sacred cause – that is, subliminally speaking, as a crusade – would, indeed, have been regarded by most of Scott's compatriots in the Irish Free State (probably including his own family) as adding blasphemy to injury. Totally on the contrary, in the propaganda of their own side Eisner's 'authentic' crusaders saw the International Brigades as a barbaric horde of priest-killers invading Spain at the behest of atheistic Communism. Even as Bill Scott fought the Fascists in Madrid's University City, thousands of men and women at home were joining a new organization, the Irish Christian Front, dedicated to the fight against Communism. The very name of the ICF was an attempt to steal enemy thunder: it was the Irish answer to the Popular Front. Mass meetings were held in public places, where the faithful crossed arms over their heads in a token pledge of crusade.[5] The enemy was Soviet but also international, the Popular Front was also the Comintern. No country was safe.

2 War of Ideals Appeals

In mobilizing human support and material resources for the conflict which began with the military rebellion of July 1936, the two competing claimants to the government of Spain drew on an arsenal of images and ideas. Of course, at first glance, the tropes of propaganda were violently opposed and starkly contrasted. In this dimension, the Republic never abandoned its advocacy of *el pueblo*, a people downtrodden by exploitative privilege and irresponsible wealth, and of a constitutional democracy threatened by a military–clerical conspiracy. The Nationalists, for their part, insisted that the legalism of the Republic was a Trojan horse for bloody revolution. When the apocalypse inevitably arrived, it would finally demolish the bastions of Church and property, those indispensable defences against chaos which had already been undermined by a generically hostile state.

No one can doubt that, ultimately – in terms of the consensual priorities of their advocates – the two 'causes' can be reduced to elemental concerns for 'order' (the Nationalists) and 'freedom' (the Republicans). Yet between these entrenched positions existed a vast no man's land of territory ripe for occupation. Expressed in a phrase which in this case is less prosaic than it may seem, both sides had much in common. In the last analysis, they fought over and for the physical reality of Spain, land and people, and their appeal was primarily to Spaniards, whose beliefs and ideals, temperaments and self-interests were the main objects of mobilization. For this reason, the conceptual thrust of propaganda, as well as its quantitative deployment, was domestic. This was especially true of the earlier period of the war when labour syndicates and political parties carried on campaigns quite independently of each other and of a (temporarily) evanescent higher authority, placing strident emphasis upon different or even contradictory notions.[6]

It is clear that propaganda themes associated with the everyday pursuit of the war effort itself could not be expected to achieve much response in the wider world. This was true, for example, of press articles, newsreels and posters which demonstrated successes in agricultural policies or munitions production, or directed the population to enlist in sectarian militias, or to beware of spies and rumour-mongers. Even more abstract desiderata such as the ownership of land or the role of education were of little wider interest. However, both sides also accorded priority to communicating the notion that the war was a kind of spontaneous national uprising against an invading foreigner.[7] The reference points here were again introspective, drawing, above all, on popular notions of Spain's war of national independence against Napoleon in the early nineteenth century. There was a potentially sympathetic audience outside Spain for appeals to aid a proud but poor people, who were being assailed by international atheism/Communism (on the one hand) or international imperialism/Fascism (on the other). Yet as the conflict developed, both historical references and the ideological subtleties of the invader's 'otherness' tended to fade, whilst the irreducible horror of his sheer and alien predatoriness achieved ever-starker profile.[8]

On the Republican side, in particular, there were ubiquitous appeals not only to the spirit of 1808, but also to a literally mythical past, stretching back to atavistic residues of the resistance of the Celtiberian city of 'Numantia' to the Roman invader.[9] This campaign drew on an intra-Hispanic patriotic profile which perhaps stiffened the sinews of Spaniards in defiance of Mussolini's legions and the Nazi eagle, but usually failed to wring the withers of foreigners outside the closed world of academic Hispanism.[10] Nevertheless, it is worth noting that the Republican pavilion at the Paris International Exhibition of 1937, famous as the first home of Picasso's *Guernica*, carried an enormous notice on its façade, purporting to be the words of President Azaña and describing his government's war aims. There was no reference to freedom, justice, or even democracy – far less to revolution. Instead, the visiting world was assured,

> Nous nous battons pour l'unité essentielle de l'Espagne.
> Nous nous battons pour l'intégrité du territoire espagnol.
> Nous nous battons pour l'indépendance de notre patrie
> et pour le droit du peuple espagnol a disposer librement à son destin.[11]

This vocabulary of 'la patrie en danger' was functionally identical to that employed on the Nationalist side.[12] Amongst the latter, more specifically, the patriotic call to arms centred upon the propaganda construct of *La Cruzada*. In this scenario, historic, Christian Spain was threatened by an international Communist conspiracy; whilst the uprising (*alzamiento*) and its political dynamic (*movimiento*) were inspired by the overriding demands of a crusade against the invading hordes of the Soviets. This programme, too, was not expected by its designers to attract a significant audience outside Spain.[13]

Nevertheless, both Valencia and Burgos displayed growing awareness of the need to stimulate foreign support via propaganda. Indeed, this constituency grew in relative importance as the military situation, and the terms of engagement of the war itself, altered during nearly three years of hostilities.[14] Selling the competing versions/visions of Spain to governments and peoples abroad had the democracies as its main target. Neither side needed to waste scarce resources on public opinion in the totalitarian countries which were its chief military allies and suppliers – indeed the question simply did not arise. The focus therefore fell on a group mainly situated in the north and west of the continental mainland, France, Great Britain, Belgium, The Netherlands and the Scandinavian nations, along with the USA.[15] A strange aberration (as already seen) was the Irish Free State, where popular feeling was so overwhelmingly pro-Nationalist that behaviourally, in the present context, it was almost a 'Fascist' dictatorship: in any case, a lost cause for the Republic.

The Spanish Civil War contains significant expression of all or most of the belief-ideals and truth-claims which achieved consensual status in western society between the philosophical renaissance of the twelfth century and the technological revolution of the twentieth. It was this that attracted intense attention from artists and writers. It has occupied so much attention since 1939 mainly because of these two contingent reasons. But whereas the Manichaean reductionism of good versus evil was the superficially staple fare of propaganda and commitment, deeper examination reveals that both texts and their readers are amazingly complex, volatile compounds of common and differential denominators. Let us work upwards from the elemental, where binary oppositions abound. Both sides pictured themselves as defending civilization against barbarism, and to this end gave maximum publicity to stories of wanton murder and destruction by the enemy. For example, Nationalist Spain was obsessed with cataloguing the murderous consequences of social revolution within the enemy zone. Throughout the war, a largely unvarying diet of relevant stories and images was directed towards sympathetic elements in Britain and Ireland – individuals, interest groups, churches and press.[16] For its part, the Republic devoted thousands of words and hundreds of images to a campaign alleging an enemy policy of indiscriminate aerial bombing of civilian targets.[17] This began with the Nationalist assault on Madrid already mentioned, and experienced a huge injection of emphasis after the terror-bombing of Guernica by the German Condor Legion five months later. By the autumn of 1936, therefore, left-wing demonstrations in British cities included the parade of relevant slogans and posters with specific Spanish provenance, whilst the right-wing (and Catholic) press carried pictures of the bodies of nuns exhibited in Barcelona and blood-chilling stories of the promiscuous horrors committed by 'red murder gangs'.[18]

Atrocity propaganda is perhaps too general a factor in any modern war to call for detailed illustration or extensive analysis *as such* in the present chapter. More striking is that the Republic put hardly less energy into convincing the world that a major war aim of the Nationalists was the destruction of Spain's artistic heritage, whilst the latter drew attention to the systematic incineration of churches and their artistic contents. These campaigns were intricately and subtly linked via thematic interplay. The constant linking of aerial bombardment of civilians (and of hospitals, orphanages and so on) with similar attacks upon art galleries, libraries and museums is a case in point.[19] In this way the basic human values of civil society were linked to the alleged essentiality of their expression in art, a link which would be recognized as valid and crucial by educated people everywhere.[20] On the other side, propaganda was able to exploit the mass destruction – this time all over Spain, not just in one world-famous spot – of medieval monasteries, Renaissance churches and Baroque convents. It might be mistaken to assume that the Nationalist concern for these losses to the national heritage was less likely to evoke universal outrage than the surface concerns of Republican propaganda.[21] Though it is true that the strictly aesthetic meaning of such losses was limited to an arcane elite, its wider significance in terms of the sentimental religious associations of Catholics, not just in Ireland, should not be overlooked. The desecration of everyday objects of affection and veneration, objects as familiar to British and French Catholics as they were to Spaniards, was cause for horror and outrage.²² Thus art on one side, religion on the other, were two faces of the same coin, icons of a dynamic propaganda discourse with an international dimension, making noises which led to sympathetic resonances in souls and hearts.²³

The genres and tropes of propaganda relevant to this chapter, and to the book as a whole, are those which we may associate with the raising of popular consciousness, material aid and (above all) foreign volunteers. Thematic distinctions between those aimed at domestic and foreign audiences are often blurred; some, indeed, may conclude that such distinctions are unimportant, or even non-existent. At government level, neither side was directly concerned with recruiting large numbers of volunteer personnel outside Spain. Indeed, in both cases the indigenous leadership was (and remained) uncomfortable with the presence of organized foreign troops. If in certain of its details a matter for negotiated adjustment, military intervention was a given, decided upon and managed by the interventionist states themselves. Outside these networks, Francoist Spain discouraged volunteer recruitment, whether of individuals or groups, and where such elements existed they were given little publicity.²⁴ The Republican government, however, had a dilemma. Having had the International Brigades foisted on it by Stalin, it was caught up in a propaganda campaign on their behalf, precisely because this suited the interests of their monopoly patron. Even were this not the case, any public attempt to combat the non-intervention policy of the democracies, which was simultaneously an attempt to end that monopoly, was of its very nature bound, if only occasionally, to produce an extreme reaction, the (literally) over-the-top emotional response of the volunteer soldier.

3 Cross and Sword, Hammer and Sickle²⁵

At Christmas 1936, nearly 700 Irishmen mustered in the Extremaduran town of Cáceres. With immense difficulty, they had been brought to Spain by General Eoin O'Duffy, whose offer of a volunteer army, originally hoped to be many thousands strong, had been accepted by General Franco. They were duly incorporated into the Legión Extranjera, the elite *Tercio* of the Nationalist army: the very force pictured by Republicans as a slavering crew of merciless bandits. In their own propaganda profile, the crusaders of the

'XV Bandera del Tercio' saw themselves as part of an international chivalry. They were Catholic anti-Communists first and Irish 'Wild Geese' only second. Almost simultaneously, a group of about eighty Irishmen arrived in the provincial capital of Albacete, base camp of the International Brigades. Likewise, these crusaders were anti-Fascists first, and members of any particular nationality or political party only second (if at all). Here, as in so many other aspects of the Spanish War's meaning, the quantitative element is vastly subordinate to the representative, symbolic significance involved.

At the highest permissible estimate, 3,500 was the total of all volunteers from the British Isles and the Irish Free State who went to serve in fighting or ancillary units of the competing Spanish armies. Relatively few of them ever sought to record their motivation for so doing; even amongst those who came back alive, and survived into old age it is rare to find more than a generalized emotion, or a reference to the broad international context being cited in explanation of the decision to enlist. To arrive at firm conclusions from such sketchy data is statistically problematic: and estimating the numbers or proportions within categories is risky.[26]

Nevertheless, common sense suggests that we can divide the volunteers into three such categories:

A. The ideologically solid: those who frankly accepted the possibility of suffering and death as a valid consequence of their fight for truth and justice.
B. Superficial idealists: those who experienced an emotional surge in favour of truth and justice, which proved (to a greater or lesser degree) temporary, and often faded away in the actual conditions met with in Spain.
C. Selfish opportunists: those to whom abstract notions were at best never a priority, and at worst meaningless.

Clearly there was some overlap between these categories, but it is a logical assumption that this would occur much more between B and C than between either/both of these two and A. Likewise, it seems likely that the first two categories were more susceptible to the influence of image and propaganda. Lastly, volunteering in category B was most likely to be caused by the short-term effect of high-profiled events, acting as a precipitant upon an existing deposit of personal beliefs. However we are concerned here with more than the representative minority of military volunteers. To the rule-of-thumb figure of 1,500[27] men and women who took this ultimate step in pursuit of individual ideals must be added many thousands of others whose (present and/or future) emotional and intellectual lives became centred on the issues and outcome of the struggle in Spain.

Despite the lifelong personal support of Martin Luther for the cause of crusade against the Ottoman, in post-Reformation Europe, ideas of crusade survived mainly in theoretical and memorial terms, mainly in Catholic countries, or at least among Roman Catholics. This culturally limited apprehension, to all intents and purposes confined to the educated elite, altered little until the late nineteenth century. But from the 1850s, the emergence of the Communist International in Europe, and the more immediate, local threat to order and property (whether real or imagined) posed by the rise of organized labour, coincided, perhaps not accidentally, with revival of interest in things medieval. The consequent elaboration of a neo-Gothic culture was widespread, if not exactly ubiquitous, among the ruling classes of western Europe. Though neo-Gothic frolic was, to begin with, a game or sport, happening on the level of entertainment as well as those of art and scholarship, it was to have profound implications for the development of Fascism, and thus for the politics of intervention in the Spanish Civil War.[28]

This provided the cultural background, the raw intellectual material, for the renaissance of the crusade concept in the twentieth century. In the Irish context, for example, whilst the Protestant Anglo-Irish built pseudo-Gothic follies in the countryside, the conspicuous rewards of business acumen and land exploitation, in equal and opposite reaction new generations (mainly from Catholic and 'dispossessed' sources) took flight in the tradition of the 'Wild Geese' to fight as volunteer mercenaries for 'freedom'. Irish exiles fought in dedicated companies both for the progressive forces of the USA and for reactionary Mexico in the Texas wars of the 1840s. The glory of the Irish 'Corcoran' Brigade which fought for the anti-slavery North in the American Civil War, was matched (or cancelled out, depending on your 'tradition') by that of the Irish Brigade which defended the Papal States against the godless forces of Italian liberalism in the same decade.[29] In conventional ideological terms, this record suggests that, unless able to focus upon a clearly identified English enemy, the crusading allegiances of

Irishmen were already rather confused. At any rate, the ideal of crusade was kept tenuously alive in Irish folk memory, linked in a vague way to legends of the Wild Geese.

In Europe generally, the ideal was seen as the military expression of a religious commitment, in which individuals and communities participate, and which is apprehended by them as both international and supranational. A working definition might be that crusades were a matter for religions of global significance. In the twentieth century, only three religions qualified: Christianity; Islam; and after 1917, Communism. The last of these, of course, refers mostly to its behavioural characteristics rather than its ontological essences. In Spain, Franco's side made a tentative attempt to advance the notion that their war had the status of a jihad for its nearly 80,000 Muslim combatants, but no historian has (so far) taken this claim seriously.[30]

On the individual level, the main motivating force behind the 6,000 or so Irishmen who (allegedly) volunteered in the first instance for General O'Duffy's Irish Brigade, was religious commitment.[31] Virtually every extant witness by a participant, even those who later became disillusioned, makes primary reference to it. All the surviving veterans interviewed by the present writer in the mid-1990s added the information that they regarded themselves as Catholics first and Irishmen only second. Not all of them actually used the word 'crusade'; but all agreed that they went to Spain to defend the Church, that is to say the right of Spanish Catholics to freedom of worship, and the physical existence of the clergy and churches upon which this right absolutely depended. They saw these rights as both inalienable and universal, and accepted Franco's claim to be defending them; thus their commitment had a clearly international dimension. In the 1930s – arguably until the 1960s – Catholicism was Ireland's only medium of international culture and communication. Just as Dublin tenement lads might feel an empathy with slum-dwellers in Barcelona, or Rhondda colliers identify with the coal miners of Asturias, so Irish farm boys felt a sense of solidarity with ordinary Catholics all over Spain. The cultural environment of the Free State in the 1930s encouraged, even conditioned, this response. A romantic-historical perception of religion predominated in every relevant medium, constituting an escapist narrative tradition instilled with suffering and heroic sacrifice. Naturally, the aspect of this culture which has excited most attention is its role in the construction of Irish nationalism after 1916. But, even leaving aside the American origins of Fenianism, this nationalism explained and legitimated itself by connection with other contemporary romantic nationalisms, the often equally Catholic nations of the age of self-determination in eastern Europe. Thus it was by no means wholly isolationist nor ethnocentric.

Under the ruling interest of the early Free State (roughly, 1923–32), the antithetical emotions stirred up by Catholic feeling shifted away from the old, and locally defeated, enemy, British imperialism, towards a new and even more insidious threat, that of International Communism. Eoin O'Duffy was himself a major player in the process by which a veritable fever of anti-Communism was whipped up in the early 1930s. This reached perhaps its fullest articulation in a celebrated booklet published in 1935 by Professor James Hogan. *Could Ireland Become Communist?* was followed by the establishment of the Irish Christian Front the following year.[32] In the summer of 1936, the cultural conditioning of the ordinary Irish Catholic, especially the male variety, was stimulated afresh by a new wave of anti-Communist propaganda, daily reportage of anticlerical atrocities in Spain, a campaign indulged by most of the popular press and the cinema newsreels. On the third Sunday of the war, a few days before before O'Duffy first called for volunteers in the pages of the *Irish Independent*, the British *Catholic Times*'s correspondent in Valladolid reported that ' "For God and Our Lady to conquer and triumph" is the battle cry of the patriots . . . The first act of the liberators on capturing a village from the Reds is to restore the crucifix in the school.'[33] The *Irish Independent*, loudest organ in the diapason of evil versus good, sent a special reporter to Spain. Gertrude Gaffney was given exclusive access to the Irish Brigade in training, and told her readers: 'I went to Caceres expecting to find the Irish Brigade composed largely of adventurers – an opinion shared by many of my neighbours. I was vastly astonished . . . to find instead a Bandera of Crusaders.'[34]

Nearly all the volunteers who left personal testimonies confirmed Gaffney's estimate, recording feelings of outrage stirred up by media treatment of the anticlerical massacres. Equally important to them, if less obvious to subsequent observers, was the wanton destruction of devotional objects of a familiar type, beloved and venerated in every Irish Catholic home, and which might be regarded as authentically popular art. Whilst atrocity stories were mostly syndicated from British press sources, there were also several horrifying eyewitness accounts by Irish expatriates who had been driven out of Spain by the Red Revolution. Of undoubted significance was that O'Duffy's volunteers were overwhelmingly from small-town, rural Ireland, and thus more susceptible to newspaper influence and communitarian Catholic feeling than were the proletarian masses of Dublin. If, as is often suggested, western Ireland was more zealously Catholic than the east, it would be significant that 70 per cent of O'Duffy's men came from Munster and Connacht. If – as widely believed – the city of Limerick was more fanatically Catholic than any other community in Ireland, then it may be significant that one in twenty came from Limerick. When volunteers arrived in Lisbon en route to Franco's Spain, they attended masses, heard sermons and visited local convents – hearing themselves praised on all sides as crusaders for the faith, and responding in suitable character. Notably, even in a textbook actually dedicated to the memory of the International Brigades, Paul Preston recognised that 'for them [O'Duffy's volunteers] this was no more nor less than a religious crusade'.[35]

However, to paraphrase an American saying, there is no copyright on ideals. In March 1937, the XV Bandera (Irlandesa) fought its only serious action against the 'red' enemy on the Jarama front. Simultaneously, the much larger Italian expeditionary force also fighting for the Nationalists (CTV) was defeated at Guadalajara. Many of the men killed and humiliated in following the Duce's great enterprise were volunteers whose main motivation for coming to Spain had been zeal for their Church, or a belief in the efficacy of Fascism – or both. In the critical stages of the battle, the Italian and largely Communist Garibaldi Battalion of Eisner's XII International Brigade played a central role.[36] Franco – perhaps he saw it as an attempt at consolation – told the Italian ambassador that 'the International Brigade have fought for an ideal, even though the ideal is a heresy'.[37] The Caudillo's statement has a triple resonance; it highlights the Nationalist claim that their war effort was a crusade against modern heresy; it supports the contention (made above) that Communism can be characterized as a heresy – that is, a movement of religious dissent; finally, and most surely of the three, it lends credence to the semi-official view of the Internationals themselves that they represented a crusading movement.

In Lewis Jones's epic novel chronicling the history of the

Rhondda coal miners, we find the outline of what historians have seen as the mythic metanarrative of the British workers' involvement in 'Spain'. Jones's story is an essentially autobiographical one, the experience of himself and his microcosmic community being taken as the paradigm of political evolution, from animal resentment of capitalist oppression towards the disciplined organization and intellectually based leadership of the Communist Party. 'Spain' is projected as the emotional and cultural climax of three generations of tragic struggle. The Party branch at 'Cwmardy' (the author's birthplace of Clydach Vale) is required to contribute its quota of one man to the British Battalion, and local leader 'Len Roberts' is selected. 'The longer Len remained away the more thrilling a legend his name became to the people of Cwmardy. He came to be regarded as a sort of chivalrous crusader linked up inevitably with the Party and Spain.'[38] Hywel Francis asserts that the series of hunger marches, a movement of which Lewis Jones was the mainspring in south Wales, and which culminated just as Madrid was being surrounded by 'Fascist' armies in October 1936, were 'pervaded by a spirit of revolutionary military discipline and crusading zeal which undoubtedly made volunteering for Spain a natural and logical extension'.[39] As a recent book on 'revolutionary armies' has argued, in much subsequent pro-Republican writing 'the wartime rhetoric surrounding the International Brigades has been perpetuated, and the saga of the volunteers time and again presented in terms of a crusade, the Last Good Fight.'[40]

A major representative figure like Ernest Hemingway, who worked as a newspaper reporter in Spain, and was (in effect) an honorary member of the Lincoln Battalion, was obsessed with the idea that their cause was a crusade for democracy. He probably got the notion in the first instance from the Communist writer Louis Fischer, who claimed to be the first American to join the International Brigades after leaving his propaganda job in Moscow in 1936, and who devoted a chapter of his memoirs to what he called the 'Holy War' in Spain.[41] At any rate, Hemingway grafted this conviction onto 'Robert Jordan', fictional hero of *For Whom the Bell Tolls*. Being with the Communists in Madrid, Jordan noted, 'was like being a member of a religious order . . . you felt you were taking part in a crusade.'[42] In the 1960s, the American scholar, Robert Rosenstone, gave his book on the Lincoln–Washington battalions a title which resonated to the toll of Hemingway's bells.⁴³ But in spite of this deep-seated allegiance Hemingway, like O'Duffy and many of his men, also admired the enemy Carlist *Requetés,* volunteer militiamen who were among the bravest nationalist troops, and many of whom came from his favourite Spanish town, Pamplona. An episode in the novel betrays his gut feeling that the Carlists, too, were authentic crusaders.⁴⁴ In the same year as Hemingway's novel appeared (1940), and with a powerful endorsement by 'Ernesto' himself, the German writer Gustav Regler, ex-commissar, Thaelmann Battalion, XI Brigade, and a veteran of Guadalajara, published his own novel about the Spanish War, *The Great Crusade.* For Regler, when civilization was at stake, neither the religious-racialist overtones nor the historical corruptions of 'crusade' mattered against the power of the word for romantic explanation and appeal.⁴⁵ The Scottish physician, Archie Cochrane, founder-member of the British Medical Unit in Spain, and the instrumental agent of its integration into the International Brigades, referred to the war as 'an idealistic crusade'.⁴⁶ One of the most valuable published testimonies, *Crusade in Spain,* carrying exactly the same title as that given by O'Duffy to his own Spanish memoir, was the work of British Battalion veteran (Patrick) Jason Gurney, a sculptor whose right hand was destroyed by a sniper's explosive bullet on the Jarama. To him, the International Brigades represented

> one of the most deeply-felt ideological crusades in the history of Western Europe . . . They were offered no reward, monetary or otherwise, except the satisfaction of their own idealism. In terms of numbers alone it was a movement comparable with the great Christian crusades of medieval times . . . The Crusade was against the Fascists, who were the Saracens for our generation.⁴⁷

All four of these International Brigade witnesses were non- or ex-Communists. Naturally, the term 'crusade' is used more sparingly by veterans who kept the Marxist faith into the Cold War and beyond. Nevertheless, the American comrade John Tisa refers to his joining 'the Spanish people's impatient crusade aimed at wiping out their medieval past'.⁴⁸ Tisa, who had a Catholic background among the Italian community of the Lower East Side, was unconsciously reaching into the semantic baggage of the New Deal decade in the USA. Before Spain, he had been deeply involved in labour disputes, demonstrations and marches, in aid of the many socio-political campaigns of the 1930s for which the word 'crusade' was routinely expropriated. In similar fashion, British workers who were later to join the International Brigades had been foot soldiers in the 'Jarrow Crusade' or later hunger marches from northern Britain or Wales to London. It is doubtless this background which explains why the term 'crusade' is used casually (and/or carelessly) here and there in the recorded interviews left by veterans and stored in the Imperial War Museum.

On both sides, the leadership set the tone. In 1935, Professor Hogan characterized International Communism as 'a phenomenon the like of which has not been seen since the early days of Islam . . . It is in essence an atheist crusade.'[49] Referring to the formation of the International Brigades, a Communist army organized and (in political terms) directed from Moscow, Frank Ryan claimed that 'so began the greatest crusade in history'.[50] Ryan, and several dozen of his men, were practising Catholics.[51] His apparent 'opposite', General O'Duffy, was also a fervent Catholic. In his original proclamation in the *Irish Independent*, O'Duffy addressed the 'thousands of young men who would cheerfully answer the call to join the crusade'. His move was inspired by an initiative from a Carlist nobleman, who wrote of 'the example to Christendom' that an Irish Brigade might offer in Spain; and the general was to experience his greatest triumph at a High Mass in thanksgiving for his crusade in Hemingway's beloved Pamplona. In seconding O'Duffy's call another would-be crusader, Tom Carew, stated that it was better to die for one's faith than for one's country. The most influential published advocacy of Franco's cause in Ireland was a pamphlet entitled *For God and Spain*, which sold many thousands of copies in 1936–7.[52] Meanwhile, one of O'Duffy's supporters claimed in the *Dail Eireann* that 'Franco was fighting to save Christendom as surely as Don John of Austria fought to save Christendom at Lepanto', adding that there was no difference between 'the young men who at present go to fight for Christianity in Spain and the crusaders who went from all over Europe to fight for Christianity in the Holy Land'.[53]

4 History, Legend, Culture

Such statements were seen by some of Ireland's writers as the acme of hypocrisy. An anonymous member of the Literary Brigade, that infant institution whose power in the culture of its people had not yet begun to compete with that of the Church, called himself 'Somhairle Macalastair'. He vituperated the O'Duffy Brigade in 1937:

> They talk of Hearth and Altar as the things that they defend
> (Which means in Fascist lingo the sweater's dividend)
> O'Duffy crowned Dictator 'midst the rolling of the drums
> And the fools that listened to him are rotting in the slums![54]

This spirit of resistance to clericalism and its radical identification with Fascism still inhabits the social context of Irish politics. These notions, and a deep suspicion of 'crusades', are reflected in Christy Moore's ballad of 1987, with its reference to Irishmen hearing 'the call of Franco/Joined with Hitler and Mussolini', and to bishops who 'blessed the Blueshirts in Dun Laoghaire/As they sailed beneath the swastika to spain.'[55]

It was Frank Ryan who first characterized the XV Bandera as dupes, fighting not for religion but for Fascism and all that it entailed, and in particular for an O'Duffyite dictatorship in Ireland. O'Duffy's side countered that the Irish Internationals were criminals, fighting not for democracy but for Communism and all that it entailed, and in particular a Soviet dictatorship in Ireland. As already remarked, both men were deeply sincere Catholics, but O'Duffy was so to an extent that would today be regarded as fanatical. His personality betrays the hallmarks of a quite common stereotype of mid-century Ireland – the frustrated or thwarted priest. His religious obedience was cynically exploited by the Irish hierarchy, though 'Maynooth' succeeded in covering the tracks later exposed by Christy Moore. After the archbishop of Dublin had welcomed the returning crusaders home in June 1937, a heavy stole of silence descended. The only clergyman to be seen at the general's state funeral at Glasnevin cemetery in 1944 was the officiating priest. Nothing was done to commemorate the XV Bandera in the annals of the Church. Yet it was Cardinal MacRory who had recommended O'Duffy to the Spanish conspirators in the first place, and other senior churchmen were active in support, both on the stage and behind the scenes. Pulpit propaganda, at least in terms of preaching the crusade, was comparatively restrained, but the largest contingent of O'Duffy's men, though leaving from Galway not Dun Laoghaire, did indeed sail under a swastika, rather than a papal banner like that of the victor of Lepanto, Don John of Austria – an artefact which their leader once saw, and coveted, in Toledo.

Moreover, when he proclaimed his crusade, the general was not unaware of the potential benefit for his own political ambitions. A few days after his proclamation in the *Irish Independent*, a correspondent to that newspaper suggested 'with a view to checking the growth of communism throughout the world . . . the establishment in every Christian city of an army of crusaders to deal with the menace to Christianity'.[56] What better place than Ireland to begin this global awakening? A dazzling vision of a warrior host, their blue shirts adorned with red crosses, seemed to rise in the general's mind. A week later he appealed for 'a couple of hundred thousand volunteers ready to fight for the Faith and for the country whether they went to Spain or not'.[57] O'Duffy always denied any intention to exploit the cause for political advancement. But politics at times compelled him to deny the cause itself. For a period after their arrival in Spain, his men were referred to in official nationalist documentation as 'La Bandera Católica Irlandesa'. O'Duffy protested to Franco that he had Protestants in his ranks from both the Free State and the North, whilst several experienced legionary officers seconded to his staff by Franco proved also to be of Irish Protestant derivation.[58] He tried to atone for this denial and to meet the prescriptions of *La Cruzada* by designing a new banner which incorporated the words 'In Hoc Signo Vinces'. In preparation for the arrival of his crusaders, all Spanish personnel who were to serve within their ranks were warned by Franco's HQ to attend church regularly, because 'the Irish are fervent practising Catholics and they are here on a religious crusade'.[59] A precisely similar apprehension was present among commissars of the British and Lincoln Battalions. When Irish refugees from the former came to join the latter at Tarazona in January 1937, the American boys were advised to go easy on jokes about nuns, holy pictures and rosaries in the interests of anti-Fascist comradeship.[60]

Easing back on the strictly religious angle, O'Duffy sought to substitute for crusading hymns the seductive calls of the Wild

Geese, music by any number of anonymous blind harpists, words by Thomas Davis and Christy's spiritual ancestor, Thomas Moore. The general had to some extent fallen under the spell of W. B. Yeats, myth-making Irish poet *par excellence*, who in the 1920s accepted the patronage of O'Duffy's party and a seat in the Free State Senate. When O'Duffy later formed the Blueshirts, a proto-Fascist organization based upon ex-army comrades of the Irish Civil War, Yeats wrote for them a set of so-called 'marching songs', which elaborated the powerful themes of the Wild Geese as indispensable elements of Irish politics and culture:

> Fail, and that history turns into rubbish
> All that great past to a trouble of fools;
> Those that come after shall mock at O'Donnell,
> Mock at the memory of both O'Neills.[61]

It was the Wild Geese, Yeats proposed, who had – as it were, by proxy – kept the national spirit alive in exile during two centuries of English oppression. O'Duffy himself began to wax lyrical on the great earls, Owen Roe O'Neill ('the hero of Benburb'), Patrick Sarsfield, and the battle of Fontenoy. This added the subtle anti-English flavour necessary to counter critics who suggested that if Irish boys wanted to sacrifice themselves in a crusade, then it should be the unceasing struggle along the border with the North, not in some far-away country of which they knew nothing. In fact, O'Duffy felt that through the reflected experience of the seventeenth century, he knew something important about Spain. Meeting his Francoist sponsors in London, he realized that the history of the Irish *tercios* and seminaries in Spain and Spanish Flanders was a living heritage. Arriving in Spain, he was profoundly moved by the eagerness of the Carlist leaders and General Mola to talk of O'Donnells and O'Neills.[62] Of course, seen from the Spanish side, this was in reality little more than a footnote to a great imperial history; upon which, doubtless, Mola and his staff had been carefully briefed for the occasion.[63] Contrariwise, the effect of the legend of the Wild Geese on many members of the XV Bandera is a matter of record. Furthermore, this is a territory of cultural reputation keenly disputed by their Republican opponents. Ryan insisted that the Irish Internationals were the true Wild Geese, and forty years later Paddy O'Daire (at one point acting commander of the British Battalion) – though recognizing the right of the O'Duffyites to fight for their ideals in Spain – passionately objected to their claim to inherit this tradition.[64]

To Irishmen, as to Spaniards, even the undoubted appeal of patriotism was no antidote to the poison of civil war. O'Duffy's men overwhelmingly derived from the Treaty Party which fought (and won) the Irish Civil War of 1922–3. They were Irish, and nationalist, but primarily Catholic: 'the word Catholic means Universal' as their catechism told them. Ryan's men were largely derived from the ex-'Insurgent', anti-Treaty side who lost out in the domestic struggle. They were Irish, nationalist, and Republican. Both groups of volunteers had claims to be 'Wild Geese' in the legendary sense, the traditional template of chosing a heroic and ideologically exemplary exile over the fate of an enduring domestic oppression. In the discourse of myth, it was not unlike opting (in La Pasionaria's famous exhortation of 1936) to die on their feet rather than live on their knees. In any case, both sides also had claims to be seen as 'Volunteers for Liberty', the XV Bandera (arguably) fighting for the relatively limited objective of liberty of worship, the Internationals (equally arguably) for a more inclusive liberal-humanist programme.[65]

Whatever cynics and sceptics alleged, many volunteers of the XV Bandera were seen by the clergy, and saw themselves as, Virgin Soldiers – a chaste bodyguard for the Queen of Heaven. They came chivalrously to save nuns and other innocent Catholic girls from the Red hordes. Their physical purity underlined and reinforced the purity of their cause. Gertrude Gaffney reassured mothers and parish priests back home that 'I never saw any of the Irishmen with girls while I was in Caceres ... All the Irishmen confessed to a tremendous respect for Spanish women: they tell you how good they are and how religious.'[66] After all, the Irish *banderistas* sprang from communities where sexual relations were limited to the narrowest permissible sphere. Even within that sacramental sanctum, sex was not supposed to be a pleasure; and, in any case, entry to Holy Matrimony was frequently deferred until the age when it was more likely to be regarded as a duty. In Spain, the *bandera*'s chaplain, Fr. Mulrean, was determined to keep the no man's land of sexual relations as deserted as the fear of mortal sin, more effective than any machine gun, could make it. Among both officers and men, Mulrean became the most unpopular man in the unit. But sexual puritanism, if admittedly of a differing ethical inspiration, also ruled in the opposite trenches. Political commissars of the International Brigades had duties of moral guardianship; keeping men away from local women – not just the *señoritas*, but also wives whose men were on active service, and even widows, was a political necessity. And it was not unknown for them to patrol trenches on the lookout for acts of homosexuality. Moreover, commissars went into battle with the men and had a high casualty rate: in this, they resembled the Carlist priests who fought alongside the *Requetés*, the Nationalist soldiers most admired by the Irish. Hence in practice, and if only wanly, the Irish legionaries reflected the crusading orders, bound by sanctions of poverty, chastity and obedience (though not that of abstemiousness). General O'Duffy set a splendid example to his men, at least in his crusade against the sin of concupiscence.

5 Going-into-History

All this was finally too much for Yeats, who was more than ever determined to clap his hands and sing (though whether from pleasure or duty is uncertain). At first, in his approach to the Spanish War, he seemed to share the partisanship (if not the perspective) of his compatriots. He told Ethel Mannin: 'I think the old Fenian in me would rejoice if a Fascist nation or government controlled Spain, because that would weaken the British Empire.'[67] Similar feelings existed elsewhere, for example in the young novelist Francis Stuart, son-in-law of Maud Gonne, and in Yeats's friend, the rabidly right-wing writer Oliver St John Gogarty. But it did not take Yeats long to become appalled by the populist, anti-intellectual excesses of the ICF; into the bargain, he decided that O'Duffy was an uncultured dolt.[68] He resisted any endorsement of the latter's Spanish adventure, and later even turned against it. His general motive was a familiar one:

> I am convinced that if the Spanish war goes on, or if [it] ceases and O'Duffy's volunteers return heroes, my 'pagan' institutions, the Theatre, the Academy, will be fighting for their lives against combined Catholic and Gaelic bigotry. A friar or monk has already threatened us with mob violence.[69]

But the essence of his feelings, if equally a protest against Irish Catholic puritanism, is in the mischievously subversive lines:

> How can I, that girl standing there,
> My attention fix
> On German, on Russian
> Or on Spanish politics?[70]

Thirty years later, the American critic Hugh Ford noted that the intellectuals he interviewed during research on his Spender-inspired book *The Poets' War*, 'were talking about a war which they considered unfinished': for many years, this was especially evident in Ireland.[71] On the Irish left, the figure of Charles Donnelly, killed in the Jarama battle fighting with the Lincoln Battalion, became as central and iconic as that of Cornford in England. Like Cornford, Donnelly was an accomplished student who had started work for a research degree in history. His choice of subject, James Connolly, Catholic-socialist 'martyr' of the 1916 rebellion, was voluble testimony to his personality and politics. But there were hugely significant differences between the two young poets. Both were sensitively conscious of privilege, but whereas Cornford merely simulated or personated the act of 'going over', Donnelly gave up academic life to be with the workers and took jobs in the kitchens of London hotels, living and working alongside Irish expatriates from the Dublin slums. More critically still, Donnelly's self-awareness also extended to the relationship of history and legend in his own choices:

> Whatever the issue of the battle is, your memory
> Is public, for them to pull awry with crooked hands,
> Moist eyes. And village reputations will be built on
> Inaccurate accounts of your campaign.[72]

Quite remarkably, this poem not only foresees the death of its author but systematically deconstructs in advance the propaganda demands which will turn his sacrifice into cultish ritual.[73] But, sure enough and soon enough, a comrade dutifully obliged, mundanely celebrating the fact

> That he who gently walked our city streets
> Talking of poetry or philosophy, . . .
> Should lie like any martyred soldier . . .
> Something has been gained by this mad missionary.[74]

Ewart Milne, who served for two years with the British Medical Unit – thus witnessing too many martyrs' deaths – was on a wavelength very close to that of Donnelly. They were afforded prematurely postmodern insights that only Irish writers could entertain in the 1930s, understandings which were uniquely related to the recent bloody disputes of their own island, and to the politically loaded historical-literary climate of their commemoration.

> We will call it Going-into-History
> And you all know History is a cruel country
> Where tiger terraces crouch drinking rivers waterless
> And sheep immobilised by sombrero shepherds' piping . . .
> It could be set in Extremadura or Cordova,
> Time crawling like inches and napoleonic wars.[75]

Not until the the last years of the twentieth century, however, did these warnings begin to seep to the marrow; and it seems no accident that peace was declared both in the Spanish Civil War and its Irish equivalent at much the same time. Brien Friel's play *Dancing at Lughnasa* approached the topic of 'crusades in conflict' with a proper ambivelance. Gerry signs up for the International Brigade (he alleges) in a Catholic church in Connemara. ' Do you offer your allegiance and your loyalty and your full endeavours to the Popular Front?' asks the comrade;

> 'I take it you are a Syndicalist?' 'No.' 'An Anarchist?' 'No.' 'A Marxist?' 'No.' 'A Republican, a Socialist, a Communist?' 'No.' 'Do you speak Spanish?' 'No.' 'Can you make explosives?' 'No.' 'Can you ride a motorbike?' 'Yes.' 'You're in. Sign here.'

But when the head of the sorority hears of Gerry's exploits, she is not amused:

> *Kate*: . . . It would be on my conscience if I didn't tell you how strongly I disapprove of this International Brigade caper. It's a sorry day when we send young men off to Spain to fight for Godless Communism.
> *Gerry*: For democracy, Kate.
> *Kate*: I'm not going to argue. I just want to clear my conscience.[76]

To Ethel Mannin, Yeats expounded another version of his neutralism. 'I have a horror of modern politics – I see nothing but the manipulation of popular enthusiasm by false news.'[77] There is some force in the contention that foreign intervention in Spain was generally much stimulated by the international media.[78] Perhaps O'Duffy and his men were indeed dupes – of the newly minted mass newspaper industry as much as of the hierarchy. It seems no accident that in the summer of 1936, several newspapers and magazines in the Free State ran features and series about Spain, stressing the religious-romantic side of Iberian history. As it happens, too, more than one Hollywood costume epic set in the medieval crusading era was on general release in small-town cinemas.[79] The 'Catholic Crusade' of 1936 was profoundly influenced by the press, and by the *Irish Independent* in particular, to the extent that suspicion lingers on that the whole shebang was an elaborate sales pitch. Like any Beaverbrook, Lombard Murphy, millionaire owner of the *Irish Independent*, perhaps saw himself as a crusader; and his editor, Frank Geary, certainly acted in the time-honoured opportunistic manner. In January 1937, for example, he procured the memoirs of 'Captain' Charles McGuinness, an adventurer who had recently deserted from the International Brigades, and now promiscuously added to the lengthening volume of 'Red Atrocity' stories. McGuinness was well endowed with the imagination indigenous to his nation, but also seems to have nurtured a less characteristic contempt for professional writers. He passed through Barcelona in late November 1936. Where Orwell had been fired by enthusiasm for the revolution, and Borkenau was merely sceptical, McGuinness went the last degree into blatant cynicism.

> Barcelona has been overrun by writers and Drawing Room Reds eager to get 'copy' at a safe distance from the firing line. But they are all within a short walk from the French, British and American Consulates, whose good services they are not loath to take advantage of when dropped by their sceptical Spanish 'comrades.'[80]

Evelyn Waugh was in many ways Yeats's converse-equivalent in England – a Catholic writer in a Protestant community who shared his neighbours' cultural distaste for the Irish. He nevertheless replied to Nancy Cunard's questionnaire that if he were Spanish, he would be fighting for Franco.[81] Perhaps reacting against the fact that (both in Britain and Ireland) Protestant religious leaders were somewhat less than ecumenical in their sympathy for the plight of Spanish Catholics, he also identified 'Christian civilization' exclusively with the Roman Church. Yet it was Waugh who created the cynical scenario (in his novel *Scoop*, 1938) of a foreign war being set up by press barons in order to boost circulation. As Lord

Copper lays it down to the less than intrepid foreign correspondent of his *Daily Beast*:

> Remember that the Patriots are in the right and are going to win. The Beast stands by them four-square. But they must win quickly. The British public has no interest in a war which drags on indecisively. A few sharp victories, some conspicuous acts of personal bravery on the Patriot side and a colourful entry into the capital. That is *The Beast* Policy for the war.[82]

~ 6 ~
Necessary Murders: The British Battalion at Brunete

The trumpets sound. Enter King Henry, Prince Henry, Prince John, Westmoreland, and others, with Worcester and Vernon, prisoners.

> K. Henry: Thus ever did rebellion find rebuke,
> Ill-spirited Worcester! did we not send grace,
> Pardon and terms of love to all of you?
> And would'st thou turn our offers contrary?
> Misuse the tenor of a kinsman's trust?
> Three knights upon our party slain today
> A noble earl and many a creature else,
> Had been alive this hour,
> If, like a Christian, thou hadst truly borne
> Betwixt our armies true intelligence.
> . . . Bear Worcester to the death, and Vernon too.
> Other offenders we will pause upon . . .
> (*Henry IV Part One*, Act V, sc. 5)

A characteristic moment from Shakespeare's version of British history vividly communicates the horror of rebellion and civil war. It carried a message which was a desideratum of Tudor propaganda. Defence of the Lancastrian monarchy and the political unity it embodied justified the summary slaughter of perfidious rebels in the moment of victory. Beyond even Shakespeare's ken was the fact that Henry IV's famous son and successor, in a moment of panic, ordered the murder of French prisoners on the glorious field of Agincourt. Shorn of the mimetic rituals of magistracy and sententiousness, the cool composition of writing and history, the casualties of battle are augmented by mutual cruelty and confusion.

> How the self-proclaimed saviours of Spain could have sunk to such depths of inhumanity defies any explanation that I am able to offer.[1]

The comment of a British Battalion veteran encapsulates feelings of righteous outrage about the conduct of the Nationalist side during the Spanish Civil War. Undimmed by the lapse of decades, such emotions are common to dedicated supporters of the Republic, and still widely subscribed by English-language writing of all genres. The expression of it quoted here refers to the battle of Brunete, and more specifically, to the XV Brigade's action on the first day of the offensive, an assault upon the village of Villanueva de la Cañada (6 July 1937). This chapter is concerned with the tragic events of that day and their mythic resonances into legend and history.

1

Brunete was the first major Republican offensive of the war. It had two strategic objectives. First, to lift the Nationalist siege of Madrid by imposing severe damage upon the enemy's Army of the Centre; second, by forcing Franco to divert his main forces from the north, to give the Republic's armies in that zone a vital breathing space. From the point of view of 'Spain', victory would bring another boon, arguably of even greater consequence. It would show a watching world that the new Ejército Popular was a modern and efficient army, capable of winning the war and, in the process, saving democracy from Fascism.[2] The situation augured well. Franco's best fighting units were committed to the northern offensive, in a mountainous region hundreds of miles away from the Madrid front; and the terrain for their attack was chosen by the Republic. Many of the International Brigade volunteers looked forward to the battle as the turning-point of the war: henceforward they would be victors, not victims. '¡No Pasarán!' would turn into '¡Pasarémos!' In the event, however, the campaign – lasting for three weeks – ended in bitter frustration, despite the enormous resources expended and the terrible casualties sustained.[3]

The Spanish Civil War was a 'total war' from the start. Both sides were desperate for victory at any cost, and instilled an uncompromising spirit of revenge into soldier and civilian alike. The new factor, which intensified the war of words and images, and vastly increased the political stakes involved, was that Brunete was the special enterprise of the Spanish Communist Party and its Stalinist associates, directors of the Soviet Union's mission in Spain. Because of its huge and multifaceted contribution to the military survival of the Republic in the winter of 1936–7, the prestige of the USSR and its indigenous affiliates (PCE and PSUC) was supreme. Stalin and the Comintern basked in the universal approbation of democrats and anti-Fascists. This quasi-hegemony of power – and actual hegemony of reputation – was based on the industry and solidarity of Comintern-supervised Party cadres. Such men were crucial not only to the prosecution of the war on the ground, but also to the recruitment of fresh 'volunteers for liberty' and the accompanying orchestra of 'Aid Spain' movements and 'end non-intervention' lobbies the world over.[4]

As we have seen, the main prize for the 'virtual' war of propaganda was the sympathy and support of the democratic nations, leading (it was hoped) to their ultimate involvement on the Republican side.[5] But for the offensive to succeed, the commitment of the real fighters on the bloody ground of Spain needed urgent renewal. Morale, made up in each volunteer from an individual mix of belief in the cause with more tangible elements – occasional leave, palatable food, American tobacco, quality weapons and (arguably paramount) mail from home – demanded an overall boost in terms of motivation and self-belief.[6] The line of public rationalization ran as follows: not content with the overwhelming quantitative advantage which they always enjoyed in terms of men and materials, Franco's armies were fighting a thoroughly dirty war. At earlier points of the war the cry had been 'Avenge Badajoz', or 'Avenge Málaga.' By now, however, new grievances, especially the supreme atrocity of Guernica, were coming to replace them in the litany of hate.

The British Battalion (the 16th) was part of the XV Brigade. For the purposes of the new offensive, the brigade was assigned to the 15th Division, which in turn formed part of the XVIII Army Corps. On the eve of the action, Brigade commander, Vladimir Copic and Commissar George Aitken issued a printed exhortation 'to all the comrades'. Each soldier was asked to bear in mind that

> we fight today to avenge Almería, Guernica and Bilbao. We fight to free MADRID as the first step in freeing Spain. We fight to free SPAIN as the first step in freeing the world from the fascist menace . . . FORWARD comrades! HURRY to the VICTORY! Put the cowardly baby killers on the run . . .[7]

The emotional effect of such manifestos on individual Brigaders was often profound. Tom Jones, from north Wales, wrote home to justify abandoning his earlier pacifism: 'I hate war with all my heart but I hate Fascist baby-killers [more].' His compatriot, Frank Owen, from 'Little Moscow' (Maerdy) – who was to be killed in the forthcoming battle – was equally fired up:

> By the time you get this you will have read of the big offensive. From now on it is to be war as it should be, Franco is not prepared for the reception that is being prepared for him, and I must say this, our side will leave very little quarter to the Fascists, for the murder of women and children has been their game, at Malaga, Almería, Guernica and Bilbao ...[8]

2

The battle zone was a wide undulating valley lying to the south of the Sierra de Guadarrama and due west of Madrid. The task of the Popular Army, which mobilized around 70,000 men, was to outflank Madrid's besiegers, threatening to isolate them from supply lines and reinforcements. Whilst it was not realistically expected to destroy this army (of some 55,000), or even to force its surrender, its withdrawal in crippled disarray would mean the release of Franco's grip on the Republic's throat. Madrid would breathe again.[9]

In order to produce this result, the army had to seize the small town of Brunete by surprise, using it as an axis to swing through ninety degrees eastwards towards Madrid. The plan required this push to join up with a complementary thrust westwards from the capital, thus completing the pincer. Having skirted several smaller, intermediate settlements under cover of night, the 11th Division under Enrique Líster duly occupied Brunete sometime before noon on 6 July. Líster set up his field command and looked for support. His immediate need was for heavy artillery and tanks, without which any further advance, and even the defence of Brunete, was doomed to failure.[10] Behind him, the 34th Division was scheduled to capture the village of Villanueva de la Cañada, six kilometres into the salient and athwart a vital connecting road running north–south. The high command was aware of the fact that, like other places near the front, Villanueva had been solidly fortified, and needed softening up prior to infantry assault. As dawn broke, it was subjected to an intensive artillery bombardment, supplemented by air strikes. Whilst its civilians took refuge in the village church, from a vantage point ten kilometres away in the Guadarrama foothills, soldiers of the three English-speaking battalions watched, awaiting their turn for action as part of the second assault wave. The men, especially veterans of earlier battles, were impressed at the weight of explosive falling on Villanueva. For the first time, the volunteers for liberty, it seemed, had might as well as right on their side.[11] But as the ground attack developed, with Soviet tanks leading the advance of Spanish infantry, Villanueva put up unexpectedly stubborn resistance. The enemy had been forewarned.

The waves of security panic which had rippled through the Republic in the weeks before the attack proved fully justified. Well in advance of D-day, Miguel Rodríguez, Miaja's intelligence chief, began to read unfavourable signs in the enemy's behaviour. On 15 June he warned that the other side, too, might be planning an attack. The scarcity of enemy deserters, from whom information might be forthcoming, made Rodríguez suspect that troops in the Nationalist front line belonged to experienced professional units, the feared Moroccan *regulares*, or perhaps shock troops of the Foreign Legion. Moreover, the second half of June brought a steady increase in the volume of traffic behind enemy lines. On 18 and 19 June, Rodríguez repeated his misgivings to the high command. Supplies, especially ordnance, had been stepped up to the network of villages on the enemy front.[12] On the very eve of attack, two anti-tank guns were dispatched to Villanueva, and men were ordered to spend the night of 5–6 July fully armed in outer emplacements.[13] The garrison comprised the Second *Bandera* of Falangists of Seville.[14] In addition to the aforementioned weapons, their commander, Miguel Pérez Blázquez, had some 700 men and twenty-four heavy machine guns, as well as two 10.5 mm cannon at his disposal. Since the Nationalists had first captured Villanueva in autumn 1936, they had constantly improved perimeter defences.[15]

The village is located on a shallow plateau in a generally flattish landscape, a feature which gave its defenders a remarkably clear field of fire. In addition to firepoints within key buildings, surrounding fields were partly entrenched, whilst an arc of barbed wire and forward machine-gun posts impeded any frontal assault from the north. This tactic was nonetheless that which Colonel Galán, commander of the 34th Division, chose to adopt. Driven by haste, and encouraged by the ballistic pulverization of his target, he relied on force of numbers, throwing two brigades and thirty tanks into the initial onslaught. It was repulsed with impunity. Several hundred casualties were incurred and about a dozen tanks knocked out. Over the next few hours, several similar attempts brought similar results. At the high command, elation over Líster's success gave way to anxiety and then to a fury of frustration. General Miaja ordered XVIII Corps commander, Colonel Jurado, to take Villanueva at all costs, even if soldiers had to be forced to the attack by threats to fire 'friendly' artillery rounds close to their ranks.[16]

Midday arrived, and the unbearable heat of the Castilian midsummer, with no sign of a breakthrough. Jurado broke down under the strain and Colonel Casado was appointed in his stead.[17] Meanwhile it was decided to reinforce the weakened brigades of the 34th Division with the fresh 15th, which had been originally intended to bypass (a captured) Villanueva in order to secure the flanks of the bridgehead to the east.[18] The XIII and XV International Brigades reached the fire zone early in the afternoon. Though they succeeded in surrounding the village, further progress was still denied. Casualties were taken in all three English-speaking battalions. By now, it was at least four hours since Líster had seized Brunete (only five kilometres away) and the whole offensive, the outcome of the battle and the future of the Republic – indeed, in the apocalyptic discourse of the war, of freedom itself – depended on breaking the bottleneck of Villanueva.[19]

At 1600 hours a Republican report described a 'furious attack taking place at this moment against Villanueva'. Another claimed that at 1930 hours 'bombers attacked the *pueblo* of Villanueva de la Cañada, unloading their missiles with great precision on the allocated targets'. A further report, printed in the government newspaper the following day, stated that 'we are maintaining close pressure on Villanueva de la Cañada and Quijorna, although the enemy is sending considerable reinforcements towards them. The fighting in these places until midnight yesterday has been extremely fierce.'[20]

During the afternoon, the British Battalion, with Fred Copeman in command, worked its way, literally marching on its stomach at times, around to the southern approaches of Villanueva. The intention was to cut off the garrison's retreat along the road to Brunete. An hour or two before sunset, the infantry companies were in tenuous occupation of positions athwart this highway. Meanwhile, such was the quantity and accuracy of incoming fire that, in defiance of strident pressure from high command, the decision was taken to await the onset of dusk before attempting the final push. Since no useful targets presented themselves, the machine-gun company, and the Brigade anti-tank battery (mostly comprising British volunteers) had so far played little part in the battle. Various members of these units busied themselves looking for water sources to replenish the flasks of their suffering comrades in advanced positions; some even settled down to catch a little sleep out of sight of enemy snipers.[21]

Inside the village – now besieged by a force of nearly 8,000 men – Pérez Blázquez had been killed along with approximately half his command. Another 100 severely wounded soldiers were taken to join the civilians in the church. One Nationalist account claims that this shelter was destroyed by bombardment, causing many further deaths. By late afternoon, Pérez Blázquez's adjutant, Captain Alvarez Lasarte, reckoned that the *bandera* had done its duty, and began to plan a withdrawal. One of his men later recalled how Alvarez managed to contact the Nationalist HQ at Brunete by field telephone, asking for permission to withdraw, and for any covering assistance available. At the other end of the line, in the offices now occupied by Líster, the Republican operator apparently believed he was speaking to a friendly officer who was defending the captured village from enemy counter-attack. According to this source, Líster promised the required assistance; perhaps he was anxious to grasp an apparent opportunity to free the logistical logjam. At any rate, not long afterwards, the defenders spotted a column on the road. Various features (including the presence of cavalry) persuaded them that help from Brunete had arrived. Survivors who were physically able prepared to move out to meet their saviours.[22]

A different perspective prevailed in the 16th Battalion. From positions in ditches along the road, and at other points of uncertain cover, they remained under severe fire. Though men were ordered (one might think, superfluously) to keep their heads down, and the light was failing, some of them spotted a group of people coming out from the town. The earliest account of immediately subsequent events was sent to the *Workington Star* by the Cardiff-based seaman, Pat Murphy. Written in hospital, it was dated only a week after the incident it described, and before the larger battle of which it formed a part had ended. Under the headline 'Workington Man's First-Hand Story of Fighting' it told an extraordinary tale:

> At dusk we could see a crowd of people emerging from the town; quite plainly the dresses of women and children could be distinguished . . . The bulk of the crowd were well-armed Italian soldiers, and when we held them up they just opened fire with machine guns, bombs and rifles. The women and children they had used as a shield were in some cases killed by the men they had been forced to protect . . . Whilst I was lying wounded I saw a number of fascists examining the wounded. They propped up our injured and shot into their breasts. Within an hour our battalion had collected these savages in . . .[23]

A second account was provided by the Welsh Communist, Jack Roberts, to the compilers of the official history of the XV Brigade, some weeks later.*[24] This corroborated Murphy's version in all essentials; taken together these two original versions by participants may be regarded as an *Urtext*.[25] In addition to printing Roberts's version under the title 'The Fascist Sortie', Frank Ryan glossed the event in his general narrative of the Brigade's battle achievements:

> At nightfall the garrison, driving women and children as cover in front of them, attempted a sortie by the Brunete road. In a fierce hand-to-hand encounter the British drove them back. Dimitrovs and British then simultaneously stormed the town and had it completely in their possession before midnight.[26]

On a small hill a few kilometres to the north-east of Villanueva ('Vértice Mocha'), a teenage member of the occupying Falangist militia had been posted as observer. He later recalled seeing that

> Villanueva was on fire. Many soldiers could be seen attacking from the south. There must have been at least three or four battalions . . . but they could not get near the village. One could guess that an effective fire was being kept up by the defenders . . . [In the evening] some Falangist survivors got out of the circle. It seems that someone had given them the uniforms of a Red unit and they were able to steal between enemy lines . . . Not more than about fourteen escaped altogether.[27]

At some point between 2200 and 2400 hours, Villanueva finally succumbed. Official Nationalist data give a total of 200 (undifferentiated) casualties among the defenders. About a dozen of the

British Battalion had been killed, with perhaps twenty wounded. On this day, at least, it seems they got off lightly compared to other units; total casualties of the XVIII Corps may well have amounted to little short of 1,000 in this sector and on this day alone.[28]

Work on clearing a path through the rubble to which Villanueva had been reduced began immediately, but twelve hours or more had been lost, and the enemy response was already in evidence. The XV Brigade spent the night of 6–7 July in or around the village, some platoons helping to flush out Falangists hiding in cellars and stables. However, at dawn the next day Villanueva again came under artillery fire, this time from Nationalist batteries. Disrupted by this, preoccupied with other tasks, torn between the need to make progress and anxiety over the wounded, it was not until later that day (7 July) that the XV Brigade was ready to move on. Its battalions headed with agonizing slowness, often ambushed by groups of retreating enemy, towards their original objective. Their mission was to secure Los Altos de Romanillos, a ridge running north–south along the further bank of the dried-up river Guadarrama, which overlooked the path of Líster's projected advance towards Madrid. It was too late. Units of the Foreign Legion, Franco's elite corps, were already in control of these heights, which now represented a crucial line of defence for the army besieging Madrid. The result was a prolonged and bloody battle of attrition around the section known as Mosquito Ridge (8–12 July). Here, the 16th Battalion was to suffer a grim fate.[29]

Having run out of trained reserves, Madrid called off the offensive on 12 July: after a lull of six days, the Nationalist counter-offensive began. Only when the latter also reached the point of exhaustion (25 July) did the orgy of mutual sacrifice cease. The net results were that the Republic had conquered some fifty square kilometres on the Madrid front, and held up Franco's offensive in the north against Santander for about four weeks. The ruins of Villanueva de la Cañada remained Republican until the end of the war nearly two years later.

3

The Popular Army as a whole had taken a severe battering. Recriminations were intense and prolonged. André Marty, main founder and political leader of the International Brigades, was recalled to Moscow to account for the setback; his assistant, Vidal Gayman, was sacked. The leadership cadre of the British Battalion, its members bitterly at odds with one another, was sent home pending the results of an enquiry by the CPGB. This reflected shock and distress resulting from the battlefield casualty count.[30] The Battalion had also been crippled as a fighting force by a spate of desertions which began in the first hours of the battle. Even worse, towards its end there had been a mutiny of the rank and file which met with unacceptable complaisance on the part of some officers. Senior British Communists were sent to Spain to report on the situation. Welsh Miners' leader Arthur Horner (for example) went to consult his colleague, Will Paynter, Marty's assistant as English-speaking base commissar. Approximately 80 per cent of the Battalion roster who had survived Brunete (some 320 men) were in hospital, in detention camps or still on the run. In effect, the British Battalion had ceased to exist.[31]

Shortly after the battle, Frank Ryan visited the front in search of material for the Brigade history of which he was editor. It seems that he met Jack Roberts and asked him to write a description of the battle for Villanueva. After receiving Roberts's account of 'The Fascist Sortie', sometime in August, he composed his own version for the *Irish Democrat*, newspaper of his party, the Irish Republican Congress.* Ryan's was the second version to appear in print, following Murphy's. Roberts's text came out in *The Book of the XV Brigade* (early 1938) and a year later a fourth reading was given in Bill Rust's history of the British Battalion sponsored by the CPGB.* Rust, like Ryan, had not been present at Villanueva; but it seems that both men made it their business to interview certain volunteers who had survived it.[32]

Though broadly consonant, the two 'original' accounts by Murphy and Roberts had certain differences of detail and emphasis. In the former, and a fortiori in later versions from the same source, the recklessly courageous author occupies centre stage. Murphy also consistently states that the enemy soldiers taking part in the sortie were Italians rather than Spaniards. Moreover, he alleges they were armed with sub-machine guns as well as rifles and grenades. Roberts is less concerned with Murphy's involvement, and makes no mention of the other two points. In fact, no Italian ground units took part in any phase of the Brunete battle.

Furthermore, as photographic records illustrate (if only by the evidence of absence) sub-machine guns were a highly unusual weapon among regular infantry troops, being issued only to certain selected units (for example, headquarters guards and elite rearguard police squads) on either side.[33]

Murphy's identification of Italians was perhaps an honest error. Two other veterans mistakenly recalled seeing Italian soldiers at Villanueva.[34] However, the involvement of Italians was useful propaganda 'proof' of Mussolini's infringement of the non-intervention agreements, and this in turn was linked to the disequilibrium in armaments, alleged key to the Republic's defeat at Brunete and elsewhere. Furthermore, in 'The Fascist Sortie', Mussolini's men were seen to be typically cowardly and pusillanimous, ready to fight only when armed with superior weapons and hiding behind women and children. The Villanueva incident confirmed that, as during the Abyssinian war, Italian Fascists were capable of any duplicity and were wholly indifferent to the fate of civilians. An important point of Republican propaganda, often reiterated since, maintained that the CTV was composed not of volunteers but of miserable conscripts, sent to Spain as unwilling instruments of the Italian dictator's search for glory.[35]

As it happens, the defenders of Villanueva (and two other nearby villages, Quijorna and Villafranca del Castillo) were indeed Fascists – but of the native, not the Italian variety. The Brigaders who died at their hands on that tragic day thus met the key requirement of martyrdom in Popular Front mythology; to have died fighting Fascism in battle. But the Brigaders' adversaries were also volunteers, men who enlisted in Seville (city and province) after the rebellion had triumphed in that region. During the war's early phases, so-called 'Seville Soldiers' – that is, rearguard regiments who discharged cushy assignments whilst the *africanistas* (professional soldiers of Franco's army) did the serious fighting – were the butt of derision amongst the latter's hardened warriors.[36] With Brunete, they began to slough off this reputation. The defence of Villanueva, by holding up the offensive for a whole campaigning day, helped provide a crucial breathing space for the organization of in-depth Nationalist resistance. Doubtless, the hands of some heroes were not spotlessly clean. The first military experiences of their unit had been in following up the African army's advance with a policy of brutal repression in the *pueblos* of western Andalusia.

But the history of the Spanish Civil War amply demonstrates that a capacity for ruthlessness, and even actual brutality, are not incompatible with political idealism. No regiment which fought in Spain ended with clean hands, and this statement does not exclude the International Brigades. In sum, by all normative criteria, it cannot be denied that the fascist defenders of Villanueva had acted on that day with as much heroism and honour as their antifascist adversaries. Except – that is – for the incident of 'The Fascist Sortie'.

No further direct corroboration of the 'human shield' story was forthcoming until Copeman's biography appeared in 1948.*[37] Here, the author's own resourceful leadership is presented as instrumental in weathering the crisis caused by 'The Fascist Sortie', and in the successful storming of the village. In subsequent years the episode at Villanueva de la Cañada became a treasured exhibit in the museum of anti-Fascist witness, taken out (as it were) for regular dusting, and often paraded at demonstrations. Over the years, as the decade-anniversaries (more recently, even half-decade anniversaries) of the war passed in review, veterans of the British Battalion were persuaded to record recollections of the war. In addition to Murphy, Roberts and Copeman, six more survivors of Villanueva, in the course of tape-recorded interviews and/or published memoirs, claimed to have witnessed 'The Fascist Sortie'.* Meanwhile, the event entered the written history of the International Brigades. In most accounts from anglophone sources, the wicked and cowardly conduct of the Nationalists has the effect of magnifying the selfless heroism of the volunteers for liberty.[38]

Finally, the story reached the cinema screen via the Loach–Allen romance *Land and Freedom* released in 1995.[39] The movie gained widespread media attention, winning prestigious prizes and attracting large audiences, especially among young people in Spain. In this version, Villanueva is transposed to the Aragon front. A POUM detachment attacks a village held by a small enemy garrison. Taking some civilians hostage, the latter, led by the parish priest, make a last stand in a church. Eventually they attempt a break-out by pushing the hostages in front of them as a 'human shield'. In the confusion soldiers and civilians are all killed and the priest is the only enemy survivor. When villagers testify to his collaboration with 'Fascist' repression, he is duly 'executed' by the freedom fighters.

This avowedly fictional episode from the Spanish Civil War ingeniously incorporates several of its key topoi of anti-Fascist myth.

For example, one of the British participants at Villanueva alleged many years later (1991) that

> the priests were up in the church firing at us with their machine guns. They came down and forced the people out . . . The civilian population, women especially, were being forced along the road while the priests were firing at us, until they got done in the end.[40]

Other accounts similarly illustrate how random elements of rumour and myth constantly refertilized the memories of veterans. The tale of parish priests occupying church towers, the better to pick off their own hapless parishioners, was apparently familiar to most rank-and-file Brigaders. It was disseminated by commissars anxious to 'explain' the widespread destruction of churches and the ban on religious observance.[41] Another addition to the *Urtext* had its origin in a notable early incident of the war. Some rebel soldiers in Madrid's Montaña barracks, under siege by the People's Militias, waved white flags. But those advancing to receive the capitulation were fired on by other defenders (in confusion and ignorance) and many died. When they tried to surrender after the barracks was stormed, dozens of officers were massacred where they stood. Thus, in some accounts, the defenders' break-out at Villanueva is embellished by the waving of white handkerchiefs. Indeed, by 1984, this new detail had even insinuated itself into a version related to the TV cameras by Jack Roberts himself.[42] In any case, tales of besieged enemy garrisons using 'human shield' tactics to escape were told widely during the war. It was alleged (for example) that the defenders of the Alcázar of Toledo had resorted to it in August 1936.[43] A similar story was used to explain the the killings of enemy officers captured by the XV Brigade during various actions in Aragon later that year, in which senior American officers were complicit.[44]

In this way, the 'Fascist sortie' arrived in the consciousness of hard-left media activists of the 1990s, fleshed out with emotional detail which tended to strengthen its power as an 'ideological weapon'. The significance of the weapon's deployment in feature films resides, of course, in the statistical fact that this medium vastly expands the target area. For every individual who derives a myth-inspired prejudice about 'Spain' from lecture theatre or written word, many thousands may be similarly affected by a film like *Land and Freedom*. Thus, in this instance, it is neither exaggeration nor distortion to state that the objectives of the Comintern in 1937, 'to continue the fight against Fascism' are still being met.[45] To the extent that Fascism may still represent a threat to human freedom, this is a consummation devoutly to be wished. But since Communism too may continue to pose such a threat, the propaganda function of anti-Fascist myth must also be critically assessed.

4

The Welsh volunteer, Leo Price, like Jack Roberts, had fought many campaigns against bosses, blacklegs and Blackshirts on the south Wales front.[46] In two interviews given in the 1970s, Price gave detailed accounts of the 'sortie'.* In response to the interviewer's prompt 'The Fascist troops had used the civilians as some kind of camouflage?', he delivered the strangely gratuitous information that

> I suppose there was so much propaganda with them [the Nationalists] like we [the Republicans] were killing everybody and everything, especially bloody nuns and priests, our bloody 'prime target' – which was a lot of bloody rubbish of course. We wasn't interested in bloody civilians, all we was interested in was these bloody German troops more than anybody. No doubt they thought there was no question of quarter. They wouldn't give it, I suppose and they wouldn't take it.[47]

Price's remarks afford a glimpse of the competitive struggle of propaganda constructs, a struggle which overlays participants' recollections of the fighting. The interests at stake in the depictive elaboration of the event at Villanueva should by now be evident to the reader. With its 'correct' perception and transmission was bound up the historical reputation of the British Battalion, of the International Brigades as a whole, and of the Comintern mission in Spain. Just as the outcome of the battle of Brunete depended, at least in part, on the capture of Villanueva, so the future of the struggle for freedom and democracy depended on the tale of 'The Fascist Sortie', along with a hundred similar myths of populist anti-Fascist culture.

As so often with the Spanish Civil War, there seems little point in asking the question, 'what actually happened?' except by way of fixing a theoretical benchmark of inquiry. No official documents exist which contribute more than contextual points. The only primary evidence is that of survivors, backed up by the secondary statements of men who were in the vicinity. But as a Russian proverb has it, 'nobody lies like an eyewitness.' How any given incident is perceived by participant or bystander, who later produces a description influenced by a range of preconditioned assumptions, often immune to sophisticated forensic techniques, is beyond the realm of useful speculation. This situation places greatest significance on the *Urtext* of Murphy and Roberts. These alone provide contemporaneous written testimony; from which later versions took their cue. (Murphy himself later added more detail concerning his own part in the skirmish.) But there is another dimension – that of 'negative' evidence. Several deposits left by British survivors of 6 July 1937 make no reference to the 'sortie'. No fewer than ten Brigaders fall into this category.

John Angus	H.K.
Jud Colman	Charles Morgan
Alec Cummings	Frank McCusker
George Gowans	Mike O'Donoghue
Walter Greenhalgh	Robert Walker[48]

Alec Cummings was in command of No. 1 (infantry) company. A Communist who later died in Spain, he was badly wounded at Villanueva. In a series of letters home during his convalescence, letters replete with propaganda material, the actual phraseology of which was often supplied by the censorship office, he failed to mention the 'Fascist sortie'. A member of Cummings's company, referred to as 'H.K.', though not apparently reporting the same event as the *Urtext*, does (however) describe a sudden and bloody flare-up in the fighting outside the walls of the village. Dundee volunteer Frank McCusker claimed that just before he was wounded he saw Italian and German prisoners being taken away.[49] Even allowing 'H.K.' and McCusker as possible exceptions, it is strange that so few who were present in the area appear to have witnessed the sortie. If they heard about it near the time, or read about it at some later stage, they failed for some reason to mention it 'in calm of mind, all passion spent'.

The Anti-Tank Battery passed through Villanueva around noon on 7 July. Fred Thomas saw 'outside the village [that is on the

Brunete road] more bodies, as the Fascists retreated'. In the gloss he added to his diary entry sixty years later Thomas recalled the story of the defenders' break-out as 'a horrible tale they [Battalion members] told us . . . This tale has become part of the legend of Brunete. I have not spoken to anyone who actually saw it happen.'[50] Evidently, soldiers had heard about the incident by the following day, but none of them had witnessed it with their own eyes. After the war, Thomas was a member of the International Brigade Association and attended celebratory occasions arranged to keep the weapon of its history bright and keen.[51] For his part, Bill Alexander was for many years secretary of the IBA. At Brunete, Alexander had also belonged to the Anti-Tanks and presumably heard the same stories as Thomas at the same time and place. His inclusion of the 'Fascist sortie' in the Battalion official history suggests he had obtained corroboration from the mouths of veterans who saw it happen: none, however, is cited.[52]

Perhaps even greater significance attaches to a letter written by Will Paynter to Harry Pollitt on 11 July. Returning to Albacete from the battle front, he gave the names of eleven Battalion members killed in the first few days of the offensive. Paynter stated: 'this is a very incomplete list of the dead, since I am informed that there are about thirty more to be added.' More details could not be obtained, 'due to the preoccupation of the leading comrades'. This indicates that Paynter had been to the front line, and had spoken to British officers about casualties, at their positions beneath Mosquito Ridge, probably on 9 July. None of his interlocutors seems to have mentioned the enemy break-out which was the ostensible occasion of most of these deaths.[53]

5

Fred Thomas's diary reference to deaths which occurred 'as the fascists retreated' towards Brunete provides the initial clue to a sketchy reality which may be conjecturally reconstructed from all the sources utilized in this chapter.

Since sources on both sides agree that towards the end of the siege, a group of defenders left the shelter of the village and took the Brunete road, the balance of probabilities is that a firefight did occur in this zone, involving the most forwardly placed members of the British Battalion. The simultaneous commotion heard by many of the latter was the coincident noise of fighting between rearguard defenders and the non-British battalions of the XV Brigade, which were storming into the village from at least two points on its further sides. Most accounts report that once the 'sortie' had been dealt with, the British mounted their own assault, by which they succeeded in entering Villanueva, thus sharing the deathless glory of its capture.

In a gloss later made on his diary entry, Fred Thomas mentions 'the bodies of women we had seen by the roadside'. Nationalist sources claim that many civilian deaths occurred as a result of the direct hit on the church. Given the frequent identification of the church tower by Republican participants as their most important target it is reasonable to suppose that XV Brigade staff called in the air strike claimed by the Valencia *parte* as taking place at 1930 hours. All save one or two of the eyewitness accounts of the 'sortie', which took place at 2100 hours or later, admit that it led to civilian deaths, with body counts ranging between only four at one extreme and the entire number of civilian hostages at the other.[54]

A similar mystery surrounds the fate of the *Falangista* militiamen who committed the crime under investigation. Recollections differ: whilst some assert that all the Fascists taking part in the shoot-out were killed, others state that some (or all) survivors were rounded up, and one account insists that some escaped 'into the surrounding fields'. Only Jack Roberts claimed complete annihilation of the guilty parties, and Frank Ryan's newspaper version repeats this detail.* Of the two Battalion histories, Rust omits reference to the point, whilst Alexander fails to support the *Urtext* to the hilt, writing that the Fascists 'were almost wiped out.'[55] If any did survive the desperate frenzy of shooting – either through being wounded, or by attempting to surrender – they knew what to expect. Frank Owen (we recall) had written in advance to his family of the enemy's probable fate at his and his comrades' hands. 'Our side will leave very little quarter to the Fascists, for the murder of women and children has been their game.'[56] Base commissar and Welsh Miners' leader Will Paynter, who (as we have seen) spent time with the Battalion only a few days after the incident, referred years later in a TV documentary to the killing of prisoners: 'Prisoners of war [he pointed out] are only taken when you are on the offensive and since the Republicans never were on the offensive they took very few prisoners and hence how could they have killed them?' Paynter's recollection of the much-trumpeted 'great offensive' of Brunete (among others) had, it seems, become a little dim.[57]

Historiographical treatment of the Villanueva incident has rarely given a hint of any untoward action by the Internationals. An exception may be detected in that given by the American academic, Cecil Eby, in his book on the American battalions of the International Brigades.

> This surprise attack from behind the skirts of women ... filled the British with a bitter rage ... Fearing prisoners would be murdered in cold blood, Captain Fred Copeman had to order his battalion out of town and allow other battalions to clear out the enemy.[58]

Versions more sympathetic to the British Battalion have it (for example) that 'Fred Copeman ... shooed the [surviving] fascists into the enthusiastic arms of Spanish friends'; or that 'many of the fascists escaped but a little later were rounded up by a Spanish unit.'[59] However, some participants remembered a different denouement. The most explicit, Frank Hillesley, told a local reporter when he got back to Reading: 'They had slaughtered old men, women and children. We went in there, lined them up, made them dig a trench and shot every one.'*[60] In the 1970s, Michael O'Donoghue of Merthyr brought back to mind that 'a lot of fellows they panicked ... We buried twenty-seven in a hole there.'[61] Another comrade, John Jones – a witness of the 'sortie' – recalled fifty years later that 'we took no prisoners because of that incident ... We shot them ... not many, ten or a dozen ... firing squad.'[62] In 1991, Charles Gowan made an indirect reference to the killings when an interviewer introduced the subject: 'Were you taking prisoners?' Gowan answered: 'No. It wasn't good policy. What could you do with them? We hadn't the forces to take them anywhere.'[63]

Perhaps 'The Fascist Sortie' as related by the *Urtexts* was a dramatic, propaganda-angled elaboration of reality. Perhaps the 'execution' of prisoners was also a fictional horror arising from the phantasmagoria of battle in the minds of elderly men thinking back over many decades. Perhaps there is some connection between the two memories. The former may have been an attempt to rationalize the failure to take Villanueva for so long despite the advantage of overwhelming odds, and also placing a dramatic-heroic gloss on events which were confused and traumatic. The latter would have been admitted by most as summary but deserved justice; or else as justified by the expediency of war. 'They play dirty, we play dirty', as Ernest Hemingway may once have put it to Lincoln Battalion commander, Milton Wolff.[64]

President Azaña discovered shortly after the event that something 'dirty' had happened at Villanueva. It was prime minister Juan Negrín's duty to report to Azaña on the progress of the war. He did not always answer questions; or occasionally, Azaña suspected, he answered them incompletely or untruthfully. On 22 July, a fortnight after the battle of Villanueva, the two men held a conference which took place after midnight. Failure after such high hopes had affected both men, and their patience became frayed. During a sharp exchange about Brunete, Azaña warned Negrín: 'I already know about the mad thing that happened at Villanueva de la Cañada.' Unfortunately, the context does not help us to know the precise nature of the 'mad thing' to which Azaña was referring.[65]

It seems reasonable to speculate, more generally, that there was a template story for soldiers to tell each other in their newspapers and at their commissar-led meetings behind the trenches. This was the tale passed on to reporters and the outside world. Often the template only faintly resembled what was set out in reports sent back to Albacete and/or to Moscow. In the meantime the atmosphere of rumour, propaganda and ignorance was just one more element of the hell in which the volunteers lived, suffered, and died. The first stage direction in *Henry IV Part Two*, the immediately consecutive scene of Shakespearean drama to that quoted from at the head of this chapter, is 'Enter Rumour, painted full of tongues'; a Republican poster (by Ramón Puyol) displayed a fantastic representation of exactly such a monster, flying through the streets, spreading morale-sapping gossip behind the lines.[66]

6

Nine months after Brunete, Frank Ryan was captured, along with hundreds of other Brigaders, during the Nationalist breakthrough on the Aragon front (March 1938). After some investigation he was charged with war crimes, tried in Burgos (Franco's wartime capital) and sentenced to death. The indictment apparently stated:

when the Republicans captured and held Brunete for a short time last summer he is alleged to have commanded firing squads of Internationals that executed Nationalist prisoners without giving them any sort of trial and to have shot down with his own pistol a number of Nationalists who were surrounded and offered to surrender.[67]

The details here seem sufficiently adjacent to suggest that Franco's government had learned of atrocities in which English-speaking units of the XV Brigade had been involved during the battle of Brunete. His biographer speculates that it may help to explain the powerful Nationalist animus against Ryan, who was the only non-Spanish member of the International Brigades ever to be formally put on trial and condemned to death by the Franco government. Another factor was the pressure on the Francoist propaganda machine to produce a symbolic demon – alien agent of the dreadful war foisted on innocent Spain by a perceived Soviet-inspired international revolutionary movement – to offer for both internal and external consumption.[68]

This pressure came (*inter alia*) from specific sources that had some political clout. When Líster's men captured Brunete they took prisoner two sisters, volunteer nurses of the medical services and members of the Falange women's group, the Sección Feminina. According to a story given wide currency in the Nationalist press, they had volunteered to stay behind with the wounded. Two staff officers died in protecting them from the 'red hordes'; the latter proceeded to use the girls as 'human shields' during mopping-up operations in the streets of Brunete. The nurses, who (according to their brother) suffered many further indignities, were daughters of the Duke of Lerma and sisters of José Larios, one of Franco's ace fighter pilots. After a highly publicized campaign, their release was obtained by an exchange deal between Burgos and Valencia. It is unlikely that news of this incident reached the British Battalion at the time of its active service on the Brunete front. But the War Commissariat in Madrid would certainly have known about the fuss being created over it during the battle's aftermath, in August, when Frank Ryan and his assistants were putting together their history of the XV Brigade.[69]

Just as the Comintern machine may have been searching for a suitable antidote to the ungallant story of the sisters, so Burgos wanted a scapegoat to offer friends and relatives of victims of

Republican war crimes, who had been encouraged to believe that gangs of foreign criminals had invaded Spain in a frenzy of bloodlust whipped up by Russian agents. Unfortunately for the Francoist public relations office, Frank Ryan (non-Communist and firm Catholic) proved badly chosen to fit this monstrous stereotype, and eventually the Caudillo, doubtless to his chagrin, was obliged to commute the death sentence.[70]

Another Irishman had not escaped. George Brown, native of Kilkenny, brought up in Manchester, was killed during the fighting outside Villanueva. One account mentions the circumstances of his death: dispatched by a Fascist officer as he lay wounded on the ground. Brown was political commissar to one of the rifle companies; the account of his death is from the hand of a surviving witness, an assiduous memorialist of the British Battalion.*[71] The crucible of anti-Fascist myth moulded George Brown into heroic martyr and memorial. Years later, an admirer sent a poem written in his memory to the International Brigade Archive in London.

> When George Brown went forward
> Towards Villanueva
> With the lads of the fifteenth
> International Brigade –
> He did not know the people
> Who were coming to greet him
> On that dust-grey road.
> And how could he know
> That hidden behind them,
> Those brotherly peasants, men, women and children
> Who came to surrender, or greet liberation,
> Were the enemy's soldiers?
> Perhaps we shall never know who they were.
> What happened eludes us.[72]

Ralph Bates, one of the band of propaganda commissars, was perhaps more conscious of the need to make weapons of war and ideology when he wrote a story of 'fictional autobiography' about his part in the battle of Villanueva. The story ends in that village, now captured by the Popular Army and under enemy fire. For shelter, Bates enters the church, the church from which so many outside had been killed, where so many inside had died, and were still dying, 'groaning and screaming in their agony'. Transported above the horror by artistic inspiration, Bates imagines himself officiating at a kind of Communist Mass, a ritual offered for the dead in which their sacrifice is sanctified by drama and poetry.

> Doctors were going among the men; the church was lit by a few acetyline flares placed in the ground. The long shadows writhed on walls, like figures in a mobile El Greco. All the church was full of the echoing litany of death. I went up to the dismantled high altar to write my report . . . Bowed over the centre of the altar, his head upon his hands, was a wounded man, blood streaming from his head. He was standing as a priest stands when he murmurs 'Hoc est corpus meum'. The man was dying . . . He seemed to be pleading the sacrifice of Spain . . . I went outside and was sick. I was not sick at the spectacle of pain but because of the unaccepted sacrifice. That it would not be accepted by the Western democracies, I foresaw, for not one of those governments had the courage even to dispense with hypocrisy . . .[73]

The last clause reveals the propaganda behind poetry and ritual. The story was to be published by an American magazine for middle-class readers, mostly women of a certain age and powerful influence in politics. They were to be seduced to action by poetry. Such is the function of myth.

Let us come back to earth with some lines of poetry which, had they been vouchsafed a reading, might not have pleased the American ladies as much as Bates's pietistic wafflings. They were the work of a rank-and-file infantryman from Suffolk who deserted during the battle of Brunete. Describing himself ironically as 'one who advanced too far', Fred Jasper composed a poem, probably intended for the 'wall newspaper' established later that year in rest billets at Ambite. The last verse reads:

> They'll never forget to this day
> How the Englishmen cleared the way
> And comrade after all it was necessary.
> For with bullets flying around
> And plenty of shit on the ground
> The Fascists I wouldn't stop to bury.

It seems unlikely that Jasper's special 'litany of death' ever saw the light of a Spanish day.[74]

~ 7 ~

Between the Bullet and the Sonnet:
Poetry and Propaganda in the Trenches

1

In the days before Christmas 1937, the British Battalion was once again preparing for battle. The 35th Division of the Popular Army, of which it formed part, had been moved into position north of the Nationalist salient around Teruel. Situated high in the eastern sierras of central Spain, the city of Teruel had been held by the Nationalists since the start of the war. It represented a constant threat, in effect the nearest enemy outpost to the Mediterranean coast, thus a spearhead which potentially could cut the Republican zone in two. In one of the best-planned operations of the war, at a moment when it was least to be expected, the Republic launched a huge offensive to sever the salient. The main thrust against Teruel by the purely Spanish elements of the Army of the East was already under way.[1]

For much of its climb into the upland regions, the battalion had been obliged to march across country. Morale was poor, and it was beginning to snow.[2] In a bid to boost confidence General Walter, C.-in-C. of the 35th Division, decided to celebrate the first anniversary of the XV Brigade with a party to which all serving veterans of the original corps were invited. The occasion was to be dedicated to the memory of Ralph Fox, 'the eminent English writer and political commissar of the English Company who was one of the first to fall'.[3] Fox, killed at Lopera a year earlier, was a Marxist literary critic, a product of Oxford University and the Lenin School in Moscow. Most of the battle-weary soldiers who attended Walter's party knew little and cared less about him, his writings, or the 'literature' which formed the subject of his criticism – despite the title of his last work, *The Novel and the People*.[4] But other writers present, and we writers who dwell on the meaning of the Spanish Civil War, care very much: and this is what makes history.

After the sustained campaigns of late summer and early autumn

1937 on the Zaragoza front, unwounded survivors of the battalion had enjoyed a lengthy rest period behind the lines in the pleasant surroundings of the upper Tajuña valley. This was a welcome respite; but the mood in the ranks was sullen, and a matter of concern to the leadership. Heavy casualties and a further spate of desertions during the battles of Quinto, Belchite and Fuentes de Ebro had reduced the battalion's numbers, whereas since the holocaust of Brunete, recruitment from home had slowed to a trickle. As yet another campaign loomed, and despite the return of several dozen men from convalescent homes on the Costa Brava – along with deserters from penal camps in less pleasant surroundings – Britons in the 57th Battalion mustered less than the formal strength of two companies. Indeed, at this point, it was 'British' only in name, for Spanish volunteer members already substantially outnumbered them.[5] The commissariat was anxious to improve collective confidence: as well as a heightened regime of 'political work', as indoctrination of the ranks was euphemistically called, much time was devoted to 'culture'. For the Brits, this involved attempts at 'guided reading', lectures and other live entertainment, including the visit of an English corps de ballet! Miles Tomalin, musician and poet, 'cultural responsible' of the British anti-tank unit, set up a 'house of culture' in the village of Mondéjar where he edited and produced a wall newspaper ingeniously called *Assault and Battery News*, successfully encouraging contributions from comrades.[6] For the Spanish companies, the basic diet was literacy courses, provided by teachers seconded from the Milicias de Cultura section of the War Commissariat in Madrid.[7] On the eve of its departure for the Teruel front, sentries posted on the approaches to Brigade HQ in nearby Ambite were issued with the password for the night:

> Challenge: Two friends . . .?
> Response: The rifle and the book![8]

2

These sentiments summed up the conceptual message of the commissars' political and cultural work; indeed, they perfectly illustrate that these objectives were two sides of the same coin. The problem was that books (as such) were often awkward companions. True, a book might stop a bullet in an emergency, in striking fulfilment of the allegorical power of the escutcheon of learning ('dominus illuminatio mea'), but as a species they were difficult to cart around in numbers. The Welsh volunteer, Edwin Greening, made what might be called the 'penultimate' sacrifice, and gave up smoking in order to use his tobacco ration as payment to comrades who were prepared to help hump a veritable library around Spain.[9] As Margot Heinemann later pointed out, a more practical medium of composition, instruction and general delight was poetry. Poems, unless of the epic-Miltonic variety, could be distributed and carried around in quantity, and on relatively few sheets of paper. 'Try carrying the manuscript of your novel around in your pack', as Heinemann graphically put it.[10] As this implies, our concern here is not so much for Golden Treasuries as for Common Pursuits; not about established anthologies but rather about new poetry, composed there and then, in billets, on the march, in the trenches, even (it has been claimed) scribbled down in the midst of battle itself.

Jack Roberts, author of 'The Fascist Sortie', had never written much more than a letter home to Abertridwr until he found himself thrown into battle at Brunete. A few days after the fight at Villanueva de la Cañada, scared and helpless under the hail of enemy metal at Mosquito Ridge, he scribbled a couple of quatrains which more than any other text encapsulated the horror of battle and the suffering of the International Brigades in the Spanish Civil War.

> Eyes of men running, falling, screaming
> Eyes of men shouting, sweating, bleeding
> The eyes of the fearful, those of the sad
> The eyes of exhaustion, and those of the mad.
>
> Eyes of men thinking, hoping, waiting
> Eyes of men loving, cursing, hating
> The eyes of the wounded sodden in red
> The eyes of the dying, and those of the dead.[11]

Unfortunately, this was not the kind of poetry which would have been regarded as making a contribution to the struggle. Dramatic, demotic, vigorous, spontaneous – all these desiderata were surely met, but the poem did not satisfy the crucial criterion laid down by

Miguel Hernández, commissar, working-class poet of the Republic: 'All theatre, all poetry and all art, has to be today, more than ever, a weapon of war.'[12] This was the locally specific version of the official 'Socialist Realism' of Soviet art. Jack Roberts, good party man and later battalion commissar, may not have known about 'socialist realism', but he knew well enough that his poem did not meet Hernández's prescription. He did not offer it for publication in *Volunteer for Liberty*, the Brigade magazine, or (apparently) even show it to anyone until he went home again to Wales.[13]

Poetry's character as the ideal medium of cogent message – epithet, image, pithy expression of feeling – marked it out for attention among the commissars. Their angle was, of course, that of propaganda and morale. Poetry was a particularly useful medium in this respect: mostly short and to the point, it came in user-friendly packets ideal for distribution and quotation. But there was more to it than this. Spain's most distinguished living poet, the pro-Republican Antonio Machado, dedicated a sonnet to the Communist warrior Enrique Líster, with the controversial conceit 'that my words might have the same value as your pistol'.[14] Machado's wish was granted a thousandfold. Sonnets were sentinels at the front; like the individual soldier on guard on his firestep in the freezing sierra, each anti-Fascist poem was the result of experience, commitment and suffering. Above all, it was widely believed that a poem, like a photograph, and – it was dawning upon many in these years – unlike a political pamphlet or a newspaper, could not lie. Poetry could thus all the more usefully incorporate the slogans of political dogma, frequently transferred from medium to medium via the cognate tissue of oral rendition. Nothing was better suited to the transmission and ingestion of key phrases, elevating nostrums, above all providing a supply of easy mottoes to shout in vilification at the enemy or in reassurance to each other, on the march or moving into battle. In principle, these could be as useful as an extra ammo pouch, as essential as a canteen of water.

Moreover, it was understood by many authoritative/didactic sources in this decade that poetry could be written by anyone.[15] So earnestly was this nostrum disseminated during the Spanish Civil War that the results demand to be physically weighed rather than aesthetically measured. The critic Serge Salaün waxes lyrical about 'la vena poética popular', 'la ola de expresión poética popular' and 'la irrupción de la poesía popular', all in a single paragraph. He attributes this phenomenon mainly to the 500 or more periodical publications of the Republican armed forces which appeared in the months after the outbreak of war.[16] Similarly, the conviction that poetry was not the elite creative preserve of the public-school element was fundamental to the poetic effort of the Brigades. Thus poetry proliferated in the English-speaking battalions.[17] Original verse written by its members still reposes among their records in New York, Moscow, Salamanca, London and elsewhere.[18] Much of it remains unpublished, despite the many collections of such material which have appeared in print over the years. In a strange way these sonnets and stanzas, doggerel and masterpiece alike, reflect the fate of the half-buried shards of metal – guns, ammunition belts, cartridges and food-cans – tons of which lie rusting away on battlefields all over Spain.[19]

The poetical simile I employ here was ubiquitous at the time. Poems were projected into the consciousness of warriors and observers alike as if they were bullets.[20] The propaganda trope was complex and many-sided. Whilst the enemy was armed to the teeth by 'International Fascism', the Popular Army – it was perennially claimed – was kept short of weapons and equipment by the pusillanimous attitude of the democracies (that is non-intervention). But whilst the Fascists had modern weaponry and ruthlessness on their side, the Republic had poems and poetry.[21] It followed that they represented 'humanity', the other side something less than human. When Spender and Lehmann asserted in the introduction to their celebrated collection of *Poems for Spain* that 'the fact that these poems should have been written at all has a literary significance parallel to the existence of the International Brigade', they were merely reiterating a notion which constituted a trope of Republican propaganda[22]

The Republic's wartime cultural mission had a wide remit, but for propaganda purposes it soon became notably concentrated on poetry and poets. Poetry was characterized as a weapon of war and its production was treated almost as a war industry. The statistical discourse of the Soviet Five Year Plans dominated propaganda material during 1937; and, as we have seen, this extended ubiquitously into the fields of education and culture. In the case of poetry, Serge Salaün, writing in the same discourse 'sobre la producción poética durante la guerra' forty years on, arrived at the veritably Stakhanovite figures of 15,000 to 20,000 published compositions, by 5,000 different authors, three-quarters of which originated in the Republican zone.[23] Rafael Alberti and Miguel Hernández were among the approved 'warrior poets'. Their verses were mass-reproduced and distributed among the men of the Popular Army. They toured the fronts, reciting aloud to the troops these blood-soaked epics, these endless litanies of suffering, struggle and vengeance. Their work was often modelled on that of Soviets like Mayakovsky, supreme bard of the Bolshevik Revolution. Alberti was photographed for the world's press in the act of hectoring an audience of new recruits, a congregation which overflowed the parade ground, men leaning from windows and crowding riskily on roofs in order to hang on his every word.[24]

Versified harangues by Alberti, Manuel Altolaguirre and others made their way into the pages of the XV Brigade 'house' magazine, *Volunteer for Liberty*. Whenever he visited the trenches, *Daily Worker* reporter Claud Cockburn (aka 'Frank Pitcairn') rarely failed to draw his readers' attention to the soldier-poets who inspired resistance. In a visionary moment 'among the German bombs' in Andalusia – for example – he 'saw a young communist poet, with books under one arm and a bag of bullets under the other, distributing books and pamphlets to men hungry for knowledge, who read them aloud to one another between the shell fire and the air raids'.[25] Many others who came to offer practical help, bringing vehicles for use as ambulances or medically related supplies (and often staying to work in the medical services) were moved to record the emotions stirred in them by instances of the poetic veracity of 'Spain'. In spring 1937 a British woman who had joined a supply mission organized by one of the 'Spanish Aid' committees visited the International Brigade hospital in Murcia.

> An American boy told me that his father had given him money to study at the Sorbonne and still thought that he was there. 'It's an odd thing', he told me when I asked him if he wanted any books. 'The only thing that you can read at the front is poetry . . . Give me poetry – other stuff is not worthwhile.'[26]

Such feelings, though expressed with sincere directness by the fighters themselves, were actually fostered by the staff intellectuals of the International Brigades. The British writer Ralph Bates, resident in Spain since the late 1920s, had attracted some attention with novels set in pre-war Catalonia. In 1936, he joined the War

Commissariat and was appointed to the XV Brigade as a cultural commissar. In the first half of 1937, he instituted a regular series of literary lectures and pep talks delivered to the boys at the front. With the military struggle nearing its end in 1939, Bates wrote an article for an American magazine in which he apostrophized 'Spain' as 'being in itself a creative source', a sort of mother or mistress of poetry. He recalled (for his middle-class, mostly female, readers) various moments of anti-Fascist communion,

> like a co-operation of the willing and loving mind in the work of the senses. In those moments perception put me in new touch with a world that was lovely, and itself pure. It is hard to describe this sensation but it is the origin of much poetry. I think now, as I thought then, of Thomas Traherne...[27]

3

This atmosphere – both real experience and pretentious nonsense – was to give rise to perhaps the greatest forcing-house of poetry ever known, a veritable dynamo of creative writing. But before going into production, the infrastructure had to be carefully assembled.[28] In February 1937, while the battle of Jarama raged, the Madrid War Commissariat headed by Luigi Longo discussed proposals for improving and centralizing the internal propaganda organization of the Brigades. A weekly magazine would be created, with editorial offices in Madrid, which would also rationalize and supervise the issue of 'local' news-sheets which had heretofore been promiscuously distributed at brigade (and even company) level. Accordingly, once serious action on the Jarama front had ceased, the XV Brigade settled down to adapt its own publicity. Forward planning would begin for a 'Book of Combat of the XV Brigade' in order record its battlefield exploits for posterity.[29] In May, a meeting of XV Brigade commissars at Morata de Tajuña agreed to set up 'cultural committees' at company level, and to provide funds for the purchase of books and musical instruments.[30] George Aitken, Brigade commissar, who chaired the meeting, was under pressure from his junior colleagues and subject to severe criticism from more senior sources in the War Commissariat on the question of poor morale, over which the British Battalion was singled out.[31] For both, the main objective of 'cultural work' was to alleviate the boredom and cynicism, along with the mounting indiscipline, that three months in the front-line trenches inevitably generated. If, perhaps, there were men at Brigade HQ who appreciated the aesthetic properties, as well as the propaganda potential, in 'culture', all were agreed that it was a necessary antidote to drinking and gambling, and the violent in-fighting which went with them.[32]

The response on the ground was immediate. The nineteen-year-old Cardiff volunteer, Sid Hamm, soon found himself appointed as 'cultural responsible' to new British recruits in their training centre at Madrigueras. In the few weeks left to him before his death at Villanueva de la Cañada, Hamm immersed himself in a sustained programme of cultural activity, helping to organize concerts, reading avidly and writing articles for the weekly flysheet. He came under the influence of Battalion intellectuals like Tomalin, Hugh Slater and fellow-Cardiffian Alec Cummings, who commanded his company.[33] With the help of Hamm and others, Tomalin soon discovered 'the talent to be found among the comrades in the line' and a scratch orchestra of mandolin, guitar, violin, flute, mouth organ and accordion was envisaged.[34] But Tomalin was also a prolific poet, and his influence, combined with that of Bates, began to tease out the poetasting instincts of the rank and file. Naturally, this began with hand-me-down verse, usually destined for the 'wall newspaper', in which an array of gripes about material conditions and moans about regulations was wrapped up in mildly sardonic diversions.

> When the going is rough
>   And the firing is tough,
> And life's end seems quite near,
> There is always some time,
>   On the firing line
> To be of comradely cheer.
>
> When the beans are cold,
>   And the bread is old –
> The coffee has a dung-like taste,
> Just remember the cause
>   You're defending and pause,
> Even beefing till you're blue in the face.[35]

By September 1937, members of the XV Brigade were being 'urged to send original poems, in English, to the *Volunteer for Liberty*, both for use in the magazine and for publication in an anthology of verse by English-speaking comrades'.[36] By this new stage, greater ambition was on display; more serious efforts, often elegizing dead comrades, offering up loss and suffering to the idea of the coming utopia, or to the prospect of future vengeance. Such proved the preferred content of poems accepted for publication in the *Volunteer for Liberty*.

> He will not see the people that shall rise
> In the new-born world for which he gave his life;
> Yet o'er his grave, a sound that never dies –
> A happier, joyous sound unmarred by strife.[37]

The author of these lines, Bill Harrington, with a lower-middle-class background in Surrey, became a regular contributor to IB publications. Arriving in Spain early in 1937, he fought through all the great battles of the war, finally being wounded in the assault on Hill 481 near Gandesa during the Ebro offensive (July 1938). Probably because he resisted the call of the Party, he was not promoted beyond sergeant, yet was the only poet from the ranks to be allocated a whole page in *Volunteer for Liberty* (on which three examples of his work appeared).[38] All the more remarkable was that, on the whole, at least, his verse failed to speak in approved slogans or commissarly clichés. Despite this, Harrington's verse was irresistible to commissar-editors like Alonzo Elliott and John Tisa, because it fulfilled a deeper political purpose. It met the requirements of the Comintern Academy for a populist style which was aesthetically pleasing, mellifluous but transparent, communicating strong emotions in simple phrases.[39]

Volunteers sometimes enclosed their poems in letters home, though only those which measured up politically were allowed through by the censors in Albacete.[40] Few other poems offered for publication in Spain by working-class writers failed to resort to the catchphrases of anti-Fascist rant – routine challenges, threats or insults offered to Franco, Hitler and Mussolini; imprecations hurled at Junker bombers or Fiat tanks; and (less colourful) condemnations of the non-intervention statesmen at home.[41]

4

Of course, all these targets were also getting it in the neck, and in similar packages, from the home-based brigade of poets like Jack Lindsay, Edgell Rickword and Randall Swingler. The primary task of this school was to stir the conscience of the nation on behalf of 'Spain', and (as a concomitant) to stimulate recruitment for the British Battalion. In August 1937, following Brunete, the CPGB realized that a whole generation of its leadership was wasting in the Spanish trenches, yet the need for replacements of the wounded, dead and deserted was pressing. For an extended period in 1937–8 the net was cast wider and less cautiously than ever, and the public-school poets were generous in handing out their specially potent version of white feathers.

> You who lean at the corner saying, 'We have done our best',
> You who shrug your shoulders and you who smile
> . . .
> To you we speak, you numberless Englishmen,
> To remind you of the greatness still among you
> Created by those men who go from your towns
> To fight for peace, for liberty, and for you.[42]

The poet John Lehmann spent much of 1936/7 in Vienna, where he helped organize 'a kind of underground railway . . . to get would-be volunteers for the International Brigade out of the country to the west'. Back in London, he 'could not help feeling the pull of Spain more and more', but the work of editing *New Writing* 'made me feel that, even at long range, I had some small if not very glorious part to play in the movement'.[43]

This role was even at the time perceived by some as not only 'not very glorious' but positively pernicious. As Cyril Connolly argued, 'a burst of felicitous militancy with the pen may send three young men to be killed in Spain; for whose deaths the author is responsible.'[44]

The issue of 'responsibility' was already a sensitive one, above all for Auden and Spender. The former's ode SPAIN was a seductive enticement to the struggle, and moreover (in my view) encapsulated the propaganda case of the Republic as faithfully as anything written by Party hacks. But his friend Connolly's warning must have seemed to many in the Party an act of Trotsky-Fascist treason, in view of the frontal attack on the left poets by the pro-Franco writer, Roy Campbell. As part of a battle of the rhyming couplets joined in the printing-basements of literary London, Campbell lambasted his enemies as middle-class cowards who recruited the workers as their vicarious hero-substitutes. In Spain, wrote Campbell, the bodies of gullible fools are piled high

> To make a huge *paella* of the plains
> A dish of rice, with corpses for the grains,
> Whom safe intriguing pedants sent to die
> And sell their scrawny mutton for a lie.[45]

Campbell's gullible fools were, however, officially his enemy's glorious and knowing martyrs. The status of martyrdom in Spain was further sanctified by the sanction of art. Great as it was to die defending the people against Fascism, to die as a poet of the people was vastly greater, for it guaranteed posthumous promotion to the 'artistocracy', the immortality of the muses, a place in the 'history' of the revolution.[46] As early as the spring of 1937, Spender, on returning from the Madrid trenches, cautioned the party against the cult of martyrdom:

> People try to escape from a realization of the violence to which abstract ideas and high ideals have led them by saying either that individuals do not matter or else that the dead are heroes . . . But to say that those who happen to be killed are heroes is a wicked attempt to identify the dead with the abstract ideas which have brought them to the front, thus adding prestige to those ideas, which are used to lead the living on to similar 'heroic' deaths.[47]

As it happened this May Day call for retreat or at least retrenchment appeared just before Auden's SPAIN, where the resolution to accept guilt by association in 'necessary murder' for the cause was coupled with profound tribute to the individual heroism of the International Brigades. Furthermore, before the war had ended, Spender himself apparently renounced his previous error by greeting a memorial volume to John Cornford with a clear recognition of the young poet's exemplary heroic status.[48] Later still, in 1950, Spender made a new and generalized characterization of the deaths of writers in Spain as a 'martyrdom', but, this time, not reckoning it as a sacrifice on behalf of any party or ideology. Rather, it was 'perhaps the greatest contribution made by creative writers in this decade to the spiritual life of Europe'.[49]

Spender's first act of equivocation was born out of his concern for the fate of Tony Hyndman, who at the time was immured in his cell in Albacete, writing his anti-heroic poem 'Jarama Front'.[50] Cecil Day Lewis, the first poet to beat the tocsin for 'Spain' – only a fortnight into the war – had also announced in 1935 that 'the stage is set for the entry of the proletarian poet'.[51] In their capacity as editors of socially prestigious left-wing poetry magazines, Rickword and Lehmann deliberately set out to sponsor working-class contributions, a policy culminating in the Spender–Lehmann *Poems for Spain* in 1939.[52] The first poem contributed by an International Brigade worker-writer to a London magazine appeared in the Communist-run *Poetry for the People* in September 1938, as the survivors of the British Battalion were fighting their last rearguard action in the Sierra Pandols.[53] In *Poems for Spain*, contributions appeared by British Battalion veterans who were not derived from normal 'literary' backgrounds (Hyndman, John Lepper and Dave Marshall) alongside others from the home front like Albert Brown, as well as the Spanish peasant-poet, Hernández. But this was still a meagre, even token, representation, hardly marking 'the entry of the proletarian poet' on the stage of 'English Literature'.[54]

5

Indeed if the poetic proles ever entered the stage at all, this event took place not in a metaphorical context but (if the neologism is permitted) in a phorical one – that is, the theatre. By the mid-thirties, no fewer than three left-inclined drama companies were flourishing in London. Auden and Isherwood wrote their plays for the Group Theatre, run by Rupert Doone, an abrasively gay and – nomenclature notwithstanding – working-class 'character'. Left Theatre was a touring group in which professionals worked for nothing or a token remuneration, and which struggled to forge links with the trade unions and the Co-operative Movement.[55] More openly committed to 'Spain' was Unity Theatre, a Communist-sponsored collective centred in St Pancras, which specialized in pedagogical-ideological drama derived from German exemplars like Ernst Toller and Bertolt Brecht.[56] In this community, ticket sellers, doorkeepers and scene-shifters were encouraged to contribute to the scripts as well as to the acting. In such circumstances, Ted Willis and other aspirant writers, working-class or lower-middle-class members of the Young Communist League, underwent a comprehensive apprenticeship in the business of theatre. Intense political activity and work for the 'Aid Spain' movement was built into this process quite naturally for many. In 1937, Jack Lindsay's *On Guard For Spain*, a species of choral poem written for declaimer soloist (with stentorian faculties or, if available, loud-hailer) and a mass of reciters was adapted to Unity's stage and soon became its staple production. Meanwhile, it was claimed that 200 branches of a new drama-orientated section of the Left Book Club had been set up.[57]

In May 1938, Ben Glaser, a Unity Theatre stalwart was with the British Battalion in their billets in the Catalan countryside. At more than three months, this rest period was the longest continuous spell that the unit ever spent out of the line. It followed the profoundly demoralizing blow dealt to the Brigades (along with the rest of the Popular Army) by their prolonged and humiliating rout in Aragon, during the Francoist offensive earlier that year. Rebuilding the military capability of the Republican armed forces represented the most formidable task the War Commissariat had faced. *Inter alia*, it called for the devising and management of a sustained programme of sporting, entertainment and cultural activities. Glaser wrote home to a friend:

> Is it possible for the [Unity Theatre] Club to send out scripts of plays that we could perform here with all 'Male Casts'[?] The Brigade is going to organise a dramatic group, which I may have to be responsible for, that is if I get released from my military duties . . . If you could get the powers that be at Unity to act on this . . . you will have the eternal blessing of all the Political Commissars of the Brigade.[58]

Another keen helper in this field – and even more anxious to escape the military side of things – was the Irish volunteer Tom O'Brien. Brought up in the tenements of dockland Dublin, O'Brien joined the Communist Party of Ireland and, ambitious to be a writer, plunged into the cultural milieu it supported. His poems soon appeared (alongside those of the teenage Brendan Behan) in the Party press, and he helped set up the New Theatre Group, working ceaselessly in the cause of 'Spain'. In April 1938, he finally succumbed to mounting moral pressure to volunteer for the

Internationals. Shortly after the Brigade finally went back into action in the celebrated Ebro offensive at the end of July, O'Brien was (apparently) wounded, and spent the rest of the campaign in hospitals and other stations behind the lines. Back in Dublin after repatriation, he got down to writing a one-act play set during the Ebro battle, with the appropriate title *The Last Hill*. Produced by the Theatre Group in September 1939, it was a purely propaganda piece, composed – in the best traditions of the British Battalion – wholly in verse of the Jack Lindsay stamp.[59] O'Brien had achieved his ambition as warrior, poet and dramatist. It will probably never be known whether such was the destiny of the anonymous Battalion cook whom the reporter Philip Jordan met during the Teruel campaign. He 'came from Bradford, he liked cooking but he wanted more than anything else to be a playwright. One day when the war was over he was going to write a knock-out and be another Mr Priestley.'[60]

6

As we have seen, the intellectual leadership of the left generally, and of the International Brigades in particular, was in these years intent on its mission of building cultural bridges with the industrial proletariat. What was later to be known to Party hacks and cultural critics as 'socialist realism', a praxis of theoretical principles adumbrated by Gorky and crudely enunciated by Radek in 1934, was achieving recognition as the way forward. Abe Osheroff, woodworker later turned part-time university teacher, claims that he and fellow-recruits to the 58th and 60th Battalions responded more readily to the proletarian poetry of the Depression than to anything written by established 'Ivy League' poets, however leftish their sentiments.[61] In Britain, the poetry critic Geoffrey Grigson called in 1938 for a demotic-domestic type of verse in which writers used 'the language in which one is angry about Spain or pleasant or unpleasant to one's wife'.[62] Cyril Connolly went so far as to suggest a double initiative: parallel induction of the working class into 'culture' and a complementary movement of the language of 'culture' towards the working class:

it is necessary for literature to approach its future custodians in a language they will understand . . . as the time for making him [the proletarian] our master grows nearer, so his education becomes more necessary since on it will depend the cultural values which he will choose to preserve.⁶³

The International Brigade commissariat concurred fully with such views. One of Ralph Bates's short stories (which are set on various battle fronts where the Brigades fought during 1937) is built around a Spanish volunteer to the XV Brigade, a peasant soldier of irreverent native wit who cannot resist subverting petty regulations. But 'Pablo' also proves to be the keenest member of the literacy classes, and after a few weeks of study he produces a beautiful ballad. 'There were defects in its meter and rhyming schemes; but [it was] as good as anything in the romancero . . . In it was the sonority and weight of the authentic folk-poem.' Shortly afterwards, Pablo is wounded by a sniper whilst helping local farmers to bring in the olive crop. The narrator/author rushes to his side, and kisses him before the medics carry him to safety.⁶⁴ Likewise, during his speech to the Congress of Anti-Fascist Writers in Madrid (July 1937), Spender paid tribute to Fox, Caudwell and Cornford, but also recognized the work of the 'hundreds of unknown writers who are members of the International Brigade', and among his Spanish colleagues singled out for praise the 'shepherd poet', Miguel Hernández.⁶⁵

As these examples illustrate, logical contortion abounded in the perceived cultural relationship between the elite and the hoi polloi, the suitor and the desired object. The teaching *illuminati* had somehow to abnegate their essential hieratic quality in the act of passing it on to the class which 'History' had selected. Yet always and inevitably 'there were defects in meter and rhyming' which the didactic classes found it impossible to ignore. In the editorial rooms of *New Writing* and *Left Review*, time expended in searching out material by proletarian poets was (apparently) further extended in 'sub-editing' the results for publication.⁶⁶ Frank Kermode's treatment of the phenomenon, though mainly in the context of abstract aesthetics, also illustrates how it could be a delicate and immensely controversial problem in practice. Under the peacetime Republic (1932–3) left-intellectuals in Madrid published a series of short stories ostensibly by 'proletarian' writers on the theme of revolution

– a series which included a contribution by Franco's politically radical brother Ramón!⁶⁷ Spender and Lehmann hinted at such difficulties in selecting *Poems For Spain:* 'We do not claim that these are the best poems . . . but we do claim that any anthology selected purely for merit would be bound to overlap.'⁶⁸ This problem existed even in the War Commissariat's offices at Madrid's Calle Velázquez (where *Volunteer for Liberty* was put together), so that despite occasional appearances by Bill Harrington and some others of his ilk, poems by accomplished Oxbridge executants like Tomalin and Wintringham still predominated in the published pages of the magazine.

Since tensions of this kind, between ideal and actual states, were to do with inherent assumptions about order and agency, they were intimately related to tensions over fundamental matters of discipline. Nearly all extended accounts of life in the Brigades make some mention of the prolonged struggle over the insistence on saluting superior officers, which became the controversial core of a systematic attempt to tighten up military discipline throughout the Popular Army after its functional breakdown at Brunete in July 1937.⁶⁹ One of those suspected by the commissariat of nurturing rank-and-file resistance to the new regulations was the Battalion commander, Fred Copeman, formerly a mutinous naval rating and bolshie building worker of formidable physical presence. In the early days of the Battalion, the fact that it was commanded almost entirely by ex British army officers, with matching accessories in terms of accents and attitudes, caused much disquiet among men who believed they had volunteered for a democratic-egalitarian fighting force.⁷⁰

Copeman had attained officer rank after showing great initative during the Battalion's first action at Jarama. His accelerated promotion in subsequent weeks – as in the case of his immediate predecessor, Jock Cunningham – was a concession to opinion within the ranks, but also obeyed the official wisdom that working men who had led comrades and inspired victory in industrial disputes could do likewise in war. Copeman's method of tackling drunkenness and bullying was effective, and he came to be appreciated by many. Despite his consciously paraded reputation as a bruiser, Copeman had deeper qualities, and Tony Hyndman, for example, remembered him as 'a soldier and poet with infinite compassion. He was the man we needed.'⁷¹ Whether or not

Copeman's mighty brow deserved the laurels of Hyndman's muse, his actions exposed the fact that the cultural policies developed with the battalion were not only largely ineffective, but arguably counter-productive. Many others agreed with Hyndman that Copeman was 'the man we needed', if only because he shared and represented their feelings about the public-school element. For the kind of culture that sophisticated minds like Tomalin, Slater and Dunbar brought to the deserving deprived was not appreciated by the majority of designated recipients. Fred Thomas noted with regret that 'by some of our more aggressive proles [artists and intellectuals] were regarded with suspicion'. Some men reacted with ribald contempt to attempts to elevate their tastes in entertainment. The audience at the ballet performance mentioned at the outset of this chapter offended its sponsor, Captain Macolm Dunbar, with 'half-suppressed guffaws and derisory comments'.[72]

Some who resented being patronized were by no means 'aggressive proles'. Tony Gilbert, for example, recalled that

> we had artists and intellectuals and not everything they said was to our liking. Some of it we didn't understand a bit, too confusing, some of the Marxist phrases, philosophy. Many East End youngsters were not accustomed to this... I knew Caudwell for a time [and] Clive Branson. To me they were completely unintelligible.[73]

Even the Cambridge graduate Tony McLean found men like Slater and Dunbar 'extremely arrogant'. 'There was some resentment among the working-class types', McLean added, who felt they had not 'come all the way to Spain to be pushed around' by public-school products.[74] Ironically, a cadre report on McLean himself objected – despite the fact that he had experience of teaching adult comrades at home – that he 'seems slightly contemptuous of the potentialities of the average "uncultural" worker, to the point of irritation'.[75] According to one historian of the British Battalion, heated feelings over this situation became so divisive as to threaten its comradely cohesion. It was Copeman who heretically opposed the theoretical nostrums of the commissariat by deliberately segregating the public-school element from the proletarians. As preparations began for what was to be the Brunete offensive, the war ministry decided that anti-tank batteries, making use of a new Soviet gun being provided in quantity, would be set up as auxiliary units at battalion level. Hopkins suggests that Copeman seized the opportunity offered to fill the British battery with public-school intellectuals and their most loyal working-class acolytes. This has been called a kind of 'apartheid', but is perhaps better interpreted in the present context as a remarkable instance of inverse snobbery, by which many commissars were surely confounded.[76]

Subsequently, Copeman led his men at Brunete with much display of heroic example but a notable absence of tactical skills and presence of mind. The disastrous effects of the battle and the defeat on the Battalion – singled out by the Albacete authorities for its total collapse of morale – led to Copeman and other leaders being summoned to Britain for investigation.[77] Though details of this process are unknown, whatever responsibility the CPGB assigned to Copeman, he was soon restored as the Battalion's commanding officer, a fact which may be regarded as illustrating the persistence of the problem discussed here.[78] Some taste of its complex flavour can be gleaned from some Battalion records captured by the Nationalist army during their breakthrough on the Aragon front in March–April 1938. Among these were examples of the incoming personal correspondence of Brigaders. Apart from family news, the main subject of these letters was sport, almost exclusively the working-class preoccupations of soccer and boxing, with local political gossip coming a poor third. 'Bourgeois culture' is simply not on the agenda. Yet paradoxically, one of the men whose home letters have survived was the Glasgow volunteer Hugh Sloan, whom Copeman had 'segregated' in the anti-tank unit, and who (like several other members) subsequently developed an interest in literature and poetry.[79]

7

Whether to be seen as weapons of war or as aids to morale, and irrespective of the extent to which they achieved the aims envisaged, in 'the most political army in history' the reading and writing of poems were political acts. Likewise, there was no distinction, at least in the minds of the commissariat, between instruction and propaganda. However, the International Brigades drew for their volunteers on largely literate cultures: with certain exceptions (Cuba, rural Poland, Ukrainian immigrants from Canada) overwhelmingly the nuclei of recruitment were urban populations from

Europe and North America. This was not always reliably the case with the Spanish battalions these men fought alongside, and which by the second winter of the war already outnumbered them.[80] As things stood, in these ranks, as in those of the (increasingly conscripted) Ejército Popular as a whole, the written word was not a reliable medium of instruction and propaganda. The problem was that alternative methods such as drama productions, film shows, concerts and poster exhibitions were expensive as well as time-consuming and labour-intensive. This helps to explain the Republic's astonishingly rapid, and (if its own publicity is to be credited) saturation-scale implementation of educational policies throughout the armed forces. The sooner the armed *analfabetos* of rural Spain were taught to read and write, the sooner they would become politically malleable and socially controllable.

From late 1936 onwards, large numbers of refugees from enemy-occupied Aragon, Andalusia and Extremadura, along with existing militia units of Catalonia and central Spain, were incorporated into the Popular Army. Education and culture were placed alongside military instruction in the barracks, especially in Madrid. Indeed, one group of cultural militiamen formed a drama company (Nosotros) which transposed training manuals into staged cameos of battle action. This proved so successful that 'improvised playwrights' were pressed into service 'as commissars and others turned their hands to dramatic composition as a means of inculcating ideas or demonstrating appropriate military practice'.[81] As in most other areas of innovation and improvement, the Fifth Regiment, originally its militia forces, later the PCE's huge umbrella organization for recruitment and training, was the cynosure of imitation.[82]

The only militia unit which survived the constant army reforms of 1936–7 (at least in name) was the Milicias de Cultura, in which several thousand university teachers, students, and recent graduates found an outlet for their ideals and their talents.[83] Antonio Candela was a peasant lad from Extremadura, conscripted by the Fifth Regiment after fleeing to Madrid among the human wave of refugees that Franco's advance pushed towards the capital in the summer of 1936. At the start of the war he had been in Badajoz as a stage-hand in one of the travelling theatres sponsored by the government; many years later he recalled with pride the work of education which went on in the Republican ranks:

One of the teachers assigned to my battalion told us how he had found a great enthusiasm amongst the soldiers for learning to read and write. One of his comrades lost his hand in battle soon after writing his first letter to his mother. The first thing he asked for when he regained consciousness in hospital was to be taught how he could learn to write with his left hand, so that he could write his second letter to his mother. It was officially announced that in the first year of the Civil War, not less than seventy-two thousand Republican soldiers had learned to read and write.[84]

The future West German chancellor, Willi Brandt, then a student observer in Spain, was also deeply impressed. He perceived a 'cultural revolution' which reached outwards from the trenches, since from local villages, 'peasants in the neighbourhood frequently come too, and take part in the discussions'. Meanwhile, behind the lines in Madrid,

> the Alerta Schools were set up. Theirs was the task of implementing the cultural, athletic and pre-military education of the fourteen to twenty-one age group . . . The Alerta movement was organised by the youth front . . . As early as the first part of summer 1937 there were 60 schools in Madrid with 10,000 pupils and 500 teachers. By the end of 1937 the number of pupils had risen to 40,000. During the terrible bombing raids on the Spanish capital, children are to be seen going round in stretcher parties. They are members of the medical battalion of the Alerta . . .[85]

In contemporary London, the *Bulletin* of the Artists' International Association also obligingly reproduced Valencia's production statistics: in only one month 13,142 soldiers had been taught to read and write; in one brigade, over 40 per cent illiteracy had been reduced to 5 per cent since the *milicianos* began work in January; meanwhile 800 new schools had been established and 150,000 copies of the 'Anti-Fascist school book' were distributed.[86] This last figure is, of course, the key to the whole project. Captain Smith-Piggot was sent to Spain by the British government to investigate Republican complaints about air raids on civilian targets. In Valencia he

> asked a Commissar of the Tank Corps what were his duties. Was it a fact that, according to the Duchess of Atholl, a large part of his time was spent in teaching the troops how to read and write. He laughed quite a long time over this and told me his main duty was propaganda to keep up the morale of the troops. He handed me a small brochure of songs he

had written for the men to sing – they were straightforward undisguised communism...[87]

Because of rather than despite these priorities, the task was addressed with fanatical earnestness. In the Spanish companies of the International Brigades, no sooner were the men withdrawn from the front, often with the sound of battle still in their ears, than they were subjected to compulsory classes. Having taken yet another battering during its outstanding contribution to the defence of Teruel, the XV Brigade was pulled out of the line at the end of February 1938. It proved a short-lived respite. The desperate military emergency now facing the Republic meant that depleted units, who were fighting in mountainous terrain often in sub-zero temperatures, had to return to action within a few days. Yet even during those precious, fearful and exhausted hours the commissars called 'a political meeting to arrange the resumption of our political and cultural work'.[88] A few weeks earlier the XV Brigade magazine had insisted that 'in loyal Spain today books are almost as important as bullets'.[89] In Ambite, during another rest period shortly before leaving for the Aragon front the previous summer, the Dimitrov Battalion reported that 'the work of struggling to throw out illiteracy from our ranks continues with great intensity, to which end our commissars never cease their pressure upon illiterate members'.[90] When the International Brigades were stood down from front-line action for the last time, Lincoln commissar John Gates immediately informed his superiors that 'literary classes have already been renewed'.[91] It was a tribute to the contribution of such efforts to Republican morale that the Nationalists identified cultural-propaganda work among their enemy as a serious obstacle to victory. They began a campaign of encouraging desertion which specifically targeted commissars.

> You know better than anyone that disaster is inevitable. When it arrives, when your leaders flee abroad, what will be your fate, you mere battalion or company commissars? You will be denounced and persecuted by your own victims, who will not forget your acts of violence. Act now! There is still time to save yourselves![92]

Some of the leading cultural commissars certainly did manage to save themselves by fleeing abroad. Rafael Alberti, poetic recruiting-sergeant-in-chief, was the best-known of such exiles, if only through his longevity.[93] From the earliest moments of the war, as

Party publicists in America put it, Alberti 'rises to address the exploited and oppressed, summoning them to arms, supporting them in their struggle for Soviet power'.[94] León Felipe, editor of the magazine *Hora de España* – whose young poets, President Azaña noted (not without a touch of his habitual sarcasm) were 'keeping alive the sacred fire' – had regularly urged Republican soldiers to die at the front. He proclaimed to potential widows and orphans that 'we will save ourselves through tears', but himself left for Mexico in 1938.[95] Miguel Hernández who encouraged the people to 'go at them face to face and die/with your face to the bullets' abandoned his wife and child and fled, but was arrested attempting to cross into Portugal, and subsequently died of tubercolosis in a Franco jail.[96] Not surprisingly, by 1938, following the rout of the Popular Army in Aragon, the Valencia press began to suggest that intellectuals, instead of making endless 'declarations' and 'manifestos' of support for the Republic, would be of more use volunteering for the front.[97]

8

When the travel writer Ted Walker visited Albacete in the mid-1980s, there was almost nothing left to betray the history of the anonymous and grimy garrison town which writers like Malraux and Louis Fischer, along with hundreds of less celebrated memorialists, described during their service with the International Brigades. Only one artefact had resisted oblivion. Although it could hardly have been more mundane or more modest, it seems nevertheless deeply symbolic. A local man pointed out to Walker

> a much-faded painted sign on the lower floor of a house that had been the Republicans' press headquarters in the Civil War. Since 1936 [*sic*], naturally, the sign had often been whitewashed over and some of the letters had chipped and flaked; but *SERVICIOS DE PRENSA REPUBLICANA BRIGADAS INTERNACIONALES* was still quite distinct.[98]

Despite the Republic's prolonged agony and utter defeat, despite the asphyxiation of its idealism and the decades of misery this meant for half the people of Spain, even despite the endless revelations of its Stalin-inspired crimes, the effort put into culture and propaganda was not wasted. This, more than anything which happened in any other dimension of the war, has fixed the tragic grandeur of the Republican cause in a sphere transcendentally above the normal processes of critical judgement. History – *pace* W. H. Auden – not only says 'alas' but also helps and pardons, with the infinite patience of the loving mother or the divinity, her son. As Auden himself was later (in effect) to claim, the spiritual tissue of this culture was composed not only of statistics, but also of more lies and more damned lies. But the International Brigade commissariat did not err in seeking to celebrate its intellectual heroes, whose biographies and obituaries constantly predominated over those of the less qualified in the pages of the *Volunteer for Liberty*.[99] Luigi Longo calculated well the potential benefits from the effort to set up its Historical Bureau, with the aim of providing the future with a scriptural story of dogmatic substance. As the bureau's director, Sandor Voros, put it: 'the popular antifascist movement will have to know the history of the International Brigades, so as to be furnished with the ideological weapons to carry on the struggle against Fascism.'[100]

These weapons are still to hand. Perhaps – though perhaps not – the post-literate culture of the third millennium will increasingly make them appear as museum pieces, pitchforks and blunderbusses of the romantic revolution. In any case, no international peacekeeping mission will ever seek to have them handed in and forged into ploughshares. At the beginning of the new century, under the centre-right government of Manuel Aznar and the Alianza Popular, Spain's longest-running industrial dispute entered its second year. The secretary-general of the PCE, Juan Ramón Sanz, apostrophized the battling strikers in the pages of the Party newspaper *Mundo Obrero*. It seems quite 'natural' that he should have employed the traditional discourse (and the *parole*) of earlier battles.

> The struggle will be a victorious Ebro,
> for our invincible legions,
> you have conquered consciences
> so that no one can betray your triumph.[101]

In a radio play, set in London, but actually produced in Belfast during the nervous years between the paramilitary ceasefires and the Good Friday Agreement, Martin Lynch presented three ageing veterans of the British Battalion who have continued the struggle for 'Spain' loyally since 1939. The comrades meet regularly in order to keep the cause alive, exchanging reminiscences about the Spanish War and, in the time-honoured tradition of the Irishman, the Welshman and the Englishman, retelling jokes at each other's expense. In flashback scenes, they are heard going into battle singing the 'Internationale' and spouting poetry. The most vivid of their memories concerns the young poet 'Eamon Downey', killed in action in Spain. To ward off the creeping cynicism which is Time's curse, they recite with holy awe the martyr's evocative lines:

> As my spirit spirals forward seeking strength
> I catch myself painting pictures of tomorrow.[102]

~ 8 ~

Conclusion: Writers, Politics, and the War for Art

> Probably the most interesting thing that has happened in the course of the Spanish conflict is the creation of that romantic and already half-legendary band of fighters known as the International Brigades. They may possibly play an important part in the history of the future.[1]

Over a million people were mobilized in the military and support units of opposing sides in the Spanish Civil War. Some 40,000 of them were foreign volunteers. Numberless others, Spaniards and non-Spaniards alike, expended upon its narrative course and final outcome, if not their life's blood, then at least precious resources of emotional feeling, of intellectual, psychological or physical energy. Such people were moved by an immense variety of causes. Many inspirations were intensely, but also essentially, private and individual, receiving their quietus with the person, and ultimately with the faded memory of his and/or hers. Of those humanitarian causes which still belong in the public domain of collective desiderata, most were eventually to be achieved in Spain – if imperfectly and (as always) precariously. In any event, these causes remain central to our perception of right human society: they include political and religious liberty, social justice, economic well-being, equality of opportunity, regional autonomy, freedom of cultural expression. Other principled objectives which seemed of equal or even greater moment in the 1930s have proved (at best) evanescent or epiphenomenal when viewed in the grand scheme of things: Communism, revolution, class struggle, authority, empire, and the enervating succubus of 'History'. But one issue has survived in the foreground of our attention as emblem and epitome of all that is good and worthwhile about the struggle for 'Spain'. What inspires human interest and mobilizes public commitment now, in the twenty-first century, about a conflict which ended in the middle of the twentieth – and which in the context of its own era of world wars is by all quantifiable comparisons dwarfed in importance – is the question of artistic expression, as medium and as issue.

Conclusion

1 Art and Power

Art is the medium which represents the Spanish Civil War, more intimately and more publicly than any other war which can be justly regarded today as a major subject of study and investigation. It is, above all, artistic representation which endows the struggle with meaning and guides its popular interpretation. Of course, in reality, Art – the relevant artistic production which has been normally made accessible to consumers, outside Spain itself, since 1945 – represents not the Spanish Civil War but 'Spain'; that is, a surgically- and strategically adapted construct, in which one-half of the nation and its people are *not* represented.[2] As we have seen, this development, a consummation of history in legend, was one devoutly wished by the leaders of the Spanish Republic, and carefully prepared, both by them and their Soviet–Comintern supporters, during the Civil War itself. In one way or another, the historical reputation of the Virtuous Republic depends upon its identification with perceived ethical (or spiritual) sanctions – a universal benediction which can only be vouchsafed by the artist. As near unanimously as makes no difference the artist is seen to endorse the Republic, both then, in 1936, and now; and, with an almost equal singularity and fervour, to condemn its alleged enemy or 'other': Fascism. Conversely, the cause of anti-Fascist 'Spain', so selflessly struggled for by artists, in return tends to confirm the status of the artist as prophet, priest, warrior, hero and guardian of the ethical order.

Irreparably damaged in the sphere of politics (and even of scholarship) by our knowledge of its crippling intellectual and moral contradictions, the myth of the Popular Front lives on unsullied in the media of the liberal-democratic world. It does so mainly because of the ethical status of 'Art' and its two domains: the currently quasi-hegemonic spiritual culture of the audio-visual arts, along with the (commensurately contracting) *cosmoi* of genre-based 'literature'. *Art and Power* was the title of a notable exhibition on London's South Bank which highlighted the relationship of the creative artist and ideology in the epoch of the totalitarian superpowers.[3] And certainly, this was the decade in which many of the great, both good and bad, began to perceive that Art itself represented a source of Power; a source that was ever expanding, but ever more volatile; and that, therefore, needed control by politics. This book has sought to outflank the Popular

Front by demonstrating how a patina of spiritual sanctity was painted over the Second Republic in order to present it as 'Spain'. We have seen that there are important senses in which the response of intellectuals and artists to 'Spain' was made in distinctly ambiguous ethical-political contexts.

In the late nineteenth century, Marxism accorded the intelligentsia a special role in the process of revolution, a role so closely analogous to as to be functionally synonymous with that of a religious priesthood in the process of salvation. Indeed, in theory the intelligentsia provided a new hierarchy, intended, in a sociological sense, to supersede the old. However, before his death even Marx came to suspect that through their association with the international workers' movement, the intelligentsia were actually seeking power for themselves.[4] The majority of those caste members investigated in this book acted not so much in the interests of abstract commitment to justice or of concrete pity for innocent sufferings (though both may have been present in some) as from a species of enlightened self-interest. During the inter-war years of general political-economic crisis, intellectuals felt themselves ever more threatened and vulnerable. Total war, revolutionary violence, Fascist oppression, economic depression, all these haunted them from without, whilst from within increasingly disruptive phases of aesthetic modernism increased their sense of isolation from society. Following the triumph of Nazism in 1933, intellectuals, for the first time generically, began to organize on an international level.[5] They foresaw the potential annihilation of their caste, and thus their social privileges and status, if what happened in Germany was to happen in Spain, France, Britain and (above all) the USSR. They adopted two majority and complementary strategies in their own defence. First, they accepted the patronage of Communism, whose programme, because manifestly intellectual in theory and content, and apparently benign in practice, seemed inherently sympathetic. Simultaneously they appealed to the proletarian masses, in the belief that the political triumph of the workers in some form was historically and mathematically inevitable, and that they could be induced to partake of the eternal values and addictive pleasures of high culture. Both these policies had failed by 1940. In a world at war, those intellectuals lucky enough to find themselves outside Hitler's New Order or Stalin's empire were forced back into the domestic, ambivalent embrace of the bourgeois state.

But it was precisely in 1936–9, and in Spain, that (as Auden called them) 'the menacing shapes of our fever' assumed terrible reality. In the Spanish context, mobilization of the intellectual often had more to it than the negative aspect inspired by fear and loathing of Fascism. It was dynamically impulsed by positive appreciation of Communism, the Party, and specifically a profound appreciation of the Soviet Union. As the Soviets defended the faith, so the faithful should defend the Soviet. It was nothing less than a teleological contract, analogous to the orthodox Thomist view of politics in the *Res Publica Christiana* of medieval Europe.

2 Intellectuals Come First

The fellow-traveller and critic Cyril Connolly was frank enough to recognize the business basis of the contract between intellectuals and the Spanish Republic. 'It is too early to say whether writers have done anything for Spain', he asserted in 1938, 'but it is clear that Spain has done an immense amount for writers.'[6] Despite this cynical sally, Connolly's book argued forcefully that Fascism, the Axis powers, essentially constituted an unholy league of international philistines – foremost amongst the 'enemies' of his title – whose main agendum was (obviously enough) the annihilation of art. The Spanish War, in particular was 'a war waged by those countries against the intelligentsia of Spain'.[7] As in many other cases of writers who, for all their genuinely deep emotions and painfully hard thinking about the dilemmas of the 1930s, ultimately failed to extract themselves from the bourgeois imperatives of liberalism, Connolly's tract is full of contradictions. In one place he advocates commitment to the People's Front *à l'outrance* on the grounds that 'the existence of any posterity capable of appreciating the arts we care for, can be guaranteed only by fighting for it, and for many who fight there will be no stake in the future but a name on a war-memorial'.[8] Yet in another he warns:

> Political writing is dangerous writing, it deals not in words but in words that affect lives, and is a weapon that should be entrusted only to those qualified to use it. Thus a burst of felicitous militancy with the pen may send three young men to be killed in Spain; for whose deaths the author is responsible.[9]

Connolly's apprehension, his sense of personal responsibility, was instilled by the fate of certain British volunteers. He, like Hugh Greene, saw that the International Brigades were 'the history of the future'; yet that future was to be contained in a public memory, enshrined in cold marble, inscribed in a granitic *nomina* of martyrs. But this felicitously postmodern moment should not lead us to conclude that the contradictions of Connolly arose entirely from a humane conscience: indeed, it was this phrase which first occurred to me when, aware of the liberal humanism of his guild (writer) and caste (Eton), I wrote, a few sentences ago, of his 'bourgeois imperatives'. His logic was not inspired by humane compassion for suffering and death, so much as a monstrous, Wellsian transmutation of Art into the be-all and end-all of politics, a process in which the shadow of beautiful and consolatory mimesis becomes the substance of mundane political concern. For Connolly, the Fascists' war in Spain was not, or at least not primarily, against landless labourers or urban proletariat, or even against democracy and liberal values, but 'against the intelligentsia'; that is, a *War Against Art*. It followed that, to the anti-Fascist, 'Spain' was a *War For Art*. To Connolly's way of thinking, in the phrase used in his reply to the questionnaire *Authors Take Sides*, 'intellectuals come first, almost before women and children.'[10] 'If You Tolerate This' was not a rhetorical prescription for humane reaction to the condition in which a young girl of Getafe was allegedly left by a Junkers 52, but rather a question of aesthetic sensibilities. In this seminar appreciation of the issues he was joined by his friend, W. H. Auden, who reported from Spain:

> Altogether it is a great time for the poster artist and there are some very good ones. Cramped in a little grey boat the Burgos Junta, dapper Franco and his bald German adviser, a cardinal and two ferocious Moors are busy hanging Spain. A green Fascist centipede is caught in the fanged trap of Madrid; in photomontage a bombed baby lies couchant upon a field of aeroplanes.[11]

Unlike his friends Isherwood and Auden, the writer Edward Upward took the decisive step and joined the CPGB. His primary allegiance, however, was to poetry, and it was for this reason that he followed Connolly's logic to its main (but unstated) political conclusion.[12] He rationalized his conversion on the grounds that the poet of today, if only he would turn to the Party, need no longer be ineffectual. Already over one-sixth of the earth the Party had led the workers to victory against the enemies of poetry and it would do the same in England.

His meticulously autobiographical novel, *The Spiral Ascent*, charts the political evolution of his *alter ego*, 'Alan Sebrill'. Here, Upward places his political evolution in a context which many would regard as bizarre beyond the realms of fiction, but which was in fact rigorously honest and exact.[13] As young students, he and a friend (probably Isherwood) vowed that 'they would be true to poetry . . . no matter what miseries and humiliations they might have to undergo for it, no matter even what crimes they might perhaps have to commit for it'. Joining the Party was one crime on the road to artistic freedom; going to Spain and joining the International Brigade was another, but further, perhaps too far, down the road.

> Why wasn't Alan himself going to Spain? If he tried to justify his not going . . . [he] could plead that by staying in England he would be saving himself as a poet: [but] poetry was being written in Spain . . . If the Fascists won they would be free to start a world war and what would become of his poetry – and of culture and civilization in general – then? He had no doubt that he ought to go to Spain; and yet . . . he knew that he would not.

While Upward struggled with his conscience, atoning for his failure to enlist in the British Battalion by striving to become an ever more obedient drone of the Party, Jack Lindsay too accepted his Original Sin – 'the indelible shame for all others save those who fought in the International Brigades'.[14] His emotions led him to a quasi-masturbatory point, as physically proximate to volunteering as he could safely get, poised on a coastal clifftop in southern England, clasping a map of Spain to his bosom, in order to write a poem for 'Spain'.[15] Cecil Day Lewis had earlier posed the rhetorically defining question for intellectuals: 'Why do we admire the communist?' After 1936, however, to be a Communist was no longer enough. For Upward and Lindsay, as for Day Lewis and Lehmann, service in the International Brigades became the new, revolutionary definition of genius: self-sacrifice for the people, the transfiguration of a poetic death in Spain – the example, *par excellence et sans pareil*, of Fox, Cornford and Caudwell. By continuing to write in the security of their studies, they could provide a liturgy of worship, the seductive scripture of belief and persuasion – in other words, propaganda. But without going to Spain, they were destined to remain merely subordinate functionaries who were to know their place at a respectful distance from the real elect. But there was another way for them to be useful, perhaps even to be truly worthy and deserving of honour.

3 The Production and Property of All

The forging of an alliance between intellectuals and the masses, like recruitment to the revolution, to the Party and to defence of the USSR, all of which overlaid and buttressed it, was a task whose urgency and practicability were alike increased by the Comintern policy of the Popular Front.[16] It was clear to the European intelligentsia, even before Karl Radek announced that writing was both the proper medium of revolution and the language of socialist realism, that the Soviet Union was the land where Art had come into its own. Were not artists more venerated and more influential there, more socially cosseted and materially enabled, than in any previous civilization? Had not Stalin himself divined and decreed that the artist was 'the engineer of the human soul'?

As Ralph Fox – *summa cum laude* of Moscow's Lenin School – had proposed, the elect status of hero and poet was fully available to the working class.[17] Both Christopher Caudwell and John Cornford had argued the same point; and it was a proposition that their martyrdom in Spain tended to consecrate. Indeed, proletarians could be seen as actually more equal in this respect, not only because (Marx's) history had selected them to inherit the earth – an evolutionary process of which the struggle in Spain was itself a part – but also because as the genetic possessors of physical courage and fraternal solidarity they were unencumbered by the coward-conscience of the sophisticated classes. As we have seen, Connolly too acknowledged that, alongside (and partly in the interests of) the struggle for 'Spain', the intellectual should lay aside the elite discourses and complex forms of 'High Art' in order to communicate with his future masters.[18] The pages of *Left Review* (1934–8) were crammed with adjurations for the intellectual to abase himself before the proles, in Orwell's metaphor to 'lose his aitches' in the service of revolution. The magazine's stated policy was that only political writing was good writing. As *Left Review*'s precursor, *Viewpoint*, had announced, 'the work of art . . . can only exist in its integrity in a classless society, in a completely communistic state . . . [Thus] art must become the production and property of all.' Day Lewis followed this up with the proclamation that 'it is in the interest of the writer to establish connections with this life [namely, of the proles] and to fight for connections *more favourable to his art*.'[19]

Again, therefore, the intellectual's action can be seen as a tactical expression of enlightened self-interest. Just as, for their part, they volunteered for the revolutionary struggle, they expected, as a sort of quid pro quo, that the people would volunteer for the fight for Art. Behind the slogans lay a contract, a mutual assurance: the middle-class intellectuals endowed the proletariat with culture, and received in exchange the physical security which came with its support. As we have seen, the alliance was made not only by the massy links of the Communist Party and the world struggle but via numberless smaller, individual links which contributed to unity and strength. Intellectuals were exhorted by Day Lewis to 'go over' to the working class: 'A living contact means the relationship between men living together. The bourgeois writer must work, eat and sleep with [the proletariat].'[20] For John Cornford and Stephen Spender this was not only a radically literalist (or if you like, fundamentalist) exercise but also a revelation of visionary significance, offering, in the persons of Ray Peters and Tony Hyndman, intimate access to an otherwise forbidden knowledge of neighbour and labour, homes and lanes, pits and pubs, smells and stories; guided experience in the underground and hitherto silent world of the great majority of the British people. Even for a recalcitrant dissenter like Eric Blair, who sought enlightenment among the dossers and drinkers of Wigan, the logic was irresistible. And from these mean streets projected the trenches of Madrid, the lines where revolution and civilization, actual in 'Spain' and the Soviet Union, potential in Britain and France, were defended. For many sincere young socialists, such as Philip Toynbee, the process seemed so natural and inevitable that any consciousness of inverse snobbery was relatively unimportant.[21] To seek authentic identification with the workers was to aim at a relationship which need be neither patronizing nor pedagogical; after all, the drive to counter the sterility of cultural deprivation was mutual to both contracting parties. Their unity (or union) promised a new and more stable moral order, which might peacefully replace the corrupt patriarchism of class and capital; indeed, this new order might even prove to be the revolution itself.[22]

Not all intellectuals were able to accept the full implications of decrees issued by Day Lewis, Radek and others. Poets and other writers whose art and aspirations cost little but their time, a daily bed and a square meal, were also sometimes able, like Jack Lindsay, to produce in a dramatic and demotic medium which could inspire large audiences for 'Aid Spain' and even for the International Brigades.[23] Painters and musicians, whose costly trades were far more dependent on capital and 'society', occupied a more awkward position in the struggle. Nonetheless, in March 1937 the Artists' International Association declared its dynamic opposition to the government's policy of Non-Intervention in Spain:

> We must END ALL FORMS OF NON-INTERVENTION. INTERVENE IN THE FIELD OF POLITICS, INTERVENE IN THE FIELD OF THE IMAGINATION. THE REVOLUTION which we can bring about must have as its objective the DEVELOPMENT OF CONSCIOUSNESS and the WIDER SATISFACTION OF DESIRE ... INTERVENE AS POETS, ARTISTS AND INTELLECTUALS BY VIOLENT OR SUBTLE SUBVERSION AND BY STIMULATING DESIRE.[24]

One of the signatories to this manifesto was the poet, painter and critic Herbert Read, an anarchist and apostle of surrealism, another the *echt*-modernist sculptor, Henry Moore. Their text seems to draw short of an endorsement of 'going over'. Rather, they prescribe a 'violent' art, going little further than the ritual dance of '*épater les bourgeois*', through modernist or surrealist works, combined with a didactic process of creating mass art appreciation, and resorting to a vocabulary which any advertising copyist would recognize. A year later Read had not moved from this position; rather, the experience of Stalinist persecution of the dissident left in Spain had refocused his determination not to compromise with the tactical compromises of the Party intellectuals over the role of the artist. Though accepting that 'the cause of the arts is the cause of revolution', Read insisted that there were positions 'which the intellectual could not decently adopt' and that it was in no way elitist or exclusivist to encourage the people in a desire for better taste, in poetry as in politics. His treatise made specific reference to the need for victory in Spain, but warned that within the Soviet Union the crackdown on artistic freedom had already begun – indeed that Radek himself, by whom 'political power was invoked to enforce an aesthetic programme', had already fallen victim to its voracious pragmatism.[25] Present in Read's mind were the events of the summer of 1937, when Communist intellectuals all over Europe and America were mobilized by the Comintern in a campaign to discredit the French apostate, André Gide, whose recent book, *Retour de l'URSS*, had provided a forbidden glimpse into actual social and political conditions in the Soviet Union. This offensive, and its accompanying aesthetic programme, were launched on the platform of Communist victory over the POUM-CNT 'insurrection' in Barcelona, which gave them a new level of influence over the Republican government, and effective control of its repressive organs of intelligence and security.

4 The Triumph of Art?

Some of his fellow-poets were even less sympathetic to the spiritual claims of the Soviets than was Read. On the quasi-Fascist (or fellow-travelling) right of the London literary scenario was Roy Campbell, a carpet-bagging versifier who had lived in pre-war Toledo, and somewhat dubiously claimed to have fought with Falangist militiamen in the early days of the Nationalist uprising. In his monotonously indignant epic, *The Flowering Rifle*, Campbell pursued a vicious vendetta against the 'pink pansy poets', branding them as paid hacks of the Jewish world conspiracy in which both capitalism and Communism collaborated:

> In that, for human serfs they both require
> Limpness, servility, and lack of fire,
> And that's the task of modern art and verse
> Whose high-paid priests are certified perverse.[26]

Of all the writers excoriated by Campbell, Stephen Spender was singled out, both for personal abuse and (it is said) on one occasion physical assault.[27] If not exactly high-paid priests of the Comintern, Spender, along with many others, dutifully obeyed its call to attend and address the Second Congress of Anti-Fascist Writers to be held in the three main cities of Republican Spain in early July 1937.[28]

The congress was consciously designed to represent the apogee of the relationship between the Republic and the world of the intellect. As ceremonial and ritual, it was the spiritual equivalent of the universal triumph prematurely celebrated by their enemies in November 1936, during what was to be the 'final assault' on Madrid. Formal recognition of the Nationalist regime by Germany and Italy had then been marked by a demonstration of power and pomp in the Plaza Mayor of Salamanca. Franco described his triple alliance as 'the bulwark of culture, civilization and Christianity in Europe. This moment', the Caudillo added, even more expansively, 'marks the peak of life in this world.'[29] As the banners of the Christian powers were carried into the square in a sweeping, choreographed movement vaguely imitative of Nuremberg rallies, repression continued behind the scenes, anyone perceived as antipathetic to 'civilization' – including hundreds of teachers – being jailed and/or shot.[30] Likewise, in July 1937, as the international synod of intellectuals assembled in Valencia, with a nervous, shuffling movement vaguely reminiscent of a League of Nations gathering, the violent persecution of POUMistas – including many teachers and journalists – was in full swing. In the wake of the Barcelona uprising, denunciations of the secret 'Trotsky-Fascist' conspiracy to undermine the Republic from within filled the newspapers; broadcasters announced the latest lurid treasons; posters adorning the walls exhorted citizens to seek out and destroy the wickedly disguised agents of Franco. The atmosphere of Muscovite menace was intensified, first by rumours of a forthcoming government offensive, and then, further, by the panic reaction of the security services to the existence of such rumours.[31] As in the city streets, so in the trenches and billets of the International Brigades. Among the latter, a dedicated branch of the SIM collaborated with commissars to indoctrinate the general positives and to detect the particular negatives in the ranks of the volunteers.[32]

An inaugural address to the congress was given by prime minister Juan Negrín on 3 July. The next day, in a clever and even courageous speech, Ralph Bates, leader of the British delegation, insisted that the war was being fought in order to awaken the Spanish people to freedom of expression in every field, after centuries of official obscurantism. For Bates, the struggle represented precisely the liberation of the masses for a renaissance of culture – a term he meant in its widest sense. Referring to a cultural construct of

Spanish history nurtured by many foreigners, and identified by Julián Juderías early in the last century, Bates argued that 'Spain's tragedy lies in the fact that "The Black Legend" was almost the truth'.[33] It was a hint, which would not have been lost on (say) the moderate Communist, José Bergamín, that the SIM and its political directors, rather than creating a new era of liberty, risked imposing a new age of oppression and censorship, like that associated historically with the Inquisition and the Index. The delegates then left for Madrid in a motorcade of expensive limousines, occasionally being delayed en route by 'spontaneous demonstrations' of delight by villagers at the benedictory presence of *los intelectuales* in their midst.[34]

Once the serious sessions started in Madrid on 5 July, it became obvious to more than one participant that the Congress was itself to be part of the suffocating security exercise, a forum for virulent propaganda against 'Trotskyism' and 'deviationism'. Some overseas delegates, led by the example of their (Soviet and Spanish) hosts, used the podium to condemn André Gide and other writers, however eminent, who might follow his crooked path into the maw of 'objective Fascism'. PCE poets such as Alberti and critics like Corpus Barga were to the fore in the witch-hunt, along with Alexei Tolstoy and Ilya Ehrenburg.[35] Others, perhaps alerted by Bates, began to read the warning signs. Loyal Communists among them were aware of the crisis of confidence over the Moscow show trials which bubbled below the surface of life in the Party. Even dedicated men, like the Dutch poet Jeff Last, on this occasion for the first time, approached their dark night of the soul. Like Bates, Last was a serving officer of the International Brigades, though, unlike him, was full of battle honours (Madrid, Jarama, Guadalajara). Yet Last evidently lacked Bates's moral courage, and devoted his speech to an elegantly dressed salad of propaganda platitudes.[36] Only after he left Spain, discussing the Writers' Congress in an autobiography which precipitated his split from the Party, did he dare to 'touch on a painful subject'. He recalled that on repeated occasions the litany of artistic victims of Fascism was recited at the congress. However,

> other names were not so much as mentioned; such names as Ottwald, Gunther, Tarassov, Rodianov, Rom, Mandelstam, Tretiakov, Bezunienski, Jossiensky, Gronski, Kliuviev? Why? Why this conspiracy of silence around the cultural reaction in Russia, about which we are all agreed in private? When we heard in Madrid that yet another school had

been bombed, [Egon] Kisch remarked 'When you hear of such horrors
... you feel inclined to defend everything that has been done on our
side, even the trials!' But does that argument really clinch the matter?[37]

Not unlike Last, Stephen Spender was later – in characteristically confessional style – to write about his profound reservations, his besetting awareness of the hypocrisy and absurdity of it all. However, his contribution from the platform in 1937 displayed no such misgivings. After paying tribute to the poets and the 'hundreds of [other] unknown writers' of the International Brigades, and condemning the vicious nature of the capitalist world, his peroration reminded 'Comrades' that 'you who are intellectuals ... have the unforgettable and infinite honour to represent the geographical centre of the struggle, to be [in Madrid] in the heart of civilization'.[38]

Mikhail Koltsov noted how, as he rose to speak on 7 July, the galleries of the Cine Goya were crowded with ordinary *Madrileños* and uniformed International Brigaders.[39] His speech may be regarded as the congress's keynote utterance. It was Koltsov's job to whip mavericks back into the herd, and he did so as brilliantly as any cossack horseman. He began by acclaiming the delegates as 'a new battalion of International [Brigaders] with glasses'. Wittily ironic on one level (especially since Koltsov himself was bespectacled) this remark was also metaphorically accurate on another. Having established a rapport with his audience, he proceeded to dress it down as if, indeed, its members were soldiers, but soldiers whose fortitude in the face of the onrushing enemy was open to question. For too long (he told them) artists had believed themselves to be specially privileged; for too long society had overvalued their work, simply because by nature it was less anonymous than the work of the masses. Koltsov then turned to attack the 'false theory' of 'expression'- meaning the intellectuals' demand for 'freedom of expression'. In the age of International Fascism, he claimed, the only artistic 'expression' which had value was that of support for the people. In a dramatic word-picture he related how in November 1936 (whilst Franco and his allies prematurely celebrated victory) Madrid's academics and artists, with their families and possessions, had fled the city rather than suffer the fate Fascism had in store for them; and how they had been specially protected by the Communist militia, the armed workers of the Fifth Regiment.[40] In this context, Koltsov was able to expose Gide as no Olympian neutral, but rather as a typically arrogant writer who had betrayed the people in the interests of his own selfish psyche and its material comfort. For an artist, Koltsov concluded, neutrality was not an option; worse than mere denial of support for anti-Fascism, it was Fascism itself.[41]

It was the difficult task of José Bergamín, president of the Alianza de Escritores Antifascistas, to sum up the Madrid proceedings. Bergamín had been chosen for this task because as a liberal and a Catholic, as well as PCE loyalist, he was the perfect front-man for the foreign delegates and the world press. He was a stereotype of the attenuated and tortured intellectual. His physical appearance testified to the actuality of the former, and he was not unconscious of the need to avoid any literal encounter with the latter. Bergamín squared the circle by praising 'liberty of thought and criticism', on the one hand, but on the other endorsing the contributions of colleagues, from platform and floor, which had excoriated André Gide.[42]

The congress was thus (*pace* Auden!) a modern version of the medieval general council of the Church, called to identify, define and condemn heresy. Moreover, its delegates were constantly reminded of the urgency of their situation by the inescapable fact that they had carefully been placed just behind the front lines of Madrid. Most of them were accommodated in the Hotel Victoria, in the Plaza Santa Ana, only a few kilometres from the perimeter trenches in the Casa de Campo. Moreover, the long-awaited battle, the first all-out offensive of the Popular Army, in the fields of Brunete not far to the west, had been deliberately scheduled to coincide with the arrival of the congress in Madrid (or vice versa, it makes no difference).[43] A huge artillery barrage began to stream towards Nationalist strongpoints early in the morning of 6 July. By the time Spender rose to deliver his address, and as the British Battalion moved forward to the attack against Villanueva de la Cañada, the enemy was responding enthusiastically and in kind against the city's defences.[44] Ears were humming, and heads were aching in the stifling heat of the auditorium. Conditions generally encouraged the delegates to reach what was, for such an occasion, an unusual degree of scholarly unanimity.

These conditions had been happily altered when, fifty years later, the now autonomous Comunidad de Valencia staged a new Writers' Conference with the aim of celebrating the achievements of 1937. In the plural Spain of 1987, with Chernobyl polluting the real atmosphere and *glasnost* permeating its ideological equivalent, the occasion was notably less dominated by feelings of solidarity than an original event whose fame had, if anything, turned into notoriety. Stephen Spender was invited to make the opening speech. Having spent half a century examining the messy entrails of his own delusionary comportment and that of fellow-intellectuals during the Spanish War, Spender was now suddenly overtaken by a renewed wave of Popular Front sentiment. He reminded his audience that in the burning of books, Fascism had itself created the hot core of anti-Fascism; and by opposing Nazism, their predecessors had synonymously and existentially asserted the freedom of artistic expression.[45] But some were unwilling to accept Spender's claims. One contributor spoke of the 'unforgivable error' made by writers like Anna Seghers (a German delegate in 1937) in giving unconditional support to Stalinism when they were perfectly aware of the persecution of intellectuals in the Soviet Union.[46] On the opposite wing, Angel Gaos, organizer of its Valencia session in 1937, insisted against its critics that the original congress had acted in a 'just cause'. Gaos launched a diatribe against US imperialism, especially condemning the pusillanimity of writers who had betrayed the cause and accepted the patronage of the CIA; which, given Sir Stephen Spender's prominence among them, was evidence of his claim to have spent many years in obscurity, 'confined by fate to a small corner of the world'.[47]

In fact it was, after all, Spender who had best understood (in 1987 as in 1937) the purpose of the conference. In advance of proceedings a manifesto had been drawn up, intended, by reflecting on the dilemmas of 1937, to encapsulate issues of ethical-political objectivity for the intellectuals of the 1980s. These sessions were evidently lively. A first draft drew attention to the coincidence – in more than just the temporal sense – between the original congress and the torture and death of Andrés Nin, leader of the POUM, at the hands of Stalinist thugs. Thus it was proposed to place alongside Max Horkheimer's dictum, 'whoever does not wish to speak of capitalism should also keep quiet about Fascism', an equal and opposite notion: 'whoever does not wish to speak about *Stalinism* should also keep quiet about Fascism.' But in the event these passages were removed from the final version by a three-to-one majority vote of the committee.[48]

A few days after the Writers' Congress of 1937 had completed its work in Spain, and international delegations were safely across the frontier, the Republican government closed down the Casa de Cultura in Valencia, where intellectuals evacuated from Madrid the previous November, amidst much publicity, had been generously accommodated. It seems that the distinguished residents had not been willing enough to accept the PCE line in speaking with one voice about the moral issues of the war. Valencia was vastly overcrowded, with thousands of homeless refugees from all parts of Spain: the Republic's intellectuals had now been granted a common cause with the people.[49]

5 Presidents, Priests and Prophets

As we have seen, prime minister Negrín formally opened the 1937 congress. Julio Alvarez del Vayo, cabinet minister and chief of the political commissariat, also attended its sessions. However, the president of the Republic, Manuel Azaña, was conspicuous by his absence – though perhaps 'inconspicuous' would be more apt. Azaña's failure to give the event his benediction passed without public comment at the time; but it represented much more than an implied criticism of the Congress's objectives. Azaña was one of Spain's outstanding intellectuals, and regarded himself in this numinous light, before a politician, even before his role as 'Father of the Second Republic' – the latter both being predicated upon the former. Since the start of the war, Don Manuel (like his intellectual adversary, Unamuno, and for similar reasons) had steadily retreated from public affairs. Yet, in terms of propaganda, he remained a salient presence among the primary constellation of Republican leaders, his portrait prominent at meetings and marches, his elevating nostrums banner-headlined in posters and papers. Azaña the writer was not invited as a delegate to the Congress. Azaña the head of state was, it seems, only invited to speak at all at a very late stage, when business proceedings had been completed. It is true that any fame Azaña had been accorded as published imaginative writer and performed dramatist had been to a large extent consequent upon his success in the field of politics since 1931. But the man himself was unlikely to make any such reflection, and even had he been so inclined, it would not have lessened the amount of his bitterness, nor the defensive venom which such displeasure customarily elicited. He confided to his diary:

> When Negrín came to see me before going to the Madrid front for the military offensive, he referred to the congress and apologized for having forgotten to mention it earlier. The whole thing was a worthless exercise. Few people attended, and even fewer of any reputation. The Spanish delegates themselves were hardly the most distinguished available. They all went off to Madrid to celebrate two meetings in a cinema, and various banquets.... I see from the newspapers that one session was presided over by Señorita León, and that in another, Corpus Barga proposed a motion of censure against André Gide. It all cost a vast amount to organize, yet on the opening day no typewriters were available, nor pencils and paper, nor even any stenographers.[50]

Behind the wounded pride of Azaña's remarks lay apparently deeper concerns about the demands of politics upon art which he characterized as 'disastrous in any case, but above all during wartime'. Directly contrary to Koltsov, he argued that 'artistic creation belongs to an independent authority ... yet no powerful movement which takes control of society fails to claim that art should be subordinate to it'.[51] In the late 1920s, when Azaña was active in intellectual circles opposed to the military dictatorship of Miguel Primo de Rivera, the work of the French critic, Julien Benda, had achieved prominence across Europe. Benda's *La trahison des clercs,* published ten years before the 1937 Congress, which warned against the increasing tendency of intellectuals to accept the tutelage of ideology, became hugely influential. In explaining his use of the medieval term 'clerk', Benda suggested that the intellectual was the modern equivalent of the priestly order, and had the same duty to his calling, that is to remain free of 'politics'.

> The modern 'clerk' has entirely ceased to let the layman alone descend to the market place. The modern clerk is determined to have the soul of a citizen and to make vigorous use of it; he is proud of that soul, his literature is filled with his contempt for the man who shuts himself up with art or science and takes no interest in the passions of the state.[52]

If Azaña (as seems likely) was apprised of Benda's warning then he gave it no heed. He carried on working for an end to dictatorship and monarchy through his pen – a campaign which met with success in 1931. Moreover, within a few years Azaña was himself translated to leadership of a government which, though democratically elected and composed mostly of liberals, nonetheless occasionally censored troublesome writers and closed down recalcitrant newspapers; that is to say, a 'powerful movement' which reckoned that intellectual concerns, like those of the Church or the army, should be 'subordinated' to the state.[53]

By a marvellous irony, Benda himself attended the 1937 congress, where he formally retracted (or recanted) his negative sanction against *l'art engagée*. Not only did he offer support to the anti-Fascist cause, but (in effect) endorsed its Comintern leadership.[54] Benda's volte-face – no pun intended – was moved by what seemed an irresistible force. The apostasy of 'clerks' in reaction to the misdeeds of Nazism after 1933 was a stream which turned into a flood after the Spanish events of 1936. Yet there remained some who refused to let themselves be carried across the ethical void. In the spring of 1937, as invitations were being issued for the Congress of Anti-Fascist Writers, Nancy Cunard, one of the Republic's most industrious supporters in the world of the arts, hit upon the novel idea of publicly sounding out opinion among British writers about the main international issue of the day.[55] Bergamín, Neruda, Auden and Spender were all consulted before the celebrated questionnaire was formulated and distributed to hundreds of recognized *savants*. The question it asked was almost consciously rhetorical, its prescriptive message in essence identical to that shortly afterwards also delivered by Koltsov in Madrid: 'It is impossible any longer to take no side.'[56]

Authors Take Sides is an unreliable document if taken at face value, since its votes were gerrymandered in favour of the result Cunard so passionately desired. There was an obvious reluctance to acknowledge the implied preference of many respondents to be included in a 'neutral' category which had been declared a priori as non-existent. (The outcome was that only sixteen were in fact categorized thus.[57]) Nonetheless, even by Cunard's reckoning, a total of twenty-one out of 148 respondents refused to be shepherded into the fold. Though six actual dissenters appeared, only one – Evelyn Waugh – was fully and unambiguously committed to the Nationalist cause. (Roy Campbell, along with others whose contrary opinion was well established, was apparently not on the mailing-list.[58]) Despite the apostasy of its own author, some of the allegedly 'neutral' authors expressed reservations along similar lines to those set out in *La trahison des clercs*. In this category, the most Olympian response was T. S. Eliot's: 'it is best that a few men of letters should remain isolated and take no part in these collective activities.' The chief clerk, however, left a necessary gloss to be made by Alec Waugh: 'There is an essential difference between the "Ivory Tower" and a standpoint "above the battle".'[59] But at the same time, reading between the lines, a more distinctive spirit can be detected among writers in all three categories.

A substantial minority referred to the essentially philistine nature of Fascism, linking support for 'Spain' with that for intellectual freedom, in a way which sometimes seems gratuitous and might even be taken as conditional.[60] One 'neutral' contributor (Charles Morgan) pointed out that intellectual freedom did not seem to figure among the aims of either contestant. Indeed, as what might be termed a 'war aim', the desire for a world in which the rights of the artist should be recognized figured at least as prominently as expressions of empathy with the suffering Spanish people. Instead of 'rights' we may justly read 'privileges'. The barely hidden agenda of many artists and critics can be deduced from Cyril Connolly's statement, which demands renewed quotation; 'Intellectuals come first, almost before women and children.' In semantic terms, if 'intellectuals come first', then the word 'almost' is simply redundant. Around the time Cunard's *Authors Take Sides* appeared (autumn 1937), concern was growing in Whitehall and the Quai d'Orsay over the fact that large numbers of neutral ships, legally trading with the Republic, were being attacked by 'mysterious' (that is Italian) submarines.[61] We may envisage a variant last reel of the film *A Night to Remember*. The black, icy waters of Fascism lap across the decks of the great Cunard liner, *SS Spain*. The cry goes up from Cyril Connolly (played by Kenneth More): 'Intellectuals first, women and children next!' With his revolver at the ready, backed up by the Fifth Regiment of Communist Militia, Connolly protects a posse of bespectacled pedants from an enraged mob of steerage-class passengers.

~ 9 ~

Epilogue: The Real Fifth Column

For all the efforts of Cunard and the Comintern, dozens of signatories to the manifesto were to abandon ship as the waters became colder and more stormy. By 1939, when, in an act as symbolic as it was cautionary, he left Europe for the USA, W. H. Auden had not only capitulated before Orwell's criticism, completely disavowing his poem SPAIN, but had also penned the celebrated lines in which he washed his hands of all political pollution:

> For poetry makes nothing happen; it survives
> In the valley of its own saying, where executives
> Would never want to tamper.[1]

All the same, in his last collaboration with Benjamin Britten, the opera-musical *Paul Bunyan* (1941), Auden provided a text which allegorizes various aspects of his 'low, dishonest decade', including the Spanish Civil War.[2] A gang of lumberjacks from many lands is engaged by the eponymous and legendary hero to clear the forests of the American frontier.

> Wanted. Disturbers of public order, men without foresight or fear . . . energetic madmen . . . the lost. Those indestructibles whom defeat can never change. Poets of the bottle, clergymen of a ridiculous gospel, actors who should have been engineers and lawyers who should have been sea-captains, saints of circumstance, desperados . . . dynamiters and huntsmen, there has been an excess of military qualities, of the resourcefulness of thieves, the camaraderie of the irresponsible, and the accidental beauties of silly songs.

One member of the team is 'Inkslinger', a writer who is able to find an artistic identity only by subjecting himself utterly to party discipline and accepting the role of agent provocateur. In words which have a familiar ring to any student of the commissariat documentation of the International Brigade, he informs on the foreman, 'Hel Helson', as a potentially subversive element: 'Keep an eye on Hel Helson. He broods too much by himself and I don't like the look on his face. And the bunch he goes around with are a bad bunch.'[3]

The experience of Stephen Spender with his own version of Hel

Helson (that is, Tony Hyndman) forced him to reconsider the nature of his commitment to 'Spain', and to politics generally. Yet the closer Spender's whole political trajectory is examined, the more bizarre and dialectically volatile it seems. It is true that he saw Hyndman as his alter ego, and that Tony was in some ways an axiomatic exemplar of the prole–poet relationship. Yet despite (or perhaps because of) his literary acculturation, Hyndman – Coldstream Guardsman turned coward and deserter – proved unable to protect either the revolution, or the person of his master. In 1936, Spender (and, in a sense, Hyndman) had written:

> The artist, I believe, will fight on the side of the workers because he wishes to bridge the gulf between his mental surroundings and the actual conditions in which the majority of men are made to live . . . because a new age of creative activity can only exist in an environment of peace and social justice . . . because his final goal is an unpolitical age, in which great works of art may be produced.[4]

As the last clause in this manifesto reveals, Harry Pollitt and his comrades of the CPGB were light years away from a true appreciation of *Forward From Liberalism*. The revolution which Spender stood for was not that of Marx, and only accidentally resembled that of Engels in that it empathized with the latter's hypothesis of 'the withering away of the state'. Though objecting (in somewhat routine fashion) to their uncompromising elitism, Spender basically sympathized with the theories of Clive Bell, one of the founders of the Bloomsbury group.[5] In 1928, Bell had developed arguments outlined by Julien Benda to even more radical conclusions. In his book *Civilization* he advocated a cultural revolution whose sole aim was to bring about a society in which creative artists would occupy a place above and apart from the rest, literally superannuated by the complaisant collaboration of labour. This was the revolution of 'artism' – the assertion, by intellectual 'artistocrats' of a political destiny, of precisely that sovereign aspiration which President Azaña described as 'an independent authority'. In the generations before Bell wrote, *savants* like Arnold, Pater and Wilde had adumbrated these 'aestheticist' nostrums. In Spain, Unamuno, Ortega y Gasset and other intellectuals, in addition to Manuel Azaña, approximated to similar utopian visions. Earlier than any, Carlyle had descried the beckoning – if distant – prospect of the Republic of Letters.

> The Man of Letters . . . is to such a degree superseding the Pulpit, the Senate, the *Senatus Academicus* and much else . . . [that it has been] recognised often enough, in late times, with a sort of sentimental triumph and wonderment. It seems to me, the Sentimental by and by will have to give place to the Practical . . . I think we may conclude that Men of Letters will not always wander like unrecognised unregulated Ishmaelites among us! Whatsoever thing . . . has virtual unnoticed power will cast-off its wrappings, bandages, *and step-forth one day with palpably articulated, universally visible power* . . . Sure enough, this what we call Organisation of the Literary Guild is still a great way off . . .[6]

It was a process by which the traditional elite, condemned by the ascendant culture of liberal democracy (and more intensely so, by the consequences of its socio-economic breakdown) to shameful consciousness and self-loathing, would cast off its mundane, corrupting accidentals, investing its material wealth for redistribution by the state. In return, the state would renew acknowledgement of its effortless superiority, now founded on the pristine basis of spiritual leadership. Spender's 'unpolitical age' was to be that of Art and the Artist, a utopia with no place for politics or ideology, or even for culture, at least as we understand it today. England was to be the Arcadian valley of the sayings of poetry, a transcendental habitation in which the hieratic artist would dispense to all the exquisite, indeed indispensable, pleasures of imaginative creation and appreciation. But this consummation has to be achieved without the willing, or even conscious collaboration of the masses: as Clive Bell confessed,

> I have not yet noticed that the soon-to-be-sovran proletariat, the working men of old England, manifest any burning desire to avail themselves of such means to civilization as they already dispose of. Rather it appears to me that their ambitions tend elsewhither . . . The British working man likes his barbarism well enough. Only he would like a little more of it . . . His notion of a glorious revolution is not the reshaping of life to bring it nearer the ideal, but a slipping into some rich man's shoes . . . The revolutionary coal-miner conceives no better life than that of the reactionary owner. [Both classes accept] the creed of the producers. Those who hold it have no use for economically unproductive work and subtle, difficult pleasures. Those who hold it have no will to civilization. But they have power.[7]

Naturally enough, given his period and preconceptions, Bell takes prevailing notions of classical Athens, a society familiar and meaningful to most males of the ruling class, as his main exemplar.

> Philanthropists seem to forget that Athenian culture was slave-supported: but he who would discover the conditions necessary to civilization must have a better memory, must remember that two-thirds – if not three-fourths of the inhabitants of Attica were slaves ... Civilization requires the existence of a leisured class, and a leisured class required the existence of slaves – of people, I mean, who give some part of their surplus time and energy to the support of others.[8]

Bell's realization that he was describing a society to which in certain respects Fascist Italy and Soviet Russia already approximated was more instinctive than deductive. He argued, somewhat tendentiously, that civilization could not be directly imposed by force, but that if social revolution and the totalitarian state were to produce the conditions for civilization, they may indeed be worthy of support by all good men – men, that is, whose ethical values were not oppressed by limiting liberalism or deadening democracy, but rather liberated by the sanctions of art and overarched by its infinite firmament.[9]

Many intellectuals were already keenly aware of the critical dependence of civilization on science. The Huxleys (Aldous and Julian) led the way here, along with others who operated in the fertile borderlands, such as C. P. Snow. Jacob Bronowski already had an appreciative private audience for his poetry, including an amount of pro-'Spain' verse which (*inter alia*) agonized over its author's failure to enlist with the International Brigades.[10] Most of these men had a Cambridge location or connection: often they were members of the 'Apostles' secret society, men who carried the missionary burden of the intellectuals' future heritage. In 1929 the physicist J. D. Bernal advanced 'the view that Marxism and Communism are not ends in themselves, but the best available means of achieving the transfer of power to the scientist'.[11] His erstwhile faculty colleague in chemistry, J. B. S. Haldane, went to Spain to advise the Republican government how to cope with mustard gas attacks – to which desperate evil, it was naturally assumed, the 'Fascists' would resort after being checked at the gates of Madrid. He told a friend who warned him to be careful that 'if only a few people like him did get killed it would make people in Britain understand what Fascism really was'.[12] Clive Bell was the father of Julian, Cambridge contemporary and friend of many 'Apostles', and of their leading figure, Anthony Blunt. Julian Bell, poet and pacifist, was killed near Villanueva de la Cañada in July 1937, some days after the Congress of Anti-Fascist Writers had moved on from Madrid. The father's chief mentor, from whose germ ideas the argument of *Civilization* was, in part, developed, was the Cambridge philosopher, G. E. Moore. Francis Cornford, Fellow of Trinity and father of John, poet and historian, was Moore's colleague.

At the time of his son's death in Spain, Cornford the elder was working on an edition of Plato's *Republic*, a book which was destined to become the vade mecum of generations of undergraduates.[13] Cornford's interpretation of the ancient text was deeply influenced by contemporary politics, and (it seems likely) by conversations with his son. He states at the outset that in the *Republic*, 'Plato's thought, from first to last, was chiefly bent on the question how society could be reshaped so that man might realize the best that is in him'. Thus Plato was a thinker of revolution, with objectives no different from those of Karl Marx.[14] Morever, it may be deduced that Spain's Second Republic – that is, the Virtuous (Athenian) Republic of its own representation – was Cornford's unspecified Platonic ideal.[15] He emphasizes that Plato's explanation of the fundamental reason for the shortcomings of the (historical) Athenian republic was the separation of the men of wisdom from politics, in other words the alienation of Art from Power. 'To Plato', Cornford noted, 'this drifting apart of the men of thought and the men of action was a disastrous calamity, indeed the root of the social evils of his time.' In Plato's own words, 'accordingly the human race would never see the end of trouble until true lovers of wisdom should come to hold political power, or the holders of political power should, by some divine appointment, become true lovers of wisdom.'[16]

By Stalin's appointment, at least, the Soviet apparatus in Spain, and the Spanish Communist Party, were anxious to be true lovers of wisdom. The Congress of Anti-Fascist Writers for the Defence of Culture provided the ideal stage to demonstrate this fact to believers and doubters alike. Through the writings of over a hundred foreign intellectuals, the news of the Republic's victories would be conveyed to the outside world in the most dramatic and affecting terms. As proceedings were under way in the claustrophobic heat of the afternoon of 7 July 1937, there was a sudden commotion outside the hall. A group of armed soldiers, stained with the sweat of battle, stormed through the doors and rushed onto the platform in front of the conference table. After what was doubtless a moment of fearful dread in the hearts of many warriors of the pen, it became apparent that the irruption represented no threat to the audience. The soldiers of the Popular Army were excitedly waving banners, and it was explained that these flags had – that very day – been captured from the enemy on the field of Brunete. They were being triumphantly presented to the literary luminaries of the anti-Fascist world, in the same spirit as similar trophies of victory have been ritually offered to the High Priests and displayed in the temples of the Gods since time immemorial.[17]

But in Moscow the stage management was otherwise. Here, intellectuals and academics were not allowed to strut and fret their hour, but simply disappeared into the darkness clutching the single permitted suitcase. Many were arrested on charges of homosexual behaviour, legalized under the Leninist constitution but now viciously proscribed by Stalin.[18] Even before the Nazi–Soviet Pact fell like a bane upon their too too solid assumptions, before Popular Fronts and Anti-Fascist associations melted into air, delegates returning to their desks and lecterns from Madrid failed to spread the word to quite the extent Koltsov and Willi Münzenberg had hoped. Though few went over to the side of André Gide (who, just before the Congress had published a second and even more condemnatory version of his offending book), most carried in their hearts reservations which if expressed in Madrid might have exposed them to charges of Trotskyism, or of being members, not of the Fifth Regiment, but rather of the Fifth Column, whom the people were encouraged to destroy on sight. Those like Spender, Last, Regler and Malraux, who had been delegates, were joined in their desertion by acolytes, like Cuthbert Worsley, who now wrote about the International Brigades:

> Those who are actually fighting, especially the ordinary infantrymen, know too much about it to feel anything but envy for those who escape, whether they desert, or resign (where that is possible), or get appointed to the base, or seconded home for duties there. Whilst those in command must use any and every method to keep those who are fighting at their posts; at the front, they will, when necessary, use revolvers; at home, when necessary, lies.[19]

Herbert Southworth once pointed out that most politically disillusioned writers of the Spanish War had their fundamental differences not with the Republic, but rather with Stalin and Stalinism.[20] True as this may be, the 'fifth column' of artists and intellectuals ultimately did more damage to 'Spain' than Stalin, Franco, Hitler and Mussolini combined – because it was damage that could never be repaired, even from the fathomless fund provided by the martyrdom of Cornford and Fox and company.

In the event, despite the perceived crisis of Fascism, and the survival strategies it inspired amongst them, nostrums about philosopher-kings and supreme legislators proved ineradicable from the intellectuals' mind-set. Of course, many must have appreciated the unmanageable contradictions in the very principle of collective subscription to programmes for individual intellectual freedom.[21] But more than this, utopian and messianic as it was, 'Artism' was inherently inimical to all other ideologically based solutions to the problems of human progress. In the four generations since Carlyle and Burckhardt, creative artists, along with their human agencies and institutional manifestations, had achieved a revolutionary access of privilege and power in western societies, mainly by occupying territory left vacant by the epic retreats of institutional religion. The new believers came to realize that artists were firmly controlled in the totalitarian states precisely because of the unique and inherent power they dispensed. They appreciated that secular dispensation of alternate praise and persecution actually served only to confirm and strengthen this power; and that because its influence was immanent and indestructible, art was not only capable of creating new states (as Walter Benjamin pointed out, in its own image) but might also resist, challenge and overthrow the state.[22] Julien Benda had established that the empire of art was not of this world; potentially infinite, its imperialism was infallibly destructive of other 'causes'. During the prolonged and universal wars of the Popular Front era, stretching from the Japanese invasion of Manchuria in 1931 to the phase of anticolonialist struggle which ended with Vietnam in 1972, the war of Art against Politics became one which was eternal, and eternally unresolved.

Which was the victor, for example, in 1963, when Michael Straight was approached by President Kennedy to head up a proposed national institute for the arts? Straight had shared 'the indelible shame' of those who heard the call of the International Brigades resonating in their souls, yet failed to answer – a kind of Petrine denial. He later acquired family connections to the Greene brothers. Like one of them, Hugh, he was convinced by the central significance of the Brigades to the cause of 'Spain' and 'the history of the future'. Like a character in a novel written by the other, Graham, during the Cold War he lived a life of inner anxiety, expecting at any moment to be 'activated' by the KGB. After returning to the USA, Straight edited a political magazine, the suitably Platonic *New Republic*, which his family had founded, and resumed the writing of poetry, a preoccupation of his Cambridge days. Now and again he sponsored ex-veterans of the War for Art in Spain (such as Stephen Spender) for visas to lecture in the USA. During the McCarthy era he was appalled by the persecution of left-wing intellectuals, exemplified for him by the experience of his brother-in-law, Gustavo Durán. One-time staff officer of the XII International Brigade, briefly head of the SIM, and part-inspiration for the hero of André Malraux's novel *L'espoir*, Durán was harassed into confessions and out of jobs until he re-emigrated to South America.[23]

But Kennedy's initiative represented a breakthrough in US political culture, the first time the federal government had ever sponsored artistic endeavour, and Straight deeply coveted the appointment. As a potential flagship government official, and mindful of Durán, Straight felt it necessary to come clean about his youthful involvement with the Comintern. The result was a sequence of events which ended, fifteen years later, with the public exposure and disgrace of Sir Anthony Blunt. At some point in the interim, Blunt and Straight were brought together again, a confrontation made necessary by the CIA investigation of the latter's past. Blunt asked his old comrade why he had decided to 'sing' after so many muted years. In a response of perfect (perhaps *too* perfect) artistic closure, Straight replied: 'Because of the Arts. Because our government finally decided to support the Arts. Kennedy was going to make me head of his new Arts Agency. That forced me to face up to it at last.'[24]

Appendix: 'Necessary Murders' – The Texts

J. Roberts[1]

It was dusk of the first day when our Battalion had advanced to within about three hundred metres of Villanueva de la Canada. Some were lying down in the ditch beside the road: five of us were taking cover behind the dung-heap on the right. Suddenly someone shouted: 'Don't fire; there are children coming from the village.' We looked down the road and saw about twenty-five people, men, women and children. In front was a little girl of about ten years of age. Behind her came an elderly woman, a boy of fourteen or so, a few old men. The remainder were young men. As they approached they shouted: 'Camaradas! Camaradas!'

Believing them to be refugees, we answered them and called them forward. Some of us were now standing, some walking to meet and welcome them. Pat Murphy, of Cardiff, was nearest to them. He approached them, telling them to lay down their arms if they had any. For answer, a revolver blazed. The Fascists, who had been driving this group of old men, women and children as cover for them, started throwing hand-grenades in our midst.

For a few minutes pandemonium reigned. It was hard to distinguish friend from foe. The Fascists had difficulty also. I saw a figure bend down, jerk up a wounded man, saw the flash of a revolver, as the Fascist despatched one of our men. 'Commandante!' yelled someone, and Fred Copeman called out in answer. A Fascist grenade lobbed towards him. It missed Fred and killed Tommy Gibbons, Battalion Secretary. We had fallen for an old trick. The crash of grenades, the barking of guns, and the shrieks of the women and children are still in my ears. But, in ten minutes it was all over; the last of the Fascists lay dead. Then, forward we charged and stormed the village.

From the other end the Dimitrovs came in. We lighted the streets with the red light of bursting grenades as we drove the Fascists before us to the centre of the town. The Dimitrovs and ourselves were within an ace of charging each other. Luckily we were shouting anti-Fascist slogans, and recognised one another in time.

The Spanish Carabineros, great fighters, were also in action, helping us. As we mopped-up, street by street, men fell. We succoured the wounded, no matter whether they were ours or the enemy. A wounded man cried out. Bill Meredith, brave young Company Commander who had been a hero at Jarama and throughout the day that was now ending in victory, bent down to attend to the cry for help. For answer he got a bullet through the heart from the wounded Fascist.

Pat Murphy's chivalry almost cost him his life. In the mêlée he was seriously wounded in the groin by a hand-grenade. Later, while going round to identify those of our comrades who had fallen, we could not help thinking of the brutality of Fascism when we found the bodies of the little girl, the elderly woman and two elderly men.

F. Ryan[2]

The final storming of the town was a desperate affair carried out just at nightfall. (The whole attack was carried out between dawn and dusk.) The Americans and ourselves were trying to find cover in flat ground a few hundred yards from the houses. Our aircraft and artillery had pounded the place well, but the church (which, of course, dominates every landscape here) kept standing. And from its tower machine-guns seriously hampered us.

Just at dusk a crowd of women, children and old men, and about forty young men, came out the road, hands outstretched, calling 'Camaradas.' Pat Murphy (Sean's old pal) and some others were behind a dung-pit. They thought the crowd were refugees. Pat got up and went to meet them, telling them to drop their arms if they had any.

Just as he approached, a revolver barked, then grenades started to fly. For five minutes there was pandemonium, guns cracking, grenades bursting, and women and children shrieking. Pat, engaged in a hand-to-hand struggle, fell into a drain with his opponent, where he dispatched him. Beside him fell a little girl of about ten years who had been at the head of the group. 'Lie quiet, girlie,' said Pat, and she smiled back as if she understood. A grenade burst in the drain and Pat was severely wounded in the groin.

In five minutes it was all over; the last of the Fascists was accounted for. When the lads went around to collect their own and the non-combatants, they found the little girl, two old women and three old men dead. It was at least a satisfaction that every single one of the Fascists who had driven them in front of them as cover was also dead.

A few minutes later the town was stormed from two opposite points. It was dark by then, with bursting grenades – it was almost all grenade work – to light the way. It was done so well that the two storming parties were within an ace of storming each other.

Hillesley[3]

The English Battalion had orders to march into the town first. We lined up across the road. Nobody fired at us and we made straight for the Fascist trenches around the village. As we were marching through – we did not think anything of it – but we saw the civilian population out in front of the trenches – women, children and old men. We got to within about 20 yards of them when the Fascists started heaving hand grenades over the heads of the civilians, and we had a hand-to-hand fight for about half an hour. When we had finished not a Fascist got away alive. They had slaughtered old men, women and children. We went in there, lined them up, made them dig a trench and shot every one. There were over 15,000 Fascists in that town. Some managed to escape over the fields, or thought they could, but we sent the cavalry after them and they were cut to pieces.

Rust[4]

At dusk a terrible incident occurred, which will be engraved for all time on the memory of those who saw it. From the town there emerged a group of people, mostly women and children, whose bright coloured dresses it was still possible to discern. Pat Murphy, a Cardiff seaman, who lay behind a heap of earth at the head of the ditch, was the first to see them and he hurried forward to find out what was taking place. Behind the civilians were a number of soldiers, mostly Italians, well armed with submachine-guns, rifles and hand-grenades. The Fascists were attempting a sortie, and were using the civilians as a screen.

But Murphy's sudden appearance caused a momentary confusion. He ordered the civilians forward to the Republican lines and called on the soldiers to halt and to put down their arms. For answer, the leader of the Fascists ran at him but Murphy fired immediately and they both fell into the ditch. Firing their submachine-guns from the hip, and throwing hand-grenades in all directions, the Fascists advanced down the road shooting some of the women and children who had not been quick enough to get out of their line of fire. Using the dead body of the Italian leader as a shield, Murphy began to fire from the ditch at the rear section of the Fascists, whom he saw peering closely at the wounded to make sure to which side they belonged and then shooting them brutally through the chest. Murphy continued firing, until he was seriously wounded in the groin by a hand-grenade. The fighting was fierce and terrible but it was all over in ten minutes. The dead lay on the roadway and mingled with the drab uniforms of the soldiers could be seen the brighter dresses of the women, whom the Fascists had used as shields. Fortunately, most of the civilians got away and some of the women courageously helped to dress the wounds of the British volunteers.

Copeman[5]
After calling the Company Commanders together, we decided to deploy the Battalion on each side of the road as soon as the sun went down, and attack.

No sooner had our companies taken up their position when a group of women appeared in sight. There must have been two dozen of them, and maybe a dozen kiddies. The women and children might be used as a screen, from behind which the enemy troops could throw hand grenades. For a moment I could not make up my mind what to do. This could be the end of the action, or on the other hand, it might only be the start.

Suddenly I heard the dull thud of hand grenades mixed with shouts and screams from the group of civilians coming down the road. There was only one answer to this. Our two remaining Ditrovs were handled by Ginger and Bill – two fine gunners. I hissed to them, 'Get ready to fire all you've got, and don't be sentimental.' At the top of my voice I yelled to our men, in the semi-darkness, 'Listen carefully. When I blow the whistle lay down and don't move.' With the next breath I blew the whistle, and Ginger and Bill let everything rip along the flat surface of the road. At least some of the women would unfortunately get it. It worked! In a few seconds the road was clear, and groping and scuffling we made our way as fast as possible to the point where the crowd had been. Not a nice sight. One old lady was dead in front. Happily she didn't know what had hit her. A few more of the women were wounded, but nearly all the Fascist troops had killed themselves. They had been carrying bags of impact grenades and these are not nice things to knock about. Only three of the men remained alive. Our own lads had obeyed the order to lie down and were safe.

We advanced towards the village. Darkness had fallen and the countryside was lit up by the flames of burning buildings. The artillery had fired its last round of the day.

L. Price[6]
So that went on till the end of the day, and then they came out in a bloody rush, men, women, kids; and I thought oh, that's all over now. I got up from where I was and walked up towards the road where they were coming down in a bloody great crowd ... They start throwing grenades and our boys start firing into them, they killed the bloody lot; men, women, kids. They all had [inaudible] pretty well – there was very few survivors as far as I could see.

S. Quinn[7]
Well, we took that village in the end but we took it twelve hours too late. There I saw the worst incident of the war. A group of civilians were pushed out of the village towards the end of the fighting, mostly women and children. We wondered what was happening until we saw they were being used as a living shield, they were screaming. It was ghastly to watch it. There were old men, babies, toddlers, and they were shot down by us because we couldn't stop. Every last one of them.

W. Gregory[8]
At dusk there was a commotion in the village and all of those around me started to peer over the top of the ditch to see what was happening. A party of women and children were slowly leaving the village and making their way down the road toward our position. They were closely packed together and casting fearful and anxious glances to left and right as they moved forward. We started yelling at them to get a move on, to get away from the village as fast as possible, to get off the road where they were so visible, to get behind our lines where they would have some protection. As they drew nearer we saw that they were being used as a human shield by a group of Fascist troops who were crouching behind them and forcing them forward, in tight formation, at bayonet-point. These

heroes then started firing at us from behind their living armour and we had no alternative but to return their fire. With great regret I have to state that quite a few of those poor women and their children were killed and wounded by both Fascist and Republican bullets which missed their intended targets. It was a side of war that I had never seen before and, thank God, I was never to see again. How the self-proclaimed saviours of Spain could have sunk to such depths of inhumanity defies any explanation that I am able to offer.

L. Rogers[9]

I lost dear ones in that battle of Brunete. Ramon especially, of Dowlais, Sid Hamm, a close friend, blown to bits.

[*What can you remember about that morning?*]

The heat was beyond ... and of course, the confrontation ... When you found the families coming out, as if surrendering, mothers, children, women coming out onto this plain, open ground, and the casualties had started to arise. This was the morning as I say that Ramon was killed, Sid Hamm was killed among a host of others. And they came out surrendering but of course it was a ruse, it was a deception, they were not surrendering at all, they were merely a blind for forces that were wanting to come on in order to annihilate us ... I remember [unintelligible phrase] and the screaming.

I was lying in this open ground. Jack Roberts was in the battle ... Jack thought I was gone, I remember him shouting out to others ... such was the nature of the open ground and a constant firing of one sort of armament or another that no movement was permissible, you couldn't move without attracting fire of some sort.

[*It has been said that there were revenge killings of POWs.*]

If this has been recorded I have no grounds to suggest it wasn't the case. But I wasn't a party to it, and I don't remember anything about it.

[*NB dotted intervals in transcription represent pauses in speech, not elisions.*]

Graham[10]

The 15th Brigade was told to advance and take the village otherwise the offensive on that sector would be delayed. At the time I was acting as runner to Major Jock Cunningham who was in command of a regiment of the English speaking battalions of the brigade. I was instructed to keep in contact with the British

Battalion and report back progress or lack of it to Jock Cunningham.

Since the Spanish unit had failed in the frontal assault, the British Battalion was under orders to go round and attack the village in the rear. We advanced with very few casualties and soon cut the road to Brunete but the fields in the rear of Villanueva were flat with no ditches or any cover. The men were exhausted with the extreme heat and lack of water. It was clear we would have to wait until dusk. This meant loss of precious time for the offensive. Suddenly in the failing light groups of women and children were seen coming from the village. Company Commander Bill Meredith from Northumberland and his commissar Bob Elliot from Blyth jumped up and shouted to the men to hold their fire. Many stood up to see what was happening. Suddenly heavy fire broke out behind the women from the fascists who had used them as a trick to escape. A dozen of our men and all the women and children were mown down. Many of the fascists escaped but a little later were rounded up by a Spanish unit. In the sortie George Brown of Manchester was wounded and then shot dead by the fascist officer. The Battalion postman, John Henderson of Gateshead was also wounded in the attack.

J. Colman[11]

Next morning we joined up with the battalion. Going down the road we passed a lot of our dead lying at the side awaiting burial. George Brown, the Manchester Communist leader, was amongst them. Apparently, the Fascists had used women and children as shields to attack the Republican troops, there were many casualties on both sides. I wasn't in the actual shooting.

Notes

Chapter 1: Introduction: The Virtuous Republic versus the Philistines

1. 'Spain 1937' by W. H. Auden.
2. Henceforward, the title of Auden's poem is normally capitalized, so as to distinguish it from 'Spain', i.e. the cultural construct which is a foreground subject of the enquiries which follow.
3. At no time has the myth had a strong profile within Spain, where majority opinion regards foreign obsession with the war as self-indulgent and somewhat bizarre; see, for example, Avilés Farré (1994). This feeling is by no means simply the product of Francoist conditioning; see Aguilar Fernández (1996), 286ff.
4. De la Cierva (1969), 5.
5. *A Prospectus for the Inauguration Overseas of the Tiananmen University of Democracy* (1990), 10. This pamphlet also quotes La Pasionaria's 'You are History. You are Legend.'
6. De la Souchère (1965), 139.
7. See, for instance, Ian Gibson's *Un Irlandés en España* (1981) which contains (*passim*) an elegy for the lost intellectual utopia of the Republic. A full, and perfectly faultless, statement of the myth of the 'Virtuous Republic' can be found in the best-selling study of contemporary Spain by Hooper (1995), 341–2.
8. The works of Stanley Payne are an exception to this rule.
9. In the less public field of 'literature', the regime became relatively lax surprisingly quickly; see Ridruejo (1979), 15–38; Jordan (1990), esp. 11–28; Butt (1978), 39–40.
10. See, for example, Orta (1986).
11. The present writer has counted the words, not including repeats. But see also Aguilar Fernandez (1996), 115–35.
12. Observed by Michael Portillo at the outset of his BBC Radio 4 series on the heritage of the Spanish War, broadcast spring 2000.
13. See Giral and Santidrián (1977).
14. See Meltzer (1978).
15. Cf. in Gibson (1981) treatments of this point on pp. 88–9, 209–10. The pro-Republican, Salvador de Madariaga, claimed that José Antonio

'was a poet, who in his dreams envisaged a Spain as beautiful as it was unreal'; foreword to Ridruejo (1976), 13.
16 See, for instance, statements by an international collection of writers and artists in Woolf and Bagguley (1967). The model was Cunard's *Authors Take Sides on the Spanish War* (1937).
17 Though Lorca's sexuality had long been an open secret, its link with his murder was demonstrated in Gibson's *La represión nacionalista de Granada y la muerte de Federico García Lorca* (1971), translated as *The Death of Lorca* (1973).
18 Inglada (2001), 86–7, 100–4, 116–20, 124–44. This superb study appeared in conjunction with an exhibition on its subject at the Reina Sofia Gallery. Ridruejo is quoted ibid. from his *Casí unas memorias* (1976 edn).

Whilst writing the present book, I told the story of Ponce de León's art, politics and death – but avoiding reference to his party affiliation – to about a dozen friends, some not wholly unfamiliar with modern Spain. All assumed that the artist was a typical left-wing victim of Fascist philistinism. This reflects our academic prejudices. When we speak of intellectuals murdered by Fascists, our voices tremble with outrage. When we speak of intellectuals murdered by Communists, our voices are muted and embarrassed. When we hear of intellectuals murdered by 'the people', we remain silent.

19 See, for instance, 'Los cuatro generales' and 'El tren blindado', in *Las canciones de las Brigadas Internacionales*, reprinted in Alvarez (1996), 359–60. This song-book was distributed to many volunteers. The 'Madrid 1936' versions of Lorca's songs have been performed and recorded countless times, usually in a heightened ideological context.
20 Cortada (1982), 173; Elsner (1972), 135; Livermore (1972), 211.
21 Lorca often posthumously accompanied Aid-Spain meetings in Britain; see e.g. Mulford (1988), 93. Later he became almost official artist of the International Brigade veterans' associations. See, e.g., examples in IBA Box 4, *passim*. His work was constantly profiled in veterans' periodical literature, anti-Franco propaganda meetings, educational work, etc. See, e.g., *The Volunteer*, journal of the Lincoln Brigade Association, *passim*
22 The most detailed account of the military confrontation is Martínez Bande (1976). There are several eyewitness accounts in English; see, e.g., the reportage of Cox (1937); memoirs of British participants include Romilly (1937/1971) and Thomas in Stradling (1998), esp. 70–8.
23 La Voz del Combatiente, 27 February 1937.
24 Muggeridge (1967), 55.

Notes

25 Ibid., 275. Cf. Sommerfield (1937), esp. 137–49.
26 See, for general reference, Robinson (1971) and Sanchez (1987).
27 Diaz-Plaja (1994), 260 ('la obsesión que tenía la izquierda republicana por la cultura no era una simple frase de propaganda.') This author's claim that the policy was vitiated by its purposes of ideological indoctrination was partly endorsed by a scholarly study appearing soon afterwards: Cobb (1995), esp. 133, 165ff.
28 Tuñón de Lara, in Garitaonandía (?1996), 331–6. In early 1938, the Republic circulated a glossy pamphlet which claimed 27,000 schools built in five years, 10,000 during 1937 alone. In contrast their enemies had closed over fifty schools: 'La República Española desarrolla la cultura', in MAE R1058/14.
29 Allison Peers (1936), 125–7.
30 Castillejo (1937/1976), 120–3. See also Castillejo's article 'Spain and the Powers: an intervention for peace?', *The Times*, 18 May 1937.
31 Cobb (1996), 238–9.
32 Allison Peers – an Anglican – was internally alienated by the atrocities (especially in his beloved Catalonia) but strove to maintain external neutrality. However, after Ramos Oliveira, then at the Spanish embassy, wrote accusing him of being 'irresponsible' and 'contemptible', matters changed. In late 1937, the Liverpool agent of the Burgos regime suggested that Peers had become 'one of the most promising elements for exploitation by our propaganda'; see the file in MAE R1057/14.
33 Garosci (1959/1981), 13–14.
34 In August 1936, the Republic obtained the signatures of nearly 100 intellectuals and artists, including Ramón Menéndez Pidal, Antonio Machado, José Ortega y Gasset and Gregorio Marañón, to a manifesto of support. The consequent publication added quotations from the works of Miguel de Unamuno and Salvador de Madariaga, implying a similar attitude; *Intellectuals and the Spanish Military Rebellion* (Press Department of Spanish Embassy in London, 1936), 9–10 and 29–32. Many subscriptions were obtained while the percussive noises of checas, roaming Madrid's smarter districts in search of fifth-columnists, rang in the signatories' ears. Of the six mentioned here, only Machado ultimately and unequivocally sided with the Republic. For the pressure put on intellectuals to declare support for the Republic, see Alvarez Lopera (1982), I, 110–2.
35 Ortega Klein (1980).
36 Ortega y Gasset (1928). In 1932, John Cornford (then adolescent) applauded an attack on Ortega's views by the Marxist intellectual, John Strachey; see Sloan (1938), 88.

37 See Ortega y Gasset (1925).
38 See Rubio and Goni (1986), 162–3. Einstein had sent a message to the 1937 Congress of Anti-Fascist Intellectuals in Madrid, referring to the 'heroic struggle of the Spanish people for freedom and human dignity'; quoted in Castells (1972), 231.
39 García Queipo de Llano (1996), 615.
40 G. Marañón, *Antonio Pérez* (1929); *El Conde Duque de Olivares: La pasión de mandar* (1936). These early exercises in 'psycho-history' were best-sellers. Abroad, Marañon's books represented Spanish historical scholarship in the same way as the novels of Victor Blasco Ibáñez – another refugee from Primo – represented its literary endeavour.
41 On Marañón's 'defection', see *El Adelanto de Salamanca*, 16 January and 14 February 1937; attacks on him followed in the Republican press, e.g. *La Voz del Combatiente*, 16 March 1937. See also the wartime correspondence of Marañón with Madariaga, printed in *El Cultural* (Madrid), 4 July 2001, 3–11.
42 See Unamuno's conversation with the Greek writer Nikos Kazantzakis (c. September 1936) recorded in the latter's *España y Viva la Muerte*, 167–71.
43 Ortíz Alfau (1986).
44 Queipo de Llano (1996), 614. One republican reporter later greeted news of Unamuno's demise with the comment 'For us, he died on 18 July' – the date of the military uprising; see *News Chronicle*, 4 February 1937.
45 The account which follows is based on that given by Luis Portilo in *The Golden Horizon* (Weidenfeld & Nicolson, 1954). I have been unable to locate a copy of this book, which is recorded as missing from the British Library; and have relied on the relevant extract printed in Payne (1963), 123–9. The writer was not present, and presumably compiled his story from the memories of others; no detailed eyewitness narrative seems to be extant.
46 'You will conquer, but you will never convince.' See, e.g., the title of a recent critical compendium, Albert (1998). After the incident, Unamuno retired to his private house and died shortly afterwards of natural causes.
47 For his epic stand against Millán, Unamuno has been honoured with his own website as one of the 'Heroes of the Twentieth Century'; see rjgeib.com/heroes/unamuno/unamuno.html
48 Taylor (1983), 169–70
49 Cockburn (1967), 161.
50 Abrahamson (1994), *passim*. 'La niña bonita', the nice-looking girl, was a familiar metaphor for the Republic.

51 Barea (1984), esp. 213–33; Koltsov, however, was much more than propaganda overlord; see 85–7 and 181–2 below.
52 Koltsov (1963), *passim*; Ehrenburg (1979), esp. 51–7.
53 See the definitive collection of Carulla and Carulla (1997).
54 The third of these examples is featured in the ingenious computer 'Screen Saver' distributed by the Abraham Lincoln Brigade Association. In spring 2001 an exhibition was held in Salamanca of wartime posters reflecting 'Cultura y educación', drawing on the Civil War Archive which is located in the city. All examples chosen to illustrate the accompanying flysheet were of Republican origin.
55 The campaign included a visit from six Labour MPs to Madrid to witness (and to bear witness to) the concern for art; see *Our Journey to Spain* (Barcelona, Seix y Barral, 1938). Many similar publications were issued: for example, *Nine Rescued Works of Art* (Barcelona, Seix y Barral, 1937), *Fascism Destroys Spain's Artistic Heritage* (Barcelona, Patronato Nacional de Turismo, 1938); Parrot (1937); Bosch-Guimpera (1937). *The Salvage of Catalonia's Historical and Artistic Patrimony* (Barcelona, Comisariat de Propaganda, 1937) claimed that 'the work of salvage of archives, libraries and objects of art was simultaneous to the first reactions of the 19 July revolution'.
56 Alvarez Lopera (1982), I, 61. See also the pamphlet in Esperanto, *La internacia fasismo detruas la arton de hispanio* (Informa Servo De Nacia Patronado Pri Turismo-Hispanio, n.d.), lavishly designed, illustrated and produced.
57 See, for instance 'Culture shall not die', report by Parisian delegate of World Student Association visit to Madrid in *Seeds of Conflict* (1975), 31–5.
58 See the diagram reproduced in Alvarez Lopera (1982), II, 195. It seems the projectiles failed to ignite. However, Goya was attacked again in the Modern Art Museum shortly after; ibid., II, 54–5.
59 Azaña (1978), 441–3. The message soon got through to the Artists' International Association in London; see *News-Sheet Bulletin*, no. 2 (January 1937), IBA Box 4/D: though it did not reach the XV International Brigade magazine, *Volunteer for Liberty*, until much later; 'The art treasures of Madrid', 25 October 1937, 6–7.
60 Delaprée (1937), 31.
61 The fundamental and comprehensive study of this process is by Alvarez Lopera (1982).
62 See, e.g., Aldgate (1979); Brothers (1997). The latter book (despite its generalized title) is almost entirely devoted to the press photography of the Spanish War and its propaganda dimensions.
63 Bates in Cunningham (1986). By autumn 1937 the government was

able to counter-attack strongly in this field: see 'Rebels order destruction of democratic literature: Nazi example followed', Spanish Press Agency, London, 2 November 1937; IBA Box 8/A1.
64 *Artists News Sheet, For Peace, for Democracy, for Cultural Progress*, no. 2; ibid., Box 4/D. Meanwhile, in contrast, the young Catalan painter Joan Brossa went to fight on the Aragon front 'with nothing but a book by Lorca'; *Guardian*, obituary, 12 January 1998.
65 Ford (1968), 183.
66 Alvarez Lopera (1982), I, 109.
67 Valleau (1982), 25.
68 Circular no. 1781, Barcelona, 22 December 1938, MAE R894/16.
69 Report datelined 8 February 1939, quoted in Ford (1968), 192. Julio Alvarez del Vayo was foreign minister in Juan Negrín's government.
70 Taylor (1983), 145; see also Alvarez Lopera (1982), II, 35–7.
71 D'Ydewalle (1946), 136.
72 Bates (1963), 354.

Chapter 2: Comrade – Lover – Victim: Cornford, Spender and Friends

1 Straight (1983), 96–7.
2 Sloan (1938), 201, 246.
3 Ibid., frontispiece. It appeared twice in the pages of the XV Brigade magazine *Volunteer for Liberty* during the war (11 October 1937 and 3 January 1938). The memorial volume's dust cover also bore the International Brigade's three-pointed Red Star symbol.
4 Straight (1983), 71. In view of this, and of the book's purpose, it is difficult to accept the author's claims that he was never a Party member.
5 Straight (1943). Following December 1941, veterans of the Lincoln Battalion were identified by US intelligence services as 'premature anti-Fascists', later adopting this tag as an ironic badge of honour. Given the context of these pages, the reader will appreciate the difficulties of interpreting a text, recorded nearly fifty years later, of a conversation between a Mr Blunt and a Mr Straight.
6 Ingram (1985), 59ff.
7 Romilly's memoir, *Boadilla*, was published by Hamish Hamilton in 1937 (I have used the McDonald edition, 1971). Romilly and Cornford, known to each other as *aficionados* of a radical London bookshop, were briefly reunited during a lull in the battle: ibid., 157, 182, and see also Ingram (1985), 142.

8   Isherwood (1976), 195–6.
9   Hyndman's published account in Toynbee (1976) is misleading about his comportment in battle. He was more candid with Tony MacLean, an acquaintance he met in Albacete; IWM AC 838/5, reel 2; cf. also, George Aitken's recollections, ibid., 10357/3, reel 2.
10 'Cuthbert said he was in a state of nervous collapse when he saw him'; Spender to W. Plomer, 2 April 1937, University of Durham, Plomer MSS 213/51/1. See also Worsley (1939), 256–61.
11 For the course of the British action at Jarama see Alexander (1986), 91–103. Romilly, unlike Hyndman, was keen for action, disliking the liaison job which he was assigned at the instance of his mother and uncle. He later became one of the few genuine cases of 'desertion *to* the front'.
12 Serrano (1989), 359.
13 Hyndman's file, RGASPI 545/6/151/2–6, includes a report by Tony de Maio, SIM agent, compiled over a year later. See also Hopkins (1998), 198.
14 Cunningham (1980), 193. One book on the Lincoln Battalion devotes a chapter ('The Massacre') to their attack on Pingarrón Heights, prefaced with a quotation from Hyndman's poem; see Eby (1969), 54.
15 Alvarez Rodríguez and López Ortega (1986), esp. introduction (1–14), printed in Spanish only.
16 See the header quotation to ch. 5 for a version of such feelings.
17 See Spender (1950), 245. (In the content material of these references Spender and Hyndman are hereafter rendered as SS and TH.)
18 Alvarez Rodríguez and López Ortega (1986), 3. An earlier translation appeared in the Spanish version of Toynbee's *The Distant Drum* (*El Tambor Lejano*, Madrid, Sedmay, 1977); this was used by Montero Barrado (1987), 96. TH's verse is also noticed by Esteban in Requena (1998), 143.
19 Spender and Lehmann (1939), 40. For critical treatment see Tolley (1975), 341; Weatherhead (1975), 66; Ford (1965), 106–7.
20 A partial exception to this observation is that during the 1970s, TH edited and contributed to the house magazine of an alcoholics' rehabilitation centre in Cardiff.
21 See above, n. 9.
22 O'Neill (1976); see also, Spender (1951 [hereafter *WWW*]), 176–7. (When he returned to Cardiff, *c.*1970, TH reverted to his first Christian name.)
23 O'Neill (1976); Shipton (1995); I owe information on TH's life to Alun Emlyn-Jones, Paddy Kitson, Terry Dimmick and Arthur Callard.
24 'For TARH' and others; see Sternlicht (1992), 30–3.

25. Spender (1936). TH appears in fictionalized form in the title story and in 'The Dead Island'. The former contains a revealing description of TH's pain at being made by a chance remark to feel like a domestic servant. The latter works out SS's concern over TH's increasing psychological dependence on himself and on alcohol. These stories clearly grew out of the intense and frequent quarrels of the two lovers, charted in *WWW*. A third story is a 'realistic' account of a political episode they experienced in revolutionary Vienna in 1934.

26. *WWW*, in which TH is called 'Jimmy Younger', forms the basis of information about the relationship (see esp. pp. 175–9, 182–6, 193–7, 212–46, where it is woven *passim* into SS's account of his involvement with 'Spain'). However, this material is compromised, to a degree well above the norm, by the conditionings of its genre. Some anti-matter is deployed in David (1992), esp. 154–94. However, TH also characterized himself imaginatively, for example, by pretending to hail from Cardiff's Tiger Bay, a feature likely to increase his exotic appeal. In fact, like Dame Shirley Bassey, who enjoys a similar attribution (hence my section title), TH was born in the less exotic surroundings of Splott, and never lived in what is now called 'Cardiff Bay'.

27. From the perspective of (say) the *London Review of Books*, SS's Maida Vale flat, where Auden, Lehmann, Day Lewis et al. often met, assumes an importance equal to that of Cliveden, the common rooms of the Cambridge Apostles or All Souls, Oxford, the cabinet table, the editorial offices of the *New Statesman* – and (of course) the Woolfs' lair in Tavistock Square. See also ch. 5.

28. See, e.g., Wood (1959), esp. 75–120.

29. For example, Splott met All Souls when SS gave a lecture in Oxford, and he and TH were entertained to tea by historian A. L. Rowse; see (1993), 181. (I owe this reference to Terry Hawkes.)

30. Gollancz, 1936.

31. On the culture of the 'rough trade', Driberg (1978), esp. 87–106 *passim*. The significance of the SS–TH story is examined in Sinfield (1997). Writing in *c*.1950, SS noted that TH 'was accustomed to be treated rough'; *WWW*, 175.

32. Quoted in David (1992), 154.

33. (1936), 10. (Hereafter *FFL*).

34. Spender (1980), 121 (SS to Isherwood, 5 October 1936). However, within a few weeks TH's flat had been occupied by a friend in need and he moved back in with SS.

35. See David (1996), *passim*. For evocative treatment of the regime which conditioned gay intellectuals into a twilight discourse of cypher and mendacity, see Mackenzie (1956), esp 170–4, an incident set in 1938.

36 In *WWW* (see esp. 204), SS recounts his first meeting Iñez Pearn as taking place after he and TH had split, which may be true. In any case, it was a *mariage de convenance*, not only in the broad political sense (where in terms of gender politics it is analogous to Auden's marriage to Erika Mann) but also in that it represented a convenient escape route *ex-hominum*.

37 Moreover, doubtless following a quarrel, TH had earlier threatened to join the Party and go to fight in Abyssinia against the Italian Fascists; see David (1992), 184. See, however, n. 40.

38 Spender (1980), 128–9 (30 December 1936).

39 Sternlicht (1992), 122.

40 *WWW*, 210–18; SS and Worsley may have secretly joined the Party at this point, since their mission was as much Comintern espionage as investigative journalism. Indeed, had they succeeded in entering Nationalist Spain, they could have ended up where Arthur Koestler found himself a month later – in a Franco death cell. In his book on *The Thirties* Malcolm Muggeridge, using privileged information, revealed that 'Mr Stephen Spender announced his departure for Insurgent territory where he proposed to operate as a spy'. The first edition (1940) carried an inserted slip stating: 'Mr Stephen Spender wishes to deny the accuracy of the author's statement regarding him on page 248.' In any case, SS's statement that 'Jimmy joined the communist party shortly after I did' is untrue. TH joined in October 1936, and SS made excuses to Isherwood for not doing likewise; *WWW*, 210–12, and cf. Spender (1980), 121–4. SS's reconfiguration has invariably been accepted by commentators.

41 Though neither set of memoirs acknowledges this, it seems not unreasonable to assume that SS had recourse to Worsley for the same reasons as TH had taken up with Giles Romilly.

42 'I Join the Communist Party', *Daily Worker*, 19 February 1937, text reprinted in Spender (1979), 80–2. The Valencia job had become vacant through the absence of W. H. Auden (see ch. 4). It had only ever been part-time, and shortly after SS arrived it vanished altogether.

43 Bell (1984), 56–7. The entry is dated 18 February 1937. Its reference to the (?) Foreign Legion is mystifying.

44 SS to Plomer (as n. 10). I am grateful to the University of Durham for permission to quote from this document.

45 PRO/FO/371/W11209/20538, 12 September 1936. The article, 'The mind of the businessman in Spain', appeared on 1 September. In Barcelona just before the war, SS and TH had received hospitality from the consul and various expatriates.

46 Pollitt addressed the British Battalion on 6 March, whilst SS visited

their lines four days later; see Graham (1987), 50–1. It seems likely that Pollitt enabled SS to see TH and negotiate with the Commissariat in Albacete.

47 TH's file, RGASPI (n. 13), noting that a report has been made against SS for recommending a deserter for a responsible job.

48 For SS's account of this trip, see *WWW*, 218ff.

49 A document in TH's Comintern file states that a medical commission had failed to find any evidence of an alleged ulcer; 'Rapport No. 681 – Cause, Hyndman, Thomas – 17 Mars [193]7'; RGASPI 545/6/151/6.

50 *WWW*, 224.

51 According to 'Rapport No. 681', 'A Valence Hyndman était arreté par la police espagnole après un rendez-vous avec le correspondent de Reuter (Barry), lequel il connait, comme il dit, por son ancien chef Stevens Bender [*sic*?] ecrivain et journaliste de gauche en Angleterre.'

52 *WWW*, 234. It seems that someone in the consulate also felt guilty at having rejected TH.

53 Once out of Spain, Spender wrote to the poet William Plomer: 'I am completely dazed by all my experiences and I can't write to you except about the very important matter of Tony's future . . .'; letter of 2 April 1937 (as n. 10).

54 Pollitt to Martin, 8 April 1937, K. Martin's Papers, University of Sussex, 14/5. (I am grateful to Sussex University and to Dr Tom Buchanan for this reference.)

55 Spender to Pollitt, 10 April 1937 (hol.), NMLH CP/Ind/Poll/2/6. All the SS–Pollitt letters cited here are addressed to 'Dear Comrade'.

56 A week later Martin and SS dined at the Woolfs'; Virginia noted: 'Harry Pollitt cuts up rough when asked to arrange Tony's and Spender's amours – not unnaturally'; Bell (1984), 79–80.

57 'Rapport No. 681'.

58 De Maio's report bears the MS note: 'Hyndaman [*sic*], Tony. Sospechoso', which may be evidence for this; ibid., 4. M. Requena (1998), 159 has 'El comunista Jimmy Younger fué acusado de trotskista', but this seems to rely only on *WWW*.

59 Tapsell to Pollitt [?May] 1937, IBA Box C/13/1.

60 'Spender . . . still has some peculiar friends. One demands cast iron guarantees that deserters are not shot! . . . [He] acknowledges that he has 4 who he is "protecting" because he thinks we will shoot them!'; Tapsell to Pollitt, *c*.10 April 1937, NMLH CP/Ind/Poll/2/6.

61 Paynter to Pollitt, 30 May 1937, IBA Box C/13/8.

62 Ibid., 15/1, unnumbered and unsigned hol. sheet.

63 'Heroes in Spain', 1 May 1937, reprinted in Spender (1979), 66–70. SS was made to atone for this, *inter alia* by chairing a meeting of writers

called to whip up support for the Republic's action against the POUM. 'From the glazed look he wore . . . I thought that Spender may have found the evening a bit of a strain'; Ambler (1986), 124–5. See also ch. 9.
64   Spender to Pollitt, 30 June 1937, IBA Box C/15/1.
65   Pollitt to Spender, 3 July 1937, ibid. (SS himself was in Spain at this point).
66   *WWW*, 243–4.
67   Leavitt (1998), 251–4.
68   Quoted in Kermode (1988), 26. (In 1950, Spender attacked Cockburn in *The God That Failed*.) A Spanish expert has lampooned SS for his confession that 'la mayor parte del tiempo que estuvó en España lo dedicó a la liberación de un amante homosexual encarcelado por desertor'; Trapiello (1994), 255–6.
69   See below, ch. 8, 178ff.
70   Toynbee (1976), 128. The hyperbole suggests the pressure SS was exerting on Pollitt.
71   List of suggested repatriations, 27 June 1937, RGASPI 545/6/53/9.
72   When SS's marriage failed he turned back to TH, who was also sought after as a casual sexual partner by Isherwood, Worsley, Tom Driberg et al.
73   Hyndman in Toynbee (1976), 128.
74   Cockburn, public schoolboy, upper-class Communist, cousin of Hugh and Graham Greene, was (however) not the only exception to this rule.
75   J. McLellan (2001A).
76   *Idem* (2001B), 175.
77   Toynbee (1976), 117–8. No sense of irony can be detected in Jump's statement – nor any awareness of *non-sequitur* in that quoted in the next note.
78   In an interview, Jump brought up the issue alongside what Orwell called 'Polcrime': 'Attitude to homosexuality was very strict [he added]. An Irish chap was sentenced to death and executed . . . because he had shot a Spaniard who had rejected his homosexual advances. That's the story I was told, anyway'; IWM AC 9524, reel 4.
79   McDougall (1986), 151.
80   For a different angle on some of these issues, though featuring the same protagonists, see K. Rothstein's website on 'British Masculinity and the Spanish Civil War', www.interchange.ubc.ca/kris/spain.htm
81   *WWW*, 222–3.
82   Wyden (1983), 255–6.
83   A file on another of Nathan's associates, John McDonald, noted: 'Chauffeur . . . Rapport criminal tres mauvais en Angleterre. A été

procureur et Sodomite', and recommended 'Deportation comme indésirable'; RGASPI 545/6/ 166/32.

84 Stradling (1999), 151, 157; denunciation of Nathan by Colonel Krieger, 21 April 1937, RGASPI 545/6/177/10–11. During an audio interview, George Aitken, one-time XV Brigade commissar, asked for the recorder to be switched off whilst he spoke about Nathan and Romilly; IWM AC 10357, reel 2. See also Ryan (1938), 188–9. Nathan was reportedly killed by a bomb dropped from a lone aircraft near Villanueva de la Cañada on the last day of the battle of Brunete.

85 However, SS told Plomer that it was Nathan's recommendation which had brought about TH's allocation to a safe job in Albacete following the Jarama crisis; see above, n. 10.

86 Leavitt (1998), 245.

87 Worsley (1971). In a prefatory 'Author's Note' the author insists, 'This is not a novel but a memoir, fictionalised.' In fact, though Worsley made a virtue of the necessity to write in cipher (mentioned above), much more is changed and invented than this claim suggests.

88 Till in the title story of *The Burning Cactus* (in 'The Dead Island' the TH character is actually nameless); Jimmy in *WWW*; Harry in Worsley's 'memoir'; Edward in Leavitt's novel. It seems that 'Tony' became a code name inside the Auden circle for the morganatic partners of its initiates; see Auden's greeting to 'the three or four Tonies' in an unpublished 'Ode to the New Year (1939)', Driberg Papers, A15 (Auden File), Christ Church, Oxford. See also Driberg (1978), 59. The Auden–Isherwood play *The Dog Beneath the Skin* (1935) contains several references to the TH–SS relationship, including a bitingly satirical scene in a nightclub; see esp. I.5.63, II.2.87 and II.2.124/6.

89 However, TH's own feeling about that day – he later spent years working for repertory companies in backstage and spear-carrying roles – was 'that was when the curtain went up, for me'; Isherwood (1976), 168.

90 Sloan (1938), 47. Unless otherwise noted, biographical details of Cornford used in sections 1 and 5 are taken from Stansky and Abrahams (1986), esp. 188–246.

91 'Left?' in Sloan (1938), 125–33. Cf the attitude of Cornford's fellow-martyr, Caudwell, to the Auden group below, 91.

92 See Weatherhead (1975), 28–9.

93 Sloan (1938), 174–8. SS read this volume for review.

94 Victor Kiernan recalled Cornford's 'telling with genuine relish, a story of Bela Kun machine-gunning five thousand prisoners during a forced retreat in the Russian Civil War; he told it not in a spirit of sadism, but in appreciation of an act of political necessity firmly carried out'; see

Sloan (1938), 124. On his selfless determination in saving the life of Jan Kurzke, see letter of Kate Kurzke, Murcia, 28 January 1937, John Strachey Papers, private possession. (I owe this reference to the kindness of Dr Tom Buchanan. The attribution of the letter to Kate Kurzke has been made by reference to corroborative materials in the IBA Archive.)

95 M. Heinemann, interview, IWM AC 9239, reel 3. This seems to have been an act of pure mendaciousness and malice.
96 See below 186–7.
97 Sloan (1938), 59–60.
98 Her possession of an ostensibly male first name is no more than the fashion of a period in which girls were often known as 'Billie' or 'Jackie', and in which Evelyn Waugh was married to a woman also called Evelyn.
99 Sloan (1938), 50.
100 Heinemann, IWM AC 9239 reel 2. As a maid of the family put it, 'what I like about John is that he always sees the funny side of life'; Sloan (1938), 19.
101 Heinemann, ibid. She later drew on all this for her novel *The Adventurers* (1960).
102 Heinemann, who later became a Cambridge don, interprets Cornford's poetry in two cognate essays: see Clark (1979), esp. 115–25, and Hart (1988), 46–64.
103 Straight (1983, 99) was told by a family member that Professor Cornford 'never liked her [Ray]'. Heinemann reveals that Cornford's mother 'was very distressed by his political attitudes – more, I think because he'd taken up with a working class girl he met in London than because of the activities themselves . . . She couldn't cope with it at all.' (At this point, like Aitken on Nathan, Heinemann asked for the recording machine to be switched off.) IWM, as n. 100.
104 Straight (1983), 99. However, it seems she was interviewed in the 1960s by Stansky and Abrahams; see (1986), 364.
105 Williams (1985).
106 Ibid., 359.

Chapter 3: Battle on the Monte Oscuro: The Surreal Landscape of Orwell's Spain

1 See chs. 7 & 8. Note that Orwell's works are cited here in the editions specified in the bibliography.
2 Williams (1984), 57.

3 Muste (1966), 168.
4 Garosci (1981), 339–54 (first edn *Gli intellettuali e la guerra di Spagna*, Turin, Eunaudi 1959).
5 *Homenaje a Cataluña* (Madrid, Ariel).
6 Spender (1950).
7 Trilling (1974, originally 1952); Chomsky (1969), esp. 86, 117; Williams (1984); Thompson (1979). In 'Outside the Whale' (originally 1960) Thompson deplored the pessimism of 'Inside the Whale', but later called Orwell's irreducible socialist humanism to his aid in attacking the greater enemy, Althusser, in the title essay (originally 1978).
8 B. Crick, *George Orwell: A Life*.
9 Sperber in Hanrez (1977), 58–61.
10 See Gutierrez Alvarez (1984), 101–12.
11 Crick (1984); Alba (1975), 150; Coll and Pané (1978), 127–41. See also the positive remarks in the best selling textbook by the Franco-Catalan historian Pierre Vilar (1992), 101.
12 Trapiello (1994), 258–9.
13 García Queipo de Llano (1996), 625.
14 Sanz de Soto (1997), 26–7.
15 On my own shelves there are no fewer than nine compendium volumes about the Spanish Civil War in which extracts from *Homage* are included. More will doubtless appear before publication of this book. Many are issued for student use as documentary source primers.
16 Stradling (1984). Some material has been incorporated into this chapter, though rarely without some alteration of place, phraseology or function.
17 Norris (1984), 7–8.
18 Alexander (1984).
19 Cunningham (1987); Monteath (1990); Horn (1990). The first of these claimed in one place (p. 504) that my methodology amounted to impugning any writer's honesty on the basis of 'a single mistake' or (at the other end of the scale of critical values) because of difference in overall interpretation between critic and subject. Only a page later, however, he stated that 'Robert Stradling's essay ... assembles quite a package of factual objections' (p. 505). Another scholar, who apparently worked independently of my essay, nevertheless reached conclusions very close to it; Iverson (1988).
20 Newsinger (1998), 57. Mr Newsinger's vicarious indignation over the reputation of a writer who has been dead for half a century testifies to Orwell's canonical status.
21 In the last sentence of *Wigan Pier*, Orwell looked forward to the day when the middle class 'may sink without further struggles into the

working class where we belong, and probably when we get there it will not be so dreadful as we feared, for, after all, we have nothing to lose but our aitches'.
22. 'A Letter from Aragon', in Sloan (1938), 247.
23. Crick (1980), 218–19; Shelden (1991), 288–9. See also Hopkins (1998), 204–9, which cites documentation from the Moscow (RGASPI) Archive.
24. See Pages i Blanch (1997).
25. *Homage*, 113.
26. 'Report on the English Section of the POUM', IBA Box C, file 13/7a.
27. *Homage*, 112–13. He told the 'Communist friend' later that 'I could not join a communist-controlled unit. Sooner or later it might mean being used against the Spanish working class'; ibid., 140.
28. 'Battalion Roll June 1937', RGASPI 545/6/47/17–19; MS table of XV Brigade losses at Brunete, ibid., 3/486/184.
29. For the 'opposition' case, see Souchy (1987). Defenders of the Republic's actions, and the role of the PCE, have emerged in Rees (1998) and Graham (1999), but their conclusions will be challenged in a forthcoming book by Frank Schauff (University of Cologne) whose paper on 'The Comintern and the Spanish Civil War: the view from the Kremlin' I attended at the University of the West of England in March 2001.
30. For a complementary account, see McNair (1979).
31. Davison (1998), 112–13.
32. 'Why I Join the I.L.P.', Davison (1998), 167 and passim. In 'Why I Write' (p. 13) he asserted that 'every line of serious work that I have written since 1936 has been written . . . against totalitarianism and in favour of democratic socialism'.
33. *The Spanish Revolution: Bulletin of the Workers' Party of Marxist Unification*, 3 February 1937, 9–10.
34. *Wigan Pier*, 149ff. Williams advises us to 'notice [Orwell's] habit of writing in these contemptuous and devaluing terms of something of which he had himself been a part'; (1984), 10.
35. McNair (1979), 15.
36. Johnson (1996), 88. As Shelden (1991, 289) points out, Edwards, who acted as correspondent for the ILP newspaper, the *New Leader*, himself deserved this jibe. Yet he also praised his rival's personal courage and initiative when reporting the attack in which Orwell's unit took part; Davison, 11, 18–20. Though it is not mentioned in *Homage*, Orwell later claimed to have been elected 'political responsible' by his company in the trenches; ibid., 138.
37. The relevant exchange with Koestler is referred to in 'Looking back', 233–4.

38 West (1989), 95.
39 All these backslidings are to be found in his various wartime essays, gathered in *England Your England and Other Essays* (1954).
40 'Eye-witness in Barcelona' (August 1937), in Davison (1998), 59; see also 'Spilling the Spanish Beans' (ibid., 41–6) and scattered remarks in book reviews, letters to newspapers, and private correspondence, ibid., *passim*.
41 See e.g. *Homage*, 198.
42 These changes of feeling and emphasis can now be tracked, thanks to the publication of Davison's edition of the *Complete Works*, vols. 11 and 12, where each piece appears in order of publication.
43 *Homage*, 7–8.
44 Borkenau (1986), 169.
45 Quoted in Horn (1990), 54.
46 Romero (1996), 43.
47 Morreres i Boix (1980), 27–38; Rocker (1986), 29.
48 Borkenau (1986), 175.
49 Seidman (1990), 175. This helps explain why the CNT eventually accepted the PCE line on discipline, and distanced itself from the POUM – a move which had obvious implications for the militias. Cf. also Fernández-Armesto (1992), 224–5.
50 One reason why I repeat this charge, first made in 1984, is that (*pace* Newsinger (1998), 57–8) it is naive to imagine that Orwell had no concept of a strategic 'higher truth' which allowed the dissemination of tactical 'lower lies'. For example, he argued that since the Communist-controlled paramilitary units behind the lines comprised well-fed, slick-uniformed men armed with the best Soviet weaponry, whilst front-line battalions were made up from starving, ragged boys carrying museum pieces, it was clear that the Republic was not serious about the war, instead angling for a compromise peace with Fascism; see, e.g., Davison (1998), 41–2, 57, 76–7. These allegations were not true in 1937, and Orwell had no evidence for them.
51 Morreres i Boix (1980); see also Thomas (1977), 656.
52 *Homage*, 156, 164–6.
53 It may also indicate that Orwell was suspected of being a security risk; see Davison (1998), 35–6.
54 'Notes on the Spanish Militias', Davison (1998), 135–45. Even during the composition of *Homage* Orwell characterized some authors as 'Trotskyists', pointing out that 'their prejudice is against the official Communist Party to which they are not always entirely fair'; ibid., 87.
55 Davison (1998), 52. See (however) above, n. 27.

56 Orwell's equivocation here was instigated by Jellinek (1938), which he reviewed in two different places in 1938, and a subsequent correspondence with the author; see Davison (1998), 172, 178, 254.
57 'Why I Write', 14.
58 'Caesarean Section in Spain', Davison (1998), 332–5.
59 Quoted in Hill (1947), 149–50.
60 'Why I Write', 10–11.
61 *Wigan Pier*, 149ff., quoted p. 179.
62 The second part of *Wigan Pier* is addressed to the leaders of British socialism just as the first part is levelled at the conscience of Orwell's own class – the petite bourgeoisie, seen as the potential 'breakthrough' constituency of the BUF.
63 'Inside the Whale', 104.
64 Sommerfield (1937); Romilly (1937); Wintringham (1940); Allison Peers (1936). Orwell reviewed the first and last of these among some twenty books about the Spanish War in 1937–40. He was impressed at times; Davison (1998), passim. For defence of the Internationals' memoirs in this context, see Klaus (1988), 6–37.
65 *Wigan Pier*, 150, 195.
66 Ibid., 30–1. When Secker & Warburg reprinted this passage in the compendium *England Your England* in 1954, they omitted the adjective 'Nancy'; see p. 191.
67 *Wigan Pier*, 161, where Auden is seen as 'a sort of gutless Kipling' and his associates as 'even feebler'.
68 W. H. Auden, 'A Summer Night'.
69 See below pp. 87–91. On the death of Bob Smillie, see Buchanan (1997), 435–61.
70 'Inside the Whale', 126.
71 Crick (1980), 207; Shelden (1991), 122–3
72 Davison (1998), 67. The context suggests Orwell was 'daring' Cunard to publish his letter verbatim.
73 The reasons for Orwell's interest in Spender remain mysterious. At any rate, he assured him: 'I don't know that I had ever exactly attacked you, but I had certainly in passing made offensive remarks about "parlour Bolsheviks such as Auden and Spender" or words to that effect.' Spender was involved with Cunard in the production of *Authors Take Sides*, and is unlikely not to have read *Wigan Pier*. His acceptance of Orwell's crooked olive-branch reveals an impeccable Oxbridge training. See ibid., 100, 130–3, 146.
74 The quotation in this sentence is from *Wigan Pier* 112.
75 Davison (1998), 136.

[76] Orwell's attitude to the popular press and its baronial associations with capitalism can be sampled in his description of the newspaper canvassers who operated in the mean streets of the industrial North as little better than slaves; *Wigan Pier*, 9–11.
[77] Ibid., 198, 201–2.
[78] Davison (1998), 132, see *passim* for examples.
[79] See below 188–9.
[80] Hopkinson (1977), 7.
[81] For the role of British newsreel companies in the Spanish War, see Aldgate (1979).
[82] Williams (1984), 58.
[83] *Homage*, 140. Fernandez-Armesto (1992, 225) observes that Orwell's initial reaction to intra-Republican division – 'aren't we all socialists?' – was 'like asking "aren't we all Christians?" at the massacre of St Bartholomew'.
[84] Davison (1998), 131.
[85] 'Why I Join the ILP', ibid., 167–9. (The caveat in this quotation is of interest.)
[86] Ibid., 261.
[87] Thompson (1979), 15
[88] 'Looking Back', 230–1.
[89] Meyers (1975), 133.
[90] See the strictures of Orwell's Catholic friend and admirer, Christopher Hollis (1956), 94.
[91] *Homage*, 173, see also 202, 213.
[92] See *Wigan Pier*, 100, where he writes about 'the histories I was given as a little boy' which explained 'that a cold climate made people energetic while a hot one made them lazy, and hence the defeat of the Spanish Armada'. See also, ch. 8, 179–80 and notes.
[93] *Homage*, 8, 19, 52, 76–7.
[94] Ibid., 79.
[95] Had Orwell inspected some local dwellings he might have been reminded of 'the Roman Catholic homes of Lancashire [where] you see the crucifix on the wall and the *Daily Worker* on the table'; *Wigan Pier*, 156. Indeed, in both Lancashire and Aragon he might also have spotted an image or statuette of the Sacred Heart – the central cult of the Traditionalist (Carlist) Communion who were the most fanatical volunteer fighters on the Nationalist side.
[96] Lison-Tolosana (1983), 44–7, 258–312; Sloan (1938), 199–200; Payne (1970), 242–4; Borkenau (1986), 94–9, 112.
[97] Review of Allison Peers's *The Church in Spain* (1937) in Davison (1998), 234. The classic study of the anticlerical murders is Montero

Moreno (1961); see also a recent and more even-handed summation of the two terrors, Juliá (1999), esp. 117–57.
[98] Shelden (1991), 308.
[99] Quoted in Meyers (1975), 149.
[100] 'Looking Back', 229–30.
[101] Taking a typically 'Orwellian' stand, Brenan, who knew the claim to be a lie, refused to sign a round robin to *The Times* organized by Sir Peter Chalmers-Mitchell, which attested that there had been no Republican atrocities in Málaga; see Gathorne-Hardy (1992), esp. 302, 315–16, 350.

Chapter 4: Battle of Heroes: Britten, Auden and the British Battalion

[1] A useful short account of the Ebro campaign in English is Henry (1999); for more detailed treatment, Martínez Bande (1988).
[2] Buchanan (1997), esp. 146–68; Fyrth (1986), esp. 133–9, 257–61; Alexander (1986), 237–55. A survey of the intellectual character of British involvement in 'Spain' will be found in Hopkins (1998), 19–125, 318–47. The atmosphere of these months amongst intellectual supporters of the Republic in both London and Barcelona is described in a near-contemporary memoir by Louis MacNeice, acquaintance of both Auden and Britten; see (1982), esp. 174–98.
[3] See the concert programmes held by BPL; also Mitchell and Reed (1991), I, 612–13 (hereafter 'L and D', all references to vol. I).
[4] Foreman (1987), 153; M. and S. Harries (1989), 97–8; for Clark's political-musical mission, see Doctor (1999) passim.
[5] See Mitchell (2000), 142–4. The score, which also utilized lines by Randall Swingler (see p. 154), was published later that year as Britten's Op. 14 (London, Winthrop Rogers).
[6] Carpenter (1992), 63. (The works by Mitchell and Carpenter cited above should also be acknowledged for background detail in this chapter, for which repeated specific references would be tedious.)
[7] Auden's role here was later acknowledged by Britten; see L and D, 378, 384. The equivocation in my sentence recognizes the contribution to Britten's literary and political receptivity made earlier by his 'unofficial' composition teacher, Frank Bridge, who was a strong pacifist.
[8] There was no movement called 'New Poetry'. I use the phrase loosely in the context of the relevant journals of the time: *New Writing*, *New Directions*, *New Signatures*, *New Country*, etc. To add to Auden's other accomplishments, he was a capable amateur pianist.

9. Carpenter (1992), 68. (This seems to quote from Britten's MS, reference not found in L and D.)
10. L and D, 434 (20 July 1936). Britten, not *au courant* with correct left terminology, refers to the military coup as a revolution, and not to the 'real' revolution which the coup itself sparked off.
11. Britten to Grace Williams, 26 April 1936, in Foreman (1987), 190; Dickinson (1988), 45
12. L and D, 434 (22 July 1936) – Britten unconsciously invoking Marx by way of protection against Fascism. The news about Barcelona, from 'the definitely pro-fascist Daily Telegraph', was incorrect.
13. Ibid., 436 (28 July 1936).
14. Ibid., 440 (24 July 1936). I am informed by Dr D. Mitchell that no trace can now be found of Britten's draft score in the BPL.
15. Ibid., 104, 435–6 (25 July 1936).
16. Quoted in Carpenter (1992), 570.
17. Quoted ibid., 84.
18. Auden and MacNeice (1967), 145–6.
19. Ibid., 238.
20. Carpenter (1992), 111, 116–17. Auden could not resist a snide remark about 'your Basque delinquent'; to Britten, January 1938, Auden file, BPL.
21. On Auden's views about Love, see Davenport-Hines (1995), esp. 115, 135.
22. Carpenter (1992), 89.
23. Interviewed in Tony Palmer's TV documentary on Britten, 'A Time There Was', BBC (1980).
24. 'FB' is Frank Bridge, who during the illness referred to 'had been delirious . . . mostly being in Spain – worrying about the revolution . . .'; L and D, 458–9.
25. Hopkins (1998), 129–30.
26. L and D, 403. See also Carpenter (1981), 118; *idem* (1992), 74; Davenport-Hines (1995), 126–7.
27. See Morris (1977), 58–9.
28. Davenport-Hines (1995), 163. In this year, Dodds, who was counsellor and confidant to both Auden and MacNeice, became Regius Professor of Classics at Oxford University.
29. Isherwood (1976), 196–7.
30. Davenport-Hines (1995), 164.
31. Isherwood (1976), 217–19.
32. Quoted in Carpenter (1981), 206–7; see also Davenport-Hines (1995), 163
33. Carpenter (1992), 89 (quoting directly from Diary MS, 1 December 1936).

Notes

34 L and D, 439.
35 'I shall be in London most of January – unless I go to Spain, with which idea I'm now toying'; to U. Nettleship, 4 December 1937, L and D, 527. I have found no other reference to this matter in Britten's papers, published or otherwise. Donald Mitchell points out that Britten did not go to Spain during the Civil War. He speculates that this remark may have been a gut reaction to the 'rapidly deteriorating situation [of the Republican cause] in Spain'; ibid., 532. But he also makes an intriguing error in his monographic study (2000, 145): 'as 1936 came to an end and 1937 began, Britten was not yet thinking of quitting the UK and following Auden to the States.' But Auden did not 'quit the UK' for 'the States' *until two years later.* Is 'the States' a slip for 'Spain'?
36 This artefact, now in the BPL, was displayed at the IWM exhibition, 'The Spanish Civil War – Dreams and Nightmares', in 2001–2.
37 L and D, 461ff.; Carpenter (1992), 90. Britten confessed the next day that he was 'feeling sore' about parting from Auden, had a drink or two that night, and was 'changing my views about life (with a capital 'S') a bit', ibid.
38 L and D, 461. The British Medical Unit had been in Spain since August 1936, so this reference was to a reinforcement and/or supply team. In any case, it seems likely that Auden had earlier been offered a job in news and propaganda, but refrained from telling his friends.
39 Carpenter (1992), 90–1.
40 See ibid., 6.
41 Isherwood (1976), 196–7
42 See ch. 2.
43 E.g. the present author's negative evidence from the relevant alphabetical file of International Brigaders in RGASPI, Moscow (545/6/101).
44 See Fyrth (1986), 49. The chief representative of the Spanish Medical Aid Committee in Spain was Peter Spencer (Viscount Churchill) who was based in Valencia. It seems inconceivable that Auden could have joined the British Medical Unit without reporting to him. In his memoirs Spencer mentions meeting Spender but not Auden; see (1964), esp. 173. Perhaps Auden obtained a pass from the Spanish embassy. He travelled directly to Valencia rather than Barcelona, which was normally at least the initial destination of visitors. This also suggests he was confident of work in the capital.
45 Connolly in Spender (1975), 68–73.
46 Koestler (1954), 336–7.
47 Cockburn's material (published 1965) is quoted *in extenso* by Weintraub (1968), 68–9.
48 In 1969, Television Wales and West screened a documentary based on

interviews with Brigade veterans Jack Roberts (see ch. 6) and Archie Cochrane (a doctor in the British Medical Unit). It included a newsreel extract showing a bullfight in an unnamed Republican city. In a middle-distance shot of a section of the audience, Auden can be identified as described in the text. This was obviously the occasion referred to in his article (see n. 49) as 'a bullfight in aid of the Spanish hospitals'. Perhaps the programme-makers were aware of the poet's ghostly presence, for they gave it the title 'The Just City' – a phrase taken from SPAIN.

49 *New Statesman and Nation*, 30 January 1937, reprinted in Cunningham (1986), 115–17. The piece was probably commissioned by Connolly, who was working for the *New Statesman*; see Martin (1969), 226.

For this hiatus in the narratology of their subject see Auden's biographers. Davenport-Hines (1995, 164–5); the leading Auden critic, Mendelsohn (1999, 196–8); and Carpenter, who compiles a partly conjectural – if well-researched – reconstruction of events (1981: 208–16). Auden's work in Valencia was propaganda. Connolly's evidence to this effect (see above) is corroborated by a young American, Kate [Kurzke], who wrote to English friends that 'I am working in American & English news service & propaganda in the Ministry of State . . . I worked some with a very nice man from the Toronto Star, and also with Auden, the poet'; letter dated 28 January 1937, John Strachey papers (see above, ch. 2, n. 94). Cockburn (as 'Frank Pitcairn') was the *Daily Worker*'s leading reporter in Spain and a loyal friend of Koltsov. My reading of SPAIN indicates that Auden was well briefed on specific components of the image of the Republic which these men had helped develop.

50 Jordan (1939), 18–9. This writer had an admirer in Harry Pollitt, who (proposing that he should write a book on the International Brigades) referred to him as 'not a member of the party though near to it'; RGASPI 545/6/155/85. His description of a night in the bar of the Hotel Victoria replicates too many details found elsewhere to be a coincidence. It also seems that Jordan had been reading *Authors Take Sides* (in particular Ezra Pound's contribution) when he composed this passage.

51 Regler (1959), 257ff.

52 Koltsov (1963). In an introductory note the publishers are cautious about the source of these documents, which was evidently in the USSR.

53 Hemingway (1976), 206–8, and esp. 371.

54 Gibson (1983), 54–72, esp. 229–32. The exact circumstances of the massacres are still uncertain – for example, whether a genuine

evacuation exercise was aborted unexpectedly, or whether its result was arranged in advance. Koltsov was the primary engine of the former, and would certainly have known about the latter.

55 For the hiatus, Koltsov (1963), 315. It seems almost uncanny that Koltsov should appear in newsreel footage used by the makers of the TWW documentary referred to above – in his case, twice.

56 It is also curious that Isherwood had entertained Hyndman and Romilly in Brussels, en route to Spain, only two weeks before he met Auden in Paris on a similar errand; see ch. 2.

57 See Carpenter (1981), 216; and cf. ch. 3. Why Auden went to Sariñena at all is a mystery. His Communist sponsors, pathologically suspicious of the CNT, would have discouraged such a destination. His chaperone, Cockburn, had the task getting the poet to *Madrid*. No letters have survived from Auden's Spanish trip. He was closely watched; either his post was intercepted, or he simply obeyed instructions to stay mum.

58 W Tapsell's report on 'Case of Comrade O'Donnell' [n.d. but March, 1937], IBA Box C 12/3. (Dr Tom Buchanan discovered this obscure reference: see 1998: 161–2. I also owe to Dr Buchanan my knowledge of the letter cited in n. 49 above.) Tapsell was informed about this incident when he was sent to check up on O'Donnell's alleged misbehaviour. He describes Auden as ' "left poet" to the Party outfit on the Aragon front'. This suggests that Auden had obtained some official appointment, presumably from the PCE. But there was no *British* 'outfit' in Aragon at this stage, since the Medical Unit had recently been relocated to the Madrid front from its original hospital at Grañén; see Fyrth (1986), 61.

Why did Auden leave the front (and, consequently, Spain) so quickly? Was he in flight from the consequences of some 'fumbled and unsatisfactory embrace before hurting'? Could it be that in this unique 'private' clause of the poem SPAIN the author registers a protest against its 'public' discourse? O'Donnell perhaps knew the answers. He was an SIM agent (Tapsell complains about 'his secret work' and 'his real chief') and had access to intelligence information; see Huber (1997).

59 The difficulties Auden experienced with Communist authorities (the feeling was, doubtless, mutual) and his awareness of the complex and vicious realities of the Republican cause (if you like, the Orwell syndrome) go some way to explain the extraordinary vehemence of his later disavowal – amounting to denial – of SPAIN. On the issues raised by Auden's equivocation, see also chs. 3 and 8.

60 Cunningham (1986), 115–17, and see below, p. 173.

61 SPAIN was first issued as a pamphlet, the fifth in a series of propaganda poems printed in Paris by Nancy Cunard and Pablo Neruda – 'Tout le produit de la vente ira au peuple de l'Espagne Républicaine.' A copy can be consulted in the British Library, Rare Books Collection (BL Cup.410.g.179), inscribed in Auden's holograph to 'Tony with love from Wystan'. This is almost certainly Tony Hyndman, the only veteran of the British Battalion with whom he was personally acquainted (see ch. 2).

62 The quotation here is not from SPAIN but the immediately preceding poem 'Danse macabre'.

63 See Vaksberg (1990), 79–80.

64 Conquest (1971), 588–92; Elorza and Bizcarrondo (1999), 374–83. The POUM 'treason trial' was almost exactly coterminous with the battle of the Ebro; Suárez (1974). See also ch. 3.

65 Althusser (1971), esp. 160–5.

66 On one occasion during his stay in Barcelona, Auden got drunk in company with Connolly, and the poet was almost arrested for urinating in the gardens of Mont Juic overlooking Barcelona; Connolly (1975), 70. Mont Juic is a well-known public park, recalled fondly by Britten and Berkeley, who a few weeks later completed their joint orchestral work with this title, based on the tunes collected in Barcelona a year earlier.

67 See Hynes (1976), 256–61, and Sullivan (1989), 229–40.

68 Caudwell (1937), esp. 138.

69 Vaksberg (1990), 94 (see also his illustration of the 'forest of hands'); Conquest (1971), 493.

70 Around this time, Bridge warned his pupil (apropos of *Our Hunting Fathers*) that his music, especially when set to such obscure texts, would not attract 'even the smaller public'; Foreman (1987), 203. Maybe this, as much as any party line, encouraged Britten to think in terms of blues and jazz idioms, which – though not yet accessible to working-class audiences – had certainly taken hold of the 'Auden Generation'.

71 Fyrth (1986), 42; perhaps Le Hot Club had not been as frigid an experience as first reported. Britten also performed at a chamber recital for Spanish Relief in Hampstead on 12 December 1938, and at a similar concert in Liverpool earlier the same year; see Harris (1998) no. 5/336.

72 Berkeley to Britten (hol. ?1938), in Berkeley File, BPL. Britten is an almost constant presence in P. Dickinson's monograph study of Berkeley's music. Though not (strictly speaking) a biography, the book makes some covert allusions to the sexual aspect of the friendship between the two men (see e.g. pp. 47–9).

73 Auden to Britten (hol., August 1938), Auden File, BPL.
74 Berkeley to Britten (?Aug. 1938), ibid.
75 Auden to Britten (typewritten, n.d.), ibid., Auden File; see Carpenter (1992), 118.
76 The Spanish War still figured in Britten's creative life in the late 1960s, when he included a poem (written in 1937) about child victims of bombing in settings of the Scots poet William Soutar, *Who Are These Children?*
77 Yet the Munich Agreement revived Auden's sense of outrage over Spain later in 1938. In an unpublished 'Ode to the New Year (1939)', he wished 'The Paralysis of the Insane/To those who sold us at München/To those who betrayed us in Spain'; Auden File, T. Driberg papers, Christ Church, Oxford.
78 Berkeley to Britten (hol., 22 October 1936), Berkeley File, BPL. Berkeley had converted to Catholicism in 1928, which underlines this equivocation. For the atrocities to which his letter refers, see Carballo (?1939).
79 Same to same (hol., 4 May 1939), ibid.
80 Same to same (hol., 3 September 1939), ibid.
81 Carpenter (1992), 136–7.
82 For the Republic's final agonies, see the useful narrative by Costa Clavell (1975).
83 Time was short, and Britten (as in his *Simple Symphony*, 1934) was already given to plundering earlier sketchbooks. Colin Matthews demonstrated that part of the score for the radio play *King Arthur* (April 1937) formed the basis of the *ostinato* second movement of *Ballad of Heroes*, which Britten entitled 'Dance of Death'; see Mitchell (2000), 165–8. My speculation about the first movement draws on this context.
84 *The Ascent of F6 and On the Frontier* (1958), 191. *On the Frontier*, first performed in November 1938, is also dedicated to Britten, with the typically enigmatic lines:

> The drums tap out sensational bulletins;
> Frantic the efforts of the violins
> To drown the song behind the guarded hill:
> The dancers do not listen; but they will.

85 Quoted in L and D, 613.
86 L and D, 64–5. Part of Britten's penance was the music for a BBC propaganda series called 'An American in England' (also 1942). A pot-pourri of Yankee songs and Sousa tunes, the broadcast was picked up by Auden, who wrote to the composer: 'I do feel sorry for you – what trash!' This is a further indication of Auden's bitterness over the loss of Britten – despite having now met his ideal love-object, Chester

Kallman; *The BBC Archive* (presented by Hermione Lee), Radio 3, 6 February 2000.

[87] Mitchell (2000), 158.

[88] 'The Hidden Heart – A Love Story in Three Pieces', Channel 4, 29 July 2001. Carpenter (1992), 583 gives the anecdote a slightly different wording. Mitchell writes: 'the storm of tears with which the composer reacted to the news of Auden's sudden death in 1973 was eloquent, even after the long years of estrangement, of the depths of the early friendship'; L and D, 384.

Chapter 5: Crusades in Conflict: Idealism, Perception, Motivation

[1] H McDiarmid, 'An English War-Poet', in Cunningham (1980), 313.

[2] Gaumont British Newsreel, no. 299.

[3] Eisner (1972), 77.

[4] Quoted in the chapter (by M. O'Riordan) on 'Ireland', in Nestorenko et al. (1975), 195.

[5] McGarry (1999), 109ff.

[6] E.g., Grimau (1979), 94, 104, 164, 187, 192.

[7] See, e.g., Abells (1973), 335ff; Buchanan (1993), 11–14.

[8] The Mongol horde of 'red savages' depicted by Burgos sources were matched by the bestial Fascists (foreign legionaries, Germans, Italians, bishops, and above all – the Moors) sketched by the other side; for the latter, see, e.g., the selection from Francisco Mateos's excoriating series 'El sitio de Madrid'; Ades (1995), 91.

[9] For poster examples of Republican patriotic discourse, see Grimau (1979), 63, 107, 204; Carr (1986), 171–2.

[10] However, the pamphlet *Spain Against the Invaders – Napoleon 1808 – Hitler and Mussolini 1936* (1938) published by the TUC, illustrated these protagonists along with a turbaned Moorish warrior. The South Wales Miners' Federation, at a special conference on 'Spain', called on the League of Nations to help the Republic 'to recover its political and territorial independence'; Francis (1984), 147.

[11] *Art Contra la Guerra* (1986), 35. Cf. Azaña (1937), esp. 18, 24. It seems that early lessons about Numantia and its suicidal resistance to Rome were drawn on by Picasso during the composition of *Guernica*; see 'Victory in Defeat', *Independent*, 26 April 1997.

[12] Lacking official recognition by France, the Nationalists were denied their own pavilion – but in this respect, at least, they seem hardly to have needed one.

13 See Prill (1998), 167–79. The first history of the conflict published in Spain was titled *Historia de la Cruzada Española* (8 vols., Madrid, Ediciones Españolas 1940–4); for a generation it was referred to in Francoist circles as 'La Guerra de Liberación' – the liberation in question being from International Communism. Southworth (1963) easily demolished some of the earlier and cruder practitioners of the tactic. But it is by no means extinguished even today in the Anglo-Saxon world; see, e.g., Carroll (1996).

14 Changes of emphasis can be monitored in the XV Brigade magazine, *Volunteer for Liberty*, which recycled propaganda material intended to be further recycled by volunteers in letters home to family, friends – and local correspondence columns; see, e.g., 'One Year of Fascist Invasion', 12 July 1937, 6–7; article on 'Madre Patria' by Teniente Valenzuela of the 24th (Spanish) Battalion, with photograph of peasants in file 'Reaping a Harvest for the New Spain', 23 April 1938, 13.

15 For the last of these, see the fascinating study by Rey García (1997).

16 Abella (1973), 355–71.

17 See the present author's study, 'Imagined Atrocity: the bombing of Getafe and Republican Propaganda in the Spanish Civil War' (forthcoming).

18 See, e.g., scattered material in Buchanan (1997), Fyrth (1986) and Hopkins (1998). Douglas Hyde, CPGB agent in north Wales, writes of men coming forward to volunteer for the British Battalion after viewing the propaganda film *Defence of Madrid*; Hyde (1952), 58–9.

19 See above pp. 18–20.

20 See Alvarez Lopera (1982), *passim*.

21 The Republican Students' Federation issued a series of posters illustrated by holy images, bearing such exhortations as 'A religious object can also be a work of art – preserve it for the national heritage'; ibid., II, 190–2; Grimau (1979), 34.

22 The British National government 'quietly contributed 500 pounds' to Cardinal Hinsley's fund for church restoration in Spain; Flint (1987), 373. It may be noted that in the 1970s, aggravated disrespect for devotional objects shown by troops in the Bogside and other Catholic districts of Northern Ireland during house-to-house searches provided a fertile source of support for the Provisionals.

23 The twin pillars of Republican propaganda – patriotic resistance to invasion and support of the world's artists in the struggle – were put in place during the Anti-Fascist Writers' Congress of July 1937. Corpus Barga addressed it on the former, whilst Soviet novelist Alexei Tolstoi elaborated the latter; see Grimau (1979), 95–102; Gamonal Torres (1987), 259–60; and Aznar Soler and Schneider (1978), III, 44–6.

24 General Miaja inadvertently put Franco's case when he told the same audience that 'nuestros enemigos pelean bajo la bandera de la civilización y el catolicismo, y para lograr esto agrupan en sus filas italianos, alemanes, irlandeses . . .'.
24 The exception here was, of course, Morocco; see Gárate Córdoba (1990). The tendency increased after the disappointing military performance of the O'Duffy Brigade. Security considerations were also important.
25 For the Irish dimension of this chapter, further material (and supporting references) can be found in Stradling (1999), passim and esp. 27–31. A more concise treatment of cognate themes is *idem* (1996).
26 My rough estimate would be an equal three-way split between the categories which follow, valid for both sides – a rationale derived mainly from my work on issues of politics and discipline within the British Battalion of the International Brigades (forthcoming).
27 This is not even an estimate but a crude, notional, working figure made up from all category A and 50 per cent of category B.
28 See, e.g, Girouard (1981).
29 Miller (1989); Jones (1971); O'Callaghan (1870).
30 Moroccan troops were often quartered in ancient Catholic cities like Salamanca, where the local newspaper devoted space to explaining (*inter alia*) that the Moors' hatred of atheistic Communism was, if anything, greater than that of the Spanish Christian; *Adelanto de Salamanca*, e.g., 17 January 1937; see also Abella (1973), 294–7.
31 O'Duffy claimed that he received 6,000 written offers to serve in Spain; see (1938), 14.
32 Hogan (?1935). With hindsight the question in question seems more ridiculous than rhetorical, but Hogan makes some incisive comments on the realities of life in the Stalinist state (see ibid., xx–xviii).
33 Quoted in *Irish Independent*, 15 August 1936. To restore the crucifix was, of course, literally an act of crusade.
34 'In War-Torn Spain: No. VIII, Spirit of the Irish Brigade', ibid, 2 March 1937.
35 Preston (1986), 92; Wharton (2002).
36 See Isaia and Sogno (1998). This book establishes that (at least) a substantial minority of the CTV were authentic volunteers. See also Granada/RTE documentary series, *The Spanish Civil War* (1983), episode 3 *Battleground for Idealists*, in which CTV veteran Renzo Lodoli recalls his ideal motivation, to fight for Christian civilization in Spain.
37 Quoted in R. Colodny's 'Preface' to Geiser (1986), vii.
38 L. Jones (1939), 326. For interpretation of the novel's 'hypothesis' see Francis (1984), *passim* and Hopkins (1998), 146–8, 291–313 and *passim*.

39 Francis (1984), 161, who also gives his key chapter the title 'Crusaders and Outcasts: The Background and Motives of the Welsh Volunteers'; see pp. 179–222 *passim*.
40 Mackenzie (1996), 120 and sources cited.
41 Fischer (1941) ch. 13 and esp. p. 366.
42 Hemingway (1976), 209–10.
43 Rosenstone (1980).
44 Hemingway (1976), 267–8. See also Castillo-Puche (1975), 95. The English Catholic writer, Graham Greene was also under the romantic influence of the Carlists and the 'wars of religion' they waged against Spanish liberal governments in the nineteenth century. In the mid-1920s he worked on a book about a young English volunteer who goes to Spain to fight for the so-called 'Traditionalist Communion'; see Greene (1972), 151–4 and *passim*.
45 (1940). Regler, too, was a cradle Catholic, born in the Rhineland.
46 E.g. in the TWW TV documentary *The Just City* (1969) (see above, p. 86 and n. 48). See also Cochrane (1989).
47 Gurney (1976), 17–18. This volunteer had come to share the elemental fear of Spanish civilians for the Moorish troops as a result of his experiences during the battle of Jarama.
48 Tisa (1985), 9.
49 Hogan (?1935), 131.
50 F. Ryan, quoted in Tisa (1985), xv.
51 See, for example, the remarks by Joe Monks in a letter of 5 February 1937; Acier (1937), 122–3.
52 De Blacam (1936).
53 Quoted in Keogh (1995), 470.
54 'Ballyseedy befriends Badajoz', *Left Review*, 12 (1936). Ballyseedy was the scene of the single worst atrocity of the Irish Civil War in 1923; the defenders of Badajoz were massacred by Nationalist troops in 1936.
55 From C. Moore, 'Vive le Quinte Brigada'; see Stradling (1999), 207.
56 *Irish Independent*, 19 August 1936.
57 *Cork Examiner*, 31 August 1936.
58 De Mesa (1998), 23.
59 Ibid., 15.
60 Herrick (1990), 64–5.
61 Yeats (1982), 322; see also Ellmann (1987), 280–1.
62 O'Duffy (1938), 6–10, 17.
63 An impressive bibliography exists concerning these aspects of Ireland's history, to which Spanish scholars have contributed. As recently as 2001 the popular magazine *History Ireland* devoted space to them, whilst a Spanish equivalent, *Historia 16*, has also visited the site.

64 Interviewed in the RTE documentary *Even the Olives are Bleeding* (directed by C. O'Shannon, 1976).
65 See Stradling (1996).
66 'Spirit of the Irish Brigade' (see n. 34).
67 Wade (1954), 881.
68 Ibid., 871.
69 Ibid., 885.
70 From 'Politics', published in *Last Poems*, 1936–9, see (1982), 392–3. Perhaps Yeats's girl was the muse of poetry, but (equally), perhaps not. See also ch. 8.
71 Ford (1965), 5–6, 114–23; see also Tierney (1973).
72 'Poem', in Cunningham (1980), 108–9.
73 Ford (1965, 123) is perhaps simplistic in suggesting that Donnelly's insights are actually 'used to deride the dedication and idealism of the Loyalist volunteers'.
74 D MacDonagh 'He is Dead and Gone, Lady: For Charles Donnelly, R.I.P.', in Cunningham (1980), 175. The last line seems implicitly to acknowledge Donnelly's ambiguity – or is it just a clumsy attempt to recuperate his legacy for the Party?
75 'Thinking of Artolas', ibid., 177.
76 Friel (1990), 50, 52. The picture is complicated by Gerry's being a Welshman – which (of course) is why he can't make explosives. For another example of healthy scepticism (or fruitful ambivalence) over relevant issues of idealism and crusade, see Jordan (1994), 87–8.
77 Wade (1954), 871.
78 See, e.g., Pike (1968).
79 Stradling (1999), 29–30.
80 'Among Those About to Die', *Irish Independent*, 8 January 1937 (last of a series of five articles, republished at http://members/lycos.co.uk/spanishcivilwar/CJMcG.htm). McGuinness's remarks should be placed alongside the fact that he himself was repatriated at public expense by the Free State consulate in Paris; see Stradling (1999), 196 and source cited. For the contrasting reports on Barcelona, see above, pp. 57–9.
81 Cunningham (1986), 57.
82 Waugh (1943), 42. The book is dedicated to Waugh's second wife, Laura, whose sister, Gabrielle Herbert, was busily raising volunteers for the 'Patriot' medical services: see Carr (1995).

Chapter 6: *Necessary Murders: The British Battalion at Brunete*

1. Gregory (1986), 71.
2. For detailed treatment of the battle (6–25 July 1937) see Casas de la Vega (1967), esp. 69ff.; Martínez Bande (1972), 120ff.; Aznar (1961), 185–233. For an account in English, Hills (1976), 137–66, based on monographs by Spanish experts; as are summaries in English-language reference sources, Thomas (1977), 710–17 and Proctor, in Cortada (1982), 94–7. A panoramic picture of the battle constructed from a mosaic of recollections by Nationalist veterans is provided in C. Revilla Cebreros (1976).
3. A recent general treatment of the International Brigades' actions is by Vidal (1998), 175ff. See also those by Catalan IB veteran Castells (1972), esp. 230ff.; Brome (1965), esp. 195–216; Johnston (1968), esp. 112–31; Delperrie de Bayac (1968), 290–319; and Richardson (1980), esp. 88–9.
4. Elorza and Bizcarrondo (1999), 329–42. Contemporary dilemmas and difficulties of subsequent interpretation are neatly encapsulated ibid., 459–63.
5. For more detailed treatment of the representative themes of propaganda, see ch. 5.
6. A sensitive discussion of the Brigades' political motivation and morale in relation to their military effectiveness is offered by Mackenzie (1997), 116–33.
7. 'To all comrades of the XV Brigade', IBA Box 22/B/8 (Capitalisation as per text). This document was quoted by Aitken's son, Ian, introducing a *Guardian* feature on the British Battalion, 10 November 2000.
8. Letters of 1 and 2 July 1937, in Francis (1984), 277.
9. Estimates vary among the authorities cited in n. 2; I have given a median figure. For topographical information and maps, Montero Barrado (1987), 71–9. Sequential campaign maps are in Martínez Bande (1972). A useful schema of the battle plan (mainly the work of non-Communist Lt.-Col. Vicente Rojo) is www.geocities.com/Athens/Troy/2630/mapas/bat_brun.jpg
10. Líster (1978), 241. Líster claimed to have taken the town at 0700hrs, but other reports indicate that it was not fully under his control until noon; Martínez Bande (1972), 138.
11. Republican superiority in the opening phase was immense. Only 2,500 enemy were within the salient established on the first day. In addition to assault divisions, Miaja had a further 20,000 men in reserve, including the XII (International) Brigade; 130 Soviet T-26 tanks, the most advanced of their day; nearly 200 artillery pieces; over 200 (mostly

Russian) aircraft; along with matching accessories in other departments. The censorship office allowed *New York Times* reporter Herbert Matthews to claim that 'it can be said that there are many tanks, many guns, and more troops than have yet been employed in this conflict'; Jackson (1972), 61–2. Yet this was the battle in which Arthur Horner described the Brigaders as fighting with 'stones against tanks'! (1960), 158. For the contrary impressions of British participants at its outset, see Graham (1999), 11–12; Thomas (1996), 33–5; Copeman (1948), 123; Shaw IWM AC 13547, reel 2.

12 Information bulletins signed by Rodríguez, 11–19 June 1937, PCE reel 15/1 (marked as folios 1–90).

13 Revilla (1976), 59–64.

14 In June 2001 the town still boasted a street named for this unit; but it was (appropriately) surrounded and outnumbered by others dedicated to artists: Picasso, Falla, Unamuno, Béquer, Gaudí, Albéniz et al.

15 Frank Thomas, a Welsh volunteer in the Nationalist army, was stationed in Villanueva during April. His unit (the VI Legionary *Bandera*) made various improvements to its fortifications; Thomas (1998), 105–9; see also map between pp. 96 and 97 of Martínez Bande (1972). Orders issued on the eve of attack warned of heavy fortifications on both flanks of the the village; RGASPI 545/3/426/218.

16 Martínez Bande (1972), 139–40 quotes a document from the 'Archivo de la Guerra de Liberación': 'C.-in-C. orders army corps chief to attack and seize Villanueva at all costs. Any units refusing to advance should be propelled forward by targeting artillery rounds to land behind them.'

17 Casado's memoirs relate that he was summoned from Valencia to replace Jurado, of whose orders and command he knew nothing, and that it took thirty-six hours for him to assume control; Casado (1939), 74–5.

18 General Order, XVIII Army Corps, 5 July 1937, RGASPI 545/3/426/218–19. Revealingly, however, it was anticipated that 15th Division might have to occupy the village if 34th was too badly damaged during its capture – seemingly a prevision induced by Rodríguez's warnings.

19 Casas de la Vega (1967), 73–4; Revilla (1976), 65–9; Martínez Bande (1972), 137; Hills (1976), 152.

20 All three *partes* (= daily reports from the fronts) are reprinted in Díaz-Plaja (1974), 351–2. See also Longo (1956), 374; Delperrie (1968), 296.

21 This paragraph is derived from a cocktail of sources about the Battalion's action, all fully referenced in the notes which follow.

Notes

22 A cavalry unit was attached to XV Brigade in late June; see Order of *Estado Mayor*, RGASPI 545/3/426/188; also Revilla (1976), 71–80. Use of cavalry by the Republicans was relatively unusual. They were ostensibly deployed here to cut down retreating enemy – but actually dealt out equally harsh treatment to Republican deserters. The unit was later annihilated at nearby Quijorna and its commander, an Italian Communist, himself deserted; Martínez Bande (1972), 140; Vidal (1998), 189; Thomas (1977), 716.

23 Photocopied page (n.d.) in Macmillan (1980). Murphy (1898–1974) had been brought up in Workington. He fought with 'No. 1 Company' in Andalusia, and later was badly wounded near Madrid – well before most of his comrades had had their baptism of fire at Jarama.

24 Henceforward an asterisk indicates those contemporary accounts from which longer, contextual extracts (with source references) are given in an Appendix, see 196–202.

25 Ryan (1938), 141–2. Roberts (1899–1979) was a miner and Communist councillor, widely known as 'Jack Russia' for his bolshie attitudes to pit managers and policemen; see Felstead (1981).

26 Ryan (1938), 132.

27 Casas de la Vega (1967), 75. Vidal (1998: 189) notes that 'in the hour before midnight, when some of the defenders, perhaps fearful of being surrounded, began to retreat, the men of the XIII and XV Brigades managed to penetrate the interior of the village'. Cf. also Longo (1956), 375.

28 Nationalist figures from Martínez Bande (1972), 140. However, Revilla (1976: 89–90) claims 400 dead, plus 160 wounded and 140 captured: considerable overlap may be assumed between the second and third of these figures. British casualties are difficult to estimate. I have collated data from Paynter's letter to Pollitt (see below, n. 53) with scattered references in survivors' recollections. Alexander (1987, 122) gives fifty casualties on the day. A contemporary list, probably by Paynter, gives eighty-three wounded in the first six days of the battle; IBA Box 21/B/3e.

29 Mosquito Ridge, occupied by the VIII Legionary *Bandera*, barred the way to the XV Brigade's main target of Boadilla del Monte, where General Varela, Nationalist GOC, had established his field HQ. Miaja ordered it taken at all costs; Franco, that it be defended to the death. In the fighting, the three English-speaking units were so badly damaged that serious consideration was given to their definitive amalgamation; J. Hinks and G. Coyle (acting commander and commissar) to Pollitt (n.d.), IBA Box 50, file 15/6.

30 Hinks and Coyle alleged that only forty-nine men remained out of 281

engaged; a little later W. Tapsell estimated forty-two out of 331: ibid., files 15/6 and 16/1.

31 Alexander (1987), 130–2; Angus (1983), 7; Horner (1960), 157–9. According to its own figures the International Brigades had 2,632 casualties and 534 desertions from 9,800 engaged; PCE reel 6, 180–4, Longo's report on 'Reorganización de las BBII', 11 August 1937. In a report to war minister Indalecio Prieto (August 1937), base commander Vidal Gayman stated that the XV Brigade was reduced to 42 per cent of its previous strength, asserting (moreover) that 'le battaillon anglais est atteint par une vague collectif de desertions qui commencé á gagner les bataillons americains. Les officiers ne sont pas exclus de ce procés de demoralisation'; García Serrano (1989), 448–9; see also Cardona (1998), 71–81. Several of the British Battalion veterans whose recollections appear in this chapter deserted during the Brunete campaign. None of them mentions this. But neither fact necessarily invalidates their value as witnesses.

32 The diary of Peter O'Connor (Lincoln Battalion) records that Ryan 'arrived from Albacete on the 27th [July]', quoted in O'Riordan (1979), 89. See also Cronin (1980), 118–23. Roberts probably delivered his manuscript to Ryan during a furlough in Madrid in the second week of August; Felstead (1981), 95.

33 Relatively few photographs show sub-machine guns – properly so-called – being carried by combatants in the Spanish Civil War. On the other hand, German machine pistols (Bergman MP18/I and MP18/II) were delivered to the Republic 'in numbers', and a consignment fell into enemy hands in late 1936; Howson (1998), 261; Turnbull and Burn (1978) illustration H. Some Nationalist officers may have carried them at Villanueva.

34 McCusker interview, McDougall (1986), 44; Adlam in *Colliers' Crusade* (BBC Wales Documentary Series, written and produced by J. Ormond, 1983), episode 2. In the same programme, Leo Price correctly identified the defenders as Falangists. If Roberts's draft had mentioned Italians, then Ryan edited them out of the published text. Cf. the *Daily Worker*'s Bill Rust, who gave currency to Murphy's error in the Battalion's official history (1939).

35 See ch. 5, esp. 110 & notes.
36 See, e.g., Thomas (1998), 119.
37 With the exception of Frank Hillesley's story (see below p. 140 and n. 60)
38 In addition to sources cited elsewhere, see Brome (1965), 202–3; Eby (1969), 131; Hoar (1969), 92–3; Elliott in Kremer and Nestorenko (1975), 68; Alexander (1986), 121; Francis (1984), 234. The only

general work which neglects the incident is Johnston (1967). In contrast, no similar study deriving from other than English or American sources has any mention of it.

39 *Land and Freedom* (directed by Ken Loach, screenplay by Jim Allen, 1995). Though the film showed mainly to art-house audiences in the UK, it was soon released in commercial video version and has been scheduled on non-subscription TV.

40 Shaw, IWM AC 13547, reel 2.

41 Stradling (1999), 193–7. Verisimilitude of detail in veterans' accounts suggests that a local citizen was regularly brought in to tell new arrivals at Madrigueras (via a commissar's translation) how the priest had turned a machine gun on women and children in the village square. Similar stories were used regularly by *Daily Worker* reporters, and were ubiquitous amongst the Republic's armed forces: see, e.g., Candela (1989), 24–7, 40–4 and *passim*. According to Alvarez Lopera (1982, I, 54) only one case has any claim to validity.

42 Thomas (1977), 244–5; Felstead (1981), 77; Sloan interview, McDougall (1986), 204; Roberts interview, *Colliers' Crusade*, episode 3, introduced by voice-over commentary that 'all his life Jack Roberts went on wondering about his first day at Brunete'. But what exactly was it he wondered about?

43 Ehrenburg (1979), 12–13.

44 See the XV Brigade journal *Our Fight*, 33 (September 1937), 2; Jack Roberts, *Colliers' Crusade*, episode 3; Zeuhlke (1996), 164. See also Carroll (1994), 155–6, 179. A regular explanation for the absence of prisoners was that enemy officers killed themselves rather than surrender: brief reflection exposes its fallacious logic. It also seems unlikely that convinced Catholics would opt for such a death, thereby condemning their souls to damnation.

45 This is ironic in the cases of Loach and Allen. The Republic's 'fight against Fascism' involved the persecution and murder of hundreds of the POUM – the party elegized in *Land and Freedom* – by Stalinist agents who labelled them as 'Trotsky-Fascists'. Indeed, this witch-hunt intensified as a result of the battle of Brunete, the failure of which was attributed to alleged co-operation between the 'Fascist Fifth Column' and the POUM in supplying intelligence to the enemy; see, e.g., Azaña (1981), II, 165.

46 Francis (1984), 232, 245.

47 Price interview, SWML, tape no. 250. See also *Colliers' Crusade*, episode 2.

48 Angus (1983), 1, 6; Colman, interview by Sanchez (1996), 77–8; Cummings, letters in IBA Box A/15/11; O'Donoghue, file in South

Wales Coalfield Collection, University of Wales Swansea, no. 3; Gowans, IWM AC 12095, reel 3; Greenhalgh, ibid., 10356, reel 2; 'H.K.', Ryan (1938), 12; Morgan, IWM AC 103622, reel 2; McCusker in McDougall (1986), 44; Walker, IWM AC 807, reel 2. I have included members of infantry companies and the machine-gun company (which was not far behind the action), but not members of the anti-tank unit, which reached Villanueva next morning, viz. Eddie Brown, John Dunlop, Chris Smith and John Londragon; McDougall (1986), 112–13, 136–7, 176–7; IWM 12290/4. Yet several men who left detailed eyewitness accounts of the sortie, on other occasions recorded interviews in which they failed to mention it, despite cognate questioning by interlocutors: e.g., Roberts himself in an interview with H. Francis (in 1969), SWML AUD 73–4; Rogers, ibid., 248; and Price in a recording from c.1980, ibid., 250.

49 Ryan (1938), 139–40, 189; McDougall (1986), 44. 'H.K.' may have been Howard King, the only survivor of Villanueva whose name begins with these initials; Kerrigan list, IBA Box D7/A1. For the command structure of the XV Brigade at Brunete, see the 'Recapitulación de Haberes, Albacete 7 de Julio 1937', AGGC, SM 1061, 105–12. Here, Cummings is placed as third in officer seniority of the 16th Battalion, a position in practice synonymous with the role of both adjutant and command of No. 1 Company.

50 Thomas (1996), 35–6. Cf. J. Colman, who was in a machine-gun detachment.*

51 Thus the last sentence of the quotation referenced (n. 50) may be legitimately taken as meaning 'I have never spoken. . .' - i.e. between 1937 and 1996

52 Alexander (1987), 121.

53 Paynter to Pollitt, 11 July 1937; IBA Box 21/B/3c.

54 The population of Villanueva and district had been about 800. In April, Frank Thomas saw 'a pleasant little village, hardly touched by the war'. Some residents (mostly shopkeepers) had stayed on, and a farmer was working in nearby fields; Thomas (1998), 105. From defenders' recollections, Revilla (1976, 62) states that 'the civil population was very sparse'; but Frank Graham says that 'out of the village came about 50 women and children . . . I remember, I was there at the time'; IWM AC 11877, reel 3.

Like Fred Thomas, Jules Paivio of the Washington Battalion spotted civilian corpses on the way out of Villanueva the day after the battle; Hoar (1969), 93. T. Jones recalled seeing bodies of women and children inside the village; *Colliers' Crusade*, episode 2. It seems unlikely that all the hostages were killed outright; equally, that none was wounded and in need of treatment. Yet in accounts of ministrations to the Brunete wounded by British members of medical units – not only those at the main rear hospital in San Lorenzo del Escorial, but also ambulance teams and field orderlies who worked near the front lines – there is no mention of a single civilian needing treatment; see, e.g., Cochrane (1989), 40–3; Stratton (1981), 43–7; the unpublished memoirs of P. Harrison ('Interesting times', MS chapter on Spain, in possession of D. Leach); McFarquahar, IWM AC 9234, reel 3 and in McDougall (1986), 85; Crome, IWM AC 9298, reel 3; Saxton, ibid., 8735, reels 5–6; Williams, ibid., 10181, reel 3 and SWML AUD 27. See also the negative evidence in Fyrth (1986), 88–94 which uses some of these sources and several others. In this context Rust's information that 'some of the women [survivors] courageously helped to dress the wounds of the British volunteers' seems to figure as something rather worse than incredible (1939, 78).

55 Alexander (1982), 121. Cf. Copeman who claims (1948, 131) that 'nearly all the Fascist troops had killed themselves'. In fact, the acting commandant, Alvarez Lasarte, was captured and spent the rest of the war as a POW. This suggests he was not held responsible for any atrocity; Revilla (1976), 71.
56 See above, p. 126.
57 *Colliers' Crusade*, episode 4.
58 Eby (1969), 131. Other accounts also imply that the 16th Battalion played little part in the final taking of the town; e.g. Bob Walker, IWM AC 807, reel 2. H. Thomas is overly patriotic in claiming (1977, 712) that Villanueva was captured by the British Battalion.
59 Hoar (1969), 92–3; Graham (1999), 2.
60 Quoted in Cooper and Parkes (2000), 75.
61 SWML Transcript 56, 6–11.
62 IWM AC 9392, reel 4. In 1976, Charles Morgan implied that prisoners were killed on the spot; ibid., 10362, reel 2. According to his IWM interview (1976) Fred Copeman made it one of his 'hard and fast rules' that 'no prisoners taken by the battalion were to be harmed'. But IB units in practice disregarded this as a counsel of perfection; transcript quoted by Hopkins (1998), 222. *The Book of the XV Brigade*, includes photographs of groups of prisoners *from the two other villages* attacked on the same day as Villanueva de la Cañada (Quijorna and Villanueva del Pardillo) being marched away; Ryan (1938), 134, 143.
63 IWM AC 12095, reel 3. This veteran confused details of incidents which took place at Villanueva (often recalled, as in this case, simply as 'Brunete') with the later street fighting in *Belchite* (September 1937) in which (however) British infantry companies were not involved.

64 Wolff (1994), 117.
65 Azaña (1978) II 163–64.
66 See illustration section, p. 6.
67 Cronin (1980), 146–7. In fact, Ryan – then XV Brigade adjutant – was present at Quinto a few months later, though he may not have witnessed the 'execution' of enemy officers; *Our Fight* (as n. 44).
68 Cronin (1980), 265.
69 Larios (1966), 128–31; Azaña (1981), II, 185; Aznar (1961), 199. Wyden (1983, 381) made a tentative connection between the incidents. Books about the Brigades written under the Franco regime are severely hostile; yet despite ideological incentive and research opportunity, none records a major case of a war crime committed by Brigade members against Spaniards. A recent investigation of atrocities, pretending to a comprehensive summation (Juliá, 1998), fails to consider some important categories of victim, among them POWs murdered on the battlefield.
70 Stradling (1999), 199–201.
71 Graham (1999), 2.
72 Anonymous poem (1946) in IBA Box 27A/ File A; published in Alvarez and López (1986), 332.
73 Bates (1963), 361–2. This essay ('Of Legendary Time') was first published in the *Virginia Quarterly Review* (Winter 1939). On Bates, see also Hopkins (1998), esp. 66–71, and Klaus (1989).
74 'A poem of the government offensive at Villanueva de la Canada', RGASPI 545/3/471. Jasper was to desert again in March 1938; see ibid., 451/65 and 157; and ibid., 6/39/65. For the wall newspaper, see ch. 7.

Chapter 7: *Between the Bullet and the Sonnet: Poetry and Propaganda in the Trenches*

1 On the battle for Teruel, see Martínez Bande (1974); for the International Brigades' actions, Vidal (1998), 229–54. In strict geographical terms, Granada was nearer the Mediterranean than was Teruel – but this had little significance strategically.
2 'Report on and recommendation re. the English [*sic*] Battalion' (17 December 1937, by W. Tapsell and W. Rust) AGGC PS Aragon 6.
3 *Orden del Día*, 22 December 1937, RGASPI 545/3/428/184.
4 Lehmann (1937); Fox (1945).
5 For the deserters, *Orden del Día*, 11 November 1937, RGASPI 545/3/428/31. Paylists for December–January 1937 record some 180

Britons and 260 Spaniards; AGGC PS Aragon 7. See also Alexander (1987), 155–60.
6. See his article, 'Culture at the Mill', *Volunteer for Liberty*, 3 January 1938, 8.
7. See below, pp. 162–4 and notes
8. RGASPI, 545/3/428/151. This was the motto of the Cultural Militias (Tuñón de Lara, in Garitaonandía (1996), 334) but was also a version of the Italian Fascist motto: 'Libro e Mosquetto, Fascista Perfetto'.
9. Hopkins (1998), 97.
10. Heinemann (1988), 46–64.
11. Spender and Lehmann (1939), 31.
12. Quoted in Esenwein and Schubert (1995), 248. On Jack Roberts, see above, ch. 6 *passim*.
13. At the time of publication its author, though identified as a Brigader, was otherwise unknown. After Roberts's death in 1980, his grandson and biographer revealed its origins. Roberts sent the poem to Spender anonymously for publication in *Poems For Spain*. See Felstead (1980), 99; Cunningham (1988), 453, 475.
14. A. Machado, 'A Líster – Comandante del Ejército del Ebro' (1938) with its notorious couplet 'Si mi pluma valiera su pistola / De capitán, contento moriría'; English translation in Kenwood (1993), 112. When I met Enrique Líster at a celebratory lunch on his return to Spain after forty years' exile in the USSR, a journalist friend urged me to 'grasp the hand that shot a hundred Fascists'. But it has been alleged that Líster's pistol was more often employed against Republican deserters and 'cowards' than the 'Fascist' enemy.
15. Arguably poetry is no longer widely perceived as an 'upper-class' medium. But in the late 1950s, when first moved by and to poetry, I was aware of negative vibes within my family and derisory reactions outside it. Indeed, an overt interest in poetry was in those days normally taken as a covert declaration of homosexualist leanings.
16. Salaün (1977), 143.
17. The Mackenzie-Papineau Battalion (No. 60) may be an exception. Compilers of a relevant anthology failed to find a single example. Nonetheless, they contrived to publish 200 pages of Canadian poems about the Spanish War, written at the time and since, a further testament to the long-term global 'harvest' of commitment. See Volpe and Albari (1995).
18. This chapter uses examples from Moscow (RGASPI 545/3/473, 474 and 478) and London (IBA Boxes 27A/a and 50/5a). Some items in the IBA collection are post-war elegies, commemorating heroes and martyrs. This has continued to form part of memorial meetings

19 sponsored by the IBA and/or various Labourist institutions. It represents a unique survival of the 1930s tradition of propaganda verse; see, e.g., *Remembering the Spanish Civil War* (1996), poems by T. Campbell, J. Jump and G. Cooney.

19 Particularly apt for Teruel, since not long ago work to extinguish a major fire in local olive fields was held up as warheads long submerged in the undergrowth began to explode; see *El Mundo*, 15 September 2000.

20 See Salaün (1977), esp. 146 ('es un arma lo mismo que una máquina de guerra') and 151 ('es ante todo un arma decisiva en el resultado de los combates').

21 In 'Sitting upon the Dead', Miguel Hernández wrote , 'I am here to defend you / with my blood and mouth / like two faithful rifles'; (1997), 62–3.

22 Spender and Lehmann (1939), 7. It is an extraordinary witness to the reputation of poetry, in connection with the British Battalion in particular, that a recent study of the International Brigades prefaces all but one of its chapters with quotations from poems by British writers; see Vidal (1998).

23 Salaün (1977), 143–4.

24 Photograph reproduced in Paz (1997), 128–9. See also the cover picture of Hernández used for the anthology, *I Have Lots of Heart* (above, n. 21). Alberti visited the Soviet Union as early as 1933, whilst Hernández was invited to tour there in 1937.

25 Cockburn (1936), 85. Cunningham (1980, 41) calls this as 'an impossibly exaggerated scenario'. But wasn't it simply 'poetic licence'?

26 Wilson (1944), 187.

27 Bates (1963), 349. (The reference is to the religious poet of the seventeenth century.)

28 See Núñez Díaz-Balarte (1996), 441–51; Almuina Fernández and Martín de la Guardia (1998), 119–31.

29 Report on meeting of 26 March 1937, RGASPI 545/3/435/1–7. *Volunteer for Liberty* was launched in May with Ralph Bates as editor. The book was to be supervised by a Historical Section, headed by a 'working-class journalist' ('periodista obrero'). This apparently referred to Frank Ryan, whose class qualifications seem dubious.

30 Allan Johnson's notes on Agenda Paper, 11 May 1937, ibid., 426/24–v.

31 Report of 16 April 1937, ibid., 435/19. See also Marty to Gallo (aka Longo), 19 April 1937 and Commissariat Report of 23 April, PCE reel 9/265.

32 Meeting of 26 March 1937 (see n. 29).

33 As Party member and student, Hamm was well qualified. Though his

diary evinces rapid disillusionment, he was potentially the perfect volunteer, keen on soccer as well as learning, and prudishly opposed to booze; Stradling (1998), 157ff. Cummings, ex-NCO in the Guards, was a typical Communist autodidact.

34 Report by 'Comrade of English Battalion' (probably Tomalin) to Brigade, 14 May 1937, RGASPI 545/3/435/77. Tomalin was a Cambridge English graduate who also studied music with Arnold Dolmetsch; see his IB file, ibid., 6/208/42–51v.

35 'Trench Spirit', anonymous MS in RGASPI, 545/3/473/25.

36 *Volunteer for Liberty*, 27 September 1937, 3. No anthology ever appeared.

37 'To a Fallen Comrade' by Bill Harrington, Cunningham (1980), 192–3. (First published in *Volunteer for Liberty*, 5 September 1938, 3 and reprinted in Alvarez and López, 1986, 96.) See also the same poet's 'To J. H.', signed MS. in RGASPI, 545/3/473/11. This was evidently rejected because too uncertain in its final exhortation; 'Your brave ideal / So soon shall peal / To herald real / Endeavour.'

38 6 October 1938, 4. For a sketch of his later career, see Bridgeman (1989), 187. An early battalion roll shows that Harrington (aged twenty-two) was not CP: IBA Box D7/A2. Repatriation lists (September 1938) include him on the full muster (as in hospital) but not on a separate list of Party members; IBA Box D7/A2 [? March 1937]; RGASPI 545/6/39/99–104 (19 October 1938).

39 Cf. the typescript poem 'Wake O World' by Sam Waitzman (Lincoln Battalion), with its convoluted metaphor and dense allusiveness, decisively marked as 'rejected'; ibid., 545/3/473/39.

40 See ibid. 437, where examples of incoming correspondence for the Lincolns acknowledge such items; e.g. 117–30, 'I read your poem "Pasaremos!", a clever verse. I have a secret yen to write if I can get out soon to stack up a dite of experience', Louise Hill to Charles [?], 26 August 1937.

41 See e.g. T. Dalton's signed MS 'The Passing of a Comrade', an elegy to Major George Nathan (killed at Brunete) in which the author glossed his own lines 'Our hearts are heavy our loss is great / Into all hearts a more bitter hate' with the marginal addition 'Against Fascism', an explanation felt necessary to assist publication; ibid. 473/32.

42 From text insert in Chandos CD recording of Britten's *Ballad of Heroes*, CHAN 8983/4 (see ch. 4), the only published version of these lines I was able to locate. Another of Swingler's exhortations to potential volunteers was: 'In your hesitant moments remember Cornford and Fox / Looking across the valleys and romantic rocks'; see *Les poètes du monde*, no. 6, ed Cunard and Neruda (Paris, 1937). One

imagines poster treatment on the lines of the First World War, e.g., 'Poets of Britain say – Go!'
43   Lehmann (1965), 283–4.
44   Connolly (1961), 116. See also below, p. 172.
45   Campbell, *The Flowering Rifle* (1938) quoted in Hoskins (1969), 52.
46   For more on this, esp. the 'artistocracy', see below, ch. 8 and Epilogue.
47   'Heroes in Spain', *New Statesman and Nation*, 1 May 1937, reprinted in Spender (1979), 69.
48   'The Will to Live', ibid. 12 November 1938, reprinted in Cunningham (1980), 263–6.
49   Spender (1950), 203.
50   See above, ch. 2
51   'Revolutionaries and Poetry', *Left Review* (July 1935), reprinted in Margolies (1998), 57. Day Lewis was responding as a Party member to the 'Radek formula' enunciated in Moscow the year before. For the powerful relationship between proletarian poetry and 'Spain' in the USA, see Guttman (1968).
52   Kermode (1989), 35.
53   'Who Wants War?', *Poetry and the People* (September 1938), 19–20. The poet, 'William Teeley', cannot be identified from Battalion records. It seems likely that the signature of St Helen's volunteer Bill Feeley – 'a lover of songs, music and poetry' according to his commander, Sam Wild – had been misread in the editorial office; see *Bill Feeley: Singer, Steel Erector, International Brigader* (1989), 4, and Feeley's file in the IBA Archive, Box A/12. An undated list of 'Bad elements' [? May 1938] registers Feeley as 'suspected Trotskyite' and Harrington as 'politically unreliable': RGASPI 3/451/156.
54   Spender and Lehmann (1939), 31–3, 40. John Lepper's background remains obscure. Perhaps his ability to write in French merely reflects the excellence of secondary state education in that era. He also claimed to be a journalist, but so did dozens of other volunteers, especially when they wanted out of the trenches; see Lepper's file in RGASPI 545/6/162/67.
55   See the chapters by A. van Gyseghem and J. Clark in Clark (1979).
56   See Chambers (1989); and Williams (1996), 16–8 for the links between Unity Theatre and the British Battalion.
57   Lewenstein (1994), 55–68; unknown correspondent to B. Glaser, 3 February 1938, AGGC PS Aragon 126; for background information, see Thuneke (1992), 199–217.
58   Glaser to C. Sevitt, 9 May 1938, IWM MS 79/4/1 (photocopy of typewritten letter). Scripts eventually arrived; same to same 14 August

1938, ibid. No details are given, but it would be surprising if they did not include *On Guard for Spain*, surely ideal for the conditions. By this time, however, the Battalion was engaged in real rather than mimetic tragedy, the Ebro campaign. Glaser's last letters were written under constant bombardment; he was killed in action on 10 September; see *Volunteer for Liberty*, 6 October 1938, 7.

59 Klaus (1994), 11–39 and 113–28. At the climax of the action a captured Italian officer commits suicide by *running backwards* into his own soldiers' fire. O'Brien was recorded as wounded on 31 July but when lists were drawn up for repatriation purposes in September, he could not be located; RGASPI 545/6/39/88.

60 Jordan (1938), 342.

61 Osheroff (1990), 13.

62 Quoted in Montefiore (1996), 82.

63 Connolly (1961), 81. Hoskins refers with only slight exaggeration to 'the slavish adulation of the working classes by gently reared intellectuals'; (1969), 55.

64 Bates (1939), 229–43 ('Jarama Ballad'). 'The romancero' is a reference to the song-book distributed to International Brigaders.

65 Aznar Soler and Schneider (1978), III, 57–9.

66 Kermode (1989), 35.

67 Santonja (1979), esp. 61–77.

68 Spender and Lehmann (1939), 7.

69 See, e.g., Johnson (1996), *passim*.

70 This factor also contributed to the mutiny of the Irish contingent at Madrigueras in January 1937: see Stradling (1999), esp. 155–62.

71 Quoted in Hopkins (1998), 181 from Spender's *World Within World*. After acquiring a second-hand copy of Copeman's autobiography *Reason in Revolt*, I found between the pages a holograph love poem written in pencil on a scrap of torn letter-paper: it begins 'And is my love come to this.' The book (a first edition) carries no indication of previous ownership.

72 Thomas (1996), 54–5.

73 IWM AC 9157 reel 5.

74 Ibid., 838, reel 2. Notably, officers were required to appoint men with degrees to act on judicial tribunals: order of 1 June 1937, RGASPI 545/3/426/117.

75 Undated report signed by 'R' (= ?W. Rowe), ibid. 545/6/171/21.

76 Hopkins (1998) has a fascinating discussion of this issue; see pp. 225–31 and sources cited. Copeman broached the subject in his IWM interview (AC 794, reel 8, 1976) rather than in the memoirs written much earlier (1948). Anti-tank units were part of the creation of 'mixed brigades' on

the template of the Red Army, and not a brainwave of Copeman's; see *Brigada Orden del Dia*, 18 June 1937, RGASPI 545/3/426/156. Hopkins's suggestion that Copeman was trying to isolate homosexuals in the anti-tank unit is not borne out by the known sexual orientations of its members. The most reliable sources are Thomas (1996) *passim*; and Hugh Sloan in MacDougall (1986), 195–239. Both served in the unit throughout its existence. Other members were the Welsh miner Jim Brewer, and Ralph Bates's brother Ronald; 'intellectual – very sincere' as Sam Wild described him; RGASPI 545/6/104/27–30.

[77] Alexander (1987), 131. The Albacete authorities were outraged by the British Battalion's comportment at Brunete; see Serrano (1989) *passim*.

[78] In the interim acting command of the battalion was held successively by two Irish proletarian comrades, Peter O'Day and Paddy O'Daire, and (indeed) the post never reverted to the 'officer class'. O'Daire, however, also later took up poetry; see IBA Box 27/A.

[79] AGGC PS Aragon 126, *passim*. These documents are often fragmentary, with random pages missing. They were evidently abandoned in the kitbags of fleeing soldiers or found in some commissars' baggage. The bundle includes a sequence of letters to Jim Arthur of the anti-tanks, which (as it happens) vividly illustrates his heterosexual preferences, and might well have been subject to censorship. Shortly before the retreats, Arthur's commander noted that censorship of mail was 'a progressively greater cause for complaint in the Battery'; A. Nicholl to Brigade commissar, 26 February 1938, ibid.

[80] These men are the true 'unknown warriors' of the Spanish Civil War. To my knowledge, no Spanish volunteer to the Brigades – from perhaps 70,000 who served – has published an account of his experiences. This contrasts sharply with the record of their foreign comrades. Is this due to the failure of the education policy discussed here, or to a general post-war disillusionment?

[81] McCarthy (1999), 207.

[82] See, e.g., *Milicia Popular, Diario del 5° Regimiento de Milicias Populares*, 109 (November 1936) displaying the autographed support of Spanish intellectuals (including Antonio Machado).

[83] Cobb (1995); Fernández Soria (?1996).

[84] Candela (1989), 98. See also Alvarez (1989), esp. 143–55 and the excellent series of field photographs between 88–9. (The author was divisional commissar of the 5th Regiment.)

[85] Brandt (1971), 141–5. This text originated as a report to the German Student Socialist organization in exile. The young Brandt naturally relied on official statistics and other copy provided.

[86] *Bulletin* of the AIA, 23 November 1937, IBA Box 8/A1.

87. R. Smith-Piggot to Foreign Office, 8 September 1938, IWM MS 70/9/1 (copy). The story reflects the fascinated horror of the 'regular' British officer on meeting a live (and probably authentically Russian) example of a mythical monster.
88. *Parte del Día*, XV Brigada, 1 March 1938, PCE reel 18/98–9. As this demonstrates, details of military action were replaced by those of 'cultural' activity in daily reports whenever troops were out of the line; see also ibid., reel 6, *Parte* of 6 August 1937, reporting the work of the loud-hailer unit broadcasting to the enemy trenches.
89. '"More and better books" is the slogan in loyal Spain', *Volunteer for Liberty*, 13 December 1937, 7.
90. Report of 17 August 1937, RGASPI 545/3/428/14.
91. Report of 30 September 1938 (in Spanish), ibid. 435/175.
92. Propaganda leaflet dropped on IB positions in spring 1938, IWM MS 598 (papers of John Peet).
93. See Alberti's obituary in *The Times*, 29 October 1999.
94. Flores (1936), 11.
95. Rosenthal (1975), esp. 31–40; Azaña (1978), II, 92.
96. Hernández (1997), 28–33. Hernández rivals Lorca in the potency of his martyrdom. A new university in Elche (Comunidad de Valencia) bears his name. A website dedicated to him received nearly 45,000 visits in under three years: sourced from *V1nedstatsbasic*. It seems that none of Salaün's 4,000 Republican poets died in battle – at least, none enjoys an explicit martyrological profile. This perhaps explains the enthusiasm in Spanish circles for Cornford, Fox, Caudwell, Donnelly and Bell, who are commemorated not only by a plaque at Madrid's Residencia de Estudiantes, but also in a bilingual edition of their relevant poetry; Cunningham (1990).
97. See Alvarez Lopera (1982), I, 113.
98. Walker (1989), 181
99. From September 1937, the English edition was edited by New Yorker John Tisa, assisted by the Cambridge linguist, Alonzo Elliott. Both men also worked under Sandor Voros and Frank Ryan on *The Book of the XV Brigade*. However, Tisa's memoirs (1985) are silent on editorial policy. The magazine's descendant, *The Volunteer*, carries obituaries of Lincoln/Washington veterans: those with an intellectual profile tend to be allocated more column inches than others.
100. 'Departmental note no. 6553', in *Page of the Base*, Albacete 22 July 1937, IBA Box 22/A.
101. *Mundo Obrero*, 117 (June 2001). In my translation I have substituted 'the struggle' for the topically specific *site of struggle* 'La Castellana', the main avenue through Madrid centre, part of which was then occupied by members of the telecommunications union *Sintel*.

[102] *Pictures of Tomorrow*, broadcast on Radio 3 (9 September 1995) and produced in Belfast by Michael Quinn.

Conclusion: Writers, Politics and the War for Art

[1] Greene (1938), 219.
[2] This hypothesis will be developed in a forthcoming book, provisionally entitled 'The Spanish Civil War Effect: Western Culture and the Cause of "Spain" since 1939'.
[3] Ades (1995); see also Becker and Caiger Smith (1995). Two other relevant exhibitions are recorded in Morris (1986) and *The Spanish Civil War* (2001).
[4] Feuer (1969), 21.
[5] British intellectuals either founded or were affiliated to the following organizations in the 1930s: National Peace Council, National Council for Civil Liberties, International Peace Campaign, Writers against Fascism and for Collective Security, Union of Democratic Control, For Intellectual Liberty, Association of Women for Intellectual Liberty, International Association of Writers for the Defence of Culture, Artists International Association, World Women's Committee against Fascism and War.
[6] Connolly (1961), 115.
[7] Ibid., 99.
[8] And again 'we are having to chose between democracy and fascism, and fascism is the enemy of art. It is not a question of relative freedom; there are no artists in fascist countries'; ibid., 110.
[9] Ibid., 116.
[10] Cunard (1937). Since the original is unpaginated, I refer where convenient to the extracts reprinted in Cunningham (1986), 51–7 (Connolly's response is at p. 52).
[11] Ibid., 116. For Connolly and Auden in Valencia, where the latter wrote about the now-famous poster, see above, ch. 4.
[12] See Upward's letter quoted in Isherwood (1978), 105.
[13] Upward's *The Spiral Ascent* is a trilogy, comprising *In the Thirties* (1962), *The Rotten Elements* (1969) and *No Home but the Struggle* (1977); I have used the Quartet Books set (1979). Quotations in this paragraph are from *In the Thirties*, pp. 19, 138, 206–7 (see also 280–2).
[14] Quoted in Thuneke (1992), 200–1.
[15] 'Looking at a map of Spain on the Devon coast' (August 1937), in Cunningham (1980), 396–9. The poem has various references to the

revolutionary significance of the breasts of young Spanish women, and to Fascists as rapists.

16 In an early *Left Review* editorial, Harry Pollitt stressed the readiness of the CPGB 'to work with anyone who is opposed to the National Government and its policy of support for Fascism abroad'; quoted in Margolies (1998), 1.

17 Fox (1945), passim and esp. ch. 8, 'The Death of the Hero', quoting Stalin on the artist at p. 84.

18 See above, pp. 158–9.

19 Both quoted in Margolies (1998), 1–5 (see also 23). These magazines were successive mouthpieces of Writers International, a 'front organization' set up by the Comintern propaganda maestro Willy Muenzenberg.

20 Quoted in Cunningham (1980), 62.

21 Toynbee, like Cornford, was a professor's son who organized student holiday parties to Welsh mining villages. He customarily spent the balance of his vacations at his parents' modest estate, with frequent visits to cousins who happened to live in nearby Castle Howard. He visited Republican Spain briefly as part of a student delegation. See 'Journal of a Naïve Revolutionary', in Toynbee (1976), 144–84.

22 Though much more should be said on this subject, for reasons of space the reader must be referred for further enlightenment to the relevant work of other scholars (and of V. Cunningham in particular).

23 Thuneke (1992).

24 AIA flysheet, IBA Box 4/D (Capitalization as per text).

25 Read (1947), 24–5, 42–3.

26 Quoted in Hoskins (1969), 47. However, Campbell certainly did fight in the anti-Fascist war of 1939–45, and was badly wounded; shedding his blood, in effect, as an ally of the mythical 'Jewish-Bolshevik conspiracy'; see Rosenthal (1975), 109; Alexander, P. (1982), esp. 171–91.

27 Cunningham (1988), 169. Meanwhile a contributor to the *Welsh Nationalist* (April 1937) noted metaphorically, in a spoof letter of literary gossip to Aunt Eira in Patagonia, that 'communist poets Auden and Spender are fighting in and out of Spain'.

28 The congress's full title was 'II Congreso Internacional de Escritores para la Defensa de la Cultura'. See publicity poster reproduced in Cunningham (1986), opp. p. 190. Comprehensive commentary upon and documentation of the congress is provided in the three volumes compiled by Aznar and Schneider (1978–9).

29 Quoted from the commentary (written by N. Ascherson) of the Granada TV documentary series *The Spanish Civil War* (1983),

episode 4, 'Franco and the Nationalists'. (The phraseology is perhaps that of Franco's adviser and brother-in-law, Serrano Súñer.)

30 Crespo Redondo (1987), 45, 215.
31 See, e.g., the account by Greene (1938), 236–44.
32 Huber (1997).
33 Aznar and Schneider (1979), 42–4. The speech was published in the (liberal) Republican daily *El Sol* on 6 July. Bates was soon afterwards removed from his posts, including editorship of *The Volunteer for Liberty*. Juderías's essay *La Leyenda Negra* first appeared in 1912.
34 Repeated and vibrant hospitality *en route* to Madrid is recorded by Spender, Silvia Townsend Warner, and several other delegates. But the shouts of 'vivan los intelectuales' were made at a cost. More usual – according to a recent estimate of material conditions behind republican lines – was 'the sad spectacle of barefooted women and children who regularly begged for the scanty leftovers of the Popular Army'; Seidman (1999), 829. For a recent and usefully complementary study of the congress, providing much extra politico-literary detail, see Thornberry (2000).
35 For the relationship of the PCE intelligentsia and the Comintern, see A. Elorza's interview, *ABC Cultural*, 17 April 1999, 16–19.
36 Address printed verbatim in Last (1939), 200–8. The author believed it to contain a sub rosa protest 'clear enough for any understanding person'; ibid., 197. His colleagues, Ludwig Renn and Gustav Regler, veterans of Nazi persecution, were also careful not to rock the anti-Fascist boat. However, the latter, commissar of the XII Brigade, who had been seriously wounded by the same shell which killed his commander (the Hungarian writer Maté Zalka, aka Colonel Lukács), later implied disgust at the congress's atmosphere; Regler (1959), 312–13.
37 Last (1939), 195–6.
38 'Camaradas, vosotros que soís intelectuales . . . tenéis el honor inolvidable e infinito de representar el centro geográfico de la lucha, de estar en el corazón de la civilización'; Aznar and Schneider (1978), 57–9. Cf. Spender's later accounts (1951), 238–44, and (1979), 71–9. Photographs of the sessions appear in Koltsov (1963) numbered 129–34; and Hanrez (1977) between pp. 336 and 337.
39 The latter were probably comrades from the XIV Brigade, the only international regiment not required for duty at Brunete; Vidal (1998), 184–5.
40 Koltsov was evidently unaware of the dialectical conflict between the moral of this tale and his earlier remarks about the social privileging of the intellectual.
41 Koltsov (1963), 435–40. Other Soviet speakers went further, openly calling for the 'liquidation of Trotskyism'; Monteath (1994A), 71.

42 Koltsov (1963), 440–1.
43 Castells (1973), 230; Monteath (1994), 69.
44 See ch. 6.
45 Alvarez Valencia (1989), I, 51. Consulting this source in the British Library, I noted that an earlier reader had not been able to desist from placing a large exclamation mark in the margin alongside the latter assertion.
46 Ibid., 193–6.
47 Ibid., 238.
48 Ibid., 16–17, 23–6.
49 See Alvarez Lopera (1982) I 104–5, where both sides of the resulting controversy are rehearsed.
50 Azaña (1978) II 141–2. Azaña recorded that Bergamín had consulted him earlier about his attending – but only for one session, and strictly *ex officio*. Bergamín then phoned on the closing day to see if the President might turn up! 'Evidently', commented Don Manuel, 'it's useless to expect anyone to organize things properly, especially matters which demand courtesy and tact'. After scornful references to ex-colleagues who *had* attended, he concluded pharisaically, 'How well I did to stay away. As I prophesied, the whole thing was a monstrosity.'
51 Ibid., 93.
52 Benda (1928), 32–3.
53 During the war the Republic of which Azaña was the (figure)head operated a policy of rigorous censorship. By 1938, its citizens were even officially banned from listening to radio broadcasts; West (1987), 34. For Azaña's egotistical approach to politics, see Stradling (1997).
54 See Jacobs (1990), 125–44. Benda had become (in the words of one Communist writer) 'un clerc de gauche'; ibid., 132. His reformation had been prefigured at the earlier London conference of the same organization just before the outbreak of war in Spain; see Bradshaw (1997), 13.
55 Cunard herself attended the congress; see Ford (1968), 171. On *Authors Take Sides*, see Chisolm (1979), 238–42.
56 Cunningham (1986), 51.
57 Vera Brittain, one of these, commented that the replies 'not surprisingly, were mainly of the kind which the editors desired to publish'; (1980), 176.
58 It is possible that awareness of its organizers' objective cautioned writers like Campbell and Wyndham Lewis against any kind of collaboration.
59 See above, n. 10.
60 Twenty-eight respondents made remarks of this kind, including

A. Calder-Marshall ('I oppose fascism as the enemy of the arts'); J. Langdon-Davies ('Art and antifascism are synonymous'); and R. Swingler ('culture has always been the directive force of man's progress ... Fascism is destructive alike to culture and human progress').

61 Cortada (1982), 369.

Epilogue: The Real Fifth Column

1 'Ode on the death of W. B. Yeats'; on Orwell vs. Auden, see above, ch. 3.
2 The quotation in this sentence is from Auden's 'September 1, 1939'.
3 Auden (1988), 21, 46, 49. In the 1930s, lumberjacks were at the forefront of union struggles against exploitation by so-called 'Fordist' bosses; see *Volunteer for Liberty*, 29 June 1937, 3.
4 Spender (1936), 37.
5 For further indications of the book's real purpose, i.e. the advancement of artists and their constituency, see ibid., 63–5, 264 and *passim*.
6 Carlyle (1841), 217 (my emphasis).
7 Bell (1938), 213–15 (but cf. 180).
8 Ibid., 175–6, 181.
9 Ibid., 190–3, 208. However none of the prophets cited here is responsible for the hypothesis of 'Artism' and the concept of 'Artistocrats', first put forward in a cognate context to that of the present book in R. Stradling and M. Hughes, *The English Musical Renaissance, 1860–1940: Construction and Deconstruction* (Routledge, 1993). Scattered circumstantial evidence in support can be found in Carey (1992).
10 Bronowski (1939); see also Heinemann (1979), 108–9.
11 Howarth (1978), 151; Kiernan (1989), 183–8. Bernal, a Jesuit-educated Irishman, later married Margot Heinemann.
12 Clark (1968), 120–1.
13 Cornford (1941, reprinted eight times to 1961).
14 See, e.g., 'The Peloponnesian War was ... a struggle between the business interests of Athens and Corinth for commercial supremacy in the West: all wars, Plato remarked, are made for the sake of getting money. And, as at other times in the world's history, the same all-powerful motive was inflaming, within the several states, the ever-present conflict between oligarch and democrat – the conflict which it was one of Plato's chief aims to extinguish.'; ibid., xiv.
15 Many founders of the Republic belonged to Madrid's club for intellec-

tuals, the Ateneo; see Stradling (1997). Cornford perhaps excuses the Spanish Republic's fall from grace during the Civil War by quoting Thucydides on Athens: 'in peace and prosperity both states and individuals are activated by higher motives, because they do not fall under the domination of imperious necessities; but war, which takes away the comfortable provision of daily life, is a hard master, and tends to assimilate men's characters to their dispositions'; Cornford (1941), xiv.

16 Ibid., xiv–xv (see also xxiv–xxv).
17 Last (1939), 199; Koltsov (1963), 434. The event (or its re-creation) was filmed for the Barcelona-based newsreel series *Espanya al Dia*, with the sequence title 'Madrid: Trofeus de la victoria arrabassats a l'enemic'; Requena (1998), 97.
18 Isherwood (1963), 248–9. See also Banting (1998), 319–29.
19 Cunningham (1986), 20. Worsley's change of heart, like Spender's (cf. above, p. 39) was inspired mainly by his friendship with Tony Hyndman. Much later he recalled that 'Spain' had 'exerted a kind of universal spiritual pull' on his generation; Worsley (1971), 190.
20 Southworth (1963), 101–5, exposing Francoist hacks who tried to make propaganda from the collected confessions of 'reformed' Communist writers (in *The God That Failed*) in the 1950s
21 Though – apart from Virginia Woolf's, vividly illustrated in Bradshaw (1997–8) – I have not actually found any articulation of it.
22 See various essays in Cubitt (1998).
23 Straight (1983), 266–72; see also the recent fictionalized biography of Durán; Vázquez-Rial (2001). McCarthy's indictment of Durán as one-time chief of the SIM (March 1950) is printed in Spanish translation at pp. 833–43 of the latter.
24 Straight (1983), *passim* and esp. 326, 335; and see above, ch. 2. Straight was conscious of the novelistic undertones of his life. The Kennedy project lapsed with the president's assassination. In 1973, however, Straight became deputy chairman of Nixon's National Endowment for the Arts. His memoirs praised Nixon highly, the president's earlier involvement with McCarthy going unmentioned. Forgive others as you would be forgiven, as the Good Book says about the Good Fight.

Appendix: 'Necessary Murders': The Texts

1 'The Fascist Sortie' in Ryan (1938), 141–2, written in 1937.
2 Q. Cronin (1980), 119–20, written in 1937.

3 'Adventures in Spain', first published anonymously in *Reading Standard*, 19 November 1937; quoted by Cooper and Parkes (2000), 275.
4 Rust (1939), 77–8.
5 Copeman (1948), 130–1.
6 SWML audio tape 250, recorded in 1974.
7 IWM AC 801/2. (Recorded in 1976 by Judith Cook: see Cook (1979), 87.)
8 Gregory (1986), 71.
9 Interview recorded by author, March 1998.
10 Graham (1999), 1–2.
11 Colman (?1995), 10–11.

Bibliography

Archival Sources and Special Collections Cited

AGGC –   Archivo General de la Guerra Civil, Salamanca
         PS – Sección Político-Social
         SM – Sección Militar
         Referenced by *legajo* (bundle) nos. and folio nos. where present.
BPL –   Britten-Pears Library, Aldeburgh.
         Referenced by correspondent.
CCL –   Christ Church Library, Oxford
         Referenced by correspondent or category.
IBA –   Archive of the British International Brigade Association, Marx Memorial Library, London. Referenced by box and file nos., plus page nos. where present.
IWM –   Imperial War Museum
         Ms. – Written Sources. Referenced by card-index nos.
         AC – Audio Collection. Referenced by index and cassette reel nos. At times, published transcripts have been used instead of, or in addition to, interview tapes. See Johnson, K. (1996) (below).
MAE –   Archivo del Ministerio de Asuntos Exteriores, Madrid Archivo Renovado and Archivo de Burgos sections. Referenced by *R(egistro* (= Dossier)), followed by *carpeta* (folder) and file nos. where noted.
NMLH –   National Museum of Labour History, Manchester
         CPGB Records, Harry Pollitt Papers
PCE –   Archivo del Partido Comunista de España, Madrid (NB These are microfilm copies of documents from Comintern Archive (RGASPI) Moscow.). Referenced by reel number and folio nos. where present.
PRO –   Public Record Office, Kew, London
         Foreign Office (FO 371), War Office (FO 889) and relevant subsections.
RGASPI – Russian Archive for the Study of Contemporary Politics and History, Moscow. Comintern Documents, International Brigades Section (545).
         Referenced by *opis* (section), *delo* (file) and *listij* (page) nos. where present.

SWML – South Wales Miners' Library, Hendrefoilan, Swansea. Audio tapes and transcripts of Welsh IB veterans.

Other Sources Cited
(Place of publication is London unless otherwise stated.)

Abella, R. (1973). *La vida cotidiana durante la guerra civil*, 2 vols. (Barcelona, Planeta).
Abrahamson, A. (1994). *Mosáico Roto* (Madrid, Compañía Literária).
Acier, M. (ed.) (1937). *From Spanish Trenches: Recent Letters from Spain* (New York, Modern Age Books).
Ades, D. et al. (eds) (1995). *Art and Power: Europe under the Dictators, 1930–1945* (Hayward Gallery).
Aguilar Fernández, P. (1996). *Memoria y Olvido de la guerra civil* (Madrid, Alianza).
Alba, V. (1975). *Catalonia: A Profile* (Hurst).
Albert, M. (ed.) (1998). *Vencer no es convencer: Literatura e ideología del fascismo español* (Madrid, Iberoamericana).
Aldgate, A. (1979). *Cinema and History: British Newsreels and the Spanish Civil War* (Scolar Press).
Alexander, B. (1982). *British Volunteers for Liberty: Spain 1936–39* (Lawrence & Wishart, 1987 edn).
—— (1984). 'George Orwell and Spain', in Norris (1984).
Alexander, P. (1982). *Roy Campbell: A Critical Biography* (Oxford, Oxford University Press).
Allison Peers, E. (1936). *The Spanish Tragedy 1930–1936: Dictatorship, Republic, Chaos* (Methuen).
Almuina, C. and Martín, R. (1998). 'Prensa y propaganda durante la guerra civil: el mito de las Brigadas Internacionales', in Requena (1998), 119–32.
Althusser, L. (1971). *Lenin and Philosophy and Other Essays* (NLB).
Alvarez, S. (1989). *Los comisarios políticos en el ejército popular de la República. Aportaciones a la historia de la guerra civil española (1936–1939). Testimonio y reflexión* (La Coruña, Edicios do Castro).
—— (1996). *Historia política y militar de las Brigadas Internacionales: testimonios y documentos* (Madrid, Compañía Literária).
Alvarez Lopera, J. (1982). *La política de bienes culturales del gobierno republicano durante la guerra civil española*, 2 vols (Madrid, Ministerio de Cultura).
Alvarez Rodríguez, R. and López Ortega, R. (eds) (1986). *Poesía Anglo-NorteAmericana de la guerra civil española: Antología bilingüe* (Salamanca, Junta de Castilla-León).

Alvarez Valencia, J. (ed.) (1989). *Congreso internacional de intelectuales y artistas, Valencia 1987*, 4 vols (Generalitat Valenciana, Consellería de Cultura, Educacio i Ciencia).
Ambler, E. (1986). *Here Lies Eric Ambler* (Fontana).
Angus, J. (1983). *With the International Brigade in Spain* (Loughborough University, Dept of Economics).
Art (1986). *Art contra la guerra: Entorn del pavelló espanyol a l'Exposició Internacional de Paris de 1937* (Palau, Ayuntament de Barcelona).
Auden, W. H. (1988). *Paul Bunyan: The Libretto of the Operetta by Benjamin Britten* (Faber).
—— and Isherwood, C. (1958). *The Ascent of F6 and On the Frontier* (Faber).
—— (1986). *The Dog beneath the Skin or Where is Francis?* (Faber).
—— and MacNeice, L. (1967). *Letters from Iceland* (Faber).
Avilés Farré, J. (1998). *Pasión y farsa; Franceses y Británicos ante la guerra civil española* (Madrid, Eudema).
Azaña, M. (1937). *Speech by His Excellency the President of the Spanish Republic* (London, Spanish Embassy).
—— (1978). *Memorias políticas y de guerra*, 2 vols. (Barcelona, Crítica).
Aznar, M. (1958–61). *Historia militar de la guerra de españa*, 3 vols. (3rd edn, Madrid, Editorial Nacional).
Aznar Soler, M. and Schneider, L. M. (eds) (1978). *Segundo congreso internacional de escritores antifascistas (1937)*, 3 vols. (Barcelona, Laia).
Banting, M. et al. (1998). 'Sexuality', in C. Kelly and D. Shepherd (eds), *Russian Cultural Studies: An Introduction* (Oxford, Oxford University Press), 311–51.
Barea, A. (1984). *La forja de un rebelde: III La llama* (Madrid, Turner).
Bates, R. (1937). 'Compañero Sagasta Burns a Church', in Cunningham (1986), 108–15.
—— (1939). 'Of legendary time', in Payne (1963), 349–62.
—— (1939a). 'Jarama Ballad' and 'Brunete Ballad', in *Sirocco and Other Stories* (New York, Random House), 229–52.
Becker, L. and Caiger Smith, M. (eds) (1995). *Art and Power: Images of the 1930s* (Hayward Gallery).
Bell, A. (ed.) (1984). *The Diary of Virginia Woolf*, vol. V: *1936–1941* (Hogarth Press).
Bell, C. (1928). *Civilization* (Harmondsworth, Penguin, 1938).
Benda, J. (1927). (trans. R. Aldington, 1928) *The Great Betrayal* (Routledge).
Blacam, A. de (1936). *For God and Spain: The Truth about the Spanish War* (Dublin, Irish Messenger).
Borkenau, F. (1938). *The Spanish Cockpit* (Pluto Press, 1986 edn).
Bosch-Guimpera, J. (1937). 'Art treasures in Spain', in *Spain Illustrated: A Year's Defence of Democracy*, no. 1 (Lawrence & Wishart).

Bradshaw, D. (1997–8). 'British writers and anti-Fascism in the 1930s', *Woolf Studies Annual* (New York, Pace University Press), 3, 1–27 and 4, 41–66.

Brandt W. (1971). *In Exile: Essays, Reflections and Letters 1933–1947* (Oswald Woolf).

Brenan G. (1943). *The Spanish Labyrinth: An Account of the Social and Political Background of the Spanish Civil War* (Cambridge, Cambridge University Press, 1990 edn).

Bridgeman, B. (1989). *The Flyers: The Untold Story of British and Commonwealth Airmen in the Spanish Civil War and Other Air Wars from 1919 to 1940* (Swindon, B. Bridgeman).

Brittain, V. (1957). *Testament of Experience* (Fontana-Virago edn, 1980).

Brome, V. (1965). *The International Brigades* (Heinemann).

Bronowski, J. (1939). *Spain 1939: Four Poems* (Hull, Andrew Marvell Press).

Brothers, C. (1997). *War and Photography: A Cultural History* (Routledge).

Brown, F. S. et al. (eds) (1989). *Rewriting the Good Fight: Critical Essays on the Literature of the Spanish Civil War* (East Lansing, Michigan State University Press).

Buchanan T. (1993). '"A far away country of which we know nothing?" Perceptions of Spain and its civil war in Britain, 1931–39', *Twentieth Century British History*, 4 (1), 1–24.

—— (1997). *Britain and the Spanish Civil War* (Cambridge, Cambridge University Press).

—— (1997a). 'The death of Bob Smillie, the Spanish Civil War, and the eclipse of the Independent Labour Party', *Historical Journal*, 40 (2), 435–61.

Butt, J. (1978). *Writers and Politics in Modern Spain* (Hodder and Stoughton).

Candela, A. (1989). *Adventures of an Innocent in the Spanish Civil War* (Penzance, United Writers).

Carballo, E. (?1939). *Prisión flotante* (Barcelona, Basa y Pagés).

Cardona, G. (1998). 'Las Brigadas Internacionales y el Ejército Popular', in Requena (1998), 71–82.

Carey, J. (1992). *The Intellectuals and the Masses: Pride and Prejudice among the Literary Intelligentsia, 1880–1939* (Faber).

Carlyle, T. (1841). 'The hero as poet' and 'The hero as man of letters', in *On Heroes, Hero-Worship and the Heroic in History* (Oxford, Oxford University Press, 1935 edn).

Carpenter H. (1981). *W. H. Auden: A Biography* (Allen & Unwin).

—— (1992). *Benjamin Britten: A Biography* (Faber).

Carr, R. (ed.) (1986). *Images of the Spanish Civil War* (Allen & Unwin).

—— (ed.) (1995). *The Chances of Death: The Spanish Civil War Diary of Priscilla Scott-Ellis* (Norwich, Michael Russell).
Carroll, W. H. (1996). *The Last Crusade: Spain, 1936* (Front Royal, Va., Christendom Press).
Carulla, J. and Carulla, A. (1997). *La guerra civil en 2000 carteles. República. Guerra civil. Posguerra*, 3 vols. (Barcelona, Postermil).
Casado, S. (1939). *Last Days of Madrid: The End of the Second Spanish Republic* (Peter Davies).
Casas de la Vega, R. (1967). *Brunete* (Madrid, Fermín Uriarte).
Castells, A. (1974). *Las Brigadas Internacionales de la guerra de España* (Barcelona, Ariel).
Castillejo, J. (1937). *Guerra de ideas en España* (Madrid, Biblioteca de la Revista de Occidente, 1976 edn).
Castillo-Puche, J. L. (1975). *Hemingway in Spain: A Personal Reminiscence of Hemingway's Years in Spain by his Friend* (New English Library).
Caudwell, C. (1937). *Illusion and Reality* (Lawrence & Wishart, 1973 edn).
Chambers, C. (1989). *The Story of Unity Theatre* (Lawrence and Wishart).
Chisolm, A. (1979). *Nancy Cunard* (Sidgwick & Jackson).
Chomsky, N. (1969). 'Objectivity and Liberal Scholarship', in *American Power and the New Mandarins* (Harmondsworth, Pelican), 23–129.
Cierva, R. de la (1969). *La leyenda de las Brigadas Internacionales* (Madrid, Ediciones El Alcázar).
Clark, J. et al (eds) (1979). *Culture and Crisis in Britain in the Thirties* (Lawrence & Wishart).
Clark, R. (1968). *J.B.S.: The Life and Work of J. B. S. Haldane* (Quality Book Club).
Cobb, C. H. (1995). *Los Milicianos de la cultura* (Bilbao, Universidad del País Vasco).
—— (1996). '"La cruzada de la cultura": the British experience of propaganda from Spain during the Civil War', *Tesserae: Journal of Iberian and Latin-American Studies*, 2/2 (Winter), 235–53.
Cochrane, A. (with Blyth, M.) (1989). *One Man's Medicine* (British Medical Journal, The Memoir Club).
Cockburn, C. (pseud. 'Frank Pitcairn') (1936). *Reporter in Spain* (Lawrence & Wishart).
—— (1967). *I Claud . . . The Autobiography of Claud Cockburn* (Harmondsworth, Penguin).
Coll, J. and Pané, J. (1978). *Josep Rovira: una vida als servei de Catalunya* (Barcelona, Vergara).
Colman, J. (?1995). *Memories of Spain (1936–1938)* (Manchester, Links Projects).

Connolly, C. (1938). *Enemies of Promise* (Harmondsworth, Penguin, 1961).
—— (1971). 'Some Memories', in Spender (1975).
Conquest R. (1971). *The Great Terror* (Harmondsworth, Penguin).
Cook, J. (1979). *Apprentices of Freedom* (Quartet Books).
Cooper, M. and Parkes, R. (2000). *We Cannot Park on Both Sides: Reading Volunteers in the Spanish Civil War 1936–39* (Reading, Reading International Brigades Memorial Committee).
Copeman, F. (1948). *Reason in Revolt* (Blandford).
Cornford, F. (ed.) (1941). *The Republic of Plato* (Oxford, Clarendon Press, Oxford, 1961 edn).
Cortada, J. W. (ed.) (1982). *Historical Dictionary of the Spanish Civil War* (Greenwood Press).
Costa, L. et al. (eds) (1992). *German and International Perspectives on the Spanish Civil War: The Aesthetics of Partisanship* (Columbia, SC, Drawer).
Costa Clavell, X. (1975). *Los últimos días de la República* (Barcelona, Bruguera).
Cox, G. (1937). *Defence of Madrid* (Gollancz).
Crespo Redondo, J. et al. (1987). *La purga de maestros en la guerra civil. La depuración del magisterio nacional de la provincia de Burgos* (Valladolid, Ambito).
Crick, B. (1981). *George Orwell: A Life* (Secker & Warburg).
—— (1984). 'Homage to Catalonia and the British Council', *Times Higher Educational Supplement*, 24 February.
Cronin, S. (1980). *Frank Ryan: The Search for The Republic* (Dublin, Repsol).
Crusells, M. and Caparrós, J. M. (1998). 'Las Brigadas Internacionales y la guerra civil española en la Pantalla (1936–1939)', in Requena (1998), 83–118.
Cubitt, G. (ed.) (1998). *Imagining Nations* (Manchester, Manchester University Press).
Cunard, N. et al. (eds) (1937). *Authors Take Sides on the Spanish War* (Left Review).
Cunningham, V. (ed.) (1980). *The Penguin Book of Spanish Civil War Verse* (Harmondsworth, Penguin).
—— (ed.) (1986). *Spanish Front: Writers on the Civil War* (Oxford, Oxford University Press).
—— (1987). 'Homage to Catalonia revisited: remembering and misremembering the Spanish Civil War', *Revue Belge de Philologie et d'Histoire*, 65, 501–14.
—— (1988). *British Writers of the Thirties* (Oxford, Oxford University Press).

—— (ed.) (1990). *Cinco escritores británicos/Five British Writers* (Madrid, Ediciones Turner).
Davenport-Hines, R. (1995). *Auden* (Heinemann).
David, H. (1992). *Stephen Spender: A Portrait with Background* (Heinemann).
—— (1996). *On Queer Street: A Social History of British Homosexuality 1895–1995* (HarperCollins).
Davison, P. (ed.) (1998). *The Complete Works of George Orwell*, Vol. 11: *Facing Unpleasant Facts, 1937–39* (Secker & Warburg).
Delaprée, L. (1936). *The Martyrdom of Madrid* (Madrid, Ministry of State).
Delperrie de Bayac, J. (1968). *Les Brigades Internationales* (Paris, Fayard).
Díaz-Plaja, F. (ed.) (1994). *La vida cotidiana en la España de la guerra civil* (Madrid, Edaf).
—— (ed.) (1972). *La guerra de España en sus documentos* (Barcelona, Plaza y Janés).
Dickinson, P. (1988). *The Music of Lennox Berkeley* (Thames).
Doctor, J. (1999). *The BBC and Ultra-Modern Music, 1922–1936: Shaping a Nation's Tastes* (Cambridge, Cambridge University Press).
Driberg, T. (1978). *Consuming Passions* (Quartet Books).
Eby, C. (1969). *Between the Bullet and the Lie: American Volunteers in the Spanish Civil War* (New York, Holt, Reinhardt and Winston).
Ehrenburg, I. (1979). *Corresponsal en la Guerra Civil Española* (Madrid, Ediciones Júcar).
Eisenwein, G. and Schubert, A. (1995). *Spain at War: The Spanish Civil War in Context, 1931–39* (Longman).
Eisner, K. (1972). *La 12a Brigada Internacional* (Valencia, Promoteo).
Ellmann, R. (1987). *Yeats: The Man and the Masks* (Harmondsworth, Penguin).
Elorza, A. (1999). 'No creo en la inocencia de los intelectuales que viajaron a la URSS en los años 30', *ABC Cultural*, 17 April.
—— and Bizcarrondo, M. (1999). *Queridos camaradas: La Internacional comunista y España, 1919–1939* (Barcelona, Planeta).
Esteban, J. (1998). 'Las Brigadas Internacionales y la guerra civil en la literatura', in Requena (1998), 133–46.
Feeley (1989). *Bill Feeley: Singer, Steel Erector, International Brigader* (St Helen's TUCURC).
Felstead, R. (1981). *No Other Way: Jack Russia and the Spanish Civil War* (Port Talbot, Alun Books).
Fernández-Armesto, F. (1992). *Barcelona: A Thousand Years of the City's Past* (Oxford, Oxford University Press).
Fernández Soria, J. M. (?1996). 'Medios de comunicación y extensión cultural en el ejército republicano', in Garitaonandía (1996), 376–401.

Feuer, L. (ed.) (1969). *Marx and Engels: Basic Writings on Politics and Philosophy* (Collins- Fontana).
Fischer, L. (1941). *Men and Politics* (Cape).
Flint, J. (1987). '"Must God Go Fascist?" English Catholic opinion and the Spanish Civil War', *Church History*, 56, 364–74.
Flores, A. (1936). *A Spectre is Haunting Europe: Poems of Revolutionary Spain* (New York, Critics Group).
Ford, H. (1965). *A Poet's War: British Poets and the Spanish Civil War* (Oxford, Oxford University Press).
—— (ed.) (1968). *Nancy Cunard: Brave Poet, Indomitable Rebel 1896–1965* (Philadelphia, Chilton Book Co.).
Foreman, L. (1987). *From Parry to Britten: British Music in Letters, 1900–1945* (Batsford).
Fox, R. (1937). *The Novel and the People* (New York, International Publishers, 1945).
Francis, H. (1984). *Miners against Fascism: Wales and the Spanish Civil War* (Lawrence & Wishart).
Friel, B. (1990). *Dancing at Lughnasa* (Faber).
Fyrth, F. (1986). *The Signal was Spain: The Aid Spain Movement in Britain, 1936–39* (Lawrence & Wishart).
Gagen, G. and George, D. (eds) (1990). *La guerra civil española: arte y violencia* (Murcia, Universidad de Murcia).
Gamonal Torres, M. (1987). *Arte y política en la guerra civil española* (Barcelona, Puvill).
Garate Córdoba, J. M. (1990). 'Los Moros en la Guerra de España', *Historia y Vida*, 23, 267– 76.
García y Queipo de Llano, G. (1996). 'Culturas en guerra', in Payne and Tussell (1996), 609–34.
Garitaonandía, G. et al. (eds) (?1996). *Comunicación, cultura y política durante la II República y la guerra civil* (Bilbao, Universidad del País Vasco).
Garosci, A. (1959). *Los Intelectuales y la guerra de España* (Madrid, Ediciones Júcar, 1981).
Gathorne-Hardy, J. (1992). *Gerald Brenan: The Interior Castle* (Sinclair-Stevenson).
Geiser, C. (1986). *Prisoners of the Good Fight: The Spanish Civil War, 1936–1939: Americans Against Franco Fascism* (Westport, Conn., Lawrence Hill).
Geli L. (1991). *Fuoco! Cronache legionarie della insurrezione antibolsevica di Spagna* (Rome, Dino).
Gibson, I. (1973). *The Death of Lorca* (W. H. Allen).
—— (1981). *Un Irlandés en España* (Barcelona, Planeta).
—— (1983). *Paracuellos – Como fué* (Barcelona, Vergara).

Giral, F. and Santidrián, P. (1977). *La República en el exilio* (Madrid, Ediciones 99).
Girouard, M. (1981). *The Return to Camelot: Chivalry and the English Gentleman* (New Haven, Yale University Press).
Graham, F. (1987). *Battle of Jarama, 1937: The Story of the British Battalion of the International Brigade in Spain* (Newcastle upon Tyne, Graham).
—— (1999). *The Spanish Civil War: Battles of Brunete and the Aragon* (Newcastle upon Tyne, Graham).
Graham, H. (1999). '"Against the state": the genealogy of the Barcelona May Days (1937)', *European History Quarterly*, 29 (4), 485–542.
Greene, G. (1972). *A Sort of Life* (Book Club edn).
Greene, H. (1938). *Secret Agent in Spain* (Robert Hale).
Gregory, W. (1986). *The Shallow Grave: A Memoir of the Spanish Civil War* (Gollancz).
Grimau, G. (1979). *El cartel republicano en la guerra civil* (Madrid, Cátedra).
Gurney, J. (1976). *Crusade in Spain* (Newton Abbot, Readers' Union).
Gutierrez Alvarez, J. (1984). 'George Orwell, el fugitivo del campo de la victoria', *Historia 16* (May), 101–12.
Guttman, A. (1968). 'The brief embattled course of proletarian poetry', in Madden (1968), 252–69.
Haigh, R. H. et al. (eds) (1986). *The Guardian Book of the Spanish Civil War* (Aldershot, Wilwood House).
Hamm, S. (1998). 'The diary of Sid Hamm', in Stradling (1998), 154–77.
Hanrez, M. (ed.) (1977). *Los escritores y la guerra de España* (Barcelona, Libros de Monte Avila).
Harries, M. and S. (1989). *A Pilgrim Soul: The Life and Work of Elizabeth Lutyens* (Faber).
Harris, K. (1998). *Books on Spain Catalogue* (Summer/Autumn).
Hart, S. M. (ed.) (1988). *'¡No Pasarán!': Art, Literature and the Spanish Civil War* (Tamesis).
Heinemann, M. (1960). *The Adventurers* (Lawrence & Wishart).
—— 'Louis MacNeice, John Cornford and Clive Branson: three left-wing poets', in Clark et al. (1979), 103–32.
—— 'English poetry and the war in Spain: some records of a generation', in Hart (1988), 46–64.
Hemingway, E. (1940). *For Whom the Bell Tolls* (Granada, 1976 edn).
Henry, C. (1999). *The Ebro 1938: Death Knell of the Republic* (Oxford, Osprey).
Hernandez, M. (1997). *I Have Lots of Heart* (Newcastle upon Tyne, Bloodaxe Books).
Herrick, W. (1968). *¡Hermanos! A Novel about the Spanish Civil War* (New York, Knightsbridge, 1990 edn).

Hill, C. (1947). *Lenin and the Russian Revolution* (English Universities Press).
Hills, G. (1976). *The Battle for Madrid* (Vantage Books).
Hoar, V. (1969). *The Mackenzie–Papineau Battalion: Canadian Participation in the Spanish Civil War* (n.p., Copp Clark Publishing Co.).
Hogan, J. (?1935). *Could Ireland Become Communist? The Facts in Full* (no place, publisher or date [Dublin, Cahill & Co., 1935]).
Hollis, C. (1956). *A Study of George Orwell: The Man and his Works* (Hollis and Carter).
Hooper, J. (1995). *The New Spaniards* (Harmondsworth, Penguin).
Hopkins, J. (1998). *Into the Heart of the Fire: The British in the Spanish Civil War* (Stanford, Stanford University Press).
Hopkinson, T. (1953). *George Orwell* (Longmans Green, 1977 edn).
Horn, G.-R. (1990). 'The language of symbols and the barriers of language: foreigners' perceptions of social revolution (Barcelona, 1936–1937)', *History Workshop Journal*, 29, 42–64.
Horner, A. (1960). *Incorrigible Rebel* (McGibbon & Kee).
Hoskins, K. (1969). *Today the Struggle: Literature and Politics in England during the Spanish Civil War* (Austin, Texas University Press).
Howarth, T. E. B. (1978). *Cambridge between Two Wars* (Collins).
Howson, G. (1998). *Arms for Spain: The Untold Story of the Spanish Civil War* (Murray).
Huber, P. (1997). 'Surveillance et répression politique dans les Brigades internationales' (unpublished paper, Lausanne Conference on the International Brigades).
Hyde, D. (1950). *I Believed: The Autobiography of a Former British Communist* (Reprint Society edn, 1952).
Hyndman, T. A. R. (1976). 'International Brigader 2', in Toynbee (1976), 121–30.
Hynes, S. (1976). *The Auden Generation: Literature and Politics in England in the 1930s* (Faber).
Inglada, R. (2001). *Alfonso Ponce de León (1906–1936)* (Madrid, Museo Nacional Centro de Arte Reina Sofia).
Ingram, K. (1985). *Rebel: The Short Life of Esmond Romilly* (Weidenfeld & Nicolson).
Intellectuals (1936). *Intellectuals and the Spanish Military Rebellion* (Press Department of Spanish Embassy in London).
Isaia, N. and Sogno, L. (1998). *Due fronti: La guerra di Spagna nei ricordi personali di opposti combattenti di sessant'anni fà* (Florence, Libri Liberale).
Isherwood, C. (1976). *Christopher and his Kind, 1929–1939* (Magnum-Methuen).

Iverson, A. (1988). 'Orwell's Spanish experience', in *idem*, *Something to Believe In: Writer Responses to the Spanish Civil War* (*The Dolphin*, 16, SEKLOS, Dept. of English, Aarthus University, Denmark), 7–28.
Jackson, G. (ed.) (1972). *The Spanish Civil War* (Chicago, Quadrangle).
Jacobs G. (1990). 'Una imagen de unidad francesa: El Congreso internacional de escritores y "La guerra justa"', in Gagen and George (1990), 125–44.
Jellinek, F. (1938). *The Civil War in Spain* (Gollancz).
Johnson, K. et al. (eds) (1996). *The Spanish Civil War Collection: Sound Archive Oral History Recordings* (Imperial War Museum).
Johnston, V. (1968). *Legions of Babel: The International Brigades in the Spanish Civil War* (Philadelphia, Pennsylvania State University Press).
Jones, L. (1937). *Cwmardy: The Story of a Welsh Mining Village* (Lawrence & Wishart, 1978 edn).
—— (1939). *We Live: The Story of a Welsh Mining Valley* (Lawrence & Wishart, 1978 edn).
Jones, P. (1971). *The Irish Brigade* (New English Library).
Jordan, B. (1990). *Writing and Politics in Franco's Spain* (Routledge).
Jordan, N. (1994). *Sunrise with Sea Monster* (Chatto and Windus).
Jordan, P. (1938). *There Is No Return* (Cresset Press).
Juliá, S. (ed.) (1999). *Víctimas de la guerra civil* (Madrid, Temas de Hoy).
Jump, J. (1976). 'International Brigader 1', in Toynbee (1976), 112–20.
Kazantzakis, N. (1977). *España y Viva la Muerte* (Madrid, Ediciones Júcar).
Kenwood, A. (ed.) (1993). *The Spanish Civil War: A Cultural and Historical Reader* (Providence and Oxford, Berg).
Keogh, D. (1995). *Twentieth-Century Ireland* (Dublin, Gill & Macmillan).
Kermode, F. (1988). *History and Value: The Clarendon Lectures and the Northcliffe Lectures, 1987* (Oxford, Clarendon).
Kiernan, V. (1989). 'Herbert Norman's Cambridge', in *idem*, *Poets, Politics and the People* (Verso), 178–92.
Klaus, H. Gustav (ed.) (1988). 'Writers and fighters: early English memoirs of the Spanish Civil War', in Lange (1988), 6–37.
—— (1989). 'Homage to Catalonia: the fiction of Ralph Bates', *London Magazine* (February–March), 45–56.
—— (1994). *Strong Words Brave Deeds: The Poetry, Life and Times of Thomas H. O'Brien, Volunteer in the Spanish Civil War* (Dublin, O'Brien Press).
Koestler, A. (1954). *The Invisible Writing: Being the Second Volume of Arrow in the Blue, An Autobiography* (Hamish Hamilton).
Koltsov, M. (1963). *Diario de la guerra de España* (Paris, Ruedo Ibérico).
Lange, B.-P. (ed.) (1988). *The Spanish Civil War in British and American Literature* (Braunschweig, Technische Universität).

Larios, J. (1966). *Combat over Spain* (New York, Macmillan).
Last, J. (1939). *The Spanish Tragedy* (Routledge).
Leavitt, D. (1998). *While England Sleeps* (Abacus).
Lee, L. (1991). *A Moment of War: A Memoir of the Spanish Civil War* (New York, The New Press).
Lehmann, J. (1955). *The Whispering Gallery: Autobiography I* (Longmans-Green).
—— et al. (eds) (1937). *Ralph Fox: A Writer in Arms* (Lawrence & Wishart).
Lewenstein, O. (1994). *Kicking against the Pricks* (Nick Hern Books).
Lison-Tolosana, C. (1983). *Belmonte de los Caballeros: Anthropology and History in an Aragonese Community* (Princeton, Princeton University Press).
Líster, E. (1977). *Memorias de un luchador: I. Los primeros combates* (Madrid, Del Toro).
Livermore, A. (1972). *A Short History of Spanish Music* (Duckworth).
McCarthy, J. (1999). *Political Theatre during the Spanish Civil War* (Cardiff, University of Wales Press).
McDougall, I. (ed.) (1986). *Voices from the Spanish Civil War: Personal Recollections of Scottish Volunteers in Republican Spain 1936–39* (Edinburgh, Polygon).
McGarry, F. (1999). *Irish Politics and the Spanish Civil War* (Cork, Cork University Press).
Mackenzie, C. (1956). *Thin Ice* (Chatto & Windus).
Mackenzie, S. P. (1997). 'The International Brigades in the Spanish Civil War: No pasaran?', in idem, *Revolutionary Armies in the Modern Era: A Revisionist Approach* (Routledge).
McLellan, J. (2001a). 'The German volunteers. public and private memories of the International Brigades', lecture given at a Day School on 'The International Brigades in the Spanish Civil War', Oxford, Department of Continuing Education.
—— (2001b). 'Remembering Spain: the contested history of the International Brigades in the German Democratic Republic' (unpublished D.Phil. thesis, Oxford University).
Macmillan, R. (1980). 'Pat Murphy 1898–1974' (unpublished project essay, Cwmbran College of Further Education).
McNair, J. (1979). *Spanish Diary*, ed. D. Bateman (Manchester, Greater Manchester ILP).
MacNeice, L. (1965). *The Strings are False: An Unfinished Autobiography* (ed. E. R. Dodds, Faber 1982).
Madden, D. (ed.) (1968). *Proletarian Writers of the Thirties* (Carbondale and Edwardsville, Southern Illinois University Press).
Marañón, G. (1929). *Antonio Pérez* (Madrid, Espasa Calpe, 1948 edn).

—— (1936). *El Conde Duque de Olivares: La pasión de mandar* (Madrid, Espasa Calpe, 1945 edn).
Margolies, D. (ed.) (1998). *Writing the Revolution: Cultural Criticism from Left Review* (Pluto).
Martin, K. (1969). *Editor: A Second Volume of Autobiography, 1931–45* (Harmondsworth, Penguin).
Martínez Bande, J. (1972). *La ofensiva de Segovia y batalla de Brunete* (Madrid, San Martín).
—— (1974). *La batalla de Teruel* (Madrid, San Martín).
—— (1976). *Frente de Madrid* (Barcelona, Caralt).
—— (1988). *La batalla del Ebro* (Madrid, San Martín).
Meltzer, A. (ed.) (1978). *A New World in our Hearts: The Faces of Spanish Anarchism* (Orkney, Cienfuegos Press).
Mendelsohn, E. (1999). *Early Auden* (second edn, Faber).
Mesa, J. L. (1998). *Los otros internacionales: voluntarios extranjeros desconocidos en el bando nacional durante la guerra civil (1936–1939)* (Madrid, Ediciones Barbarroja).
Meyers, J. (ed.) (1975). *George Orwell: The Critical Heritage* (RKP).
Miller, R. R. (1989). *Shamrock and Sword: The Saint Patrick's Battalion in the US–Mexican War* (Norman, Oklahoma University Press).
Mitchell, D. (1981). *Britten and Auden in the Thirties: The Year 1936* (new edn, Woodbridge, Boydell Press, 2000).
—— and Reed, P. (1991). *Letters from a Life: Selected Letters and Diaries of Benjamin Britten*, 2 vols. (Faber).
Monteath, P. (1990). 'Problematising history: Orwell's Spanish experience', *Melbourne Historical Journal*, 20, 112–25.
—— (1994). *Writing the Good Fight: Political Commitment in the International Literature of the Spanish Civil War* (Greenwood).
—— (1994a). *The Spanish Civil War in Literature, Film and Art: An International Bibliography of Secondary Literature* (Greenwood).
Montefiore, J. (1996). *Men and Women Writers of the 1930s: The Dangerous Flood of History* (Routledge).
Montero Barrado, S. (1987). *Paisajes de la guerra: Nueve itinerarios por los frentes de Madrid* (Madrid, Comunidad de Madrid).
Montero Moreno, A. (1961). *Historia de la persecución religiosa en España, 1936–1939* (Madrid, Biblioteca de Autores Cristianos).
Morreres i Boix, J. (1980). 'Las milicias populares en Cataluña, 1936–1937', *Historia* 16, 55, 27–38.
Morris, F. (ed.) (1986). *No Pasaran! Photographs and Posters of the Spanish Civil War* (Bristol, Arnolfini Gallery).
Morris, J. A. (1977). *Writers and Politics in Modern Britain* (Hodder & Stoughton).
Muggeridge, M. (1940). *The Thirties: 1930–40 in Great Britain* (Hamish Hamilton).

—— (1967). *The Thirties: 1930–1940 in Great Britain* (Collins edn).
Mulford, W. (1988). *This Narrow Place: Sylvia Townsend Warner and Valentine Ackland: Life, Letters and Politics, 1930–51* (Pandora).
Muste, J. M. (1966). *Say That We Saw Spain Die: Literary Consequences of the Spanish Civil War* (Seattle, University of Washington Press).
Nestorenko, I. et al. (1975). *International Solidarity with the Spanish Republic, 1936–1939* (Moscow, Progress Publishers).
Newsinger, J. (1998). *Orwell's Politics* (Macmillan).
Norris, C. (ed.) (1984). *Inside the Myth: Orwell, Views from the Left* (Lawrence & Wishart).
Núñez Díaz-Balarte, M. (1996). 'La prensa en las Brigadas Internacionales', in Alvarez (1996), 441–51.
O'Callaghan, J. C. (1870). *History of the Irish Brigades* (Dublin).
O'Duffy, E. (1938). *Crusade in Spain* (Dublin, Browne & Nolan).
O'Neill, D. (1976). 'A Cardiff footnote to the Spanish Civil War: Tom's days of sunshine and despair', *South Wales Echo*, 2 August.
O'Riordan, M. (1979). *Connolly Column* (Dublin, New Books).
Orta, F. M. (1986). *The Last Pharaoh* (Weidenfeld & Nicolson).
Ortega y Gasset, J. (1925). 'On Fascism', in *idem*, *Invertebrate Spain* (Allen & Unwin, 1937), 190–201.
—— (1928). *La rebelión de las masas* (Madrid, Castalia, 1998 edn).
Ortega Klein, A. (1980). 'La decepción política de Ortega' *Historia*, 16 (48), 67–78.
Ortiz Alfau, A. M. (1986). *Bilbao en la obra de Unamuno* (Bilbao, Temas Vizcainos).
Orwell, G. (1936). *The Road to Wigan Pier* (Harmondsworth, Penguin, 1962 edn).
—— (1938). *Homage to Catalonia and Looking Back on the Spanish War* (Harmondsworth, Penguin, 1966 edn).
—— (1954). *England, Your England and Other Essays* (Secker & Warburg).
Osheroff, A. (1990). 'Reflections of a Civil War veteran', in Perez and Aycock (1990), 9–17.
Pages i Blanch, P. (1997). 'Marty, Vidal, Kleber et le Komintern: Ce que nous apprennent les archives de Moscou' (unpublished paper, International Brigades Conference, Lausanne).
Parrot, L. (1937). *Panorama de la culture espagnole* (Paris, Éditions Sociales Internationales).
—— (1937a). *The Salvage of Catalonia's Historical and Artistic Patrimony* (Barcelona, Comisariat de Propaganda).
Payne, R. (ed.) (1963). *The Civil War in Spain, 1936–1939* (Secker & Warburg).
Payne, S. (1970). *The Spanish Revolution* (Weidenfeld & Nicolson).
—— (1987). *The Franco Regime, 1936–1975* (Madison, University of Wisconsin).

—— and J. Tussell (eds) (1996). *La Guerra Civil: Una nueva visión del conflicto que dividió España* (Madrid, Temas de Hoy).

Paz, A. (1997). *The Spanish Civil War* (Paris, Editions Hazan).

Perez, M. and Aycock, W. (eds) (1990). *The Spanish Civil War in Literature* (Lubbock, Texas Technical University Press).

Pike, D. W. (1968). *Conjecture, Propaganda and Deceit: The International Crisis over Spain, 1936–39, as Seen in the French Press* (Stanford, California Institute of International Studies).

Preston, P. (1986). *The Spanish Civil War* (Weidenfeld & Nicolson).

—— and Mackenzie, A. L. (eds) (1996). *The Republic Besieged: Civil War in Spain, 1936– 1939* (Edinburgh, Edinburgh University Press).

Prill, U. (1998). 'Mitos y mitografía en la literatura fascista', in Albert (1998), 167–79.

Read, H. (1938). *Poetry and Anarchism* (second edn, Freedom Press, 1947).

Remembering (1996). *Remembering the Spanish Civil War* (Aberdeen, Aberdeen Trades Council).

Rees, T. (1998). 'The high-point of Comintern influence? The Communist Party and the Civil War in Spain', in Rees and Thorpe (1998), 143–67.

—— and Thorpe, A. (1998). *International Communism and the Communist International 1919–43* (Manchester, Manchester University Press).

Regler, G. (1959). *The Owl of Minerva* (New York, Farrar, Strauss and Cudahy).

—— (1940). *The Great Crusade* (New York, Longmans).

Requena Gallego, M. (ed.) (1998). *La guerra civil española y las Brigadas Internacionales* (Cuenca, Universidad de Castilla-La Mancha).

Revilla Cebrecos, M. (1976). *De esos tenemos tantos como el que más* (Madrid, Del Toro).

Rey García, A. (1997). *Stars for Spain: La Guerra Civil Española en los Estados Unidos* (La Coruña, Edicios do Castro).

Richardson, R. (1982). *Comintern Army: The International Brigades in the Spanish Civil War* (Lexington, Kentucky University Press).

Ridruejo, D. (1962). *Escrito en España* (Buenos Aires, Losada).

—— (1976). *Casi unas memorias* (Barcelona, Planeta).

—— (1979). 'La vida intelectual española en el primer decenio de la postguerra', in idem, *Entre literatura y política* (Madrid, Seminarios y Ediciones), 15–38.

Robinson, R. (1971). *The Origins of Franco's Spain: The Right, the Republic and Revolution, 1931–36* (Newton Abbot, David & Charles).

Rocker, R. (1937). *The Tragedy of Spain* (ASP, 1986).

Romero, L. del (1996). *De Fuentedodos a Fuenteovejuna: Memorias de un comisario de guerra* (Barcelona, Nossa y Jara).

Romilly, E. (1937). *Boadilla: A Personal Record of the English Group of the Thaelmann Battalion in Spain* (McDonald, 1971).

Rosenstone, R. (1980). *Crusade of the Left: The Lincoln Brigade in the Spanish Civil War* (Lanham, MD, University Press of America).

Rosenthal, M. (1975). *Poetry of the Spanish Civil War* (New York, New York University Press).

Rowse, A. L. (1993). *All Souls in My Time* (Duckworth).

Rubio, F. and Goni, J. (1986). 'Un millón de títulos: Las novelas de la guerra de España', in Tamames (1986), 153–69.

Rust, W. (1939). *Britons in Spain: The History of the British Battalion of the XVth International Brigade* (Lawrence & Wishart).

Ryan, F. (ed.) (1938). *The Book of the XV Brigade* (Sunderland, Graham, 1986).

Salas Larrazábal, R. (1973). *El Ejército Republicano*, 4 vols (Madrid, Editorial Nacional).

Salaün, S. (1977). 'La expresión poética durante la guerra de España', in Hanrez (1977), 143–54.

Salvage (1937). *The Salvage of Catalonia's Historical and Artistic Patrimony* (Barcelona, Comisariat de Propaganda).

Sanchez, D. (1996). 'North-west volunteers to Spain 1936–39' (unpublished BA dissertation, Dept. of Hispanic Studies, University of Manchester).

Sanchez, J. M. (1987). *The Spanish Civil War as a Religious Tragedy* (Notre Dame, Notre Dame University Press).

Santonja, G. (ed.) 1979). *La novela proletaria (1932–1933)*, 2 vols. (Madrid, Editorial Ayuso).

Sanz de Soto, E. (1997). 'Les écrivains et la guerre d'Espagne', *Le Monde Diplomatique* (April), 26–7.

Seeds (1975). *Seeds of Conflict, Series 3: The View from the Left* (Nendeln, Klaus Reprint).

Seidman, M. (1990). 'The Unorwellian Barcelona', *European History Quarterly* 20 (April), 163–80.

—— (1999). 'Quiet fronts in the Spanish Civil War', *The Historian*, 61 (Summer), 821–41.

Selden, M. (1991). *Orwell: The Authorised Biography* (Heinemann).

Serrano, C. (ed.) (1989). 'El "informe" de Vital Gayman sobre "La base de las Brigadas Internacionales"'. *Estudios de Historia Social* (July 1937), 315–459.

Shipton, M. (1995). 'Top poet saved gay lover from the firing squad', *Wales on Sunday*, 19 November.

Sinfield, A. (1997). 'Stephen Spender's bit of rough: some arguments about art, AIDS, and subculture', *European Journal of English Studies*, 1 (I), 56–72.

Sloan, P. (ed.) (1938). *John Cornford: A Memorial Volume* (Cape).

Sommerfield, J. (1937). *Volunteer in Spain* (New York, Knopp).
Souchère, E. de la (1965). *An Explanation of Spain* (New York, Vintage Books).
Souchy, A. et al. (1987). *The May Days: Barcelona 1937* (Freedom Press).
Southworth, H. R. (1963). *Le mythe de la croisade de Franco* (Paris, Ruedo Ibérico).
Spain (1938). *Spain Against the Invaders: Napoleon 1808, Hitler and Mussolini 1936* (United Editorial).
Spanish (2001). *The Spanish Civil War: Dreams and Nightmares* (Imperial War Museum).
Spencer, V. A. (Peter) (1964). *All My Sins Remembered* (Heinemann).
Spender, S. (1936). *The Burning Cactus* (Faber).
—— (1936a). *Forward from Liberalism* (Gollancz).
—— (1951). *World Within World* (Hamish Hamilton).
—— (ed.) (1975). *W.H. Auden – A Tribute* (Weidenfeld & Nicolson).
—— (1979). *The Thirties and After* (Fontana).
—— (1980). *Letters to Christopher*, ed. L. Bartlett (Santa Barbara, Calif., Black Sparrow).
—— (et al.) (1950). *The God That Failed: Six Studies in Communism* (Hamish Hamilton).
—— and Lehmann, J. (eds) (1939). *Poems for Spain* (Hogarth Press).
Sperber, M. (1977). 'Los escritores ingleses', in Hanrez (1977), 47–61.
Stansky, P. and Abrahams, W. (1966). *Journey to the Frontier: Two Roads to the Spanish Civil War* (Constable, paperback edn, 1986).
Sternlicht, S. (1992). *Stephen Spender* (New York, Twayne).
Stradling, R. (1984). 'Orwell and the Spanish Civil War: a historical critique', in Norris (1984), 103–25.
—— (1996). 'Battleground of Reputations: Ireland and the Spanish Civil War', in Preston and Mackenzie (1996), 107–32.
—— (1997). 'History and the triumph of Art: Manuel Azaña's vision of Spanish democracy', in Stradling, Newton and Bates (eds), *Conflict and Coexistence: Nationalism and Democracy in Modern Europe – Essays in Honour of Harry Hearder* (Cardiff, University of Wales Press), 132–58.
—— (ed.) (1998). *Brother against Brother: Experiences of a British Volunteer in the Spanish Civil War* (Stroud, Sutton).
—— (1999). *The Irish and the Spanish Civil War, 1936–1939: Crusades in Conflict* (Manchester, Manchester University Press).
Straight, M. (1943). *Make This the Last War: The Future of the United Nations* (New York, Harcourt-Brace).
—— (1983). *After Long Silence* (Collins).
Stratton, H. (1984). *To Antifascism by Taxi* (Port Talbot, Alun Books).
Suarez, A. (1974). *Un episodio de la revolución española: El proceso contra el POUM* (Paris, Ruedo Ibérico).

Sullivan, R. (1989). 'History and desire: Auden's "Spain" and Caudwell's Illusion and Reality', in Brown et al. (1989), 229–40.
Tamanes, R. (ed.) (1986). *La guerra civil española: Una reflexión moral, 50 años después* (Barcelona, Planeta).
Taylor, A. J. P. (1983). *A Personal History* (Hamish Hamilton).
Thomas, F. (1996). *To Tilt at Windmills: A Memoir of the Spanish Civil War* (East Lansing, Michigan State University).
Thomas, F. H. (1998). 'Spanish legionario: a professional soldier in Spain', in Stradling (1998), 35–153.
Thomas, H. (1977). *The Spanish Civil War* (Harmondsworth, Penguin, 3rd edn).
Thompson, E. P. (1979). *The Poverty of Theory and other Essays* (Merlin Press).
Thornberry, R. S. (2000). 'Writers take sides, Stalinists take control: the Second International Congress for the Defense of Culture (Spain 1937)', *The Historian*, (Spring), 589–605.
Thuneke, J. (1992). 'Jack Lindsay's mass declamation "On guard for Spain" (1937) and the speech chorus tradition of the Workers' Theatre Movement (1926–1936)', in Costa et al. (1992), 199–222.
Tierney, W. (1972). 'Irish writers and the Spanish Civil War', *Eire Ireland* 7 (3), 36–55.
Tisa, J. (1985). *Recalling the Good Fight: An Autobiography of the Spanish Civil War* (South Hadley, Mass., Bergin & Garvey).
Tolley, T. (1975). *The Poetry of the Thirties* (Gollancz).
Toynbee, P. (ed.) (1976). *The Distant Drum: Reflections on the Spanish Civil War* (Sidgwick & Jackson).
Trapiello, A. (1994). *Las armas y las letras: Literatura y guerra civil (1936–39)* (Barcelona, Planeta).
Trilling, L. (1952). 'George Orwell and the Politics of Truth', in R. Williams (1974), 62–79.
Turnbull, P. and Burn, J. (1978). *The Spanish Civil War 1936–39* (Osprey).
Upward, E. (1979). *The Spiral Ascent* (Quartet Books).
Vaksberg, A. (1990). *Stalin's Prosecutor: The Life of Andrei Vyshinsky* (New York, Grove Weidenfeld).
Valleau, M. (1982). *The Spanish Civil War in American and European Films* (Ann Arbor, UMI Research Press).
Vázquez-Rial, H. (2001). *El soldado de porcelana* (Madrid, Punto de Lectura).
Vidal, C. (1998). *Las Brigadas Internacionales* (Madrid, Espasa Calpe).
Vilar, P. (1992). *La guerra civil española* (Barcelona, Crítica).
Volpe, N. and Albari, M. (eds) (1995). *Sealed in Struggle: Canadian Poetry and the Spanish Civil War* (Tenerife, University of La Laguna).
Wade, A. (ed.) (1954). *The Letters of W. B. Yeats* (Hart-Davis).

Walker, T. (1989). *In Spain* (Corgi edn).
Waugh, E. (1941). *Scoop: A Novel about Journalists* (Harmondsworth, Penguin, 1943 edn).
Weatherhead, A. K. (1975). *Stephen Spender and the Thirties* (Lewisburg Pa., Bucknell University Press).
Weintraub, S. (1968). *The Last Great Cause: The Intellectuals and the Spanish Civil War* (New York, Weybright & Talley).
West, W. J. (1987). *Truth Betrayed* (Duckworth)
—— (ed.) (1989). *Orwell: The War Commentaries* (New York, Schocken Books).
Wharton, B. (2002). 'La última cruzada: El papel de Limerick en la Guerra Civil Española', *Investigaciones Históricas* (forthcoming).
Williams, C. et al. (1996). *Memorials of the Spanish Civil War: The Official Publication of the International Brigade Association* (Stroud, Sutton).
Williams, R. (ed.) (1974). *George Orwell: A Collection of Critical Essays* (Englewood Cliffs, Prentice-Hall).
—— (1984). *Orwell* (Fontana-Flamingo).
—— (1985). *Loyalties* (Chatto & Windus).
Wilson, F. (1944). *On the Margins of Chaos: Recollections of Relief Work in and between Three Wars* (John Murray).
Wintringham, T. (1939). *English Captain* (Harmondsworth, Penguin, 1940 edn).
Wood, N. (1959). *Communism and the British Intellectuals* (Gollancz).
Wolff, M. (1994). *Another Hill* (Urbana and Chicago, Illinois University Press).
Woolf, C. and Bagguley, J. (eds) (1967). *Authors Take Sides on Vietnam* (Peter Owen).
Worsley, T. C. (1939). *Behind the Battle* (Robert Hale).
—— (1967). *Flanelled Fool* (Hogarth edn., 1985).
—— (1971). *Fellow Travellers: A Memoir of the Thirties* (London Magazine Editions).
Wyden, P. (1983). *The Passionate War: The Narrative History of the Spanish Civil War* (New York, Simon & Shuster).
Ydewalle, C. d' (1946). *An Interlude in Spain* (Readers' Union).
Yeats, W. B. (1982). *Collected Poems* (Macmillan).
Zuehlke, M. (1996). *The Gallant Cause: Canadians in the Spanish Civil War, 1936–1939* (Vancouver and Toronto, Whitecap Books)

Index

Abertridwr 147
'Aid Spain' movement 27, 34, 74–5, 92, 125, 150, 157
Aitken, George 125, 151
Alba, duke of 18
Albacete 28, 36, 37, 38, 39, 41, 42, 53, 81, 99, 105, 138, 141, 153, 156, 162, 166
Alberti, Rafael 90, 150, 165–6, 180
Alcubierre 71
Alexander, Bill 50–1, 52, 72, 138, 139
Alianza de Escritores Antifascistas 182
Alianza Popular 167
Allen, Jim 134
Allison Peers, E. 10, 63
Almería 125, 126
Altolaguirre, Manuel 39, 150
Altos de Romanillos, Los 131
Alvarez del Vayo, Julio 20, 37, 39, 41, 184
Alvarez Lasarte, Captain 129
Ambite 144, 146, 165
American Battalion 28, 87
Andalusia 5, 133, 150, 163
Angus, John 137
Anti-Fascist Writers' Congress 19, 40–1, 44, 159, 178–82, 184–5, 186, 192–3
Anti-Tank Battery 137, 138
Antología Bilingüe 29, 30
Aragon 26, 35, 44, 45, 48, 50, 54, 60, 63, 71, 74, 87, 134, 135, 141, 157, 162, 163, 165, 166
Arnold, Matthew 189
Arriba 5
Art and Power (exhibition) 170
Artists' International Association (AIA) 19, 164, 177

Assault and Battery News 146
Astray, Millán 14–15
Asturias 108
Ateneo (Madrid) 11
Atholl, duchess of 164
Auden, W. H. x, 1, 32, 34, 44, 49, 56, 64–5, 76–95, 99, 154, 155, 156, 167, 172, 173, 182, 186, 188
Auden group 32, 41, 64, 65, 66
Authors Take Sides in the Spanish Civil War 44, 65, 173, 186–7
Azaña, Manuel 8, 12, 102, 141, 166, 184–6, 189
Aznar, Manuel 167

Badajoz 125, 163
Baker, Josephine 84
Banting, John 19
Barcelona 4, 20, 33, 35, 36, 49, 52, 53, 54, 57–60, 71, 74, 75, 77, 78, 87, 89, 93, 100, 104, 108, 121, 178, 179
Barga, Corpus 180, 185
'Barraca, La' 5, 9
Basque Country 11, 14
Bates, Ralph 19, 21, 40, 143–4, 150–1, 152, 159, 179–80
Behan, Brendan 157
Belchite 146
Belfast 167
Bell, Clive 189, 190–1, 192
Bell, Julian 33
Benda, Julien 185, 186, 189, 192, 194
Benjamin, Walter 194
Bergamín, José 180, 182, 186
Berkeley, Lennox 78, 79, 80, 92, 93–4

Index

Bernal, J. D. 191
Bilbao 14, 125, 126
Blair, Eileen 53, 54, 71–2
Blair, Eric, *see* Orwell, George
Blockade 19–20
Bloomsbury group 189
Blunt, Anthony 25, 27, 46, 192, 195
Boadilla 27, 44
Borkenau, Franz 57, 58, 121
Brandt, Willi 164
Branson, Clive 161
Brecht, Bertolt 156
Brenan, Gerald 73
Britain 74, 103, 104, 106, 121, 162, 171, 176
British Battalion 27, 28, 30, 36, 40, 41, 42, 50, 53, 55, 63, 74, 76, 81, 84, 87, 91, 94, 100, 111, 112, 115, 116, 123, 125, 128–44, 145–6, 151–2, 154, 156, 157, 158, 160, 161, 162, 174, 182
British Council 16
British Medical Unit 85, 112, 119
Britten, Benjamin 75–84, 89, 92–5, 99, 188
Brockway, Fenner 55
Bronowski, Jacob 191
Brooke, Rupert 82
Brown, Albert 156
Brown, George 143
Brunete 43, 53, 74, 124, 126–44, 146, 147, 154, 160, 161, 162, 182, 193
Burgos 12, 14, 17, 103, 141, 142, 173
Burckhardt, Jacob 194
Byron, Lord 25, 82

Cáceres 105, 109, 117
Cambridge 25, 44, 45
Camp Lucas (Mahora) 38
Campbell, Roy 66–7, 154–5, 178, 186
Candela, Antonio 163–4
Cardiff 27, 31, 129, 152
Carew, Tom 113
Carlists 112, 113, 116, 118

Carlyle, Thomas 189–90, 194
Carpenter, Humphrey 92
Casado, Colonel 128
Castile 5
Castillejo Duarte, José 10
Catalan Communist Party, *see* Partido Socialista de Unificación Catalana
Catalonia 9, 19, 20, 58, 74, 75, 78, 94, 150, 157, 163
Catholic Times 109
Caudwell, Christopher 85, 88, 91, 159, 161, 174, 175
Cervantes, Miguel de 7
Checa 6, 10
Chomsky, Noam 49
Churchill, Winston 27
Cisneros, Hidalgo de 39
Clark, Edward 75, 76
Cochrane, Archie 112
Cockburn, Claud 40, 59, 85, 86, 150
Colman, Jud 137
Comintern 37, 41, 53, 57, 59, 65, 75, 81, 85, 86, 100, 107, 125, 136, 142, 153, 170, 175, 178, 186, 188, 195
Committee of Anti-Fascist Militias 58
Common, Jack 69
Communism 26, 35, 44, 48, 52, 57, 63, 70, 100, 102, 103, 108, 109, 110, 113, 114, 115, 120, 136, 169, 171, 172, 178, 191
Communist Party 25, 26, 27, 39, 43, 51, 59, 60, 172, 175, 176, 177, 180
Communist Party of Great Britain (CPGB) 27, 32, 34, 35, 36, 37, 38, 39, 40, 50, 51, 55, 56, 63, 68, 74, 80, 84–5, 87, 90, 91, 111, 132, 153, 154, 162, 173–4, 189
Communist Party of Ireland 157
Communists 2, 7, 8, 25, 26, 32, 38, 45, 46, 48, 60, 72, 73, 85, 94, 100, 137, 156, 174, 178, 181
Condor Legion 18, 104

Confederación Nacional de Trabajo (CNT) 19, 53–4, 59, 60, 85, 87, 178
Connolly, Cyril 34, 65, 85, 154–5, 158–9, 172–3, 175, 187
Connolly, James 119
Co-operative Movement 156
Copeman, Fred 128, 134, 140, 160–2
Copic, Vladimir 125
Cornford, Frances 25, 44, 46
Cornford, Francis 25, 46, 192
Cornford, James 45, 46
Cornford, John 8, 25–7, 35, 42, 43–5, 46, 47, 52, 71, 81, 88, 119, 155, 159, 174, 175, 176, 192, 194
Corpo Truppe Voluntarie (CTV) 52, 110, 132–3
Cossío, Manuel 9
Costa Brava 146
Cummings, Alec 137, 152
Cunard, Nancy 19, 20, 44, 65, 121, 186, 187, 188
Cunningham, Jock 160

Daily Telegraph 59
Daily Worker 35, 59, 86, 150
Dartington Hall 26, 46
Davis, Thomas 116
Day Lewis, Cecil 32, 44, 81, 90, 91, 156, 174–5, 176, 177
Delaprée, Louis 18–19
Dimitrov Battalion 165
Dodds, E. R. 81, 82–3
Domingo, Marcelino 9
Donnelly, Charles 119–20
Doone, Rupert 156
Dublin 100, 108, 110, 119, 157, 158
Dun Laoghaire 114, 115
Dunbar, Malcolm 161
Durán, Gustavo 6, 19, 195
Durruti, Buenaventura 4
d'Ydewalle, Charles 20–1

Ebro, the 74, 153, 158, 167
Eby, Cecil 140

Edwards, Bob 55–6
Ehrenburg, Ilya 17, 90, 180
XVIII Army Corps 125, 128, 131
Einstein, Albert 12
Eisner, Alexei 99–100, 110
Ejército Popular, *see* Popular Army
11th Division 126
Eliot, T. S. 187
Elliott, Alonzo 153
Engels, Friedrich 189
Extremadura 163

Falange 3, 5, 6, 70, 127, 130, 131, 139, 142, 178
Fascism ix, 2, 7, 11, 17, 18, 30, 32, 48, 51, 53, 54, 56, 57, 68, 69, 70, 77, 89, 90, 102, 107, 110, 114, 118, 124, 136, 149, 155, 167, 170, 172, 180, 181–2, 183, 187, 194
Fascists 4, 5, 7, 16, 28, 29, 72, 77, 93, 100, 111, 112, 126, 133, 133, 138, 139, 140, 144, 149, 171, 173, 191
Federación Anarquista Ibérica (FAI) 87
Felipe, León 166
Fenianism 109, 118
Ferrere, Claude 20
Festival of Music for the People (London) 75, 94–5
Fifth Column 5, 6, 53, 61, 188–95
XV Bandera del Tercio, *see* Irish Brigade
Figueras 20
First World War 82
Fischer, Louis 49, 111, 166
Ford, Hugh 119
For God and Spain 113
Foreign Legion 127, 131
Fox, Ralph 85, 145, 159, 174, 175, 194
France 74, 75, 103, 171, 176
Francis, Hywel 111
Franco, Carmen 14
Franco, Francisco 3–4, 6, 7, 10, 11–12, 13, 14, 15, 16, 17, 18, 19, 20, 28, 49, 61, 65, 70, 71, 73, 74,

81, 86, 94, 99, 100, 105, 108, 110, 113, 115, 121, 124, 125, 126, 131, 133, 142, 143, 153, 154, 163, 166, 173, 179, 181, 194
Franco, Ramón 160
Francoism 3–4, 9, 13, 15–16, 51, 70, 74, 105, 114, 116, 143, 157
Friel, Brian 120
Fuentes de Ebro 146

Gaffney, Gertrude 109, 117
Galán, Colonel 127–8
Gandesa 153
Gaos, Angel 183
Garibaldi Battalion 110
Garosci, Aldo 10–11, 49, 50
Gates, John 165
Gayman, Vidal 132
Geary, Frank 121
Generalitat de Catalunya 57, 58
Generation of 1898 14
Geneva 20
Germany 3, 4, 10, 56, 69, 179
Gerona 71
Gibson, Ian 86
Gide, André 178, 180, 181–2, 185, 193
Gilbert, Tony 161
Glaser, Ben 157
Glasgow 28
Gogarty, Oliver St John 118
Gollancz, Victor 51
Gonne, Maud 118
Gorky, Maxim 158
Gowan, Charles 140
Gowans, George 137
Goya, Francisco 16, 18, 20
GPO Film Unit 76
Granada 4, 9
Greene, Graham 195
Greene, Hugh 173, 195
Greenhalgh, Walter 137
Greening, Edwin 147
Grigson, Geoffrey 158
Group Theatre 156
Guadalajara 37, 52, 53, 110, 112, 180
Guadarrama, Sierra de 126, 127

Guernica 79, 104, 125, 126
Gurney, Jason 112

Haldane, J. B. S. 191–2
Halifax, Lord 59, 72
Hamm, Sid 152
Harrington, Bill 153, 160
Heinemann, Margot 45–6, 147
Hemingway, Ernest ix, 21, 86, 111–12, 113, 141
Hernández, Miguel 148, 150, 156, 159, 166
Highway, The 61
Hillesley, Frank 140
Historical Bureau 167
Hitler, Adolf 18, 32, 114, 153, 171, 194
Hogan, James 109, 113
Hollywood 19, 121
Hopkins, J. 161–2
Hopkinson, Tom 67
Hora de España 166
Horkheimer, Max 183
Horner, Arthur 132
Huesca 52, 87
Huxley, Aldous 191
Huxley, Julian 191
Hyndman, T. A. R. x, 27–9, 30–43, 44, 45, 47, 77, 85, 87, 88, 156, 160–1, 176, 189

Ibárruri, Dolores (La Pasionaria) vii, 117
Iceland 78, 80, 81
Independent Labour Party (ILP) 52, 55–6, 69
International Brigade Association (IBA) 138, 143
International Brigades: XI 6, 7, 8, 99, 112; XII 7, 27, 41, 99, 100, 110, 195; XIII 128; XIV 43; XV 19, 27, 40, 124, 128, 129, 130, 131, 132, 135, 139, 142, 145, 148, 150, 151, 152, 157, 158, 159, 165; XXXVII 8; and *passim*
International Society of Contemporary Music Festival (Barcelona) 77

Ireland 43, 100, 103, 104, 106, 107–9, 110, 113, 114–15, 119, 121
Irish Brigade (XV Bandera) 105–6, 108, 109–10, 113, 114–18, 120
Irish Christian Front (ICF) 100–1, 109, 118
Irish Democrat 132
Irish Independent 109, 113, 115, 121
Irish Republican Congress 132
Isherwood, Christopher 27, 32, 33, 34, 80, 82, 83, 84, 92, 94, 173, 175
Italian Fascist Army, *see* Corpo Truppe Voluntarie
Italy 4, 56, 179, 191

Jarama 7–8, 28, 29, 36–7, 42, 63, 87, 91, 110, 112, 119, 151, 156, 160, 180
Jarrow Crusade 113
Jasper, Frank 144
Jellinek, Frank 61
Jiménez, Alberto 10
Jones, John 140
Jones, Lewis 110–11
Jones, Tom 125–6
Jordan, Philip 86, 158
Juderías, Julián 180
Jump, John 42
Junta Delegada del Tesoro Artístico 19
Jurado, Colonel 128

Kennedy, John F. 194, 195
Kermode, Frank 159
Kerrigan, Peter 37
Kisch, Egon 181
Koestler, Arthur 49, 54, 56, 85, 86, 90
Koltsov, Mikhail 17, 86–7, 90, 181–2, 185, 186, 193
Kopp, Georges 54
Korean War 49

Lambert, Constant 75
Land and Freedom 51, 134, 135

Largo Caballero, Francisco 69
Larios, José 142
Last, Jeff 7, 8, 180–1, 193
Lawrence & Wishart 50
Leavitt, David 40, 43
Left Book Club 33, 35, 51, 157
Left Review 19, 27, 159, 175–6
Left Theatre 156
Lehmann, John 32, 149, 154, 156, 160, 174–5
Lenin, Vladimir I. 62, 90
Lenin Division 52, 60
Lepper, John 28, 37, 156
Lérida 71
Lerma, duke of 142
Levinski, Benjamin 54
Lewis, Wyndham 66
Limerick 110
Lincoln Battalion 21, 111, 115, 119, 141, 165
Lindsay, Jack 154, 157, 158, 174–5, 177
Lisbon 110
Listener, The 45
Líster, Enrique 126, 128, 129, 131, 142, 148
Loach, Ken 134
London 6, 31, 33, 35, 37, 44, 75, 83, 87, 89, 92, 116, 149, 154, 155, 164, 167, 170, 178
London Symphony Orchestra 75
Longo, Luigi 151, 167
Lopera 145
Lorca, Federico García 4–5, 6, 9, 16, 19
Luzuriaga, Lorenzo 10
Lynch, Martin 167–8

'Macalastair, Somhairle' 114
McCarthy, Joseph 49, 195
McCusker, Frank 137
McGuinness, Charles 121
Machado, Antonio 148
McLean, Tony 161
McNair, John 55
MacNeice, Louis 32, 78
MacRory, Cardinal 114
Madge, Charles 44

Madrid 2, 3, 4, 5, 6, 7, 9, 12, 14, 19, 17, 18, 27, 28, 29, 33, 37, 40, 53, 77, 81, 86, 89, 94, 99, 100, 104, 111, 124, 125, 126, 131, 135, 142, 155, 159, 163, 164, 173, 176, 179, 180–2, 184, 185, 186, 191, 192, 193
Madrigueras 152
Maerdy 126
Málaga 125
Malraux, André ix, 6, 166, 193, 195
Manchester Guardian 20, 61
Mann, Erika 78
Mann, Thomas 73
Mannin, Ethel 118, 120
Manzanares, the 6
Marañón, Gregorio de 12
Marshall, Dave 156
Martin, Kingsley 37, 38
Marty, André 53, 131–2
Marx, Karl 171, 175, 189, 192
May Events 53–4, 60, 69, 89
Mayakovsky, Vladimir 150
Merthyr Tydfil 140
Miaja, General 127, 128
Milicias de Cultura 163
Milne, Ewart 119–20
Miranda del Ebro 20
Mitchell, Donald 95
Mola, General Emilio 99, 116
Monde, Le 50
Mondéjar 146
Montaña barracks (Madrid) 5, 135
Monte Oscuro 48, 55
Montflorite 71
Moore, Christy 114, 116
Moore, G. E. 192
Moore, Henry 177
Moore, Thomas 116
Mora, Constanza de la 39
Morata de Tajuña 151
Morgan, Charles 137, 187
Morrerres i Boix, J. 60
Moscow 6, 37, 58, 89, 111, 113, 132, 141, 149, 175, 180
Mosley, Oswald 32, 45
Muggeridge, Malcolm 8
Mulrean, Fr. 117

Mundo Obrero 167
Münzenberg, Willi 193
Murcia 150
Murphy, Lombard 121
Murphy, Pat 129–30, 132–3, 134, 137
Mussolini, Benito 32, 37, 102, 110, 114, 133, 153, 194

Nathan, George 42–3
Nationalists xi, 2–3, 4, 7, 12, 13, 15, 16, 18, 19, 35, 37, 48, 69, 70, 74, 101, 102–5, 110, 112, 118, 123, 124, 127, 129, 130, 131, 133, 134, 139, 141–2, 145, 162, 165, 178, 179, 182
Negrín, Juan 8, 41, 72, 94, 141, 179, 184, 185, 186
Neruda, Pablo 186
New Republic 195
New Statesman 37, 39, 40
New Theatre Group 157–8
New Verse 44
New Writing 154, 159
New York 4, 149
News Chronicle 36, 61
Nin, Andrés 183
Non-Intervention Committee 7
'Nosotros' 163

O'Brien, Tom 157–8
O'Daire, Paddy 116–17
O'Donnell, Hugh 53, 87
O'Donoghue, Michael 137, 140
O'Duffy, Eoin 105, 108, 109, 110, 112, 113, 114, 115–17, 118, 120
Old Mill (Snape) 92
O'Neill, Owen Roe 116
Orr, Charles 55
Ortega y Gasset, José 11–12, 13, 90, 189
Orwell, George (Eric Blair) x, 35, 45, 48–73, 87, 88, 90, 121, 175, 176, 188
Osheroff, Abe 158
Owen, Frank 126, 139
Owen, Wilfred 82

Pamplona 112, 113
Paris 6, 12, 84, 89, 92
Paris International Exhibition (1937) 102
Partido Comunista de España (PCE) 39, 58, 124, 163, 167, 180, 182, 184, 192
Partido Obrero de Unificación Marxista (POUM) 52, 53–4, 55, 58, 59–60, 61, 69, 71, 87, 89, 134, 178, 179, 183
Partido Socialista de Unificación Catalana (PSUC) 53, 54, 58, 59, 60, 87, 124
Pater, Walter 189
Paynter, Will 39, 132, 138, 139–40
Pears, Peter 80, 92, 93, 95
People's Militias 135
Pérez Blázquez, Miguel 127, 129
Pérez de Ayala, Francisco 12
Peters, Ray 45, 46, 47, 176
Picasso, Pablo 88, 102
Pingarrón, Sierra de 28
Poetry for the People 156
Pollitt, Harry 35, 36, 37, 38, 39, 41, 44, 52, 55, 93, 138, 189
Ponce de Léon, Alfonso 5–6
Popular Army (Ejército Popular) 53, 59, 74, 77, 124, 126, 131–2, 143, 145, 149, 150, 157, 160, 163, 166, 182, 193
Popular Front ix, 2, 9, 13, 54, 61, 68–9, 75, 85, 89, 95, 100, 101, 120, 133, 170–1, 172, 175, 183, 194
Prado Museum (Madrid) 18, 19
Pravda 58, 86
Preston, Paul 110
Price, Leo 136
Primo de Rivera, José Antonio 3, 4, 70
Primo de Rivera, Miguel 6, 11, 12, 13, 14, 185
Puyol, Ramón 141

Quijorna 128, 133
Quinto 146

Radek, Karl 91, 158, 175, 177, 178
Ranke, Leopold von 67
Read, Herbert 177–8
Regler, Gustav 7, 56, 112, 193
Renn, Ludwig 7, 41–2
Republicans xi, 3, 5, 7, 13, 71, 74, 81, 87, 88, 89, 101, 102, 103, 104–5, 111, 116, 117, 124, 125, 126, 127, 128, 129, 131, 133, 139–40, 141, 142, 143, 145, 149, 157, 163–4, 165, 166–7, 178, 184, 191
Rhondda Valleys 45, 108, 111
Rickword, Edgell 154, 156
Ridruejo, Dionisio 5, 6
Roberts, Jack 130, 132, 134, 135, 136, 137, 139, 147–8
Rodríguez, Miguel 127
Roman Catholicism 8–9, 71, 72, 93, 101, 104, 107, 108–9, 110, 112, 113, 114–15, 117, 118, 120, 121, 186
Romero, Luis del 58
Romilly, Esmond 27, 63, 81, 100
Romilly, Giles 27, 28, 34, 43, 85
Rosenstone, Robert 111–12
Rotha, Paul 80
Rust, Bill 132, 139
Ryan, Frank 113, 114, 116, 117, 130, 132, 139, 141 3

Salamanca 13, 14–15, 16, 149, 179
Salaün, Serge 148–50
Santander 131
Sanz, Juan Ramón 167
Sariñena 87
Schopenhauer, Arthur 7
Scott, Bill 100
Second World War 27, 68, 95
Seghers, Anna 183
Seidman, Michael 58, 59
Servicio de Inteligencia Militar (SIM) 179, 180, 195
Seville 127, 133
Sheldonian Theatre (Oxford) 16
Snow, C. P. 191
Slater, Hugh 152, 161
Sloan, Hugh 162

Index

Smillie, Bob 64, 65, 72
Smith-Piggot, R. 164–5
Socialist Party of America 55
Solidaridad Internacional Antifascista 69
Sommerfield, John 8, 63
Southworth, Herbert 194
Soviet Artists' Congress (1934) 91
Soviet Union (USSR) ix, 1–2, 3, 17, 25, 51, 52, 58, 58, 69, 72, 89, 91, 95, 100–1, 103, 114, 124, 142, 149, 170, 171, 172, 175, 176, 178, 180, 183, 192, 191
Spanish Medical Aid Society 53, 85
Spender, Stephen x, 30, 31–43, 44, 45, 47, 49, 55, 56, 65, 67, 77, 87, 91, 119, 149, 154, 155–6, 159, 160, 176, 178–9, 181, 182, 183, 186, 188–9, 190, 193, 195
Springhall, David 37
Stalin, Joseph ix, 2, 46, 54, 55, 56, 64, 72, 86, 89, 90, 91, 105, 124–5, 171, 175, 177, 183, 192, 193, 194
Straight, Michael 25, 26–7, 46, 194–5
Stuart, Francis 118
Swingler, Randall 154

Tablet, The 70
Tapsell, Wally 37, 38, 53
Tarazona 115
Taylor, A. J. P. 16, 20
Teruel 42, 145, 146, 158, 165
Thaelmann Battalion 41, 112
Thomas, Fred 137–8, 139, 161
Thompson, E. P. 49, 70
Thomson, Rita 78, 95
Tisa, John 112–13, 153
Toledo 135, 178
Toller, Ernst 156
Tolstoy, Alexei 180
Tomalin, Miles 146, 152, 160, 161
Toynbee, Philip 31, 176
Trend, J. B. 19
Trilling, Lionel 49, 72

Unamuno, Miguel de 13–14, 21, 184, 189

United States of America 25, 26, 95, 103, 107, 112, 183, 188, 195
Unity Theatre 156–7
Universidad Complutense (Madrid) 6, 9, 11
University City (Madrid) 6–7, 8, 21, 100
Upward, Edward 173–5

Valencia 17, 28, 35, 36, 37, 39, 58, 75, 85, 86, 87, 94, 103, 139, 142, 164, 166, 179, 182–3, 184
Valladolid 109
Valley of the Fallen 3
Varela, General José 7
Vienna 154
Vietnam War 5
Viewpoint 176
Villafranca del Castillo 133
Villanueva de la Cañada 124, 126–31, 132–5, 136, 137–41, 143–4, 147, 152, 182, 192
Volunteer for Liberty 148, 150, 152–3, 160, 167
Voros, Sandor 167
Voz del Combatiente, La 7–8

Wallington 71
Walker, Robert 137
Walker, Ted 166
Walter, General 145
War Commisariat (Madrid) 146, 150–1, 157, 160
Waugh, Alec 187
Waugh, Evelyn 121–2, 186
'Wild Geese' 106, 107, 108, 115–17
Wilde, Oscar 34, 84, 189
Williams, Raymond 46, 48, 49, 68
Willis, Ted 157
Wintringham, Tom 63, 160
Wolff, Milton 141
Woolf, Leonard 35
Woolf, Virginia 33, 35–6
Workers' Music Association 75
Workington Star 129
Worsley, Cuthbert 28, 34, 35, 36, 43, 193

Writers' Conference (Valencia, 1987) 182–3

Yeats, W. B. 116, 118–19, 120, 121

Young Communist League 157

Zalka, Maté 7
Zaragoza 87, 146